Lecture Notes in Artificial Intelligence 2446

Subseries of Lecture Notes in Computer Science
Edited by J. G. Carbonell and J. Siekmann

Lecture Notes in Computer Science
Edited by G. Goos, J. Hartmanis, and J. van Leeuwen

Springer

Berlin
Heidelberg
New York
Barcelona
Hong Kong
London
Milan
Paris
Tokyo

Matthias Klusch   Sascha Ossowski
Onn Shehory (Eds.)

Cooperative
Information Agents VI

6th International Workshop, CIA 2002
Madrid, Spain, September 18-20, 2002
Proceedings

 Springer

Series Editors

Jaime G. Carbonell, Carnegie Mellon University, Pittsburgh, PA, USA
Jörg Siekmann, University of Saarland, Saarbrücken, Germany

Volume Editors

Matthias Klusch
DFKI GmbH, German Research Center for Artificial Intelligence
Stuhlsatzenhausweg 3, 66123 Saarbrücken, Germany
E-mail: klusch@dfki.de

Sascha Ossowski
University Rey Juan Carlos, School of Engineering (ESCET)
Campus de Mostoles, Calle Tulipan s/n, 28933 Madrid, Spain
E-mail: S.Ossowski@escet.urjc.es

Onn Shehory
Haifa University, IBM - Haifa Research Labs
Mount Carmel, Haifa, 31905 Israel
E-mail: onn@il.ibm.com

Cataloging-in-Publication Data applied for

Die Deutsche Bibliothek - CIP-Einheitsaufnahme

Cooperative information agents VI : 6th international workshop ; proceedings /
CIA 2002, Madrid, Spain, September 18 - 20, 2002. Matthias Klusch ... (ed.). -
Berlin ; Heidelberg ; New York ; Barcelona ; Hong Kong ; London ; Milan ;
Paris ; Tokyo : Springer, 2002
    (Lecture notes in computer science ; Vol. 2446 : Lecture notes in
    artificial intelligence)
    ISBN 3-540-44173-5

CR Subject Classification (1998): I.2.11, I.2, H.2, H.3.3, H.4, C.2.4, H.5

ISSN 0302-9743
ISBN 3-540-44173-5 Springer-Verlag Berlin Heidelberg New York

Springer-Verlag Berlin Heidelberg New York
a member of BertelsmannSpringer Science+Business Media GmbH

http://www.springer.de

© Springer-Verlag Berlin Heidelberg 2002

Typesetting: Camera-ready by author, data conversion by PTP-Berlin, Stefan Sossna e.K.
Printed on acid-free paper   SPIN: 10871063   06/3142   5 4 3 2 1 0

Preface

These are the proceedings of the Sixth International Workshop on Cooperative Information Agents (CIA 2002), held at the Universidad de Rey Juan Carlos in Madrid, Spain, September 18–20, 2002. It was colocated with the Third International Workshop on Engineering Societies in the Agents World (ESAW 2002).

Since 1997 the annual CIA workshop series has aimed to provide an open forum for all parties interested in the research and development of intelligent information agents for the Internet and Web. Each event in this renowned series attempts to capture the intrinsic interdisciplinary nature of this research area by calling for contributions from different research communities, and by promoting open and informative discussions on all related topics.

In keeping with its tradition, this year's workshop featured a sequence of regular and invited talks of excellence given by leading experts in the fields related to information agent technology. These talks covered a broad area of topics of interest, such as information agents for mobile computing environments as well as information gathering, exchange, management, and collaborative recommender systems. Other topics included agent interaction and communication, negotiation strategies for purchasing relevant information, and agent-based distributed knowledge management.

As last year, the workshop issued two awards for best paper and best system innovation to acknowledge particularly significant advances in research and development, respectively, in the area of information agents. This year the *CIA System Innovation Award* and the *CIA 2002 Best Paper Award* were sponsored by the Spanish Association for Artificial Intelligence and Elsevier Science, respectively.

CIA 2002 featured 4 invited, 15 regular, and 8 short papers selected from 59 submissions. The result of the peer-review of all contributions is included in this volume, rich in interesting, inspiring, and advanced work in the research and development of intelligent information agents worldwide. All workshop proceedings to date have been published by Springer-Verlag as Lecture Notes in Artificial Intelligence Vols. 1202 (1997), 1435 (1998), 1652 (1999), 1860 (2000), and 2182 (2001).

The CIA 2002 workshop was organized in cooperation with the Association for Computing Machinery (ACM), and was supported by the French National Institute for Research in Computer Science and Control (INRIA). We are very much indebted to our sponsors whose financial support made this event possible and contributed to its success. The sponsors of CIA 2002 were: Spanish Ministry for Science and Technology, Spain; Universidad de Rey Juan Carlos, Spain; Elsevier Science, The Netherlands; Whitestein Technologies, Switzerland; IBM Research, Israel; Swiss Life AG, Switzerland; AutoDesk Inc., USA; and AgentLink II, (European Network of Excellence for Agent-Based Computing).

We are also grateful to the authors and invited speakers for contributing to this workshop, and to all members of the program committee and external reviewers for their very careful, critical, and thoughtful reviews of all submissions. Finally, a deep thanks goes to the brave members of the local organization team in Madrid for their hard work in providing CIA 2002 with a convenient location, and an exciting social program.

September 2002   Matthias Klusch, Sascha Ossowski and Onn Shehory

Co-chairs

Matthias Klusch   (DFKI, Germany), General Chair
Sascha Ossowski   (University Rey Juan Carlos, Spain)
Onn Shehory   (IBM Research, Israel)

Program Committee

Wolfgang Benn   (TU Chemnitz, Germany)
Federico Bergenti   (University of Parma, Italy)
Sonia Bergamaschi   (University of Modena, Italy)
Cristiano Castelfranchi (NRC Rome, Italy)
Brahim Chaib-draa   (Laval University, Canada)
Rose Dieng   (INRIA, France)
Frank Dignum   (University of Utrecht, The Netherlands)
Tim Finin   (University of Maryland at Baltimore, USA)
Mike Huhns   (University of South Carolina, USA)
Toru Ishida   (University of Kyoto, Japan)
Catholijn Jonker   (Free University of Amsterdam, The Netherlands)
Larry Kerschberg   (George Mason University, USA)
Yasuhiko Kitamura   (Osaka City University, Japan)
Sarit Kraus   (University of Maryland, USA)
Daniel Kudenko   (University of York, UK)
Victor Lesser   (University of Massachusetts, USA)
Mike Luck   (University of Southampton, UK)
Pablo Noriega   (CSIC, Spain)
Werner Nutt   (Heriot-Watt University, Edinburgh, UK)
Eugenio Oliveira   (University of Porto, Portugal)
Lin Padgham   (RMIT, Australia)
Ana Paiva   (TU Lisbon, Portugal)
Michal Pechoucek   (TU Prague, Czech Republic)
Paolo Petta   (Austrian Research Institute for AI, Austria)
Alun Preece   (University of Aberdeen, UK)
Omer F. Rana   (University of Wales, UK)
Ulrich Reimer   (Swiss Life AG, Switzerland)
Volker Roth   (Fraunhofer IGD, Germany)
Heiko Schuldt   (ETH Zurich, Switzerland)
Sandip Sen   (University of Tulsa, USA)
Amit Sheth   (University of Georgia, USA)
Carles Sierra   (CSIC AI Research Lab, Spain)
Munindar Singh   (North Carolina State University, USA)
Von-Wun Soo   (National Tsing Hua University, Taiwan)

Robert Tolksdorf   (TU Berlin, Germany)
Steven Willmott   (EPFL Lausanne, Switzerland)
Mike Wooldridge   (University of Liverpool, UK)
Makoto Yokoo   (NTT Communication Science Lab, Japan)
Eric Yu   (University of Toronto, Canada)
Franco Zambonelli   (University of Modena, Italy)
Ning Zhong   (Maebashi Institute of Technology, Japan)

Local Organizing Committee

Holger Billhardt   Alberto Fernández
Vicente Matellán   Sascha Ossowski
Ana Pradera   Juan-Manuel Serrano

Table of Contents

Invited Contributions

Information Agents for Mobile Computing Environments

Issues of Interaction and Negotiation

Information Gathering and Collaborative Filtering

Agent-Based Information and Knowledge Management

Issues of Agent Communication and Cooperation

Agents, Crawlers, and Web Retrieval*

Ricardo Baeza-Yates and José Miguel Piquer

Center for Web Research
Dept. of Computer Science, University of Chile
Blanco Encalada 2120, Santiago, Chile

`{rbaeza,jpiquer}@dcc.uchile.cl`

Abstract. In this paper we survey crawlers, a specific type of agents used by search engines. We also explore the relation with generic agents and how agent technology or variants of it could help to develop search engines that are more effective, efficient, and scalable.

1 Introduction

The Web has become the largest easy available repository of data. Hence, it is natural to extract information from it and Web search engines have become one of the most used tools in Internet. However, the exponential growth and the fast pace of change of the Web, makes really hard to visit a significant portion of the Web, and even harder to revisit that portion to keep a collection that accurately represents the changes in Web pages, and hence retrieve relevant documents. Therefore, Web retrieval is a practical and interesting research challenge.

Web search engines have three standard components: crawlers, spiders or robots (input), Web database and index (storage) and query resolver and interface (output) [3, chapter 13]. We define a Web database as a collection of Web objects (HTML pages, images, etc.). Current architectures are centralized, with all components running together using parallel processing (typically a farm of PCs).

The main problem of this architecture is scalability, and crawlers are its bottleneck. Crawlers cannot cope with exponential growth and then this decreases Web coverage and Web freshness (having current page content). Another problem is the paradigm used to obtain the input. It is well known that interruptions are better than polling when dealing with slower devices. In practice, Web servers are slower devices, so instead of pulling information from them (only if it has changed or it is new), would be much better that they push the information to the search engine. This idea is explored further later.

We first survey crawlers and we present a taxonomy based in three coordinates. Then we briefly survey agents, and in particular agents as searchers for specific information. We continue with the application of agents and/or pushing technology to improve Web search engines. Finally, we end with some concluding remarks. Related surveys are [2] for Web search engines including crawling and [14] for focused crawling.

---

* Funded by Millennium Nucleus Center for Web Research, Mideplan, Chile.

M. Klusch, S. Ossowski, and O. Shehory (Eds.): CIA 2002, LNAI 2446, pp. 1–9, 2002.

2   Crawlers

All search engines available on the Internet need to traverse Web pages and their associated links, to copy them and to index them into a Web database. The programs associated with the page traversal and recovery are called crawlers. The main decisions associated with the crawlers algorithms are when to visit a site again (to see if a page has changed) and when to visit new sites that have been discovered through links. The parameters to balance are network usage and Web server overload against index accuracy and completeness.

As Web crawlers are mostly used by search engines, their inner components are usually well guarded secrets and only benchmarks [51] are revealed. Some exceptions (in chronological order) are: RBSE Spider [26], Internet Archive [8], SPHINX [40], Google Web crawler [44], Mercator [29], and a parallel crawler [17]. Other papers deal with page ordering for crawling [21, 42], mirroring [16], Web server overloading [55, 54], keep the collection up to date [22, 20, 18], dynamic pages [49], and knowing how Web pages change over time [19, 7, 24]. Recent work focuses in high performance, scalability, and flexibility [43, 5, 25, 15, 52, 45].

The main goals of a crawler are the following [11]:

1. The index should contain a large number of Web objects that are *interesting* to the search engine's users.
2. Every object on the index should *accurately represent* a real object on the Web (content through time).
3. Generate a representation of the objects that capture the most significant aspects of the crawled object using the minimum amount of resources.

We can model different crawlers using three coordinates that are Web page attributes[11]: quality, quantity, and freshness.

Quality refers to the intrinsic semantic value of the object. Quality can be estimated in many ways [21]: link analysis such as Pagerank [44] (link popularity), similarity to a driven query (focused crawling or a searching agent), accesses to that page on the index (usage popularity), and location-based: by the perceived depth (eg. number of directories on the path to the Web object) or by domain name, IP address or geography.

Quantity depends on the size and format of the information being stored for every object. This depends on the representation chosen. If the complete object is stored, it is high. If only a few keywords are stored, it is low.

Freshness relates to the accuracy that the stored representation reflects the current Web page content, because as Web updates are common, freshness decreases fast with time. Freshness can be estimated quite precisely if the last modification date of the Web page is informed by the Web server [18], using the work in [7].

The proposed taxonomy covers many particular cases, as shown in Figure 1.

It must be noticed that the goals mentioned before compete between them, because the crawler must decide between going for a new page, not currently on the index, or refreshing some page that is probably outdated in the index. There

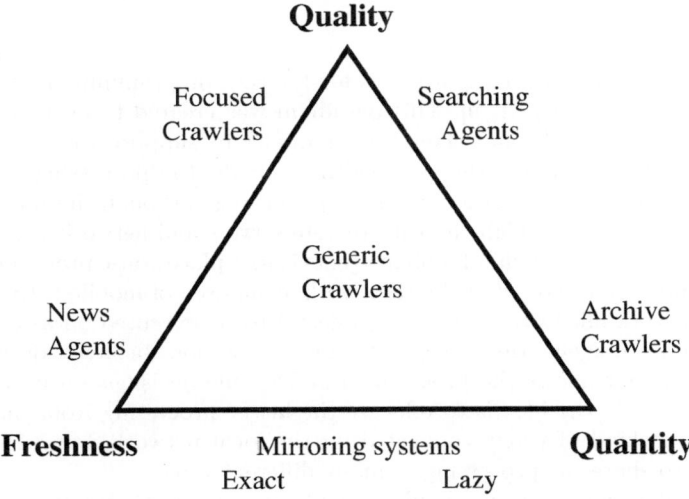

Fig. 1. Different crawlers in the model by Castillo and Baeza-Yates [11].

is a trade-off between quantity (more objects) and quality (more up-to-date objects). In addition, many new pages will appear as URLs in new or modified pages.

Previous work tends to separate two very similar problems and to mix two very different problems [11]:

- The two similar problems are the index freshness and the index quality according to other metrics (eg. link analysis). It will be better to think in terms of a series of scores associated to different characteristics of the documents in the collection, weighted accordingly to some priorities that will vary depending on the usage context of the crawler. As some goals are contradictory, the software must decide amongst, for instance, trying to discover new pages or updating existing ones. In this case, we need some way to tell the crawler how to decide between these alternatives.
- The two different problems that are commonly mixed are the problem of short-term efficiency (that is, maximizing the bandwidth usage and be polite with servers [34]), and long-term efficiency (ordering the set to favor some important pages).

One solution to this contradictory goals is to use a short-term scheduling that deals with bandwidth usage, politeness, etc; and a long-term scheduling that deals with quality, quantity, and freshness [11].

3   Agents

One of the most promising approaches for Internet programming is the mobile-agent paradigm[36, 58, 31, 9]. This paradigm was created to overcome the inadequacy of the traditional client/server model to support wireless networks and mobile devices, where the bandwidth available, the processing capacity of the end device and many other resources are scarce, although the Internet does provide access to other high-capacity remote servers and networks.

In general, the idea behind mobile agents is to replace static programs (clients and servers) with a more flexible framework, composed of mobile active objects. This framework allows to send code (objects) to be executed on a remote machine. The word agent tries to suggest some autonomous behavior or even some intelligence, that allows the program to make some decisions on its own. In a wireless network, the idea is to relocate the heavy processing from the end device to some kind of proxy connected on the local network, but with enough flexibility to share the processing in many different ways.

An ideal agent platform should provide enough functionality to allow an active object to replicate itself, to migrate from one machine to another, to spawn new parallel threads, to handle references to many objects on many different sites, to support partial failures and to guarantee a reasonable level of security for every participant.

A fully functional and flexible agent platform is not yet available, but many well-known platforms do exist today[10, 35, 33], providing most of the base functions needed to develop real distributed applications. The complexity associated with the agent paradigm includes security (how to allow execution of unknown code in a safe way)[57], thread migration[1], object migration[48, 56], replication[28], garbage collection[47], etc. However, it seems reasonable to believe in a future where the agent paradigm (implemented for different languages and in different platforms) will be globally available.

Even if agents were designed for wireless network and mobile devices, their flexibility makes them suitable for any distributed application. In general, they allow to split computation in a very flexible way, allowing to optimize network usage and/or load balancing.

4   Searching Agents

Another approach is to design personal searching agents, instead of using the search engine/crawler technology. This is also called a focused crawler in the Web search engine field. The idea is to code in an intelligent agent all the personal interests (that could have been learned following the user Web navigation[37] or the user search behavior). The agent will spawn itself and navigate by its own the net, selecting the most interesting links as the user would do. Once a day, for example, the agent will report its findings to the user, who will evaluate them to further refine the agents searching criteria. Other early work on this includes [4].

Here, the problem is that a global agent infrastructure is needed to test and to deploy such a solution. A first test, that can be explored today, is to develop a program that uses the existing search engines (for example a meta-search engine like Copernic)to search pages on the user's behalf, copying them, and further selecting the most interesting to report them to the user[46]. One main issue here when having pages to process, is to explore many of them (breadth-first search) or to exploit the best of them (depth-first search). Preliminary results show that seems better to explore [46].

Focused crawling was introduced by Chakrabarti *et al.* [12] to collect topic-specific Web pages. The idea is to do a "best-first" crawl instead of "breadth-first" or "depth-first". "Best" could be defined in many ways. For example could be a global link based measure such as Pagerank [44] or the similarity of the page to a topic described by a query. After that, several implementations and results were published [13, 23, 39, 41]. In particular, Rennie and McCallum [50] studied reinforcement learning by using feedback, while Menczer and Belew [38] used evolutionary adaptation by local selection, and selective query expansion by internalization of environmental signals. Kluev [32] uses a vector space model and clustering techniques.

A related idea is topic distillation in the Web [12, 30], where instead of looking for a topic, we extract the topics currently on the Web. Searching agents can also be used for filtering information, an important task when dealing with information overload, as well as Web mining. Evaluation of topical crawlers can be found in [53].

5   Towards the Perfect Web Search Engine

The agent technology could improve the crawler's effectiveness allowing some co-operation from the server, lending some processing cycles to the crawler. In general, the existing crawlers perform their work without cooperation from the Web servers, they must transfer the pages using standard HTTP protocol through TCP ASCII connections, and poll them to see if a page has been modified.

It is more efficient to send an agent to the server, where it can locally search for new pages, links and modified pages. It can also pack them all together in a batch compressed file to be transferred to the search engine. The main search server could interact with the remote agent to decide if it is worth to transfer the existing batch based on decisional parameters such as the number of files, importance of them, etc. The intelligence of the crawler can then be distributed between the main search engine and the existent agents. Brandman *et al.* [6] study the impact on the bandwidth when Web servers publish metadata of their Web pages, such as actualization dates, size, etc. They show that there are savings and also the freshness of the pages increases. A similar paper focuses on freshness [27]. However, we can go one step further and instead of only pulling information, we can push it.

The interaction then drifts from pulling pages to pushing changes. As usual, the other extreme is also not efficient, as pushing too much will overload the centralized server. Hence, the best solution is that the server negotiates in advance with the agent when and how to send a message warning that a batch of changes is ready (or even better, that the changes to the index needed are already computed and available). Then, the main server will pull whenever possible those changes. This implies again a long-term scheduling, which may find more changes when really visits a Web server that pushed a warning. Nevertheless, this scheduling is simpler as we have more information, and we do not need to worry about politeness as we are sure that all accesses are not frequent and they are always successful.

In general, Web servers will want to cooperate in this architecture, because today it is an accepted value to be indexed on a popular search engine. On the other hand, even if they are spending CPU cycle on the search engine behalf, they are not being polled by the crawler, thus they are effectively diminishing their Web server access load.

As a first testing stage, while a global available agent platform is not available, a simple server, associated to the Web server, could be developed to provide a similar functionality and measure the performance improvement. As we already mentioned, small changes to the Web server have been suggested to enable cooperation with search engines[6, 27], but they lack flexibility and they interfere with the crawler policies. Agents could improve a lot this behavior, enabling their algorithms to priorize pages to be embedded in the agents code. In this sense, the agent is an important component of the crawler's algorithm, and its logic follows a particular search engine's policies.

6   Concluding Remarks

In this paper we have tried to formalize how agents could be used to improve Web search engines and we have surveyed, to the best of our knowledge, the main results on crawler and agent technology applied to Web retrieval. We are currently implementing and deploying a distributed architecture that follows the ideas of the previous section, as part of the objectives of our new Center for Web Research (www.crw.cl).

We end by pointing out that there is still a lot to do, and the interaction of information retrieval, artificial intelligence, and Web technology, is just starting. Only taking the best of them we can tame this world wide beast.

References

1. Anurag Acharya, M. Ranganathan, and Joel Saltz.   Sumatra: A Language for Resource-aware Mobile Programs.   In J. Vitek and C. Tschudin, editors, *Mobile Object Systems: Towards the Programmable Internet*, volume 1222, pages 111–130. Springer-Verlag, Heidelberg, Germany, 1997.
2. A. Arasu, J. Cho, H. Garcia-Molina, and S. Raghavan. Searching the Web. ACM Transactions on Internet Technologies, 1(1), June 2001.

3. R. Baeza-Yates and B. Ribeiro-Neto, *Modern Information Retrieval*, Addison-Wesley, England, 513 pages, 1999.
4. M. Balabanovic and Y. Shoham, Learning Information Retrieval Agents: Experiments with Automated Web Browsing, in AAAI Spring Symposium on Information Gathering, Stanford, CA, March 1995.
5. Paolo Boldi, Bruno Codenotti, Massimo Santini, and Sebastiano Vigna. Trovatore: Towards a highly scalable distributed web crawler. In Proc. of 10th International World–Wide Web Conference, Hong Kong, China, 2001. Poster session (Winner of the Best Poster Award).
6. O. Brandman, J. Cho, H. Garcia-Molina, and N. Shivakumar. Crawler-friendly web servers. In *Workshop on Performance and Architecture of Web Servers (PAWS)*, June 2000.
7. B. Brewington, G. Cybenko. How dynamic is the Web?, Proc. WWW9, 2000.
8. M. Burner. Crawling towards Eternity - Building An Archive of The World Wide Web, Web Techniques, May 1997. http://www.webtechniques.com/-archives/1997/05/burner/.
9. L. Cardelli, Mobile Computation, In J. Vitek and C. Tschudin (Eds), Mobile Object Systems: Towards the Programmable Internet, Vol 1222, LNCS, Springer-Verlag, 1997.
10. D. Caromel, W. Klauser, J. Vayssiere. Towards seamless computing and metacomputing in Java. *Concurrency, Practice and Experience* 10, Sept 1998.
11. Castillo, C. and Baeza-Yates, R. A New Model for Web Crawling (poster), WWW11, Honolulu, 2002.
12. Chakrabarti, S., van der Berg, M., and Dom, B. Focused crawling: a new approach to topic-specific Web resource discovery. In Proceedings of 8th International World Wide Web Conference (WWW8), 1999.
13. Chakrabarti, S., van der Berg, M., and Dom, B. Distributed hypertext resource discovery through examples, VLDB, 1999, 375-386.
14. Chakrabarti, S. Recent results in automatic Web resource discovery, ACM Computing Surveys, 1999.
15. Cho, J. Crawling The Web: Discovery and Maintenance Of Large-Scale Web Data, Ph.D. thesis, Stanford University, 2001.
16. J. Cho, N. Shivakumar, H. Garcia-Molina. Finding replicated Web collections, In Proc. of 2000 ACM International Conference on Management of Data (SIGMOD) Conference, May 2000.
17. J. Cho, H. Garcia-Molina. Parallel Crawlers, WWW11, 2001.
18. J. Cho, H. Garcia-Molina. Estimating Frequency of Change, Technical Report, Dept. of Computer Science, Stanford University, 2001.
19. J. Cho, H. Garcia-Molina. The Evolution of the Web and Implications for an Incremental Crawler, VLDB conference, pages 200-209, 2000.
20. J. Cho, H. Garcia-Molina. Synchronizing a database to improve freshness. Proc. of ACM SIGMOD, pages 117-128, 2000.
21. J. Cho, H. Garcia-Molina. Efficient crawling through URL ordering. Proc. WWW7, 1998.
22. E.G. Coan, Jr., Zhen Liu, Richard R. Weber. Optimal robot scheduling for Web search engines. Technical Report, INRIA, 1997.

23. M. Diligenti, F. Coetzee, S. Lawrence, C. L. Giles, and M. Gori. Focused Crawling using Context Graphs, Proc. of 26th International Conference on Very Large Databases, VLDB 2000.

24. F. Douglas, A. Feldmann, B. Krishnamurthy, J.C. Mogul. Rate of Change and other Metrics: a Live Study of the World Wide Web, USENIX Symposium on Internet Technologies and Systems, 1997.

25. Jenny Edwards, Kevin McCurley, and John Tomlin. An Adaptive Model for Optimizing Performance of an Incremental Web Crawler. In Proceedings of the Tenth International World Wide Web Conference, pages 106–113, May 2001.

26. D. Eichmann. The RBSE spider: Balancing effective search against Web load, Proc. of 1st WWW conference, 1994.

27. V. Gupta and R. Campbell. Internet search engine freshness by web server help. Technical Report UIUCDCS-R-2000-2153, Digital Computer Laboratory, University of Illinois at UrbanaChampaign, January 2000.

28. D. Hagimont and D. Louvegnies. Javanaise: distributed shared objects for Internet cooperative applications. In *Middleware'98*, The Lake District, England, 1998.

29. A. Heydon, M. Najork. Mercator: A scalable, extensible Web crawler., World Wide Web, 2(4):219-229, 1999.

30. V. Katz and W.-S. Li. Topic distillation on hierarchically categorized Web documents. In Proceedings of the 1999 Workshop on Knowledge and Data Engineering Exchange, IEEE, 1999.

31. J. Kiniry, D. Zimmerman A Hands-on Look at Java Mobile Agents, *IEEE Internet Computing* 1(4):21–30, July-August 1997.

32. Kluev, V. Compiling document collections from the Internet, *SIGIR Forum* 34, 2000.

33. R. Koblick, Concordia, *Communications of ACM* 42(3):96-99, March 1999.

34. M. Koster Robots in the Web: threat or treat, *ConneXions* 9(4), 1995.

35. D. Lange, M.Oshima. Programming and Deploying Java Mobile Agents with Aglets. Addison Wesley, 1998

36. D.B. Lange and M. Oshima, Seven Good Reasons for Mobile Agents, *Communications of ACM* 42(3):88–91, March 1999.

37. H. Lieberman. Letizia: An Agent That Assists Web Browsing. In 1995 International Joint Conference on Artificial Intelligence, Montreal, CA, 1995.

38. F. Menczer and R. Belew. Adaptive retrieval agents: Internalizing local context and scaling up to the web. Machine Learning conference, 1999. Later in *Machine Learning* 39, 200, 203-242.

39. F. Menczer, G. Pant, M. Ruiz, and P. Srinivasan. Evaluating topic-driven web crawlers. In Proc. 24th Annual International ACM SIGIR Conference on Research and Development in Information Retrieval, 2001.

40. R. Miller, K. Bharat. SPHINX: A framework for creating personal, site-specific Web crawlers, Proc. of WWW7, 1998.

41. Mukherjea, S. WTMS: A system for collecting and analyzing topic-specific Web information, WWW 9, Elsevier, 2000.

42. M. Najork, J. Wiener. Breadth-first search crawling yields high-quality pages, Proc. of WWW10, 2001.
43. Marc Najork and Allan Heydon. On High-Performance Web Crawling. Chapter 2 in J. Abello et al. (editors), Handbook of Massive Data Sets, Kluwer Academic Publishers, 2002.
44. L. Page, S. Brin. The anatomy of a large-scale hypertextual Web search engine. Proc. of WWW7, 1998.
45. G. Pant and F. Menczer. Myspiders: Evolve your own intelligent web crawlers. *Autonomous Agents and Multi-Agent Systems* 5(2):221–229, 2002.
46. G. Pant, P. Srinivasan, and F. Menczer. Exploration versus exploitation in topic driven crawlers. In Proc. Second International Workshop on Web Dynamics, 2002.
47. Jose M. Piquer. Indirect distributed garbage collection: Handling object migration. *ACM Transactions on Programming Languages and Systems (TOPLAS)*, 18(5):615–647, September 1996.
48. Michael Philippsen and Matthias Zenger. JavaParty — transparent remote objects in Java. *Concurrency: Practice and Experience*, 9(11):1225–1242, 1997.
49. S. Raghavan, H. Garcia-Molina. Crawling the Hidden Web, 27th International Conference on Very Large Data Bases, September 2001.
50. Rennie, J. and McCallum, A. Using reinforcement learning to spider the Web efficiently, Int. Conf. on Machine Learning, 1999.
51. Search Engine Watch, http://www.searchenginewatch.com/reports/.
52. V. Shkapenyuk and T. Suel. Design and implementation of a high-performance distributed Web crawler. In Proceedings of the 18th International Conference on Data Engineering (ICDE'02), San Jose, CA Feb. 26–March 1, pages 357–368, 2002.
53. Padmini Srinivasan, Gautam Pant, Filippo Menczer. Target Seeking Crawlers and their Topical Performance, 25th ACM SIGIR, Finland, August 2002.
54. J. Talim, Z. Liu, Ph. Nain, E. G. Coffman. Controlling the robots of Web search engines, Joint international conference on on Measurement and modeling of computer systems, 2001.
55. P.N. Tan, V. Kumar. Discovery of Web Robots Session Based on their Navigational Patterns, Available on-line at http://citeseer.nj.nec.com/443855.html
56. E. Tanter, J. Piquer. Managing References upon Object Migration: Applying separation of Concerns SCCC'01, Punta Arenas, Chile, IEEE Press, Nov 2001.
57. Giovanni Vigna, Protecting Mobile Agents through Tracing, 3rd ECOOP Workshop on Mobile Object Systems, 1997.
58. D. Wong, N. Paciorek, D. Moore. Java-Based Mobile Agents. *Communications of ACM*, 42(3):92–95, March 1999.

Intelligent Interfaces for Information Agents: Systems, Experiences, Future Challenges

Kenji Mase

ATR Media Information Science Laboratories, Kyoto 619-0288, Japan,
mase@atr.co.jp,
http://www.mis.atr.co.jp/~mase/

Extended Summary

The key issues of intelligent interfaces for information agents, such as "context awareness," "personalization," "multi-modality," and "embodiment" are discussed with several examples of research prototype systems. We investigate various intelligent interfaces and present, in this paper, the design detail of the interface prototypes which are developed for the purpose of multi-modal interaction and communication.

The cellular phone system with internet connectivity has provide us with the mobility of telephony, computing and networking. We focus to the mobile "Intelligent Interfaces" with agents in this article as the successor of mobile computing and networking. This article presents the examples of mobile intelligent interfaces along with our experiences of realization and discuss for future challenges.

New paradigms of interface, such as the Perceptual User Interface (PUI) and the Real-World Oriented Interface (RWI), have been recently introduced following the flourishing years of the Graphical User Interface (GUI). PUI is a computer interface with perceptual sensors such as computer vision and speech recognition. These sensors work as the eyes and ears of the computer to interpret the user's situation and intention from multi-modal interactions(figure 1). RWI is a computer system that exploits the interactions and contexts (figure 2) of users with yet-computerized objects in the real world such as a desk, a book, and stationary. It connects objects and events in the real world to the computer world, i.e. cyberspace.

Both PUI and RWI consume a lot of computing power for interface functions such as sensing and interpreting. This consumption can be greater than the power necessary to accomplish the main task. For instance, the PUI may needlessly view an empty office until someone enters. The RWI may uselessly watch the stationary objects in a room all day. Toy Interface is a novel modeled real-world oriented interface that uses objects with toy-like shapes and attributes as the interface between the real world and cyberspace (see Figure 4). Because toys successfully represent real world objects including humans and events, they can become very good tangible interfaces that provide an intuitive metaphor.

M. Klusch, S. Ossowski, and O. Shehory (Eds.): CIA 2002, LNAI 2446, pp. 10–13, 2002.
© Springer-Verlag Berlin Heidelberg 2002

This research was supported in part by the Telecommunications Advancement Organization of Japan.

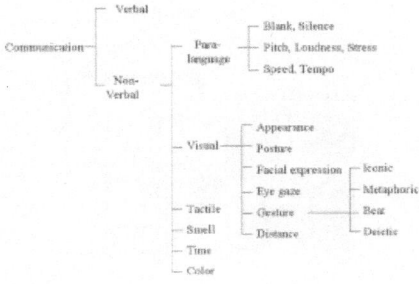

Fig. 1. Elements of multi-modal communication

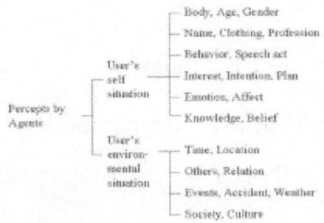

Fig. 2. User's various contexts

Fig. 3. C-MAP: Context-aware Mobile Assistant Project - An example of personalized interface agent[1]

12   K. Mase

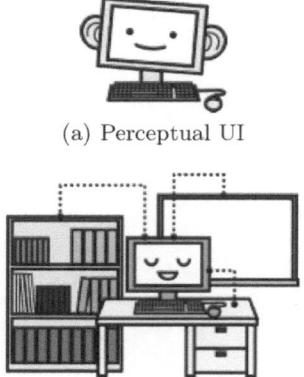

(a) Perceptual UI

(b) Real-World oriented Interface

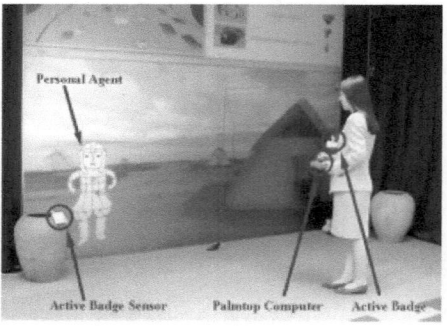

(c) Toy Interface

Fig. 4. PUI, RWI and Toy Interface

Fig. 5. Combination of PUI (gesture interface) and Interface Agent[2]

References

1. Sumi, Y., Mase, K.: Digital assistant for supporting conference participants: An attempt to combine mobile, ubiquitous and web computing. In: UbiComp 2001, Atlanta (2001)

Fig. 6. Communication Aids: AgentSalon[3]

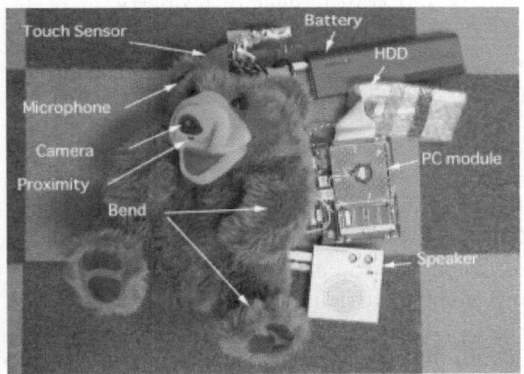

Fig. 7. Stuffed-toy intelligent interface[4]

2. Kadobayashi, R., Nishimoto, K., Mase, K.: Design and Evaluation of Gesture Interface of an Immersive Walk-through Application for Exploring Cyberspace. In: Proc. of The Third International Conference on Automatic Face and Gesture Recognition (FG'98), Nara, Japan (1998) 534–539
3. Sumi,Y. and Mase,K.: AgentSalon: Facilitating Face-to-Face Knowledge Exchange through Conversations Among Personal Agents, The 5th International Conference on Autonomous Agents (Agents 2001), pp.393-400, May 2001.
4. Yonezawa, T., Clarkson, B., Yasumura, M., Mase, K.: Context-aware sensor-doll as a music expression device. In: Proc. CHI2001 extended abstracts, Seattle (2001) 307–308

Electronic Institutions: Future Trends and Challenges
(An Extended Abstract)

Pablo Noriega and Carles Sierra

Artificial Intelligence Research Institute —IIIA,
Spanish Council for Scientific Research —CSIC,
08193 Bellaterra, Barcelona, Catalonia, Spain.
pablo@iiia.csic.es, sierra@iiia.csic.es

1. There are situations where individuals interact in ways that involve:
   - *Commitment.* Interactions usually involve some promises of future actions, payments and transference of property, or other forms of obligations among participants
   - *Delegation.* Participants may act in representation of someone else.
   - *Repetition.* The same type of interaction is performed repeatedly, possibly involving different individuals, usually involving different items, issues or concerns.
   - *Liability and Risk.* The achievement of the interaction involves some sort of interest or gain for participants, and usually some transaction costs as well. Consequently, there is some risk involved that may be allocated more or less explicitly to participants.

   These situations involve participants that are
   - Autonomous.
   - Heterogeneous. Having different goals, different rationales, different moral standings.
   - Independent. Act regardless of a shared loyalty, a common authority or previous agreement.
   - Not-benevolent. One cannot assume they will be moved by the common good or any altruistic aim or consideration. These participants are probably self-motivated, egoist and may even be willing to injure other participants if doing so yields any benefits to themselves.
   - Not-reliable. Likewise, they may act as if they are able and capable, but even unknowingly, they may fail to act in any expected way out of their own will.
   - Liable. Although the characteristics above may seem overwhelmingly pessimistic, one should realize that participants ought to be liable for the damage they inflict to others.
2. Such situations are not uncommon: Markets, medical services, armies are but ready examples of forms of collective problem solving, coordinated tasks, and communities in which participants interact under the type of features mentioned above. Many more exist and many have proven successful for dealing with their intended goals for a very long time.

M. Klusch, S. Ossowski, and O. Shehory (Eds.): CIA 2002, LNAI 2446, pp. 14–17, 2002.

3. In such situations, it is not uncommon to resort to a trusted third party whose aim is to make those interactions effective by establishing and enforcing conventions that standardize interactions, allocate risks, establish safeguards and guarantee that certain intended actions actually take place and unwanted situations are prevented. Such is the intuitive notion of an *institution*, as we normally use the term when we refer to the *institutional* character of markets, political organizations, religious communities or families. Similar intuitions underlie theoretical approaches to institutions such as the economic-theoretic, sociological, legal and psychological ones.

4. While having entities that facilitate commitment making among individuals have proven useful over time, those functions that institutions provide for human interactions become ever more pertinent when we consider the possibility of letting participants to be not only humans, but software agents as well.

5. If we grant that institutions serve to articulate agent interactions, one can then say that the crucial purpose of an institution is to facilitate, oversee and enforce commitment-making among participants in a repetitive situation. Further analysis of these issues is worth undertaking. At least five concerns underlie the commitment-making functionality of an institution.

   - *Manage the identity of participants.* Validate access to the institution of only those agents that qualify, and only to those activities they may be entitled to participate in. In the case of software agents, make sure that adequate management is made of delegated authority or capabilities, and avatars, clones, and other forms of invalid replication of identities are properly expressed and taken care of. In the case of mixed-environments where humans and software agents interact. distinguish between internal (or *staff*) agents, and external agents.

   - *Define and validate requirements on participant capabilities.* The institution should make explicit the different roles that may be played by participants, that is the type of actions and commitments that an individual external agent is entitled to perform and entailed to satisfy. Make explicit, also, the requirements in terms of capability (behavioural competence, expertise, legal authorization, availability of resources, etc.) that external agents need to satisfy in order to participate in the institutionally regulated interactions.

   - *Establish interaction conventions.* This function requires from the institution to make explicit the intended meaning of all communications exchanged within the institution. In order to fix such meaning, all entities that intervene in the socially shared interactions need to be made explicit beforehand, as well as the conventions that determine what communications are needed, when and who can exchange them. Special attention has to be paid to those interactions that are repetitive, thus defining a protocol or adequate guidelines for the effective execution of those actions and their intended effects, exceptions and corrective procedures. Naturally, the choice of interaction conventions should take into account value considerations, usually transparency, accountability and efficiency are paradigmatic. Issues such as privacy, transaction costs, information asymmetries and the degree of integration of anciliary interactions ought to be taken into account for these purposes.

- *Facilitate effective interactions.* The institution has to see to it that participating agents can achieve their intended goals within the institution, and ideally in a better way than they could by themselves without resorting to the institution. Hence, the role played by the institution should result in better trust and accountability for the agent interactions, should make encounters more likely, encounters more successful, and outcomes more productive for all participants. These aims can be achieved through different means, namely by the institution imposing regularity on the interactions, making the enactment of the interactions known and foreseeable, facilitating the presence of apt participants, and enforcing interaction conventions that are efficient for achieving the intended goals of all participants. In this respect, it should be noted that, at least in principle, the institution should make an effort to stay neutral with respect to the interest of any one of the participants, or giving any undue advantages to any type of participant.

- *Enforce satisfaction of commitments.* First through the design and implementation of mechanisms and devices that achieve adequate record keeping, risk allocation, safeguards, and liability underwriting among all participants. Next, by making an explicit standardisation of protocols, pre-conditions and post-conditions that govern commitment making within the institution. Finally, through the implementation of appropriate enforcement, corrective or compensatory mechanisms that may range from staff agents, supervisory devices, corrective measures, pre-epmtive safeguards, fines, insurance, bonds or guarantees, etc.

6. We have proposed to address those functions through the idea of *Electronic Institutions*.

7. We have defined an Electronic Institution as an entity that has three main components:

- *Dialogical Framework.* Where most ontologic aspects of the institution are addressed: the language used to communicate and the intended meanings of illocutions, terms and entities that may be invoked in those communications *within the institution.*

- *Performative Structure.* The conventions that establish the flow of interactions and the intended social consequences of the actions that take place within the institution.

- *Norms for Individual Behaviour.* The conventions to which individual agents are subject to while acting within the institution. These conventions address the preconditions that need to be satisfied by a given participant in order to establish a commitment, and the effects such commitments may have on the individual's existing commitments and ulterior behaviour.

8. We have developed and tested these ideas in a number of projects (e.g. Fishmarket, SMASH, MASFIT, SLIE, ISLANDER). And they seem to be fruitful.

We will expand on these ideas in our talk. We would also like to invite interested readers to look into the following references that expand on the ideas mentioned in this extended abstract [1,2,4,3,6,5].

References

1. E-Institutor URL . http://e-institutor.iiia.csic.es.
2. P. Noriega. *Agent Mediated Auctions: The Fishmarket Metaphor*. Number 8 in Monografies de l'IIIA. IIIA-CSIC, 1999.
3. P. Noriega and C. Sierra. Auctions and multi-agent systems. In Matthias Klusch, editor, *Intelligent Information Agents*, pages 153–175. Springer, 1999.
4. J. A. Rodriguez-Aguilar. *On the design and construction of Agent-mediated Institutions*. Number 14 in Monografies de l'IIIA. IIIA-CSIC, 2002.
5. C. Sierra and P. Noriega. Agent-mediated interaction. from auctions to negotiation and argumentation. In Mark d'Inverno, Michael Luck, Michael Fisher, and Chris Preist, editors, *Foundations and Applications of Multi-Agent Systems: UK-MAS 1996-2000*. Springer, in press.
6. Carles Sierra, N. R. Jennings, Pablo Noriega, and Simon Parson. A framework for argumentation-based negotiation. In *Proceedings of the 4th International Workshop on Agent Theories, Architectures and Languages (ATAL-97)*, 1997.

Making Peer Databases Interact – A Vision for an Architecture Supporting Data Coordination

Fausto Giunchiglia and Ilya Zaihrayeu

DIT – Dept. of Information and Communication Technology
University of Trento, 38050 Povo, Trento, Italy
{fausto, ilya}@dit.unitn.it

Abstract. Our goal in this paper is to study the problem of the interaction among databases in a peer-to-peer (P2P) network. We propose a new approach, that we call *"data (base) coordination"*, that rejects the assumption, made for instance in data integration, that the involved databases act as if they were a single (virtual) database, modeled as a global schema. From an operational point of view, the distinguishing feature of data coordination is that many of the parameters (metadata) influencing the interaction among peer databases are decided at run time. For any given query, the involved databases interact using the most "appropriate" (virtual) schema. This is crucial for dealing with the strong dynamics of a P2P network. We provide four basic architectural notions and hint how they are the building blocks of a possible distributed implementation capable of coordinating databases in a P2P network.

1. Introduction

"Peer-to-peer is a class of applications that take advantage of resources – storage, cycles, content, human presence – available at the edges of the Internet. Because accessing these decentralized resources means operating in an environment of unstable connectivity and unpredictable IP addresses, peer-to-peer nodes must ... have significant or total autonomy of central servers." (Quote from Clay Shirkey [20])

Among many others, the definition given above is the one providing quite a suggestive view or peer-to-peer (P2P) computing. Many examples of P2P computing already exist; take for instance Napster [16], a shared directory of available music and client software which allows, among other things, to import and export files; Gnutella [7], a decentralized group membership and search protocol, mainly used for file sharing; or Groove [9] a system which implements a secure shared space among peers. In this context, JXTA [11] is an important project which aims at creating a common platform that makes it simple and easy to build a wide range of distributed services and applications in which every device is addressable by a peer.

In such an application domain, the question which arises is whether there is a role for peer databases, also called P2P databases, by which we mean a database able to operate in a P2P environment, and therefore to interact with its peers, with a modality coherent with the spirit of P2P computing. Very little work has been done on this

M. Klusch, S. Ossowski, and O. Shehory (Eds.): CIA 2002, LNAI 2446, pp. 18–35, 2002.
© Springer-Verlag Berlin Heidelberg 2002

problem, see for instance [8], mainly concentrating on data placement. It is still an open issue whether the development of P2P databases is simply a new problem domain where we can apply existing database technology, and in particular that developed for data integration [10], or whether the solution of this problem requires the development of new ideas, new theory, and new technology.

We believe that the development of P2P databases does require such new developments. Our goal in this paper is to argue in favor of this thesis, discuss domain characteristics and solution desiderata, and to provide the first guidelines of a possible architecture. We propose a new approach, that we call *data (base) coordination*, that rejects the assumption, made in previous approaches, most noticeably in data integration, that the involved databases act as if they were a single (virtual) database, modeled as a global schema. We talk of coordination, very much in the spirit of [15], as further elaborated in [17], meaning that ...

"... Coordination is managing dependencies between interacting databases."

From an operational point of view, the distinguishing feature of data coordination is that many of the parameters (metadata) influencing the interaction among peer databases are decided at run time. The involved databases are not integrated to implement an *a priori* defined global schema, but, for any given query, they coordinate in order to define and use the most "appropriate" (virtual) schema. This is the crucial feature which allows us to deal with the strong dynamics of a P2P network.

The paper is structured as follows. In Section 2, we articulate the database coordination problem as four related but orthogonal subproblems: database integration, database coordination, providing good enough answers, and tuning coordination over time. In Section 3 we hint at a possible architecture implementing data coordination and introduce its four basic notions, namely: interest groups, acquaintances, coordination rules, and correspondence rules. In Section 4 we provide the highlights of a query answering algorithm. In Section 5 we develop an example. We conclude with a description of some of the many open research problems (Section 6) and with some final remarks (Section 7).

Two observations. First, while we believe that the ideas described in this paper apply to both query answering and update propagation, this paper mainly focuses on the former problem. The latter problem is discussed only sporadically, and never thoroughly. Second, in this paper, after providing the basic intuitions, we concentrate on the issues concerning a possible implementation architecture. As also discussed later, our proposed architecture can be seen as an implementation of the *Local Relational Model (LRM)*, a new model and proof-theoretic framework which provides a foundations to the coordination of P2P information sources [19].

2. The Database Coordination Problem

We articulate the database coordination problem in four steps, starting from data integration up to the issue of how to tune coordination over time.

2.1   Database Integration

Let us consider the following example scenario. Consider the situation where John, a person living in Toronto, is described in the database F of his family doctor, in the database P of a pharmacy, and also in the database H of the hospital where he once received medical treatment.

In the scenario hinted above the databases are completely *autonomous* and independent of one other. They are independent in their language, contents, in how they answer queries, ... They may be incomplete, overlapping, semantically heterogeneous, mutually inconsistent, ... Nevertheless it is definitely worthwhile to integrate their information and to exchange queries and updates. Consider the following examples.

Example 2.1: John is admitted to the hospital. As a consequence, H becomes "acquainted" with F for the purpose of retrieving his case history, and also for updating F with a new record corresponding to the medical checkup or aid taken when the treatment is over.

Example 2.2: The pharmacist administrating P prescribes a drug to John and, as a result, a new record is added to P. A new corresponding record should appear in F as well. Therefore, P gets acquainted with F and F can be updated.

We can suppose that John always goes to the same pharmacy and hospital. In this case, once the databases get acquainted, it is possible to reuse the same data integration mechanisms for query and update exchange. If one can also predict what F, P, and H are, as it can be the case, then one can decide that it is worthwhile, at design time, once for all, to implement the integration among these three databases. For this kind of problems existing technology, for instance in data integration [10], may suffice.

2.2 Database Coordination

In a P2P environment things can get much more complicated. Consider the following further example.

Example 2.3: John goes to a ski resort in another country, for instance Trentino in Italy. Unluckily, here he has an accident; for instance, he breaks a leg, and he must get medical aid to the resort's medical office. This office, in turn, has its own database M which now needs to get involved. M may need to query H for the purpose of retrieving treatment details of a similar past accident. Furthermore, when John returns home, a new record from M should appear in F. However the acquaintance between M and F does not need to be maintained for ever, since the two databases will probably not need to coordinate again, and can eventually be dropped.

In situations like that described in Example 2.3 the design and development of data integration mechanisms for randomly acquainted databases which may need to communicate only a few times, becomes impractical.

We have (at least) three kinds of unpredictable run time factors, which influence the answer to a given query in a P2P network, namely:

1. *Network (dependent) variance:* the network changes over time. This may happen for many reasons, for instance: there is a different set of peers; due to their autonomy, some databases change their interaction with their peers; or, the interaction mechanisms change.

2. *Database (dependent) variance:* for any given P2P network, different databases, even if asked the same query, and at the same time, will provide different answers. While trying to provide a "global" answer, a database queries other peer databases. However each database queries the network from "its point of view". It may involve different databases (a subset of those available) or, even keeping the same set of databases, it may activate a different form of interaction with, as a result, different data passed around.

3. *Query (dependent) variance:* different queries, even if posed to the same database, will impose different points of view on the network. As above in item 2, depending of the specific query, we may cause different databases to be involved or different forms of interaction among databases.

In our opinion, network, database and query variance, are the three fundamental elements of variability which must be considered in a P2P scenario. In order to solve these kinds of problems we need new and extremely flexible mechanisms for database interaction, that we collect under the heading of *database coordination.*

Notice that, in this context, it makes very little sense to speak of a global schema, as it is commonly done in the data integration literature [10]. The main conceptual reason for rejecting this notion is that we cannot think of a set of P2P databases just as a particular implementation of a single (virtual) database, this being the underlying assumption which motivates the definition of a global schema. Consider the effects of the three kinds of variance defined above on a global schema. Network variance forces us to assume that the global schema changes over time. Database variance forces us to assume that we have a global schema for each database (access point?) in the P2P network. Query variance forces us to assume that we have a global schema for each distinct query. That is, if we make the global schema assumption, we are able to explain how any specific query posed to a specific database in a specific instant in time will be answered. However, we cannot explain how the dynamics influence the answer to a query, this being the main issue in a P2P network.

From a foundational point of view, any theory developed under the assumption of a global schema, and under the implicit assumption that the global schema is fixed, prevents us from the studying the dynamics of a P2P network. As far as we know these two assumptions have never been relieved, in particular in the data integration literature, see for instance [10, 12]. Rejecting this hypothesis requires a new kind of semantics. It is no longer possible to see the global schema as a view of the local database (global-as-view approach) or, vice versa, the local databases as views of the global database (local-as-view approach). For instance, we can no longer assume that there is a unique universe containing all the elements of the single databases. The mappings among elements may change over time, or may be different depending on the query or on the database answering the query. This topic is not discussed in this paper. A new semantics, called the *Local Relational Model,* based on the *Local Models Semantics* [6, 4], which provides the foundations for the coordination of P2P databases is given in [19, 1].

From an implementation point of view, we believe that the previous work on data integration can be partially re-used in this framework. Once one fixes the query, the database it is posed to, and the P2P network, then it should be possible to implement coordination using some variation of the existing data integration algorithms. However, for this to happen, two steps must be taken:

1.   a specific set of parameters (metadata) must be defined which can be used to model network, database and query variance;

2.   the existing algorithms for data integration must be modified and parameterized as functions of the defined metadata.

2.3   Good Enough Answers

Moving from data integration to data coordination, it becomes hard to maintain a high quality level in the answers that the P2P network is able to provide. By high quality level we mean the fact that data can flow among the databases preserving (at the best possible level of approximation) soundness and completeness. In this context, soundness means that the data provided by the local databases satisfy the global schema (but they are not necessarily complete, some of them can get lost in the coordination). Completeness has the dual meaning. In the data integration literature, completeness is often given up, still maintaining the request of soundness. In a P2P environment, completeness and soundness will be very hard to achieve. This will happen in limit cases, for instance with low dynamics, simplified interaction among the databases, and if and when there will be interest in investing a substantial amount of money in the solution of the problem.

One area where there will often be interest in getting very high quality data integration is the medical care domain. There are however many other application domains where this is not the case. One such example is tourism. This domain, is not life critical, and in many cases the small dimension of a single business (hotel, campsite, ...) does not justify big investments. Consider the following example.

Example 2.4: When planning his vacation in Trentino, John goes to a local agency, which unluckily can not offer John anything from their own database. Instead the agency searches for single operators in the Trentino region (hotels, ski resorts, etc), starts communication sessions with some of them, and queries for the necessary information (e.g., prices, conditions, availability).

Compared with the medical care example, the dynamics will have a much higher impact on the quality of the answer. We have network variance: the relevant databases are much more unstable in their being active and coordinated in the network, nodes come and go (for instance depending on the season), and so on. We have database variance: John travels around and queries different databases. The same query will get different results since each database will implement different degrees of coordination with the others, and so on. Thus, for instance, a query about hotels made to a hotel database will likely get an answer that is better than the answer obtained from a campsite database. We also have query variance: if you ask a query about campsites to a campsite database you will likely get a better quality answer than if you ask this database a query about hotels, and dually for the hotel databases. Depending on the query, certain coordination mechanisms may or may not be activated. However, in this application, the agency doesn't need the best possible answer. It simply needs some answer. As long as, for instance, it gets a hotel John likes, this is good enough. Compared to the previous example, much lower quality data coordination will probably suffice.

The medical care and tourism domains are just examples. Things can get even more radical and complex when one thinks of applications where some of the nodes are mobile and where coordination happens on an even more occasional basis, for instance due to the physical proximity of two mobile peers. (As from the quote in the introduction, these kinds of situations should be quite usual in a P2P network.) In these situations, and for certain kinds of applications, almost any answer will suffice, as long as there is one. In a P2P environment, in terms of quality of answers, it is possible to go from one extreme to the other. On one extreme, it may be usual to get poor quality answers. This may happen because the databases interact partially or do not interact at all or, even worse, they pass around data which are wrong (for instance because of unsolved problems of semantic heterogeneity). On the other extreme, there will be a tight coordination and it will be possible to achieve or, at least, approximate soundness and completeness. Between these two extremes there is a continuum of answers of different quality.

The problem of the quality of the answers must be dealt with by developing the notion of *"good enough answer"*. The intuition is that an answer will be good enough when it will serve its purposes given the amount of effort made in computing it. A lot of research needs to be done on this topic. Here it is worth pointing out that, when trying to get good enough answers, one can work to produce the best infrastructure but also, for any given infrastructure, to spend a lot of time in the run time query answering. A theory of what it means to be a good answer should take into account both these factors and relate them to how the query results are used.

2.4   Tuning Coordination over Time

In order to implement database coordination, a lot of metadata needs to be produced and maintained. Due to the strong dynamics of a P2P network, this is a crucial and hard task to perform. A node will never know the full list of its peers, it will never know everything about them, and its knowledge will be hard to maintain and will easily become obsolete. There will likely be a need of tuning and sometimes improving, on each single peer, the quality of the interaction (for instance, with the help of learning algorithms, metadata editors, and so on. See later). There is an obvious trade-off between the quality of the answers and the effort made in maintaining coordination.

3. Hints of a Possible Architecture

A P2P network consists of an open-ended number of nodes (or peers), where each peer is uniquely identified by its *id* or *address*. In our approach each peer has a local database, and an extra layer, called the *P2P layer*, or, also, the *LRM layer*. The LRM layer interacts with the local database and interfaces it with the P2P network. The resulting architecture, first published in [1], is shown in Figure 1.

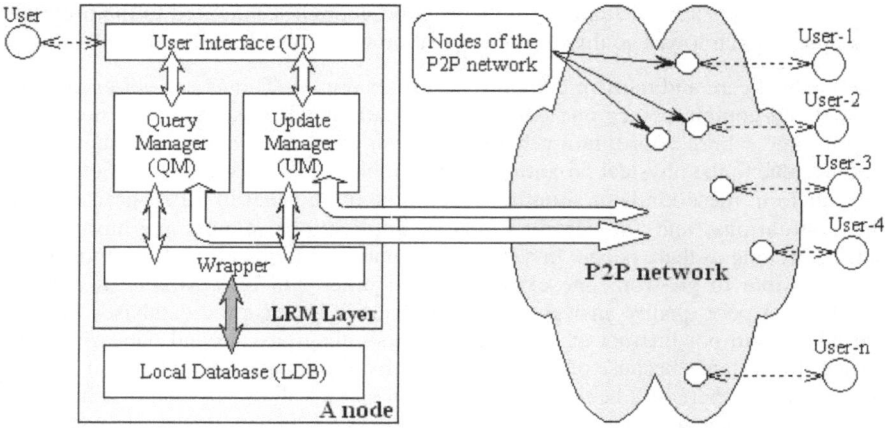

Fig. 1. First level architecture

The *LRM Layer* is the P2P functionality layered on the *Local Database* (LDB). *User Interface* allows the user to submit queries which will then be answered by the local database and the peer databases, to receive results and messages from the other nodes, and to control the other modules of the LRM Layer. *Query Manager* (QM) and *Update Manager* (UM) are responsible for query and update propagation. *Wrapper* is a translation layer between QM and UM, and LDB. Peers communicate through QM and UM using XML messages (white arrows). Inter-module communication is also XML-based, as shown again by the white arrows. The communication language between Wrapper and LDB is LDB-dependent (it could be SQL, for example).

The main functionalities for coordinating P2P databases are implemented within QM and UM. These functionalities are implemented using four basic notions, described below.

Interest Groups. In most cases, nodes know very little of the other nodes of the P2P network, and in particular about the *topics* about which their peers are able to answer queries. Intuitively, medical care, tourism, tourism in Trentino, are all possible topics. A topic could be formalized as keywords, a schema, an ontology, or as a context [5], as used in [2]. We introduce the notion of *(interest) group* and define it as a set of nodes which are able to answer queries about a certain topic. A node can belong to multiple groups. The notion of group is introduced with the main goal of computing, for any given input query, the *Query Scope* (QS) – the set of nodes a query should be propagated to. The definition of a group must satisfy two complementary requirements. First, groups help deal with the complexity and the high number of nodes of a P2P network. Instead of searching for single nodes which could answer its input query, a node looks for one or more groups according to their topic. This, of course, means that the input query must be associated with a topic (this could be done by the user or by the system itself). Second, groups are used to compute a bound on the number of nodes in the query scope, therefore guaranteeing termination. Thus, topics should be general enough to capture most of the "relevant nodes", but not too general, to avoid inefficient query answering. At the moment we are supposing that each group will have a node, called the *Group Manager* (GM) which is in charge of the management of the metadata needed in order to run the group.

Acquaintances. *Acquaintances* are nodes that a node knows about and that have data that can be used to answer a specific query. A node is an acquaintance of another node only with respect to (possibly, a schematic representation of) a query. Acquaintances can therefore be thought of as links from one node to another, labelled by a (schematic) query. If a node is an acquaintance, then there must be a way to compute how to propagate a query, to propagate results back, and to reconcile them with the results coming from the other acquaintances. Crucial for these tasks are *coordination rules*, and *correspondence rules*, as defined below.

The schematic representation of queries used in acquaintances is conceptually different from the topic associated with a group. A node can be part of a group without being an acquaintance of all the nodes in that group. One example is the case where a node gets a query about hotels in Italy and chooses the group with topic "tourism in Italy". However one of the nodes in that group is a campsite. Conversely, we may have a node which is acquainted with the node that gets a user query asking about hotels, but it belongs to the group with characteristic topic "tourism in Austria".

The intuition is that a node will try to propagate a query to the acquaintances in QS. This is in turn may activate the recursive propagation of the query to the acquaintances of the acquainted nodes. This will happen until the query is propagated to all reachable acquaintances. In general not all the nodes in QS will be queried, this happening when there is node which cannot be reached by the transitive propagation of queries along acquaintance links.

Coordination rules. Each acquaintance may be associated with one or more *coordination rules*. At run time, nodes use coordination rules which specify under what conditions, when, how and where to propagate queries or updates. One possible implementation of coordination rules is as *ECA rules* [3]. A triggering *Event* can be an update or a query coming from the user or from another node; *Condition* refers to properties of the update or query (e.g., the type of query and/or which data items are referenced by the query), and *Action* can be the translation and propagation of a given update or query to a particular acquaintance.

Consider Example 2.3 and suppose that M has a schema "Accidents". Then one possible coordination rule, relating M to H, is as follows:

Event: "Query to 'M:Accidents'"
Condition: "Value of First Name attribute in the body of the query is 'John'"   (1)
Action: "Translate that query using Correspondence Rules and send it to H"

(1) is a simple coordination rule which launches query propagation to H when a query posed to M contains 'John' as a search criterion. It is easy to think of more complex coordination rules, for instance, rules which can selectively extract information from one of two databases, or rules which do some filtering, and so on.

Correspondence rules. Each acquaintance is associated with one or more *correspondence rules*. Correspondence rules take care of the semantic heterogeneity problem. They are implemented as rewrite rules and are called by coordination rules, in the body of the code implementing their action and condition components. Correspondence rules are used for the translation of queries and query results. They can be used, for instance to translate attribute or element names. In this latter case we also call them *Domain Relations* [19].

Consider the coordination rule in (1). Then we may have the following rewrite rules concerning attributes:

$$
\begin{array}{lcl}
\text{Address\_Reason} & \rightarrow & \text{Disease} \\
\text{Treatment\_Taken} & \rightarrow & \text{Treatment\_Desc} \\
\text{Prescription\_Given} & \rightarrow & \text{'None'} \\
\text{Date} & \rightarrow & \text{In}
\end{array}
\tag{2}
$$

Where "None" means that there is no corresponding attribute. Similarly, the following domain relations are applied for rewriting element names:

$$
\begin{array}{lcl}
\text{Value (Address\_Reason)} & \rightarrow & \text{Value (Disease)} \\
\text{Value (Treatment\_Taken)} & \rightarrow & \text{Value (Treatment\_Desc)}
\end{array}
\tag{3}
$$

In the above example values are translated without modifications, but it is easy to think about more complex translations when, for instance, dates are converted to different formats, currency conversion, and so on. In practice, this is a very hard task which involves a lot of data scrubbing and transformation and which occupies a substantial amount of all the data integration projects.

4. Answering Queries

Reconsider Figure 1. The process starts when a node, let us call it *n1*, receives a user query with an indication that this is a *global query,* namely a query whose answer should be computed asking not only the local database but, also the "reachable" peers in the network. Below a list of problems which must be dealt with to answer a global query.

1. *n1* computes the query topic, maybe with the help of the user;

2. *n1* matches the query topic with the topics of the known groups and, as a result, computes one or more groups that could provide meaningful answers;

3.   *n1*, with the help of QM, computes QS;

4. *n1* may not be acquainted with any of the nodes in QS, or, more in general, the acquaintances graph may not be connected enough. In order to solve this, a

Getting Acquainted Protocol needs to be activated whose main goal is to learn coordination and correspondence rules between *n1* and the nodes in QS, or between any two nodes in QS. The getting acquainted protocol will presumably involve database schema exchange, schema matching [18], coordination and correspondence rules derivation from the results of matching, and, probably, some other phases.

5.   Exploiting coordination and correspondence rules, *n1* sends the query to the acquaintances in QS. For efficiency reasons, this should be done in parallel. Here, various non trivial issues arise. In particular:

    a.   Not all the nodes in QS are acquaintances of *n1*. To maximize the query results, and exploiting the fact that coordination and correspondence rules tell us how to propagate queries forwards and results backwards, the acquaintances of the acquaintances of *n1* can be *transitively* queried. This originates a propagation mechanism on the graph of acquaintances.

    b.   The acquaintances graph may be a DAG, namely have multiple paths between two nodes. As a consequence, a node can be queried more than once. This requires the implementation of mechanisms for avoiding multiple answers and multiple query propagations.

    c.   The acquaintances graph may have cycles. Loops must be avoided.

    d.   Not all the nodes in QS may be reachable by the acquaintances graph. We have to stop for one of two reasons: we have reached all the nodes in QS, or the nodes in QS which have not been reached yet cannot be reached.

Problem a. can be dealt with by implementing, inside each node, automated query propagation mechanisms. The implementation of coordination rules as ECA rules is one possible solution (see example above). Problems b. and c. can be dealt with by associating each query with a unique identifier. Any node receiving the same query twice will discard it. Problem d. can be dealt with by supposing that a node, for instance GM, knows QS and which nodes have been involved by the propagation mechanism (for instance because they send this information to it). GM seems a good choice as it is the node with the most information about its peer nodes, and all the nodes know about it;

6.   All the nodes involved send their results back to *n1*. This is applied recursively until all the results have been propagated back to *n1*;

7.   Reconcile all the results and answer the user query.

The basic algorithm hinted above can be made more efficient. Some of the possible extensions are listed below. QS can be recursively computed, for instance by the nodes answering the query; this may lead to better answers. It is possible to use intermediate nodes that are not part of QS but that, via the appropriate coordination and correspondence rule, can propagate the query; this may allow to reach otherwise unreachable nodes. Data reconciliation can be done at the intermediate nodes; among other things this can make the process faster, for instance by avoiding the propagation of duplicate information coming from different nodes. And so on.

5. A Medical Care Scenario

Let us instantiate the intuitions described above to Example 2.3 above. For simplicity we assume that all databases are relational, each consisting of one relation, and that SQL is the language used.

5.1 The Three Databases

Let us suppose that the relations of the databases *F, H* and *M* are as follows:

F: Prescription (PatID, P_Name, Illness_Desc, StartDate, RecoveryDate, Treatment, Type, Prescriptions);
H: Patients (PID, Name, Disease, Treatment_Desc, In, Out);
M: Accidents (P_id, FN, LN, Address_Reason, Treatment_Taken, Prescription_Given, Date);

PatID, PID and P_id are the patients' identifiers; P_Name and Name are their full names; FN and LN are their first and last names; Illness_Desc, Disease and Address_Reason are their medical problems; Treatment, Treatment_Desc and Treatment_Taken are descriptions of the prescribed treatments; Prescriptions and Prescription_Given are the descriptions of prescribed drugs; StartDate, In and RecoveryDate, Out are the start and end dates of a treatment; Date states when certain treatment was given; and, finally, Type specifies where a treatment was conducted, a value from the set {"Home", "Hospital"}. The three databases are heterogeneous. They use different relation and attribute names to represent similar concepts, different formats for patients' ids and dates, and they also contain different data.

Let us assume that the databases keep the following items:

F:Prescription

PatID	P_Name	Illness_Desc	StartDate	RecoveryDate	Treatment	Type	Prescriptions
8	John	Flu	Mar 13, 02	Mar 15, 02	None	Home	Nasol
2	Eric O'Neill	Headache	Jan 06, 02	Jan 06, 02	None	Home	Aspirin
8	John	Leg fracture	Nov 11, 01	Dec 23, 01	Leg put in plaster	Hospital	Rest at home

H:Patients

PID	Name	Disease	Treatment_Desc	In	Out
P12	John	Abscess	Surgical operation	Mar 7, 2002	Mar 14, 2002
P10	Mary	Arm fracture	Plastering	Feb 12, 2002	Feb 17, 2002
P12	John	Forearm dislocation	Bandage	Jan 08, 2002	Jan 13, 2002

M:Accidents

P_id	FN	LN	Address_Reason	Treatment_Taken	Prescription_Given	Date
A12	Paolo	Traverso	Back injury	None	Heating ointment	01.22.02

5.2   The Acquaintances Graph

Let us now suppose that the following query is asked to M, where 'A13' is the new id for John in M:

Q_M =   <u>Select</u> FN, LN, Address_Reason, Treatment_Taken, Prescription_Given, Date   (4)
<u>From</u>   "M:Accidents"
<u>Where</u> Address_Reason <u>Like</u> ('%Fracture%' <u>Or</u> '%Dislocation%') <u>And</u> PID = 'A13'

with the indication that this is a global query and that its topic is

$$T= \text{"Medical care in Canada"}$$

The intuitive meaning of query (4) is that the search should be propagated to some nodes presumably in Canada which are supposed to store information on John's case history. Note that Q_M is stated in the language of M.

Let us further suppose that, after some search (possibly guided by the user), T is matched with the topic "Medical care in Toronto" of the interest group $G = \{F, H, P\}$, with H being G's GM. Notice that M is not part of G. However this is irrelevant to our purposes. We can further suppose that H is acquainted with F and that P is acquainted with F. This situation is reported in Figure 2 below.

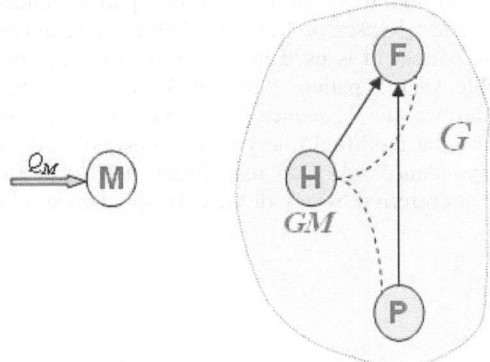

Fig. 2. Initial state

The dashed lines between H and F, H and P stand for the network connections used for the propagation of the metadata needed in order to manage the group and its services. As from Section 4, these connections can, for instance, be used to propagate to H all the data needed in order to guarantee termination for any set of nodes QS which is a subset of G.

Let us suppose that GM computes and sends back to M a query scope QS = $G = \{F, H, P\}$. To start the coordination session, M must get acquainted with one of the nodes in G. We can reasonably assume that it is decided that M must get acquainted with H.

At this point the *Getting Acquainted Protocol* is activated. The schemas of M:accidents and H:patients are matched. They both have the structure of a depth 1 tree. The two structures can be easily matched once the elements are matched, for instance by applying, among others, linguistic techniques.

As a result a set of coordination rules are learned. They are:
COOR#1

(5)

Event:	M:Q
Condition:	Q: (Address_Reason $\in$ <u>Select</u> OR Treatment_Taken $\in$ <u>Select</u>) AND (PID = 'A13' $\in$ <u>Where</u>)
Action:	Q = Apply (Q, Corr#1);
	Q = Apply (Q, Corr#2);
	Q = Apply (Q, Corr#3);
	Q = Apply (Q, Corr#4);
	Q = Apply (Q, Corr#5);
	Q = Apply (Q, Corr#6);
	Q = Apply (Q, Corr#7);
	Q = Delete_not_Mapped (Q);
	Send (Q, H).

COOR#1 is the rule identifier. **COOR#1** propagates the input query to **H**. It triggers when a query Q is submitted to **M**. In the condition part we check whether the select part of Q refers to Address_Reason or Treatment_Taken (these attributes are shared with **H**), and whether the patient id is used in the query condition part and it is equal to John's id (a possible shared patient between **M** and **H**). The action part of the coordination rule defines the sequence of query modification operations, and it concludes by sending the modified query to **H**. Apply (Q, Corr_rule) returns Q after applying the correspondence rule Corr_rule. Delete_not_Mapped (Q) eliminates those attributes which are not referred by any of the correspondence rules.

COOR#2

(6)

Event:	M:R_H
Condition:	None
Action:	R_M = Null;
	R_M = Apply (R_H, Corr#8);
	R_M = Apply (R_H, Corr#9);
	R_M = Apply (R_H, Corr#10);

COOR#2 propagates results back from **H** to **M**. There is no need to apply domain relations. **COOR#2** calls correspondence rules which indicate which value should be assigned to which attribute in **M**.

A set of correspondence rules are also learned. Below is a set of rules for translating attribute names in a query:

Corr#1:	P_id	→	PID	
Corr#2:	FN	→	Name	(7)
Corr#3:	LN	→	Name	
Corr#4:	Address_Reason	→	Disease	
Corr#5:	Treatment_Taken	→	Treatment_Desc	

The following translate object and schema names:

Corr#6:	'M:Accidents'	→	'H:Patients'	
Corr#7:	'A13'	→	'P12'	(8)

Note that the matching between *H* and *M* is not perfect, and, in particular, that the attribute date is not translated. We expect that the getting acquainted protocol will not be able to produce the best possible match in many cases.

Finally, a set of rules needed for the translation of results are also learned. Note again that there is also no mapping of date related attributes.

Corr#8:	Name	→	FN	
Corr#9:	Disease	→	Address_Reason	(9)
Corr#10:	Treatment_Desc	→	Treatment_Taken	

5.3 Query Propagation

Finally, when an "appropriate" acquaintances graph has been built, the propagation algorithm can be started. The resulting data flow is given in Figure 3 below.

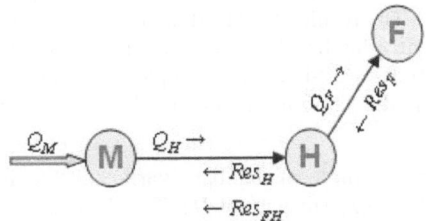

Fig. 3. Query answering

According to the rules given above Q_M gets translated to Q_H as follows:

$$Q_H = \underline{\text{Select}} \text{ Name, Disease, Treatment\_Desc} \tag{10}$$
$$\underline{\text{From}} \text{ "H:Patients"}$$
$$\underline{\text{Where}} \text{ Disease } \underline{\text{Like}} \text{ ('\%Fracture\%' } \underline{\text{Or}} \text{ '\%Dislocation\%') } \underline{\text{And}} \text{ PID = 'P12'}$$

H computes the following answer to Q_H

$$\text{Res}_H = <\text{'John', 'Forearm dislocation', 'Bandage'}> \tag{11}$$

which is then sent unmodified to *M* (even if at *M* the same values are related to different attributes).

Following the transitivity mechanism described in Section 4, H translates Q_H and propagates it to F as Q_F. Since H and F are from the same group we can suppose that we have correct and complete coordination and correspondence rules. Let us suppose that Q_H is translated to Q_F as follows:

$$Q_F = \text{Select P\_Name, Illness\_Desc, Treatment} \\ \text{From \quad "F:Prescriptions"} \\ \text{Where \quad Illness\_Desc Like ('\%Fracture\%' Or '\%Dislocation\%') And PID = '8'} \tag{12}$$

F returns to H the following query answer:

$$\text{Res}_F = \text{<'John', 'Leg fracture', 'Leg put in plaster'>} \tag{13}$$

These results are translated at H, propagated back to M, where all the results are reconciled and presented as:

$$\text{Res}_H{}^M = \text{<'John', 'Forearm dislocation', 'Bandage'>} \tag{14}$$

$$\text{Res}_{FH}{}^M = \text{<'John', 'Leg fracture', 'Leg put in plaster'>}$$

5.4 Variance and Good Enough Answers

Consider the results in (14). They are incomplete and some fields (LN and Date) present in Q_M are missing in the answer. Nevertheless, these results are good enough since they still serve the needs of M. LN and Date are not critically important for M for treatment purposes, moreover John can likely provide approximate dates.

Let us now consider an example of network variance. Suppose that F is down and cannot answer queries. The results produced are even more incomplete due to the fact that $\text{Res}_{FH}{}^M$ is not present. Whether they are good enough, it depends on what it will be possible to do with only $\text{Res}_H{}^M$. Since, in Example 2.3 John breaks a leg, much it will depend on whether it is the same leg as in $\text{Res}_H{}^M$. John will be able to produce this information.

Let us now consider an example of database variance. Recall Figure 3 and suppose that M gets acquainted with F (instead of H). The database variance is caused by the change in the acquaintance path (F, instead of H, is queried). M poses, in the language of F, a query Q_F which requests the same data as Q_H. However, the answer is different since F has a different 'vision' of the world. More concretely, it is not acquainted with H. We have:

$$\text{Res}_F{}^M = \text{<'John', 'Leg fracture', 'Leg put in plaster'>} \tag{15}$$

Very likely this answer will be good enough.

Let us conclude with an example of query variance. Let us suppose that we ask Q_M as above with "John" substituted with "Mary". Mary is not a shared patient between H and F and, therefore, there are no coordination rules for her and there is no query propagation to F. Notice that a value in an attribute changes the query propagation tree. We have the following answer:

$$\text{Res}_F^M = \quad <\text{'Mary', 'Arm fracture', 'plastering'}> \tag{16}$$

This will likely be a good enough answer.

6. Research Problems

The ideas described in this paper are very preliminary. A lot of work needs to be done to make these ideas concrete and to be able to evaluate their usefulness. In this section we articulate, at the current state of the art, some of the open and relevant research problems. We do not consider the many issues which need to be dealt with at the theoretical level, and in particular, what we consider crucial future developments of the LRM. For a preliminary discussion about this, see [19].

Groups. A lot of issues need to be dealt with. Some of them are as follows: we need to verify the role of the group manager, to define what a topic is, and to define the services associated to a group, we need techniques for group discovery, for associating a node to a group, for maintaining the group metadata, for propagating (part of) them in the P2P network and/or to the member nodes, ..., and so on. At the moment we are evaluating whether the JXTA group mechanisms can be reused, at least in part, to implement our own interest groups.

Query answering and update propagation. This is still open space. As from above, an interesting issue is how much of the existing technology in data integration, and in particular of the LAV/GAV technology [10], we will be able to reuse and to adapt to the P2P problem domain. Similarly, concerning the implementation of coordination rules, we should be able to leverage the existing work on active databases and ECA rules, see for example [3].

Maintaining coordination metadata. We foresee two basic mechanisms for maintaining and developing metadata. The first is by (semi) automatically learning them from navigating the network. We will need to develop sophisticated *matching* techniques capable of computing the most appropriate group topic and the query scope, and to learn coordination and correspondence rules. Most of the time the match will be only partial and not perfect. The general area of matching is definitely not mature. However a lot of material can be found in the literature, see for instance [18, 13, 14]. The second is the development of (graphic) editors which should allow a user to develop, in a computer supported way, the desired metadata. To this extent, it is important to notice that coordination and correspondence rules are the procedural implementation of *coordination formulas,* as defined in [19]. Coordination formulas are indexed first order formulas and are the declarative specification of coordination and correspondence rules. Also topics, if we take them to be labeled graphs, can be developed using an editor similar to that described in [2].

7. Conclusion

This paper is a first investigation of the problem or how to make databases interact in a P2P network. P2P networks are characterized by high dynamics and by the fact that nodes are autonomous. We have characterized the problem as having four main dimensions:

1. We must integrate data coming from autonomous, most often semantically heterogeneous databases. This problem is very similar to the data integration problem widely studied in the literature;
2. We must deal with network, database, and query variance. This requires us to define a new set of metadata and to define algorithms whose behavior changes in dependence on these data. This is why we talk of data coordination, as distinct from data integration;
3. We will almost never get correct and complete answers. We must be content with answers which are good enough;
4. There is a need to tune metadata. This is requires in order to cope with the dynamics of a P2P network.

We have provided the guidelines of an architecture which supports coordination among peer databases. This architecture is based on four basic notions: interest groups, acquaintances, coordination and correspondence rules. We have listed what we consider to be the most relevant research problems in this domain. The theory underlying and motivating the architecture and notions discussed in this paper is described in [19].

Acknowledgements. The ideas described in this paper have matured thanks to the close interaction with Phil Bernstein and John Mylopoulos. Phil Bernstein asked a lot of hard questions. John Mylopoulos suggested that coordination formulas could be implemented as ECA rules. We also thank Paolo Bouquet, Gaby Kuper, Matteo Bonifacio and Luciano Serafini for the many stimulating discussions.

References

1. Bernstein, P.A., Giunchiglia, F., Kementsietsidis, A., Mylopoulos, J., Serafini, L., and Zaihrayeu, I. "Data Management for Peer-to-Peer Computing: A Vision". WebDB02 – Fifth International Workshop on the Web and Databases, 2002.
2. Bouquet, P., Dona', A. and Serafini, L. "ConTeXtualized local ontology specification via CTXML". MeaN-02 – AAAI Workshop on Meaning Negotiation. Edmonton, Alberta, Canada, 2002.
3. Dayal U., Hanson E.N., and Widom J. "Active Database Systems. Modern Database Systems: The Object Model, Interoperability, and Beyond". W. Kim, (Ed), Addison-Wesley, Reading, Massachusetts, 1994.
4. Ghidini, C., and Serafini, L. "Distributed First Order Logics". Frontiers of Combining Systems 2 (Papers presented at FroCoS'98). Dov M. Gabbay and Maarten de Rijke, (Eds), Research Studies Press/Wiley. ISBN 0863802524 (hardback).
5. Giunchiglia, F. "Contextual reasoning". Epistemologia, special issue on "I Linguaggi e le macchine". Vol. XVI, pages 45-364, Tilgher-Genova, Italy, 1993.

6. Giunchiglia, F., and Ghidini, C. "Local Models Semantics, or Contextual Reasoning = Locality + Compatibility". KR'98 –Sixth International Conference on Principles of Knowledge Representation and Reasoning. Morgan-Kauffman, 1998. Long version: Ghidini, C., and Giunchiglia, F. "Local Models Semantics, or Contextual Reasoning = Locality + Compatibility". Artificial Intelligence. 127(3):221-259, 2001.
7. Gnutella, see http://www.gnutellanews.com .
8. Gribble S., Halevy A., Ives Z., Rodrig M., and Suiu D. "What can Databases do for Peer-to-Peer?". WebDB01 –Fourth International Workshop on the Web and Databases, 2001.
9. Groove, see http://www.groove.net .
10. Halevy, A. "Answering queries using views: a survey". VLDB Journal 2001.
11. JXTA, see www.jxta.org.
12. Lenzerini, M. "Data Integration: A Theoretical Perspective". PODS 2002: 233-246, 2002.
13. Madhavan J., Bernstein P. A., and Rahm E. "Generic Schema Matching Using Cupid". Proc. VLDB 2001, 2001.
14. Magnini, B., Serafini, L. and Speranza, M. "Linguistic Based Matching of Local Ontologies". MeaN-02 –AAAI Workshop on Meaning Negotiation. Edmonton, Alberta, Canada, 2002
15. Malone, W.T., and Crowston, K. "The Interdisciplinary Study of Coordination". ACM Computing Surveys, Vol. 26, No. 1, 1994.
16. Napster, see http://www.napster.com.
17. Perini, A., Susi, A., and Giunchiglia, F. "Designing Coordination among Human and Software Agents". SEKE'02 – Fourteenth International Conference on Software Engineering and Knowledge Engineering, 2002.
18. Rahm E., and Bernstein P. A. "A survey of approaches to automatic schema matching". The VLDB Journal 10: 334–350, 2001.
19. Serafini, L., Giunchiglia, F., Mylopoulos, J., and Bernstein, P.A. "The Local Relational model: Model and Proof Theory". IRST Technical Report 0112-23, Istituto Trentino di Cultura, December 2001.
20. Shirkey, C., see http://www.shirky.com/#p2p.

Tourists on the Move

Mikko Laukkanen, Heikki Helin, and Heimo Laamanen

Sonera Corporation
Sonera Corporate R&D
P.O.Box 970, FIN-00051 Sonera, Finland
{Mikko.T.Laukkanen,Heikki.J.Helin,Heimo.Laamanen}@sonera.com

Abstract. In a nomadic environment a user may access same services
as she would using her desktop computer, but she could do so anywhere,
at any time and even using a variety different kinds of devices. This kind
of environment places new challenges on the architecture implementing
the services, because a set of parameters, such as different kinds of mobile networks, varying Quality of Service, characteristics and limitations
of the mobile device and the user's location, have to be taken into account. In this paper we present an architecture, which addresses these
issues. We have implemented the architecture as a multi-agent system,
which consists of middle-agents specialized in monitoring and controlling
network connections, content adaptation based on both mobile device
characteristics and the QoS of the network connection and a scalable
user interface, which supports multiple mobile devices. Together these
agents form a multi-agent system, which allows the services to adapt to
the changes in the nomadic environment.

1 Introduction

The progress in the mobile network technologies and mobile devices changes
the way in which people access services. A user may access same services as
she would using her desktop computer, but in the nomadic environment she is
able to do so anywhere, at any time and even using a variety of different kinds
of devices. This kind of environment places new challenges on the architecture
implementing the services, because a set of parameters, which usually could have
been ignored in the wireline environments, has to be taken into account. Mobile
networks introduce parameters such as different kinds of wireless networks, high
variability in the Quality of Service (QoS), and characteristics and limitations of
the mobile devices. In addition, contextual parameters, such as user's location,
direction and speed, as well as time of day should be considered. However, of
the contextual parameters, we deal only with the location.

In this paper we present an architecture, which addresses these aforementioned issues. We have implemented the architecture as a multi-agent system,
which consists of middle-agents specialized in monitoring and controlling network
connections, content adaptation based on both mobile device characteristics and
the QoS of the network connection, and a scalable user interface, which supports

M. Klusch, S. Ossowski, and O. Shehory (Eds.): CIA 2002, LNAI 2446, pp. 36–50, 2002.
© Springer-Verlag Berlin Heidelberg 2002

multiple mobile devices. The services are implemented as agents, which either implement a service by themselves or wrap some existing service. Our multi-agent system is hosted by MicroFIPA-OS and FIPA-OS agent platforms, but the architecture is not dependent on the agent platform, and in fact, could run even without a platform. However, our architecture does not include a directory service, where agents can advertise their capabilities; therefore, we assume that the service is available. We are also in the process of adding support for JADE-LEAP [3] and JADE [2] agent platforms.

We believe that software agent technology is an ideal methodology to design and implement a middleware, which addresses the challenges in the nomadic environment. Agents are able to re-actively sense changes in the environment and autonomously act based on them. For instance, upon detecting that the throughput of the underlying network connection drops dramatically, an agent specialized in the wireless communication may make a decision to change from the current network technology to another. Once changed, the agent may inform other agents about the new QoS, who are therefore able to react based on the changing QoS, for instance by applying content adaptation.

This paper reflects the work being done in the CRUMPET[1] project, which is funded by EC IST[2] 5th framework. The aim of the CRUMPET is to implement, validate, and trial tourism-related services for nomadic users [18]. The services utilize different wireless networks, such as GSM, GPRS, and WLAN. We have chosen tourists as the target end-users, because we believe that tourism and the environment, where the tourists are, and will be in the future, can be considered as a good example of a nomadic environment. More and more people combine several purposes with travelling, such as business, education, and leisure. These kind of tourists may not invest a great deal of time in pre-planning their trips, but prefer having location-based, personalized, and just-on-time services at their destinations.

Adaptive applications in mobile computing is a topic under an active research. Therefore, in Section 2 we will first describe the related work on the area. In Section 3 we describe how the nomadic environment differs from the stationary environment in terms of service deployment. Section 4 presents our architecture for providing agent-based services for nomadic users. In Sections 5, 6 and 7 we describe the core parts of our architecture in more detail. These are device independence, network monitor and control functions, efficient agent communication in the wireless environments and content adaptation based on the mobile device capabilities and network QoS. Finally, Section 8 concludes this paper and describes our future plans on improving the architecture.

2   Related Work

Recently, a number of research efforts have looked at supporting nomadic users and applications, but only a few of those are agent-based. In [1], Al-bar and

---

[1] CReation of User-friendly Mobile services PErsonalized for Tourism.

[2] European Commission, Information Society Technology.

Wakeman give a survey to the constraints of mobile computing and the different kinds of adaptation spaces. In addition, a number of adaptive frameworks are reviewed. Al-bar and Wakeman identify three main constraints in mobile computing: mobile device, network and mobility constraints. We will address all of these in this paper.

JADE-LEAP is a lightweight agent platform targeted at small devices such as PDAs and phones. JADE-LEAP is based on an open-source agent platform JADE. To date, JADE supports bit-efficient agent communication [5,8], but in the JADE-LEAP it is not included. However, the bit-efficient communication support could be used in JADE-LEAP also. Our architecture is not dependent on the agent platform, and we are in the process of adding support for JADE and JADE-LEAP to host the agents in our architecture.

RAJA (Resource-Adaptive Java Agent Infrastructure) [4] is a generic architecture, where domain-specific functionality is separated from resource and adaptation concerns. It is divided into system and applications levels. The system level provides resource management services implemented by a set of agents. The application level implements domain-specific computation, and contains two kinds of agents, Basis Agents and Controller Agent. Controller Agents are attached to resource-unaware Basis Agents to provide the adaptation support. Controller Agents in turn make use of the system level services.

Monads project [16] has implemented an agent-based architecture providing adaptive services. The principal idea is that nomadic applications are offered information about the future quality of the connection, and they are supposed to adjust their behavior to meet the forthcoming situation. Our system operates only on parameters of present time, which is enough when there is no upper bound to the delays from changing for instance content encoding. If we were to support for instance adaptive streaming video, the only option to guarantee low delays is to predict the changes in the environment. In such a case, our system and its network monitoring functionality could be extended by the prediction mechanism from the Monads system.

Korolev *et al.* proposes a lightweight scheme for negotiating client's capabilities in the context of end-to-end content adaptation for wireless Web access [14]. Their method resembles W3C's CC/PP [19], but is much less complex than the CC/PP, because they have simplified the framework by dividing the variety of mobile devices in a few relatively large categories. In this sense Korolev's scheme is like ours; however, in addition to device adaptation, our architecture supports also adaptation to changing network QoS.

3   Deploying Services for Nomadic Environments

Nomadic environment differs from stationary environments in four fundamental ways. Firstly, the user is situated in an environment, where there may be multiple data communication networks available. Because of the variety in the characteristics of the networks, for instance the QoS may change dramatically based on the user's location. The architecture has to provide means to manage accesses to multiple data communication networks, allow seamless roaming between them and provide information about the QoS of the network connections.

Secondly, the user may access the services using a variety of different mobile or stationary devices. The characteristics and limitations of the device dictates the constraints on how the user is able access the services and what kind of content the user is provided with. For instance, a service providing only JPEG-encoded color images is useless to a user who is accessing the service with a WAP phone, if the images are not transcoded to a format the WAP phone understands. Thus, the architecture should support adaptation, or the services themselves should be able to adapt the content to meet the limitations of the device.

Thirdly, although the user can access the same kind of services as with her desktop computer, the nomadic environment promotes the concept of just-on-time services, which are made available to the user based on her current location. Furthermore, making the service available to the user could be controlled or biased by the user interests. User interests could be composed of for instance preferences for the quality and format of the content, usage of the different networks in various situations, and filtering the available services based on user preferences, location, and time of day. Modeling the user's interests and matching them to the services is an important issue when providing just-on-time services.

Fourthly, the mobile networks and devices are developing rapidly, which has to be taken into account when implementing the services. The architecture should be scalable and open in order to allow modifications and updates to the existing services and creation of new services easily.

In our architecture we address these issues by specialized agents, which hide the complexity of the networking, deal with variety of mobile devices, and provide information about the user's location. Together these agents form a multi-agent system, which allows service agents to adapt to changes in the nomadic environment. The architecture is extendable in terms of new kind of services by introducing new agents to the system. In the next section we will have a more detailed look at the architecture.

4   Architecture for Supporting Applications in Nomadic Environments

The general architecture for supporting applications in the nomadic environment is shown in Figure 1. The users access the system using a (mobile) device, which can either host User Agent (UA) and Communication Agent (CA), or act only as an interface to the system. The former is usually the case with laptop and handheld computers, whereas the latter with WAP phones and Web kiosks. The mobile devices connect to the Access Node through a wireless access network, which can be for instance GSM, GPRS or WLAN. The Access Node is the central part of the system. It is a logical entity in the fixed network, which has two main functions; it allows the mobile devices to access the services, if the mobile devices

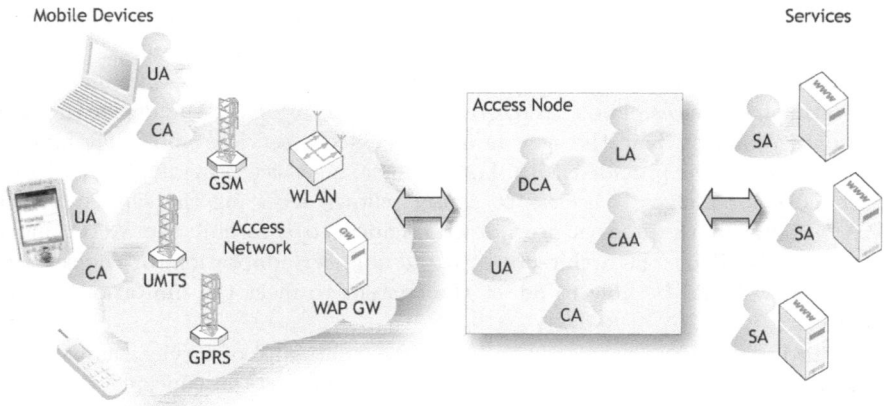

Fig. 1. The main components of the architecture

are not able to access the services by themselves, and it hosts the agents that enable the services to adapt to the nomadic environment.

On the agent level the architecture is divided into three logical agent planes as shown in Figure 2. The CA on lowest plane hides the complexity of the underlying network infrastructure and provides agents on the upper planes with information about the QoS of the network connections and a message transport protocol for exchanging agent messages over the wireless network. The CA is discussed in Section 6.

Middle-agents on the middleware plane provide support for the service agents. This support comprises of content adaptation, agent-level session management, and support for location-awareness. Middle-agents are independent on the application that the agents on the service plane implement. Dialogue Control Agent (DCA) is a service broker, with which the UA maintains an agent-level session. Together with the directory service (Directory Facilitator (DF) in FI-PA terminology [7]) the DCA knows about the available services, and is able to broker the requests from the UA to the correct service agent. It should be noted that the directory service is omitted in both Figure 1 and 2. Location Agent (LA) wraps functionality related to location-awareness. It can provide the location of a mobile device, it can draw maps of any coordinate in various formats (depending on the mobile device profile) and it can calculate distances between coordinates. Content Adaptation Agent (CAA) adapts the content based on the mobile device capabilities (device adaptation), network QoS (QoS adaptation), and the user preferences. In the device adaptation the CAA operates on mobile terminal profile, which is provided by the UA, whereas in the QoS adaptation the CAA uses the QoS information from the CA. The user preferences are provided by the UA. A detailed description of the CAA is given in Section 7.

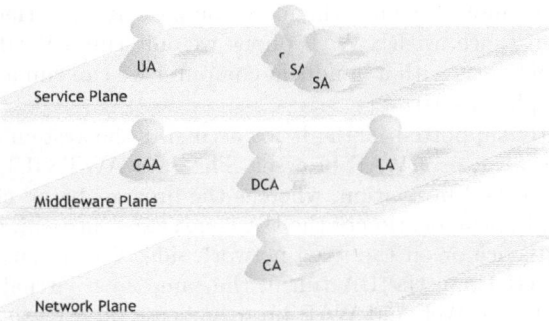

Fig. 2. The logical division of the agents between network, middleware and service planes

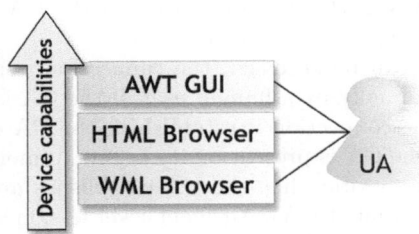

Fig. 3. The relation between the mobile device's capabilities and the complexity of the user interface. As can be seen from these three examples, the interface can range from a simple WML browser to an Java AWT GUI

Service Agents (SA) implement a certain application area, which in our case is services for a tourist domain. The UA is an agent, which provides the user interface for the human user. Based on the mobile device, the user interface can be presented for example as Java AWT GUI, HTML or WML. We will have a more detailed look at the UA in Section 5.

In the following sections we will concentrate on the network and middleware planes by describing the services the CA, the CAA and the UA provide to the service agents on the service plane.

5   Accessing the Services in Device-Independent Way

The User Agent (UA) provides the user interface for a human user. Because there is a large variety of different mobile devices available, and we believe that the variety will be even bigger in the future, we allow the user interface to scale based on the mobile device capabilities. Figure 3 shows the idea of scaling; the more capable the mobile device, the more complex user interface we are able to run on it. For instance, with a WAP phone we only run a WML browser on the mobile device, whereas with a handheld computer we can run a Java application providing a graphical GUI.

The currently supported methods for accessing the system are a Java AWT GUI, a Web browser, or a WAP browser. The Java AWT GUI accesses the UA directly using method invocation, whereas the browser-based clients use HTTP interface. The physical location of the UA is not fixed, instead, it may run either on the mobile device or on the fixed network side. When using the Java AWT GUI, both the GUI and the UA run in the same Java virtual machine on the mobile device. In the Web and WAP browsers' case on the other hand, the user interface and the UA may run either on the same device or be distributed so that the user interface runs on the mobile device and the UA on a fixed network node. It must be noted that in this case the device cannot benefit from the services the Communication Agent (CA) provides. Therefore, we do not address the communication between the user interface and the UA in our architecture, but leave it out of the scope of this paper.

Before the services can be accessed, the connection is made to the Access Node by the CA, or manually by a human user, if the CA is not present on the mobile device. Once the connection is established, the CA on the Access Node (and on the device, if the CA is present on it) begins to monitor the QoS of the connection to the device. After this, the UA establishes an agent-level session with Dialogue Control Agent (DCA). An agent-level session is initiated, suspended, resumed and closed by the UA, and the possible network level disconnections do not affect the life-cycle of the agent-level session. Depending on which kind of user interface a request is coming from, the UA determines the correct device profile. During the session establishment and resume, the UA sends the device profile to the DCA, which in turn informs this to Content Adaptation Agent (CAA). Once the CAA knows the current device profile, it is first of all able to adapt the content to be best-suited for the device in use, and secondly, it is able to either request QoS information or subscribe to the changes in the QoS of the mobile device from the CA. Once the agent-level session is established, the actual service access can take place.

In Figure 4, an example service access procedure is depicted in the cases of a Java AWT GUI, a Web browser, and a WAP browser. In the example a tourist asks the system for her current location. The user interface makes a service request, which in the Java AWT GUI's case is a method invocation, the Web browser's case HTTP-request for a HTML page, and the WAP browser's case HTTP-request made by a WAP gateway. In the example, a sample of a HTTP request is shown. Having received the request, the UA constructs the correct device profile and attaches it to the agent message destined to the appropriate service agent. When the service agent eventually replies to the request, the reply message is routed via the CAA, which adapts the output according to the device profile. The CAA and the adaptation are discussed in Section 7.

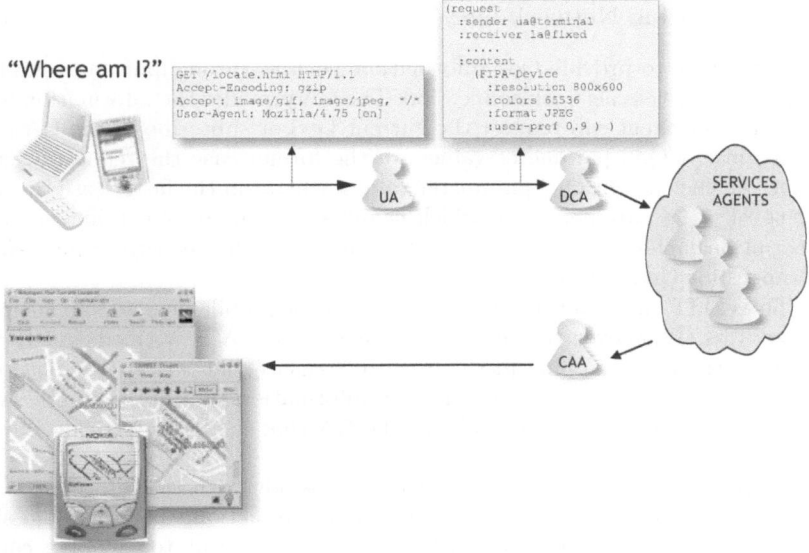

"Where am I?"

```
(request
  :sender ua@terminal
  :receiver la@fixed
  .....
  :content
    (FIPA-Device
      :resolution 800x600
      :colors 65536
      :format JPEG
      :user-pref 0.9 ) )
```

```
GET /locate.html HTTP/1.1
Accept-Encoding: gzip
Accept: image/gif, image/jpeg, */*
User-Agent: Mozilla/4.75 [en]
```

UA   DCA   SERVICES AGENTS

CAA

Fig. 4. This figure shows a scenario, where a user asks the system for her location. Based on the device, the UA assigns a device profile and delivers the request to the service agent. The reply from the service agent is adapted by the CAA according to the device profile

6   Supporting Middle-Agents in Wireless Environment

The Communication Agent (CA) on the network plane supports the agents on the upper planes in terms of providing information about the QoS of the network connection and wireless link connection type, enabling seamless roaming between different network technologies, and taking care of delivering agent messages in the wireless environment. The network plane is divided into the following three logical functionalities:

- Monitoring the QoS of data transmission.
- Controlling the underlying data transmission connections.
- Implementation of Wireless Message Transport Protocol (WMTP) tailored for delivering agent messages in wireless networks.

The first two functions are implemented by the CA, whereas the WMTP is either used as a standalone process or plugged in to an agent platform, if such is used. Within the CRUMPET project we are using versions of MicroFIPA-OS [15] and FIPA-OS [17], which we have plugged the WMTP in to. In the following, we discuss these functionalities in more detail.

6.1   Monitoring Network QoS

The CA is able to provide QoS information, such as throughput and round-trip time, of the wireless network connection. The CA provides the information in two ways; another agent can request the current QoS or subscribe to the CA about changes in the QoS parameter values. In the former case the requesting agent receives all the current QoS parameter values, wheras in the latter case the agent may specify the parameters, of which changes it is interested in knowing. The subscription includes a set of constraints, by which the subscriber may specify the ranges for QoS parameter changes.

The WMTP maintains a mapping between the mobile devices and their current address. Whenever the mapping changes, the CA is notified and the CA advertises the new mapping in the directory service (DF in a FIPA platform). Any agent interesting in getting the QoS information to a given mobile device may then ask the directory service for the CA that is able to provide the QoS information.

The proper place for the CA is at the same side with the information producer. For instance, in a Web browsing type of interaction, the CA would sit on an access node, where it is able to provide QoS information to agents or components, which adapt or select the most appropriate format for the content to be delivered to the mobile device.

6.2   Controlling the Underlying Network Connections

Service and middle-agents, and of course human users, should not be bothered about the characteristics of the underlying network connections, because these kinds of agents are usually interested in having their agent messages delivered to their peer agent. In addition, in the future, and already to date, there will be multiple access networks available. The CA hides the complexity related to the connecting to the networks and roaming between them. Agents may explicitly ask the CA to open a communication channel or activate a message transport protocol to another agent or agent platform, but the CA is also able to initiate these actions autonomously.

The autonomous operation of the CA is based on the network QoS, the human user's preferences, and the CA's own knowledge for instance on how to connect to the networks. For instance, let us consider the following scenario. A tourist is on a tour in a foreign city and her mobile device is connected to a GPRS network. She arrives at a location, where there is a public WLAN coverage available. The CA knows that the tourist prefers a WLAN over the GPRS because of the higher throughput, and knows the parameters for accessing the WLAN. Therefore, it decides to autonomously change from the current GPRS network to the WLAN. After a while the tourist moves away from the WLAN coverage and the CA detects that only a GSM network would be available. The CA looks up the tourist's preferences again and finds out that the access to the GSM network is too expensive for her. The CA informs the tourists that she is moving away from the WLAN coverage and once exited altogether, she will not have a network access available anymore. The tourist decides to stay on the WLAN coverage to complete the task she is working with, and only after that resumes her tour.

Currently our CA supports access to GSM, HSCSD, GPRS, WLAN and wired ethernet networks. Furthemore, the CA is able to use Bluetooth to connect to other Bluetooth-enabled devices, such as mobile phones. In addition, adding support for an access to new networks is easy.

6.3   Agent Communication in Wireless Environment

Because the mobile device is usually connected to a wireless network, the agent communication should be tailored in order to provide an efficient usage of scarce and fluctuating data communication resources. For this reason we have implemented a Wireless Message Transport Protocol (WMTP) that allows both efficient and reliable communication between the mobile device and the access node. The WMTP is based on FIPA Agent Message Transport Protocol for HTTP Specification [6] and is fully compliant with it, but extends it to be better suited for wireless networks. When designing the WMTP we concentrated on improving the following:

- Minimize the number of round-trips, because latencies in the wireless wide-area networks tend to be large.
- Implement reliability in the form of message sequence numbering.
- Recover from (sudden) disconnections by supporting sessions.

Having an efficient and reliable MTP for wireless environments is not enough to provide sufficient communication facilities for agents communicating over a wireless connection. The encoding of messages should also be bit-efficient. For message envelope and ACL we use the bit-efficient transport encoding as specified by FIPA [5,8]. These encoding options reduce significantly the transfer volume over the wireless link comparing to other standard encoding options. In [12] we analyzed these encoding options in more detail.

We use XML for the actual message content. However, it is well known that XML is a highly verbose syntax, and therefore unsuitable to be used in environments where slow (wireless) links are involved. Given this, we use binary-XML [20] whenever a message is sent over a wireless link. The binary-XML reduces the transfer volume significantly comparing to standard XML. However, it is still only a sub-optimal solution. For example, the size of a binary-XML encoded message content is similar to that of a s-expression encoded FIPA-SL [9] message. Although using the binary-XML encoding gives an acceptable performance, we are still looking for better and more efficient solutions for encoding the message content.

The communicative behaviours of interacting agents also affect the amount of bits transmitted over wireless links. Therefore, conversations between communicating agents need to be well designed in order to minimize the amount of bits to be transmitted over a wireless link. The challenge can be split into two domains: Firstly, when there is a common, often used conversation pattern, for example for electronic auctions, it is possible to specify a standardized conversation protocol. Now, the conversation protocol should be designed so that the number of round-trips is minimized. Secondly, when agents' interactions do not follow any common, often used pattern, agents themselves need to decide what to communicate, to whom, when, and how. There are many research challenges, such as how to evaluate the value of communication [11], how to obtain just-on-time information about the QoS of wireless data communications, and how to make the decision process fast enough. These issues remain for future research.

7   Adapting the Content Based on the Environment

The Content Adaptation Agent (CAA) applies both device and QoS content adaptation. Whereas the device adaptation is about adapting the output based on a device profile, the QoS adaptation is about modifying the output according to the QoS of the current network connection. The CAA separates the device and QoS adaptations into two separate independent processes. There are four reasons for this:

1. Some devices, such as WAP phones, are only able to fetch content from an URL, and do not allow software to be uploaded on them.
2. QoS adaptation should use as accurate estimate about the current QoS as possible; thus, the QoS adaptation should be applied as close to the actual content delivery as possible.
3. Having the QoS adaptation as independent process allows the CAA to be used as a transcoding proxy in normal Web-browsing.
4. Having the device adaptation as an independent and non-mandatory process allows the services, if they prefer so, to apply the adaptation by themselves; a service could have for instance pre-encoded video clips for different kinds of devices.

In this section we will describe how the CAA performs both the device and QoS content adaptation.

7.1   Formatting the Output Based on the Device Profile

In Figure 5 the components of the CAA can be seen. For the device adaptation the device profile and the actual content are fed in as parameters. Based on the device profile the CAA chooses the best-matching template for the adaptation. The templates represent the static part of the output, which is "filled" with the actual content. The adapted content is created and stored to a local cache, and after this the content itself or a URL pointing to the content is returned. For instance, a device, which runs a Java AWT GUI-enabled User Agent (UA), prefers to have the content itself (because the Java AWT GUI is able to render the output itself), whereas a HTML browser fetches the content using the URL.

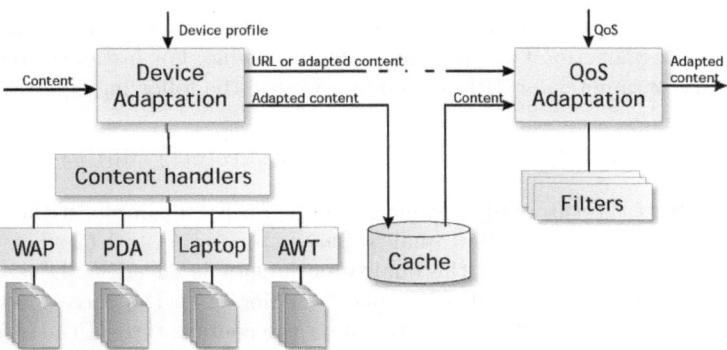

Fig. 5. The internal structure of the CAA. The components in device adaptation are on the left side, whereas the components of QoS adaptation on the right side. In the middle there is the cache, to which the device adaptation stores the adapted content and from which the QoS adaptation reads the content to be adapted

The URL to the content is stored to local cache in both of the cases. This makes it possible to change devices during an agent interaction. For instance, we could think of a scenario, where a user first initiates an operation using a certain device. Then the device is disconnected from the network, but the operation is left running on the service side. After a while, the user reconnects using another kind of device and resumes the operation. In this case, the result of the operation is formatted according to the profile of the current device.

7.2   Adapting the Content on the Fly

The QoS adaptation functionality in the CAA can be seen as two roles. Firstly, the CAA acts like a traditional web proxy, that is, it receives requests to fetch a web object and either forwards them to web servers located at the fixed network or to the local cache, where the results of the device adaptation has been placed in. Additionally, the CAA performs necessary transformation, transcoding, and information abstraction for the web objects that are fetched to the mobile terminal.

Secondly, in conjunction with the UA and the CA, the CAA controls how and what kind of adaptation (transformation, transcoding, and information abstraction) is performed. The CAA receives information about the current QoS from the CA, but instead of using only QoS, the CAA allows the user to bias the adaptation process by giving feedback using a preference value, which is for simplicity implemented as a floating point number ranging from 0 to 1; the bigger the preference value, the better the quality. The preference value can be updated at any time independently of the adaptation process.

The quality parameters the CAA uses in the QoS adaptation depend on both the network connection QoS and the preference value. For instance, to calculate the quality parameter for JPEG encoding we use the following equation:

$$quality = \lfloor ((tp/2) + (preference\_value^2) * 10) \rfloor \tag{1}$$

where tp is the throughput value in kbytes/s. For example, if the throughput is 9.6 kbytes/s, the actual quality parameter is 7 (GSM case), and if the throughput is 43.2 kbytes/s, the quality parameter is 24 (HSCSD case). Once the CAA has calculated quality parameter, it looks up the correct adaptation filter (in this case the JPEG filter) based on the content type of the object, and passes the quality parameter to it. After the adaptation, the filter returns the adapted object, which is in turn returned to the client.

8   Conclusions and Future Work

In this paper we discussed how the nomadic environment introduces new challenges in designing and implementing services for nomadic users and how the service access will change as compared to the desktop environment. A new set of parameters, such as varying QoS of the network connections, sudden disconnections, limitations and variability in the mobile devices and the user's current location, affect, when, where, and in which format a service is made available to the user.

We described our architecture that we have implemented to address the aforementioned issues. The architecture is targeted at today's and future tourists, who prefer accessing just-on-time kind of services during their trip instead of spending time on pre-planning the trip. The architecture is implemented as a multi-agent system consisting of agents on both mobile device and on the fixed network side. Tourists access the system using a mobile device ranging from a simple browser in a Web-kiosk to a high-end handheld device capable of hosting agents. Based on the device in use, the output shown to the tourists is adapted to be suited for her device. In addition, the output is adapted based on the QoS of the network connection.

Our multi-agent system is hosted by MicroFIPA-OS and FIPA-OS agent platforms, but we are in the process of adding support for JADE and JADE-LEAP as well. In the future we will continue working with the system by adding new features to it and improving the existing parts. We will look at standard ways, such as CC/PP [19] and FIPA-Device Ontology [10], to be used in profiling the mobile devices, and technologies such as DAML [13], to represent ontologies in the system.

The work has been done in the CRUMPET project, which will end on October 2002. Some parts of the system is already available as open-source, and we are planning to release most of the remaining parts as open-source after the CRUMPET project has ended.

Acknowledgements. The work presented in this paper originates from the EU-funded project CRUMPET (IST-1999-20147). Therefore, we would like to thank the partners of the CRUMPET project.

References

1. Adnan Al-bar and Ian Wakeman. A Survey of Adaptive Applications in Mobile Computing. In *Proceedings of the 21st International Conference on Distributed Computing Systems Workshops (ICDCSW'01)*, pages 246–251. IEEE Computer Society Press, April 2001.
2. F. Bellifemine, A. Poggi, and G. Rimassa. JADE — A FIPA-compliant agent framework. In *Proceedings of the 4th International Conference on the Practical Applications of Agents and Multi-Agent Systems (PAAM-99)*, pages 97–108, 1999.
3. Federico Bergenti and Agostino Poggi. A FIPA Platform for Handheld and Mobile Devices. In John-Jules Meyer and Milind Tambe, editors, *Pre-proceedings of the Eighth International Workshop on Agent Theories, Architectures, and Languages (ATAL-2001)*, pages 303–313, August 2001.
4. Yun Ding, Rainer Malaka, Christian Kray, and Michael Schillo. RAJA – A Resource-adaptive Java Agent Infrastructure. In Jörg P. Müller, Elisabeth Andre, Sandip Sen, and Claude Frasson, editors, *Proceedings of the 5th International Conference on Autonomous Agents*, pages 332–339. ACM Press, New York, NY, USA, May 2001.
5. Foundation for Intelligent Physical Agents. *FIPA ACL Message Representation in Bit-Efficient Specification*, October 2000. Specification number XC00069, available at: http://www.fipa.org/.
6. Foundation for Intelligent Physical Agents. *FIPA Agent Message Transport Protocol for HTTP Specification*, October 2000. Specification number XC00084, available at: http://www.fipa.org/.
7. Foundation for Intelligent Physical Agents. *FIPA Abstract Architecture Specification*, August 2001. Specification number XC00001, available at: http://www.fipa.org/.
8. Foundation for Intelligent Physical Agents. *FIPA Agent Message Transport Envelope Representation in Bit Efficient Specification*, August 2001. Specification number XC00088, available at: http://www.fipa.org/.
9. Foundation for Intelligent Physical Agents. *FIPA SL Content Language Specification*, August 2001. Specification number XC00008, available at: http://www.fipa.org/.
10. Foundation for Intelligent Physical Agents. *FIPA Device Ontology Specification*, April 2002. Specification number XC00091, available at: http://www.fipa.org/.
11. Piotr J. Gmytrasiewicz and Edmund H. Durfee. Rational Communication in Multi-Agent Environments. *Autonomous Agents and Multi-Agent Systems*, 4(3):233–272, 2001.
12. Heikki Helin and Mikko Laukkanen. Towards Efficient and Reliable Agent Communication in Wireless Environments. In Matthias Klush and Franco Zambonelli, editors, *Cooperative Information Agents V, Proceedings of the 5th International Workshop CIA 2001*, number 2182 in Lecture Notes in Artifical Intelligence, pages 258–263. Springer-Verlag: Heidelberg, Germany, September 2001.
13. J. Hendler and D. L. McGuinness. The DARPA agent markup language. *IEEE Intelligent Systems*, 15(6):67–73, November/December 2000.

14. Vladimir Korolev and Anupam Joshi. An End-End Approach to Wireless Web Access. In *Proceedings of the 21st International Conference on Distributed Computing Systems Workshops (ICDCSW'01)*. IEEE Computer Society Press, April 2001.
15. M. Laukkanen, S. Tarkoma, and J. Leinonen. FIPA-OS Agent Platform for Small-footprint Devices. In John-Jules Meyer and Milind Tambe, editors, *Pre-Proceedings of the Eighth International Workshop on Agent Theories, Architectures, and Languages (ATAL'01)*, pages 314–325, August 2001.
16. P. Misikangas, M. Mäkelä, and K. Raatikainen. Predicting Quality-of-Service for Nomadic Applications Using Intelligent Agents. In A. L. G. Hayzelden and R. A. Bourne, editors, *Agent Technology for Communication Infrastructures*, chapter 15, pages 197–208. John Wiley & Sons, 2001.
17. S. Poslad, P. Buckle, and R. Hadingham. FIPA-OS: The FIPA agent platform available as open source. In *Proceedings of the 5th International Conference on the Practical Application of Intelligent Agents and Multi-Agent Technology (PAAM 2000)*, pages 355–368, April 2000.
18. S. Poslad, H. Laamanen, R. Malaka, A. Nick, P. Buckle, and A. Zipf. CRUMPET: Creation of User-friendly Mobile Services Personalised for Tourism. In *Proceedings of 3G 2001 - Second International Conference on 3G Mobile Communication Technologies*, March 2001.
19. W3C. *Composite Capability/Preference Profiles (CC/PP): A User Side Framework for Content Negotiation*, July 1999. W3C Note, available at: http://www.w3.org/.
20. Wireless Application Protocol Forum. *Binary XML Content Format Specification*, November 1999. Version 04-Nov-1999.

An Agent-based Approach for Helping Users of Hand-Held Devices to Browse Software Catalogs*

E. Mena[1], J.A. Royo[1]**, A. Illarramendi[2], and A. Goñi[2]

[1] IIS Depart., Univ. of Zaragoza, Maria de Luna 3, 50018 Zaragoza, Spain
{emena,joalroyo}@posta.unizar.es
[2] LSI Depart., Univ. of the Basque Country, Apdo. 649, 20080 San Sebastián, Spain
{jipileca,alfredo}@si.ehu.es
WWW home page: http://siul02.si.ehu.es/

Abstract. Considering the existing tendency toward the use of wireless devices we propose in this paper a new service that helps users of those devices in the (tedious, repetitive and many times costly in terms of communication cost) task of obtaining software from the Web.

The goal of the service is twofold: First, to allow users to obtain software by expressing their requirements at a semantic level. For that the service deals with an ontology, specifically created for the service, that contains a semantic description of the software available at different repositories. Second, to guide users in the task of browsing the ontology in order to select the adequate software.

The service has been developed using mobile agent technology. A software obtaining process based on adaptive agents, that manage semantic descriptions of available software, presents a qualitative advance with respect to existing solutions where users must know the location and access method of various remote software repositories. In this paper we describe the main elements that take part of the service and some performance results that prove the feasibility of the proposal.

Keywords: Mobile information agents, Ontologies, Adaptive information agents, Mobile computing.

1 Introduction

Working with any kind of computer (desktop, laptop, palmtop), one of the most frequent task for the users is to obtain new software in order to improve the capabilities of those computers. For that, a well-known solution is visiting some of the several websites that contain freeware, shareware and demos (such as Tucows [12] or CNET Download.com [1]). However, that approach can become cumbersome for naive users —they may not know: 1) the different programs

---

* Supported by the CICYT project TIC2001-0660 and the DGA project P084/2001.
** Work supported by the grant B131/2002 of the Aragón Government and the European Social Fund.

M. Klusch, S. Ossowski, and O. Shehory (Eds.): CIA 2002, LNAI 2446, pp. 51–65, 2002.

that fulfil their needs, 2) the features of their computers, and, 3) the websites where to find the software— and can become annoying for many advanced users. Moreover, if those users use a wireless device, the time expended to find, retrieve and install the software should be minimized as much as possible in order to reduce communication cost and power consumed.

Taking into account the previous scenario we propose in this paper a Software Retrieval Service that allows users to find, retrieve and install software. This service presents two main features: 1) *Semantic Search*: the service allows users to express their software requirements at a semantic level and helps them to browse customized software catalogs in order to select the adequate software. For that, the service makes use of an ontology (specifically created for the service) that contains a semantic description of software available in different repositories, and so it makes transparent for users most of the technical details related to the software retrieval task. 2) *Analysis of user behavior*: the system "observes" users information requests in order to anticipate their needs and even learns from its mistakes to improve its future behavior with those users. So it offers a customized and adaptable service to users putting a special emphasis on optimizing communication time.

The Software Retrieval Service takes part of ANTARCTICA [3], a system that provides users of wireless devices with a new environment that fulfils some of their data management needs. ANTARCTICA follows the widely accepted architecture for mobile computing [11] and so it deals with users of wireless devices and hosts situated at the fixed network that we call GSNs[1].

The implementation of the service is based on the agent technology [10]. Four main agents participate in the service (see Figure 1): *Alfred*, the user agent situated at the user computer who is an efficient majordomo that serves the user and is on charge of storing as much information about the user computer and the user her/himself as possible; the *Software Manager* agent (situated at the closest GSN[2]) that prunes the software ontology taking into account the user requirements; the *Browser* agent, which is created at the GSN and then it moves to the user computer to help her/him to navigate the pruned ontology and select the wanted software; new information requested by the user will be retrieved by the *Catalog Updater* agent, which is created by the Browser to update the user software catalog; and the *Salesman* agent which carries the selected program to the user computer and installs it whenever possible. The interactions among these agents are explained in detail in [6].

Two main tasks take part when dealing with the service: 1) to prune the ontology in order to present to the user a software catalog containing only that part related to her/his requirements (to avoid confusing the user and overloading her/his computer), and 2) to attend user refinements on such a catalog trying to predict future user behavior (to minimize network communication). The re-

---

[1] The *Gateway Support Node (GSN)* is the proxy that provides wireless users with different services like the Software Retrieval Service.
[2] There exists one Software Manager agent on each GSN.

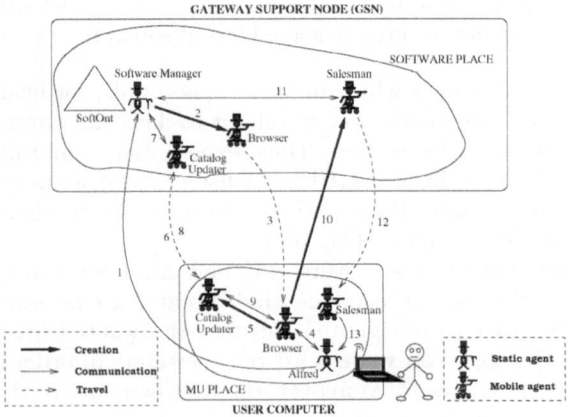

Fig. 1. Main architecture for the Software Retrieval Service

sponsible for those tasks are the Software Manager and the Browser agents, respectively.

Concerning related work, to our knowledge, agents have not been widely used for software retrieval. In [4] they explain a mechanism to update several remote clients connected to a server taking advantage of mobile agents capability to deal with disconnections; however this work is more related to *push technology* than to services created to assist users in the task of updating the software on their computers. In the Ariadne project [5] they work on automatic wrapper construction techniques and build an ontology on top of each website in a semi-automatic manner. OntoAgents [2] allows the annotation of websites to perform a semantic search; data can be accessed using a web browser or performing a search that is managed by agents, which consider the different terms in the website. In these last two projects they use agents, not for retrieving software but accessing websites.

In the rest of the paper we detail the behavior, knowledge and adaptability of the Software Manager and Browser agents, which are the key of the success of the Software Retrieval Service. In Section 2 we explain how the initial interaction of the user with Alfred is performed. In Section 3 we describe how the first pruned ontology (the first catalog) is obtained. In Section 4 the catalog browsing is detailed including the analysis of the user behavior. We compare the software retrieval service with a Tucows-like approach in Section 5, and some conclusions appear in Section 6.

2   Initialization of the Software Retrieval Service (SRS)

Alfred is an efficient majordomo agent, situated at the user computer, that serves the user and is on charge of storing as much information about the user

computer, and the user her/himself, as possible. Let us start with the situation
in which the user wants to retrieve some kind of software. Two cases can arise:

1. The user exactly knows which program s/he needs, for example, JDK1.4.0
   for Win32, and also knows how to ask for it. This can happen because s/he
   is a usual client of this service. Thus, expert users could directly pose the
   request, with the help of a GUI, as a list of constraints *<feature, value>*
   describing the software they need. In the example the data entered would
   be *[<name, JDK1.4.0>, <OS, Win32>]*.
2. The user only knows some feature of the program, for example, its purpose.
   In this case, the user needs some kind of catalog concerning the software
   available, in order to navigate it and find the wanted program. With the
   help of a GUI, users can write a list of constraints in order to express their
   needs the best they can[3]. Moreover, the user can specify the level of detail
   (expressed as a percentage) that s/he wants in such a catalog, the more detail
   the bigger catalog. Advanced users could be interested in many features of
   software while naive users could only be interested in just a few, such as a
   brief description, the name of the program and the OS needed to install it.

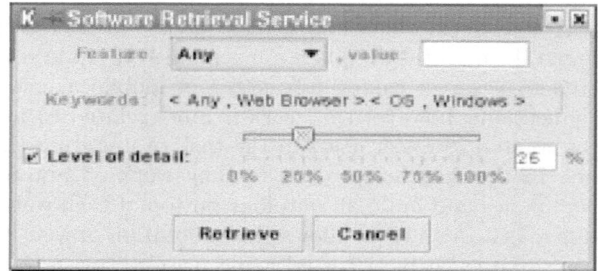

Fig. 2. Alfred's GUI for the Software Retrieval Service

It is also possible that the user does not know any feature of the software.
S/he could have seen it in the past but now is not able to remember the
name, the exact purpose, etc. However, if s/he would see it again s/he could
recognize it. Even in this case, the system will help the user as we explain
in Section 3.1.

   In addition to the constraints and the level of detail (if specified) Alfred
can add more constraints concerning the user computer (e.g. OS, RAM memory, video card, etc.) and previous executions of the service (e.g. previous web
browsers downloaded). Indeed, all the information provided by the user is stored
by Alfred. Thus, with each user request, Alfred stores more information about

---

[3] The information provided can be imprecise. In Figure 2, the user does not know
neither the web browser name nor the concrete Windows version of her/his computer.

the user computer and about the user; a detailed description of the *knowledge* managed by Alfred can be found in [6].

After the user specifies her/his requirements, Alfred sends a software catalog request to the *Software Manager* agent residing at the GSN.

3   Obtaining a Software Catalog: The Software Ontology and the Software Manager

After receiving a request of Alfred (on behalf of the user), the Software Manager agent performs two main tasks: 1) To obtain a catalog corresponding to the user request, and 2) To create an agent that travels to the user computer, presents the catalog to the user, and helps her/him to find the wanted software.

For the first task, we advocate using an ontology, called *SoftOnt*, to describe *semantically* the content of a set of data sources storing pieces of software. This ontology will be stored in all the GSNs that belong to the ANTARCTICA system. The SoftOnt ontology, which stores detailed information concerning the available software accessible from the GSN, is managed by the Software Manager (one per GSN). So, instead of users having to deal directly with different software repositories, the system uses an ontology to help users to retrieve software. Structurally, SoftOnt is a rooted acyclic digraph whose inner nodes store information about software categories and whose leaves store information about programs.

In [7] we explained the process used for building the SoftOnt ontology. However, due to space limitations we summarize here the main steps involved in that process: the *translation* and the *integration* steps. In the translation step, specialized agents analyze HTML pages corresponding to several software repositories on the web, like Tucows [12]. Fortunately, those pages classify the different pieces of software in several categories and so, the specialized agents take advantage of those categories to create ontologies (one ontology per website) and they transform subcategories in websites into specializations in ontologies. In the integration step, the ontologies obtained from the different software repositories are integrated into only one ontology. Taking into account that in the considered context (software repositories) the number of data sources is low and the number of categories is not very high we advocate building only one ontology. Moreover, as the vocabulary heterogeneity problem on the context is limited, the process of integrating the ontologies can be automatized using a thesaurus for the automatic vocabulary problem resolution.

Therefore, *the SoftOnt ontology constitutes the main knowledge managed by the Software Manager agent and the pruned ontology (customized to each user) constitutes the main knowledge managed by the Browser agent.*

3.1   The Software Manager: Ontology Pruning

The SoftOnt ontology must be pruned in order to obtain a first software catalog to present to the user. This pruning process is very important due to three reasons: 1) it avoids presenting the user categories and pieces of software that cannot be installed on the user computer (different OS, or other restrictions); 2) it avoids presenting very specialized categories and pieces of software that could surely make naive users spend more time reading the catalog, and consequently, finding the wanted software; and 3) it minimizes the communication cost by sending interesting information only.

The Software Manager is able to prune an ontology by considering different parameters:

- *Node to prune.* The Software Manager will only consider the subtree defined by the specified node and their underlying nodes. To prune the whole ontology, the node to prune should be the root node of the ontology.
- *Keywords.* They are a list of constraints *<feature, value>* that nodes in the result must satisfy.
- *Level of detail.* It is a percentage that indicates the amount of data that should be included in the result; for example, a level of detail of 30% indicates that only the 30% of the ontology should be included in the result. If keywords are specified, the level of detail is applied on the set of nodes satisfying the keywords.
- *Pruning strategy.* It indicates *which* nodes of the ontology will be selected, it is the selection criteria. Several pruning strategies have been implemented in our prototype:
  - *The most requested nodes.* The Software Manager updates global[4] statistics about the retrieval of each node in SoftOnt. Every time that a node is included in the catalog for some user, its count is increased. Thus, when this strategy is used, the most requested nodes are selected first.
  - *The most requested nodes by the user.* The Software Manager also stores which nodes are sent to each user (user statistics). Thus, by using this strategy the Software Manager selects first those nodes requested for the user in the past.
  - *The proportional strategy.* In this strategy, brother nodes[5] have the same priority. In other words, when a node must be pruned using a certain level of detail of $n\%$, then all the immediate descendants of such a node will be pruned using a level of detail of $n\%$. This strategy is very useful when the system has no idea of what the user is looking for, as it does not favour any concrete branch.
  - *The heaviest strategy.* In this strategy, the nodes with more underlying pieces of software are selected first. This strategy is based on the idea that the user could be looking for a software under very populated categories, like games.
- *Node type.* The pruning strategy could consider only nodes that represent software categories, nodes that represent pieces of software, or both. Thus, the *node type* parameter can be 'categories', 'programs', or 'nodes', respectively.

---

[4] Once a day, Software Managers on different GSNs can share and update their statistical information about the retrieval of each node in SoftOnt.

[5] Brother nodes are those with at least one common father node.

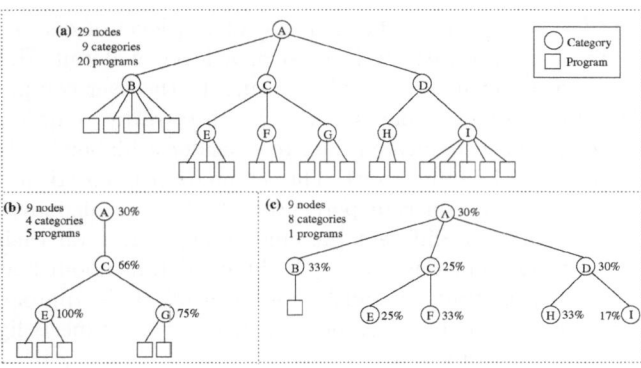

Fig. 3. Pruning an ontology: (b) with heaviest and (c) proportional strategies

Figure 3 shows the difference between two pruning strategies, when the node to prune is 'A', no keywords, level of detail is 30% and node type is 'nodes'. Notice that, independently of the pruning strategy, a level of detail of 30% indicates that only the 30% of the ontology must be obtained (9 nodes, in the example).

In the initialization of the service, the parameters sent by Alfred are: the level of detail for the whole ontology and some keywords; both parameters are optional for the first time. For future catalog refinements, the parameters sent by Alfred are: the node to prune, the level of detail for that node, and (optionally) new keywords. The rest of parameters are estimated by the Software Manager as explained in the following. Therefore, when the Software Manager is invoked to perform a prune of the SoftOnt ontology, the following steps are followed:

1. *Selecting the node to prune.* For the first catalog it will be the root node of SoftOnt, as the first time we consider the whole ontology. In future catalog updates, the user can request pruning a concrete node (see Section 4.1).
2. *Choosing the node type.* If no keyword and no level of detail was specified by the user, only categories will be included in the first catalog: the user has provided no information about what s/he wants, therefore the system will only include categories in the first catalog to help the user to choose first the kind of software wanted. In other case, the catalog will include both categories and program nodes.
3. *Pruning the SoftOnt ontology using keywords*, if any was specified by the user (pruning using keywords is very selective). Let us call $Ont_{keywords}$ to the ontology after considering the keywords:

$$Ont_{keywords} = \begin{cases} prune(SoftOnt, keywords) & \text{if any keyword} \\ SoftOnt & \text{otherwise} \end{cases}$$

Only nodes of the kind selected in step 2 which fulfill all the keywords will be included in the result.

4. *Setting the level of detail.* If the user specified a level of detail, the system must provide her/him with at least such a level of detail. However, as a remote connection must be opened to return to the user computer the catalog requested, system estimates if it is worth to retrieve more information than what it has been requested, i.e., to consider a higher level of detail to avoid future network connections. This estimation is based on the current network status and a concrete percentage $\%_{incr}$ specified by Alfred (different users could have different increments depending on their expertise, computer, network connection, etc.). Technical details about how this increment is obtained in run-time can be found in [9]. This approach improves the efficiency of the system when the user successively requests lightly higher level of detail of the some node.

If the user did not specify a level of detail (only possible for the first software catalog), the Software Manager will consider a level of detail of $\%_{incr}$.

5. *Applying a pruning strategy on $Ont_{keywords}$*, using the parameters obtained in the previous steps. For the first catalog, the proportional pruning strategy is selected, because it prunes brother nodes proportionally, which is a good idea for the first catalog. In future catalog updates, the system will automatically select the most suitable strategy (see Section 4.2). Let us call Ont_{pruned} to the result of this task.

6. *Obtaining an incremental answer.* The first catalog will be the complete Ont_{pruned}. Moreover, to avoid sending data that are already on the user computer, the Software Manager stores the ids of the nodes sent to each user[6] ($nodes_{user_i}$) and, in future catalog updates, it removes those nodes from the catalog obtained. Thus, only the *new* information is sent.

7. *Compressing the catalog obtained.* The information obtained in the previous step can be compressed to reduce the use of the network when sending a catalog to the user computer. In [9] we show when it is worth to compress the catalog by considering the catalog size, the current network status and other parameters measured in run-time.

Notice that, even when the user did not specify any keyword or level of detail, the system automatically sets during steps 1, 2, 4, and 5 the most appropriate values for the parameters needed to perform a prune (node to prune, node type, level of detail, and pruning strategy).

3.2   Creating the Browser agent

After the first catalog is obtained the Software Manager creates a Browser agent initialized with such a catalog. This specialized agent will travel to the user computer and help the user to find the wanted software as explained in the next section. It is important to stress that, although the Software Manager could have

---

[6] This information is also stored by the Browser agent at the user computer, thus when the user changes to another GSN (*handoff*) the Browser tells the new Software Manager which are the nodes already retrieved.

selected a level of detail higher than the specified by the user, the Browser will exactly show to the user what s/he asked for. The rest of the information can be used by the Browser as a buffer to perform future catalog updates, as explained in Section 4.3.

4   Catalog Browsing: The Browser Agent

Once on the user computer, the Browser agent presents the catalog as a rooted acyclic digraph (see Figure 4) where nodes are software categories (shaded nodes represent nodes whose descendants are hidden). In order to help users, under each node in the catalog there is a bar that represents graphically: 1) how much information about that node is shown (in middle grey); 2) how much information about that node is available at the user computer (in light grey); and 3) how much new information about that node could be requested to the Software Manager (in dark grey). For example, concerning the node 'Linux' in Figure 4, the Browser is showing the 10% of all the information available in the ontology, the 58% is available at the user computer, and the 42% remaining could be remotely requested to the Software Manager.

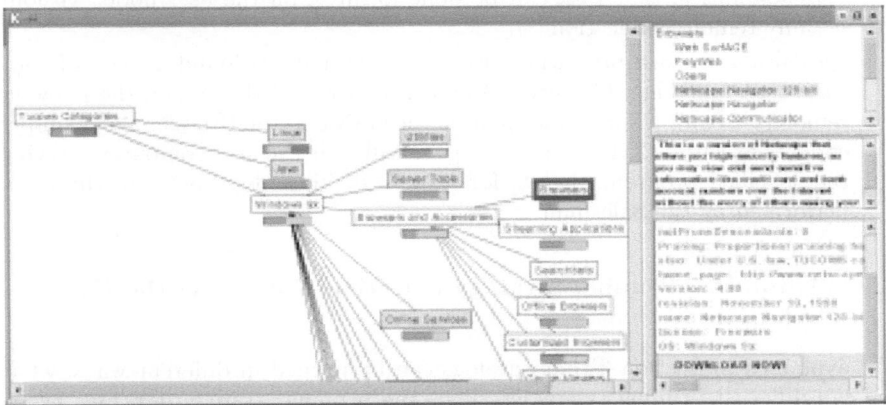

Fig. 4. Browsing the catalog

In the following we explain the different actions that the user can perform on the catalog, how the Browser analizes the user behavior to anticipate future actions, and how the catalog refinements that request new information about some node are managed.

4.1   Navigating the Catalog: User Actions

The following are the different actions that a user can perform after studying the catalog presented:

- *To ask for information about a node.* Just by left-clicking on a node, the Browser shows (on the right side of the GUI) all the features of such a node, including the list of programs under it.
- *To open/close a node.* By double clicking on a node, its immediate descendants are shown/hidden.
- *To prune some node.* By right-clicking on a node, the user has the possibility to specify a new level of detail for that node or provide new constraints for that node and its descendants. Thus, different actions can be performed:
  - *To request less detail of a node*, when too many descendants below that node are shown, which makes the task of finding the wanted software too confusing for naive users.
  - *To request more detail of a node*, as the user could suspect that the wanted program could be under such a node. The Browser could have the requested information (no remote communication would be needed) or not (the Browser will have to remotely request those data to the Software Manager at the GSN). Sections 4.3 and 4.4 detail this task.
  - *To provide new constraints*, as the user could have remembered some feature of the wanted program therefore could want to provide a new constraint (a new pair *<feature, value>*). As the Browser has pruning capabilities, that task can be done locally[7], on the user node, without any remote connection.
- *To download a program*, when user has (fortunately) found a piece of software that fulfils her/his needs. As a consequence of this action the Browser remotely creates a Salesman agent on the GSN and the Browser agent simply ends its execution. The Salesman agent will visit the user computer carrying the specified program. See [8] for a more detailed description of the tasks performed by the Salesman.

4.2   Automatic Pruning Strategy Selection: Analyzing the User Behavior

We explained in Section 3 that catalogs can be pruned in different ways, what we call different pruning strategies. Thus the pruning strategy indicates *which* nodes of the ontology will be selected. The result of applying different pruning strategies is different although the same number of nodes is selected. Therefore, different pruning strategies select first certain kind of nodes (the most frequently requested, those with more programs, etc.).

In order to minimize the number of user refinements, i.e., the number of user actions needed to find the wanted software, the Browser tries to anticipate future user actions by analizing her/his past behavior. Thus, the Browser stores the nodes in which the user had some interest in the past. When the Browser detects that the user seems to follow a pattern that corresponds with the nodes that would have been selected by some of the available pruning strategies, then that pruning strategy will be used in the next prune.

---

[7] In our prototype, different constraints are joined by a logical AND operator.

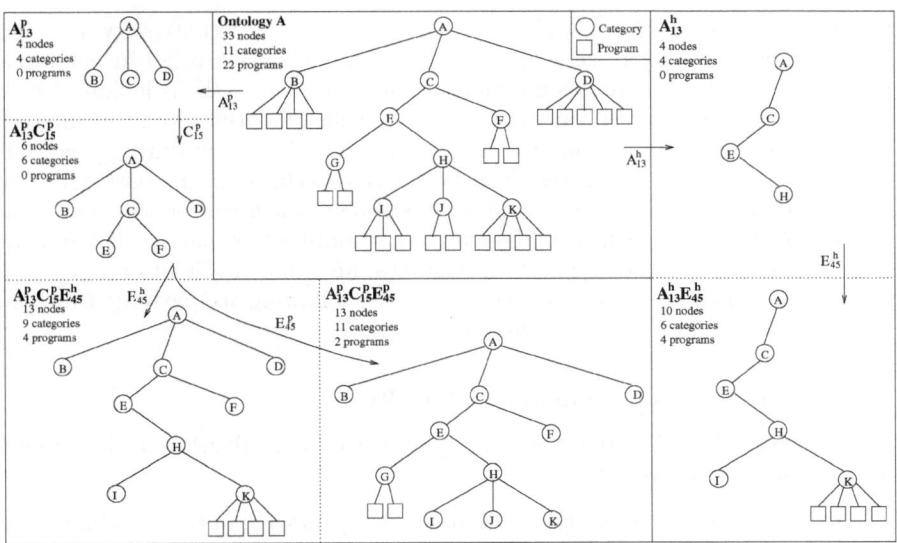

Fig. 5. Analyzing the user behavior and selecting new pruning strategies

In Figure 5 we show how the catalog changes with different pruning strategies. We use the following notation to indicate the different prunes: N_{lod}^{str} means that node N was pruned using the *str* pruning strategy (abbreviations: 'p' = proportional, 'h' = heaviest) and a level of detail of *lod*%; for example, $< A_{13}^p C_{15}^p E_{45}^h >$ represents the result after 1) pruning node A proportionally and a level of detail of 13%, 2) pruning the resulting node C proportionally and a level detail of 15%, and finally 3) pruning node E using the heaviest strategy and a level of detail of 45%. In this example a threshold of three[8] is used to change the pruning strategy, and the proportional prune is used by default. 1) In $< A_{13}^p >$ we show the first catalog presented to the user (the whole is pruned for the first catalog). 2) The user requests a higher level of detail of node C; the pruning strategy remains the same as in the first prune, and the result is $< A_{13}^p C_{15}^p >$. And 3) the user requests a higher detail about the node E; it is the third time that the user selects the path that would have been shown if the root node would have been pruned using the heaviest strategy ($< A_{13}^h >$). Therefore the Browser selects the heaviest pruning strategy in order to make easier to the user the task of finding the wanted software, as s/he seems to be interested in nodes with many programs; the result is $< A_{13}^p C_{15}^p E_{45}^h >$. With the proportional strategy the result would be $< A_{13}^p C_{15}^p E_{45}^p >$. Notice that if the user was looking for programs under node K, the heaviest strategy would have selected those nodes just in two

---

[8] The default threshold should be a small value, three or five, and that threshold will increase each time the Browser detects an error in its estimation. The system stores a threshold for each user and pruning strategy.

user refinements ($< A^h_{13}E^h_{45} >$; however, selecting the heaviest strategy from the beginning is a very risky choice, there exist many chances to fail in helping a user for which the system has no information about what s/he is looking for.

Therefore, the Browser counts the nodes for which the user shows any interest and, whenever the user seems to follow a recognized pattern during a certain time, the corresponding strategy will be selected. Whenever the user does not follow the pattern of the current pruning strategy, the Browser will select the proportional strategy (which is the least risky) until a new pattern is followed. The Browser "remembers" previous mistakes, and the threshold of a rejected strategy is augmented anytime the user stops following its pattern; thus the Browser tries to improve its predictions.

4.3   Treating a New Refinement Locally

Some actions selected by the user can be performed by the Browser itself, without using network resources:

- *The user requests to open/close a node.* The Browser simply shows/hides the descendants of such a node, no new information is needed.
- *The user requests a lower level of detail of some node.* As no new information is needed and the Browser has pruning capabilities, it prunes the selected node by considering the level of detail indicated by the user. In this case, the bar corresponding to that node will indicate now that less information is shown; however, the indicator that represents the Browser buffer about that node will remain the same (because the amount of information locally available is still the same).
- *The user requests a higher level of detail below the buffer limit.* Again, the Browser has already all the needed information and can prune the catalog properly.

Notice that, by using the Browser pruning capabilities and the Browser buffer, many user refinements can be performed without using network connections. Nevertheless, if the requested refinement cannot be performed using the information currently available to the Browser, then the new information must be requested remotely to the Software Manager as explained in the following subsection.

4.4   Treating Refinements that Implies Using the Network

Some refinements requested by the user cannot be performed by the Browser itself: the user can request information that the Browser does not have, so a remote request to the Software Manager is necessary. For that task, the Browser creates a *Catalog Updater* agent[9], whose goal is to retrieve from the GSN the

---

[9] The Catalog Updater could be remotely created on the GSN; however if that remote creation fails due to network instability, the Browser should retry such a task. Creating the agent locally permits the Browser to depute the Catalog Updater to manage network communications

needed information, by requesting the Software Manager to prune the node subject of the user refinement with the specified level of detail and keywords.

To achieve its goal, the Catalog Updater agent can follow two alternatives: 1) a remote call from the user computer to the Software Manager at the GSN, or 2) to travel to the GSN, to communicate with the Software Manager locally, and travel back to the user computer. To select a choice, the Catalog Updater considers the number of retries needed to maintain a network connection open during a certain time (see [9] for details about this estimate). The Catalog Updater chooses one of these two alternatives *in run-time*, as the network status is estimated right before a remote connection is needed.

As explained in Section 3, new catalogs are returned in an incremental way (only new information is retrieved to optimize communication costs). Thus, the Catalog Updater merges the previous user catalog with the new information properly, and then finishes its execution. In this way, notice that the Browser upgrades its knowledge with each user refinement, making less frequent the need for remote connections. So, future refinements can be attended faster and avoiding the use of the network.

5   Performance Evaluation: SRS vs. Tucows

In this section we compare the use of the Software Retrieval Service (SRS) with the use of Tucows[10]. Figure 6 shows a real sample session with the two systems: (a) the network use and user refinements using Tucows to find a certain software (a CAD tool), and (b) the same situation when using SRS. Axis-x represents time in minutes; lines above axis-x represent access to the network and lines below axis-x represent user refinements (the longest line represents the moment in which the user found the wanted software).

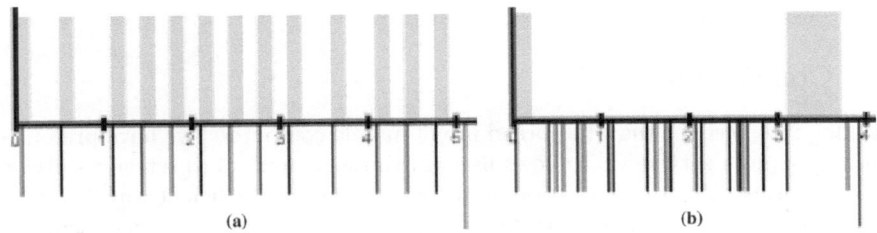

(a)   (b)

Fig. 6. Network use and user refinements using (a) Tucows and (b) SRS

We can observe that in Tucows (Figure 6.a) there is a network access for each user refinement which makes necessary a continuous connection to the net-

---

[10] Data was obtained after testing both software retrieval methods by different kinds of final users. Each user retrieved several pieces of software, first with the SRS and then with Tucows. Most of the users already knew Tucows.

work. However, in SRS (Figure 6.b), as the system is able to manage some user refinements without remote access, there exist long time gaps for which SRS did not access the network. This feature makes the system more robust to temporal network disconnections, and enables considering an automatic mechanism that decides to disconnect the user computer from the net, to reduce the cost of GSM wireless connections.

In Figure 7 we show how the total time was spent in different tasks (a) when using Tucows and (b) when using SRS. Axis-x shows the different software that users looked for, and axis-y shows the average time spent. Notice that, although using Tucows can sometimes be faster, using SRS reduces the network communication cost (for example in Figure 7, when looking for a DBMS).

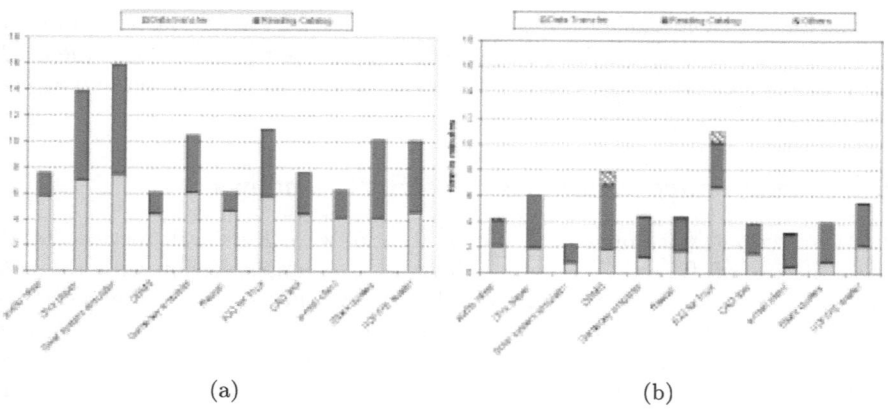

(a)   (b)

Fig. 7. Time-consuming tasks for different (a) Tucows and (b) SRS sessions

6   Conclusions

Taking into account the widespread use of mobile computers, we have presented in this paper a service that allows users of those computers to retrieve software from existing software repositories in an easy, guided and efficient way. Easy, because the service allows users to express their software requirements at semantic level, i.e., they express what they need but not how to obtain it. Guided, because the service, using specialist knowledge-driven agents, only presents to the user those software categories related to her/his requirements (a customized catalog) and helps her/him to browse those categories until the wanted software is found. Finally, it is efficient because, although the service can be used on any kind of computer, it puts on a special emphasis on mobile users, saving wireless communications. The reported performance results, obtained using the implemented prototype, corroborate this when comparing the service with a more classical way of obtaining software, such as accessing the Tucows website.

7 Acknowledgements

We would like to thank V. Pérez his priceless help in the implementation of the prototype. Special thanks to many anonymous users that tested our system for performance evaluation.

References

1. CNET Inc., 1999. http://www.download.com.
2. G. Wiederhold et al. Ontoagents. http://WWW-DB.Stanford.EDU/OntoAgents/.
3. A. Goñi, A. Illarramendi, E. Mena, Y. Villate, and J. Rodriguez. Antarctica: A multiagent system for internet data services in a wireless computing framework. In *NSF Workshop on an Infrastructure for Mobile and Wireless Systems, Scottsdale, Arizona (USA)*, October 2001.
4. IBM Corporation. TME 10 Software Distribution - Mobile Agents SG24-4854-00, January 1997. http://www.redbooks.ibm.com/abstracts/sg244854.html.
5. C.A. Knoblock, S. Minton, J.L. Ambite, N. Ashish, I. Muslea, A.G. Philpot, and S. Tejada. The ariadne approach to web-based information integration. *To appear in the International the Journal on Cooperative Information Systems (IJ-CIS) Special Issue on Intelligent Information Agents: Theory and Applications*, 10(1/2):145–169, 2001. http://www.isi.edu/info-agents/ariadne/.
6. E. Mena, A. Illarramendi, and A. Goñi. A Software Retrieval Service based on Knowledge-driven Agents. In *Fith IFCIS International Conference on Cooperative Information Systems (CoopIS'2000), Springer series of Lecture Notes in Computer Science (LNCS), Eliat (Israel)*, September 2000.
7. E. Mena, A. Illarramendi, and A. Goñi. Automatic Ontology Construction for a Multiagent-based Software Gathering Service. In *proceedings of the Fourth International ICMAS'2000 Workshop on Cooperative Information Agents (CIA'2000), Springer series of Lecture Notes on Artificial Intelligence (LNAI), Boston (USA)*, July 2000.
8. E. Mena, A. Illarramendi, and A. Goñi. Customizable Software Retrieval Facility for Mobile Computers using Agents. In *proceedings of the Seventh International Conference on Parallel and Distributed Systems (ICPADS'2000), workshop International Flexible Networking and Cooperative Distributed Agents (FNCDA'2000), IEEE Computer Society, Iwate (Japan)*, July 2000.
9. E. Mena, J.A. Royo, A. Illarramendi, and A. Goñi. Adaptable software retrieval service for wireless environments based on mobile agents. In *2002 International Conference on Wireless Networks (ICWN'02), Las Vegas, USA*. CSREA Press, June 2002.
10. D. Milojicic, M. Breugst, I. Busse, J. Campbell, S. Covaci, B. Friedman, K. Kosaka, D. Lange, K. Ono, M. Oshima, C. Tham, S. Virdhagriswaran, and J. White. MASIF, the OMG mobile agent system interoperability facility. In *Proceedings of Mobile Agents '98*, September 1998.
11. E. Pitoura and G. Samaras. *Data Management for Mobile Computing*. Kluwer Academic Publishers, 1998.
12. Tucows.Com Inc., 1999. http://www.tucows.com.

Large Scale Peer-to-Peer Experiments with Virtual Private Community (VPC) Framework

Tadashige Iwao[1], Makoto Okada[1], Kazuya Kawashima[2], Satoko Matsumura[2],
Hajime Kanda[2], Susumu Sakamoto[2],
Tatsuya Kainuma[2], and Makoto Amamiya[3]

[1] Service Management Laboratory, Fujitsu Laboratories Ltd.,
4-1-1 Kamikodanaka, Nakahara-ku, 211-8588 Kawasaki, Japan
{iwao, okadamkt}@flab.fujitsu.co.jp
[2] 2nd Development Division, Fujitsu Prime Soft Technologies Ltd.,
1-16-38 Aoi, Higashi-ku, 461-0004 Nagoya, Japan
{kawashima, matsumura, h-kanda, susumu, kainuma}@pst.fujitsu.com
[3] Graduate School of Information Science and Electrical Engineering,
Kyushu University,
6-1 Kasuga-Koen, Kasuga, 816 Fukuoka, Japan
amamiya@is.kyushu-u.ac.jp

Abstract. This paper describes service models for peer-to-peer services in a mobile environment. These days, mobile devices such as PDAs and mobile telephones have the power and the capability to support a variety of services independently. In the near future, peer-to-peer services, for mobile devices in a mobile environment, will be commonplace. However, the performance of these devices is not comparable to those of PCs. The CPU performance of mobile devices is ten times less than those of PCs. Likewise, the data storage capacity of mobile devices is quite limited. Thus, it is difficult for these devices to provide peer-to-peer services such as file sharing and the access of CPU power. Hence, we propose suitable peer-to-peer service models for mobile devices. We have performed a large-scale experiment, with six hundred participants. This paper also contains the results and discussions of this experiment.

1 Introduction

Recently, the performance of mobile devices, such as PDAs and mobile phones, has increased enough to provide a wide variety of services independently. In the near future, peer-to-peer services will be commonplace for mobile devices. The peer-to-peer services on mobile devices will enable people to use them in a mobile environment. However, performance of these devices is not comparable to those of PCs. CPU performance of mobile devices is ten times less than those of PCs. In addition, the data storage capacity of mobile devices is limited. Hence, it is difficult for these devices to provide peer-to-peer services such as file sharing and the access of CPU power. Hence, a study must be conducted to determine what kinds of services are suitable for peer-to-peer services on mobile devices. In

M. Klusch, S. Ossowski, and O. Shehory (Eds.): CIA 2002, LNAI 2446, pp. 66–81, 2002.

addition, we must determine if ordinary people really do use peer-to-peer services on mobile devices, and whether there is a need for the exchange of information under such a mobile environment. Experiments using real systems can provide the answers to these questions.

Current major peer-to-peer systems such as Gnutella[1], Napster[2], and SETI@home[3] focus on PCs, and do not provide services for the mobile environment. These systems are popular on the Internet, and have thousands of users. Gnutella and Napster provide file sharing in a peer-to-peer format. Users of these systems find other peers who have the files they want. These systems focus on PCs because of the large data storage requirements. Also, SETI@home is a project that performs calculations to find signals of extra-terrestrial origin by using PCs, in which the owners of the Internet-connected PCs give consent to participate in the project. The software that performs these calculations operates as a screen saver, since the calculation places a heavy load on the PC during use. These kinds of applications need high CPU performance, and are not suitable for mobile devices such as PDAs and mobile telephones. It is difficult for mobile users to use applications which saps the performance of PDAs and mobile telephones. Thus, file sharing and accessing of computing power are not suitable for the mobile environment. In a mobile environment with low power devices, only basic information browsing if possible. Therefore, one possible peer-to-peer service is the simple exchange of information among peers in a mobile environment. In addition, information that depends on physical locations will be of use in a mobile environment. In such a situation, the location-dependent information may change according to users. For example, permitting only the regular members to view the flight information from airports. It is not enough to represent information only as HTML because the changing information, according to authentification of users, is not only given as HTML. It is required that the information, in peer-to-peer services in a mobile environment, manages itself according to the location and users. We therefore need service models of peer-to-peer services in a mobile environment.

We provide a framework, called *Virtual Private Community* (VPC)[4,5] in which each unit of information is an agent, that can manage itself, controls access rights and interacts with other agents autonomously. Agents in VPC are activated according to users' attributes that also includes the location of users. VPC also provides collaboration among agents in an ad-hoc network under mobile environments. The peer-to-peer services are defined as *policy packages* that consist of rules to activate agents, agent definitions called *roles*, and contents for the services. VPC is realized by VPC platforms (VPC-Ps) that manage users' attributes, and decide which agents to activate according to the rules in the policy package and users' attributes. Large-scale experiments were conducted with practical applications using VPC for a period of two weeks. About six hundred people participated in the experiment.

Section 2 describes the foundation of peer-to-peer services and discusses suitable services of peer-to-peer services in a mobile environment. Section 3 describes details of VPC. Section 4 describes peer-to-peer services in VPC, and section

5 shows the practical application of a VPC prototype system to peer-to-peer services in a large-scale experiment.

2   Foundation of Peer-to-Peer Services in a Mobile Environment

The exchange of information among peers is the most important feature in peer-to-peer services. Information is provided by, and used by, the peers in a peer-to-peer environment. There are two phases in treating the information; the propagation, and the utilization of information. The propagation of information is performed by the transfer of information from one peer to another. This behavior is the reason why file sharing systems, such as Gnutella and Napster, are called peer-to-peer systems. In the utilization of information phase, there are two models; a stand-alone model and an interaction model. A stand-alone model involves the use information off-line, such as playing music files. This model does not require interaction with other peers. An interaction model involves the interaction among peers to use applications such as chat, network games, and groupware. The number of peers involved in the interaction may be small or large, and the interaction should be conducted in a peer-to-peer manner. In addition, the copyrights of the information that is exchanged must be protected. There must be strict controls for information access, and only approved users should be able to access the information. In addition, the privacy of the peers must also be protected.

Peer-to-peer systems should not only support the propagation phase but also the utilization phase as well. Gnutella and Napster do not have policies for each contents (information) used in the utilization phase, and caused serious problems with copyright issues. On the other hand, if policies that define how to use and access information are provided in central servers, the peers always need to refer to the servers, even if the information is propagated among the peers. That causes problems of scalability and utilization. Servers will become overloaded if peers were required to access the central server for each information, causing the load to exceed the threshold. SETI@home is categorized as a stand-alone mode in the utilization phase, and the system is not a peer-to-peer in the propagation phase since the data is sent from a central server. Therefore, this system does not cause centralization of access while the calculations are being performed. It also does not centralize the user authentification process from the viewpoint of user privacy protection. In order to ensure that a person is a regular user of the information, the authentification server needs to have the user's attributes, password, and so on. Users have to send some personal information to the server to get authentification; the user information is not secure in this phase. It is also a concern that peers cannot use the information in a stand-alone mode. Hence, there should be a policy that defines how to use and access the information.

One methodology is to make the information an agent that decides its own behavior among the peers in the propagation and utilization phases. The agent propagates among the peers, and authenticates users in the users' own mobile devices, and not from central servers. The agent also interacts with other propagated agents that work with other peers. The agent may change itself according to peers by the result of authentification, and copyright information. In order to make this a reality, we need a framework for the agent.

3   Virtual Private Community (VPC)

Our framework, called *Virtual Private Community* (VPC), enables information in peer-to-peer services to act as an agent. VPC provides a mechanism that defines an agent behavior, authenticate users, and executes agents. Necessary agents for a peer-to-peer service are defined in a policy package that consists of a condition rule to decide active agents according to users, a set of agents(called *roles*), and necessary information(contents) for the service. Agents communicate with each other through communities that are created by agents who have accepted the policy packages. Services are offered by interaction among agents in communities. For example, in a music retail service, a policy package contains two agents, an authorized agent which can play the complete music file, and a trial agent which can play only part of the music file. Users who have purchased the music file can listen to the music through authorized agents.

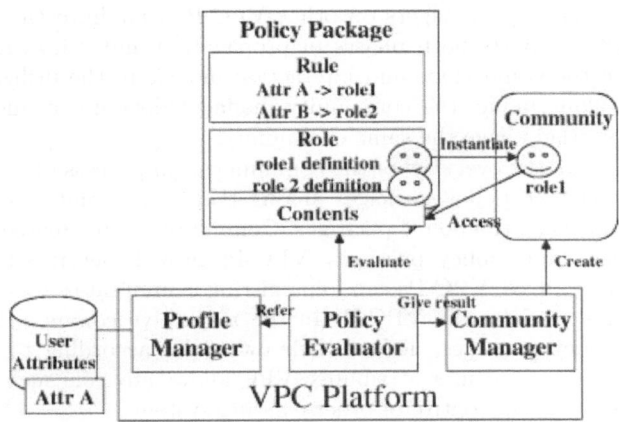

Fig. 1. Basic Model of VPC

3.1   VPC Basic Model

Figure 1 shows a basic model of VPC. In the basic model, a policy package defines the agents, condition of activation for each agent, and information that is treated by the agents. Agents are activated by *VPC platforms* (VPC-Ps) that manage user attributes, evaluate policy packages according to the user attributes, decide

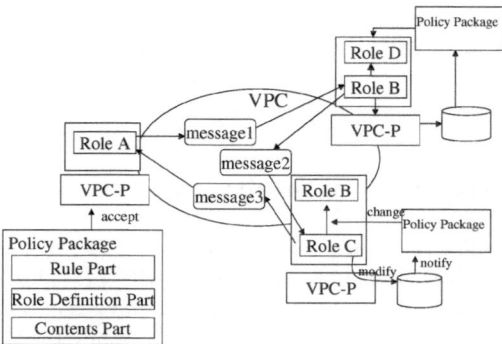

Fig. 2. VPC communication overview

appropriate roles, and create the community. The agents access contents in the
policy packages, in which the agents are defined.

Main parts of a VPC-P are a profile manager, a policy evaluator, and community manager. A profile manager manages the user profile in anti-tamper
devices such as Java Card [6]. A policy evaluator decides roles depending on the
user attributes. A community manager executes selected agents, and connects
with other community managers on other VPC-Ps that have the same policy
packages. VPC supports both phases of propagation and utilization, and also
supports both the stand-alone and interaction models in the utilization phase.
In the stand-alone mode, the community manager does not connect with the
others, even if others have the same community.

Figure 2 shows the overview of the communication process of VPC. VPC-Ps
are able to exchange policy packages among themselves, and to communicate
with each other using the policy packages. Communities are created by VPC-Ps
that accept the same policy packages. VPC-Ps provide services by collaboration among themselves. VPC-Ps can join existing communities by accepting the
policy packages used by the VPC-Ps in the respective communities. VPC-Ps
analyze the policy packages, deduce their own roles according to the rules of
the policy packages, and user attributes. VPC allows any role such as database
access, calculation, and control of other existing systems.

A community consists of VPC-Ps that accept a particular policy package.
Thus, VPC-Ps form communities by connecting to each other. Communities
consist of sub-communities on each VPC-P. Entities of a community reside on
distributed VPC-Ps that connect the community.

3.2   Policy Package

Figure 3 depicts a structure of policy packages. A policy package consists of a set
of rules as a condition table, a set of roles as transitions, and a set of contents. A
rule consists of a condition and role names. A condition is described with logical

expressions using attributes. An attribute consists of a database name, a variable name, and the value of the variable. A role consists of a role name, a program name, and an initialization method. A content consists of a content name, and content path that locates the real content data. Content includes program codes that implements roles. A policy package is written in XML.

Policy packages are encoded by S/MIME [7]. S/MIME enables VPC to detect falsification of policy packages by checking hash codes of policy packages. When VPC detects falsification of policy packages, the VPC discards the policy packages.

```
<policy package>  ::= <rules> <roles> <contents>
<rules>           ::= <rule> | <rule> <rules>
<rule>            ::= <condition> <role names>
<role names>      ::= <role name> | <role name> <role names>
<condition>       ::= "TRUE"
                    | "and" <condition> <condition>
                    | "not" <condition>
                    | "eq" <attribute> | "<" <attribute>
<attribute>       ::= <variable name> <value>
<roles>           ::= <role> | <role> <roles>
<role>            ::= <role name> <program name> <init description>
<contents>        ::= <content> | <content> <contents>
<content>         ::= <content name> <content path>
```

Fig. 3. Structure of Policy Packages

3.3   User Profiles

A profile manager has access interfaces for roles. User profiles are stored as a variable and its value, or as digital certificates of PKI[8]. Roles and a policy evaluator are able to access data through a profile manager by specifying the variable name.

A profile manager evaluates expressions of variables and values. A profile management part has corresponding evaluation modules for each database. It evaluates given expressions using the evaluation modules. Therefore, the profile management part allows evaluation of expressions that use types.

3.4   Evaluation of Rules in Policy Packages

A policy evaluator deduces roles by evaluating rules in policy packages according to users' attributes. A policy evaluator refers to conditions of rules in policy packages, evaluates each term of each condition with a profile manager, and decides appropriate roles for the user. Then, it compares a list of current active roles and deduced roles, installs necessary roles that are not currently active into sub-communities, and removes unnecessary roles from the sub-communities.

A policy evaluator requests evaluation of each term of conditions in a rule of a policy package to a profile manager. The profile manager accesses the specified variables in a term, and gets a value for specified variables. Then, it evaluates the term with the value, and returns TRUE or FALSE as a result. The policy evaluator combines the results, and decides the validity of the condition. The policy evaluator deduces appropriate role names by evaluating all conditions in the rule according to users' profiles.

The policy evaluator gets role programs with deduced role names from the policy package. Role programs are Java objects in VPC-Ps. The role assignment part creates instances of role programs with initialization according to init description in the policy package, and adds them into corresponding communities.

A user has a set of attributes $A = \{a_1, ..., a_n\}$. A rule part of a policy is a set of activation rule $W = \{c_1 \rightarrow r_1, ..., c_i \rightarrow r_i\}$. A activation rule consists of a pair of a condition, that is combination of attributes ($c_k = a_{k_1} \wedge ... \wedge a_{k_n}$), and a role r_k to activate. A evaluator $E(A, W) = \{r_k | c_k \rightarrow r_k \in W, c_k \vdash A\}$ is a function that determines a set of roles according to users' attributes and activation rules. A predicate $c_k \vdash A$ means $\forall a_{k_i} \in elements(c_k) \wedge a_{k_i} \in A$. A function $elements(c_k)$ returns a set of attributes used in c_k. Roles that are assigned for users are given by the evaluator E with activation rules.

3.5   Interaction among Roles in Communities

Collaboration among agents in communities is performed by message passing and the messages have to be accepted by appropriate roles in order to enable the collaboration. Our framework adopts the mechanism of collaboration among roles developed by Field Reactor Model [9] that is a coordination model [10] based on Dataflow Computing [11]. The Field Reactor Model (FRM) provides a method of flexible collaboration among agents by employing pattern matching.

VPC-P provides pattern invocation that is based on FRM. The patterns in VPC-P correspond to patterns in FRM and pattern invocation provides a method of invoking functions of roles without signatures of functions and addresses of roles. When a message of a pattern is sent into a community, VPC-P automatically invokes the appropriate functions. As well, values returned from the functions are put into the community as messages. Collaboration among roles is constructed as a chain of message passing and the roles do not require the specification of addresses of roles to invoke. VPC-P allows the user to define patterns and roles.

Role calculation is performed according to the following; a set of patterns that are used in a community C is $P = \{p_1, ..., p_m\}$. There are roles $R_1, ..., R_n$ in community $C(C = \{R_1, ..., R_n\})$ and a role R_k is expressed as $R_k =< I_k, f_k, O_k >$. f_k is a function that has pattern $I_k (\in P)$ as an argument and returns pattern $O_k (\in P)$. The pattern matcher $M(m)$ checks whether a message m matches the pattern of function f_k, and if there is success, then it invokes function f_k. Then the function f_k returns messages as its values with this process being described by $M(m) = \{\cup_{i=1}^n O_k | I_k = m\}$. Thus the computation between roles in the community C proceeds as $M(m), \forall m_n \in M(m_{n-1})$. The community

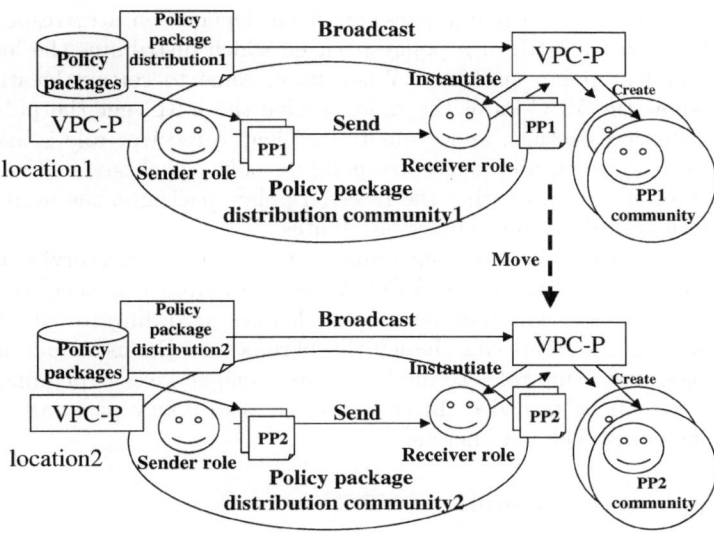

Fig. 4. Location dependent services

C repeats this process until complete collaboration among roles is created. This method of collaboration is similar to the coordination model such as Linda [12].

Patterns of roles are object types. A VPC-P allows any Java objects as roles and messages. VPC-Ps provide type match invocation that is a method, in which methods of objects are invoked when the same type of messages as an argument of the methods are put in the communities. Return values of the methods are put back in the communities when the return values are not null. The methods of roles are merely declared as normal methods.

4 Peer-to-Peer Services with VPC

VPC makes information agents act as roles in a policy package. Authorized users that have certificates can see and use the information through assigned roles. In addition, VPC-P supports location dependent services; Figure 4 shows an overview of location dependent services. In VPC-P, location dependent services are also described as policy packages. The policy packages contain roles for browsing a list of services that are provided at the location, and for downloading the policy packages. A kind of "meta-level" policy package can manage several other policy packages through roles. Roles to obtain policy packages act as gate keepers of each policy package. Only users who have certificates can reach the inner part of policy packages. This mechanism allows adaptation of services not only depending on location, but also depending on time, context in a service, and so on.

VPC-Ps that have a policy package which depends on a corresponding location, broadcast a URL of a policy package which distributes the location of these dependent policy packages. When users come to certain locations such as a hotspot, the VPC-Ps of the users receive the URL, get the policy packages distribution package, and evaluate it. Then, a receiver role is assigned to VPC-Ps of the users, and gets corresponding policy packages to the location. By the receiver role evaluating the received policy packages, the users may see information according to the users' attributes.

In order to provide services depending on time, context in a service and so on, attributes that are managed by VPC-Ps include parameters such as time and context in a service. The parameters switch roles according to rules in policy packages. Also, the roles can change the parameters. By using parameters to switch roles, and using roles to modify parameters, services depending on time and context can be provided. In this case, rules in policy packages should be defined including such parameters.

4.1   Application Examples of VPC

This section shows typical examples of VPC. There are two examples; retail of music for stand-alone mode and secure file sharing for interaction mode. In the music retail example, users who bought the music can listen to the full part of music with high quality. Other users who do not buy the music can listen to part of the music with low quality. In the secure file sharing example, only authorized users can join in a file sharing community, and share files such as the customer database file and specification of new products. The users also can communicate with each other using chat. The example is similar to Groove[13].

The music to sell is packed as a policy package that contains "fullplayer program" with decryption for regular users, "partplayer" for non regular users, encrypted music data, and a rule to assign "play music" for regular users. The rule part of the policy package of the service is the following:

```
<cond>PKI0EA02</cond><role>fullplayer</role>
<cond>''not"<cond>PKI0EA02</cond></cond><role>partplayer</role>
<cond>''not"<cond>PKI0EA02</cond></cond><role>buymusic</role>
```

"PKI0EA02" is a PKI certificate that is for buying the music. If users have that certificate, then they can have "fullplayer" role. "buymusic" is a role to buy the music, and installs "PKI0EA02" certificate to user's profile when users buy it. Even though users copy this policy package among them, only regular users can listen to the music.

In secure file sharing example, users can create a secure community, in which users exchange files and communicate with each other by chat. Only users who are authorized can join in the community. The rule part of the policy packge of the example is the following:

```
<cond>PKI0120E</cond><role>requester</role>
<cond>PKI0120E</cond><role>responder</role>
<cond>PKI0120E</cond><role>chat</role>
```

Fig. 5. General view of the shopping center

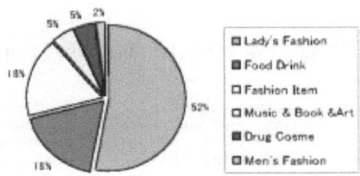

Fig. 6. Categories of shops

"PKI0120E" is a PKI certificate that is published by the community authority. Only the users who have the certificates can join in the community. In the community, there are three roles: "requester", "responder", and "chat". "requester" is a role to request the files which the users desire. "responder" is a role to answer the inquiry. "chat" is a role to communicate among users. The users who do not have the certificate are not able to join in the community since no roles are assigned. In addition, other users who do not join in the community are not able to understand message in the community since the messages are encrypted by those roles.

5   Experiment with Practical Application

We have performed large-scale experiment on VPC in an underground shopping center in Nagoya city (Japan) for two weeks. This experiment aimed to make sure of the effectiveness of a new peer-to-peer (p2p) service and a p2p medium using VPC in a stand-alone mode.

In the experiment, each user has a PDA that is WindowsCE, and users get information, such as special bargain price information of shops around the user, depending on the user's location, through a wireless LAN. The information of the service is provided as a policy package with VPC. Users can see the information that matches the user's attributes. For example, the information in a drug store has two contents, cosmetics for ladies and shaving lotion for gentlemen. When

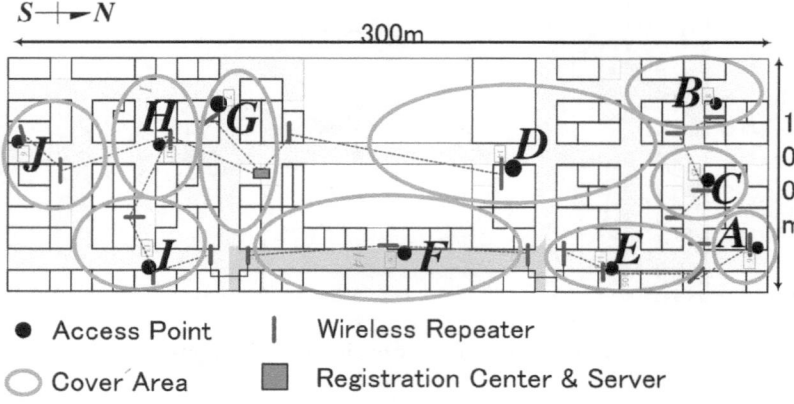

Fig. 7. Overview of the shopping center

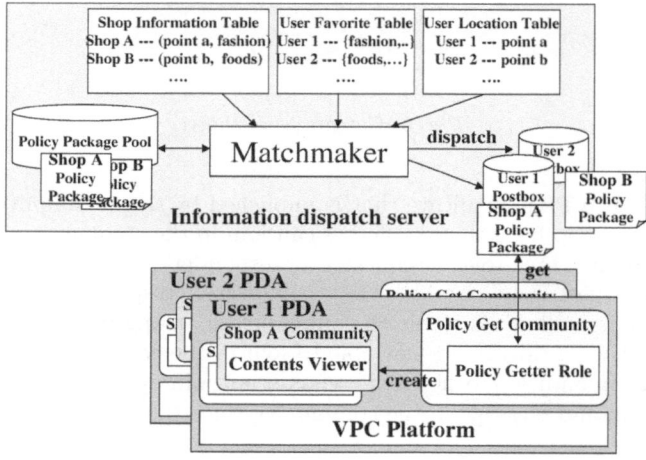

Fig. 8. System overview

the user is a woman, she can see the cosmetics information. We employed a bingo game as a user interface in order to make the experiment more attractive for users. A bingo card for each user is given during registration. Each set of information includes its own ID that is a bingo number. Users can exchange given information(policy packages) among them. When users win the game, they can get a coupon that is only able to be used in the shopping center.

Figure 5 shows a scene in the shopping center. Categories of shops in the shopping center are shown in figure 6. This experiment had been broadcasted by some TV media, FM radio stations and newspapers. About six hundred people participated in this event, thanks to the media.

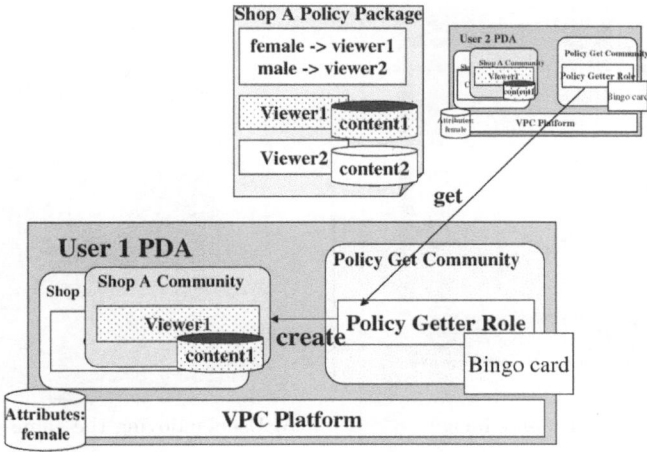

Fig. 9. Exchange information among peers

5.1 System Overview

Figure 7 shows an overview of the shopping center and location of wireless LAN access points. The size of the shopping center is about 300m x 100m. There are 107 shops in it. We employed 802.11b for wireless LAN. Ten access points are set in this area. Each access point is connected by wireless LAN repeaters. The number of repeaters is twenty. Each access point covers an area in which about ten shops reside, and manages MAC addresses of PDA terminals. Channels of access points are different from neighborhood in order to avoid interference. Users are registered at the registration center when they begin the game.

A system overview is shown in figure 8. The system consists of a server, which sends information to each user, and VPC that works on user's PDA terminals. We could not prepare PCs or PDAs for each access point because it is too expensive and is against the fire prevention laws in Japan. Therefore, we decided to use a server and to multiplex it. The server has policy packages of all the shops and three tables; shop information table, user favorite table, and user location table. A user location table maintains connections between PDAs and access points. A user favorite table has a set of users' favorite categories, and is created for each user during registration. The shop information table has pairs of shops' locations and the categories for each shop. The main module is a matchmaker that decides policy packages to send for each user according to matching user's location and favorite with shop information. The server has a postbox for each user inside it, and dispatches corresponding information within the area, in which users exist, to the users' postboxes. Users' VPC-Ps get delivered policy packages and evaluate them.

Figure 9 shows diagram of exchange of information among peers. A "policy get" community that has a "policy getter" role is to exchange information among peers and to get information from the server, and is activated on the PDA

(a) Display image   (b) Users enjoying the game

Fig. 10. Game

terminals. The role also inquires other peers by broadcasting messages periodically. When the user wants information and other peers indicate will giving the information, the two "policy getter" roles on both users' VPC-Ps exchange the information each other. The "policy getter" role also checks the user's postbox periodically. The "policy getter" role creates shop communities, when it gets new policy packages from the postbox or other peers. A "viewer" role that enables a user to see its contents (HTML) is activated. The "viewer" role is changed according to user's attributes.

5.2   Results and Discussion

Figure 10 (a) shows a display image on PDA, and (b) shows users enjoying the game. About six houndred users came to participate in the experiment. Figure 11(a) shows the numbers of persons per generation. The numbers of women in the teens and 20s are far greater than for any other generation since many shops target this generation. Also, the number of men in their 20s and 30s are greater than for any other generation of men. Figure 11(b) shows the change in the numbers of players per a day. It also shows the total numbers of information exchanges, and the numbers of repeat players of the game. The total players and repeat players increased day by day. The increase in the number of repeat players was especially remarkable. In the questionnaire that players filled out after the game, we found one of the sources; girls from high school and junior high school had come again several times, and joined this experiment after hearing about it from their friends. It is natural that the numbers of players were on weekdays compared on the weekend. The information exchanges did not increase, and were almost constant (10-15) from the first day.

The followings are user comments:

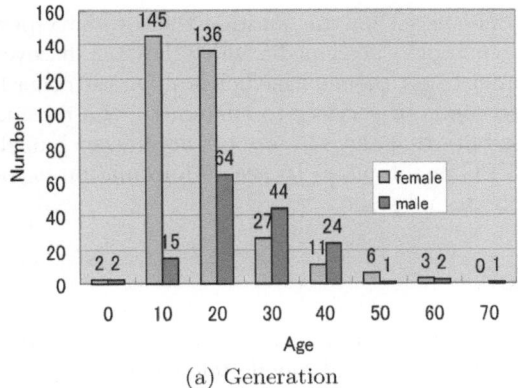

(a) Generation

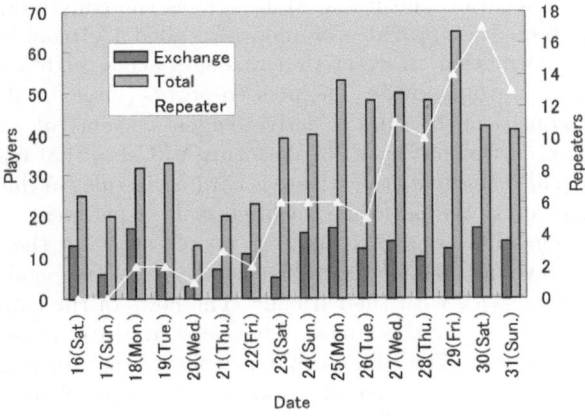

(b) Change in the numbers of players per a day

Fig. 11. Results

- It is a lot of fun as a game.
- I am interested in the time services.
- I want to exchange information more.
- I need to exactly pinpoint information by location.

The followings are shop owners' comments:

- P2P services may be new advertisement media.
- We want to use these services as new market tool to focus on specific customers.
- PDAs are not popular for ordinary people. We require these services with mobile phones.
- Please perform this event for a year.

We have got one answer for the question that ordinary people use or require p2p services. The customers need media which they can discover goods or services they require in order to get them with efficiency. On the other hand, shop owners want to advertise goods or services to customers who are interested in. There are sufficient possiblity that the p2p services become such media. Especially, the p2p services in VPC enable users to access information according to location, time, service context, and so on.

6   Conclusion

This paper proposed peer-to-peer service models for a mobile environment with mobile devices such as PDAs and mobile telephones. Very restricted mobile devices are not suitable for file sharing and the renting of CPU power. In a mobile environment, information browsing is basic. Also, the information may change according to the location and users. Moreover, as the copyright of information needs to be protected, we provide a framework, called a Virtual Private Community, to make information an agent that manages access rights, and to interact with other agents autonomously. The peer-to-peer services are defined as policy packages that consist of the rules to activate agents, agent(role) definitions, and contents. VPC is carried out by VPC platforms(VPC-Ps) that manage users' attributes and decide the agents to activate according to rules in the policy package and users' attributes. We performed a large-scale experiment with a practical application using VPC about six hundred people enjoying the experiment. In the experiment, young ladies (teens-20s) came again and again, and enjoyed this peer-to-peer service with their friends. The news of the experiment spread through the grapevine for these ages. They also freuently exchanged information among themselves. The i-mode that is web browser for mobile telephones of DoCoMo Ltd. in Japan increased explosively from people of these ages, and has thirty million users now. There is possibility that peer-to-peer services will become very popular due to the influence of people of these ages.

Acknowledgments. This work was done under a grant to the "Research on Management of Security Policies in Mutual Connection" from Telecommunications Advancement Organization (TAO) of Japan.

References

1. Fernando Bordignon and Gabriel Tolosa, Gnutella: Distributed System for Information Storage and Searching Model Description,
   http://www.gnutella.co.uk/library/pdf/paper_final_gnutella_english.pdf (2000)
2. Napster: http://www.napster.com. (1998)
3. By Eric Korpela, Dan Werthimer, David Anderson, Jeff Cobb, and Matt Lebofsky:SETI@Home: Massively Distributed Computing for SETI. Computing in science & engineering, January/February 2001 (Vol. 3, No. 1), pp. 78–83, http://www.computer.org/cise/articles/seti.htm, IEEE (2001)

4. T. Iwao, Y. Wada, S. Yamasaki, M.shiouchi, M. Okada, and M. Amamiya, "A Framework for the Next Generation of E-Commerce by Peer-to-Peer Contact: Virtaul Private Community", WETICE2001, pp. 340–341, IEEE (2001)
5. T. Iwao, Y. Wada, S. Yamasaki, M. Shiouchi, M. Okada, and M. Amamiya, "Collaboration among Agents in Logical Network of Peer-To-Peer Services, SAINT2002, pp. 6–7, IEEE (2002)
6. Sun Microsystems, "Java Card 2.1.1 Platform", http://www.java.sun.com/products/javacard/javacard21.html,
7. B. Ramsdell, Editor, "S/MIME Version 3 Message Specification", http://www.faqs.org/rfcs/rfc2633.html, 1999
8. Stephen Kent, and Tim Polk, "Public-Key Infrastructure", http://www.ietf.org/html.charters/pkix-charter.html, 2000
9. Tadashige Iwao, Makoto Okada, Yuji Takada and Makoto Amamiya, "Flexible Multi-Agent Collaboration using Pattern Directed Message Collaboration of Field Reactor Model", LNAI 1733 pp. 1–16, PRIMA'99
10. G. A. Papadopoulos and F. Arbab, "Coordination Models and Languages", Advances in Computers Vol. 46, pp. 329–400, 1998
11. Amamaiya, M., Hasegawa, R.: Dataflow Computing and Eager and Lazy Evaluation, New Generation Computing, 2, pp. 105–129, OHMSHA and Springer-Verlag (1984).
12. Carriero, N. and Gelernter, D. "Linda in Context", Communications of the ACM Vol. 32-4, pp. 444–458, 1989
13. Groove: http://www.groove.net/ (2000)

A Cognitive Architecture for the Design of an Interaction Agent

Ana García-Serrano[1] and Javier Calle-Gómez[2]

[1] Artificial Intelligence Department, Technical University of Madrid, Spain
[2] Computer Science Department, Carlos III University of Madrid, Spain
{agarcia,jcalle}@isys.dia.fi.upm.es

Abstract. The paper is focused on the Interaction Agent designed to provide an Advanced Human Computer Interaction in the on-going project VIP-ADVISOR[1]. The problem addressed is the identification of the components of the cognitive architecture needed and in particular, introduces a model for the intentions underlying any interaction as a key point for dialogue management required to perform successful interactive process. A detailed case study and the first evaluation performed are described using the current prototype for advice-giving in an e-commerce scenario.

1. Introduction

This paper proposes a theoretical framework for the modelling of the different cognitive components taking part in an Advanced Human Computer Interaction (HCI) for the development of an advice-giving assistant.

In order to reach a coherent management of the complete interactive process (i.e. the dialogue), three major subtasks were identified: the interface related ones, the dialogue management, and the intelligent content generation [1]. In our proposal the whole interactive process is performed by an agent-based system: (i) The interpretation of the user and generation of the system utterances are the *interface agent* main tasks; (ii) The identification of the coherence of the discourse pieces is the responsibility of the *interaction agent*; (iii) The selection of content for system interventions according with the circumstances (i.e. user requirements, and others) is performed by the intelligent *agent*, that includes a knowledge-based system incorporating the domain knowledge (figure 1).

The work presented in this paper is devoted to the design and deployment of the interaction agent. The remaining sections of this paper are organised as follows. First is presented in detail the components of the interaction agent cognitive architecture. In the third section is included a detailed example to show the interactive process management in the global system. Finally some details about the evaluation aspects taking into account for the prototyped interaction agent are given.

---

[1] VIP-ADVISOR project IST-2001-32440

M. Klusch, S. Ossowski, and O. Shehory (Eds.): CIA 2002, LNAI 2446, pp. 82–89, 2002.
© Springer-Verlag Berlin Heidelberg 2002

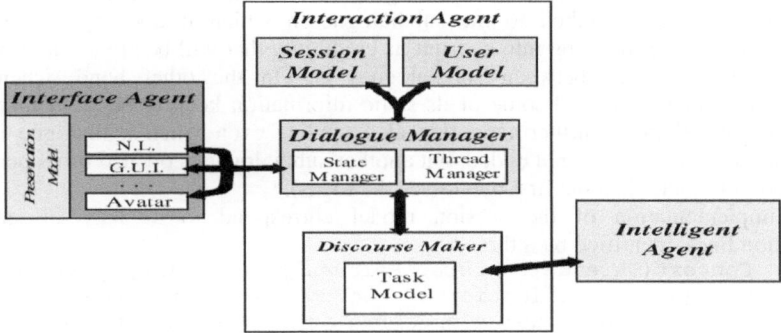

Fig. 1. Agent-based system

2. The Cognitive Architecture for the Interaction Agent

For the description of the components of the architecture of the interaction agent, first step is to characterise the information involved during the dialogue-based interaction.

The Trindikit architecture [2] is a set of tools for the development of dialogue management systems, developed during Trindi and Siridus projects [3]. This architecture provides a dialogue control based in 'information states' [4]. There will be a 'global information state', and the target is to get it to some particular requirements. This scope is very useful for interaction systems that require obtaining a great deal of information from the user for the dialogue to success. Siridus extends its scope to dialogues in which the task is not predefined, so first is established a communicative task between two interlocutors, followed by the accomplishment of that task. Finally, it should be mentioned that this system brings into account prosodic features (stress, intonation or emphasis) with the acquired information.

The TRAINS family is a full series of progressively improved prototypes of an interactive planning assistant in a simplified transportation domain [5]. Later versions have added robustness, module independence in the architecture, and domain knowledge for constructing better plans in more complex domains as TRIPS project [6].

In our design, the dialogue direction and motivation, *the dynamic information*, has to be settled and, in a complementary way, *the static information* is used as the information dressing the global interaction by providing the semantic content details.

2.1 The Session Model and User Model

The static information within a session can be divided into atomic pieces according to the representative part of the speech, so any 'Inform' act should be interpreted as at least a piece of static information. For any other act, there should be extracted its representative part (if any) and included as new static information pieces.

The interventions are organised in dialogues and subdialogues, hence the static information should be linked to the subdialogue in which it does appear. This information is accessed taking into account its credibility that will be higher inasmuch as shorter the distance between subdialogues is. On the other hand, when a subdialogue comes to an end some of its static information keep to be valid for the precedent subdialogue. Furthermore, this also applies even when a dialogue just losses the focus (this is, it is not ended, but another subdialogue is opened or reopened somewhere else, and then the first one losses the focus).

The implementation of the session model correspond to a 'bag' of static information lines, identified by a thread:

```
Context(Thread, Feature, Relevancy, Certainty, Value).
Thread: identification of the context is related to.
Feature and Value: a specific attribute and its value
Relevancy: is needed for inheritance processes
Certainty: represents the trust in the value
```

In this model, the identity of the user is a continuous process along each session in which any information acquired regarding the user will be used to influence the whole interaction process. This sort of User Model, register links between values for the significant user features observed during system's life, through all sessions held with different kind of users. When starting a new session, the user is unknown, but he will probably match with a 'class' or a group of users. Hence, when some information about the user is needed, the feasible values for that feature would be bounded, and even there could exist some predominant one.

2.2 Dialogue Manager

As aforementioned, the *dynamic information* refers to the underlying intentions and motivations during the dialogue. Within each subdialogue, it could be established a discourse line or 'thread' that carry the intentional information of that dialogue. Each thread should be related to its precedent ones, and at the same time could give raise to new minor threads which accurate intentional interpretations. It could be established that dialogues can be organised with a tree structure. Thread modelling provides, consequently, a mechanism for organising, interpreting and planing dialogues, following the intentions shown by the user interventions and system's own intentions, raised either from a thread grammar or motivated by the result of some component in the dialogue (for example, when is needed extra information, a new thread will be yield for acquiring that information from the user).

Apart from intentional processing, several pragmatic studies point out the existence of predefined protocols and interchange of elements that are commonly used for certain purposes. One of these is the organising principles [7], to understand the dialogue as a shared co-operative social task in a way that the steps in the dialogue are the illocutive elements that are performed by the interlocutors by turn. Subsequently, there will exist a set of patterns for each kind of dialogue that any interaction should fit to a pattern of its class. Those patterns will be named 'scripts', and the sort of dialogue is better known as 'dialogue game'. The user/system interventions could be seen as steps through the dialogue according to some particular set of rules named 'adjacency pairs'. This dialogue management is known through the bibliography as 'dialogue games' [8]. They are complementary to an intentional management as the thread model. Along any communicative process, the receiver is continuously searching for his interlocutors plan of interpretation. When both of them coincide at the same plan, it can be said that they have reached a commitment [9,10].

The thread model designed will observe three components: the user thread (regarding user intentions, as they are acquired and interpreted), the system thread (how system introduces new threads as a reaction to the user ones and its own definition), and finally the thread joint (depicting that common ground).

thread *(Intention, Object, State, Guide, Id, Father)*
Intention and *Object*: the action and object
State: information to link a thread to a game playing.
Guide: who opened the thread
Id: sequential number of creation of threads
Father: identification of the predecessor thread

The intentions and objects observed in the analysed corpus were modelled with the following threads:

Thread	Object
Command	Purchase, search
Request	Data, confirmation, product
Solve	Command, request, data, approve, deny
null	

When a new thread comes, first is to decide if that thread already exists in its branch (that means that the discourse follows an existent thread). If not, it will be a new thread. This thread could close a previous thread or just be a new one:

the thread...		will close the thread...	
Solve	command	Command	*
Solve	request	Request	product
Solve	data	Request	Data
Solve	approve	Request	Data
Solve	deny	Request	Data
Solve	approve	Request	confirmation
Solve	deny	Request	confirmation

The State Manager that supports the thread management in the Dialogue Manager is implemented as an automaton that is used also before interpreting an intervention of the user, providing a prediction of the feasible paths the user can make by his own.

The transitions in the automaton may come from user moves (normal motions), or without them. When they arise with no explicit move by the user, they could be due to three different sources, which lead to three kinds of motions: λ-motions (ellipsis, when is postulated that the user had omit a step of the script), π-motions (for linking dialogues and sub-dialogues), and event-motions (or ε-motions, when they are due to an interruption of the system). The implemented transitions were acquired from corpus analysis, and some of them are shown next grouped by sort of steps: user steps, user null steps (made with no explicit discourse), system null steps, and event steps (caused by some event from the task model).

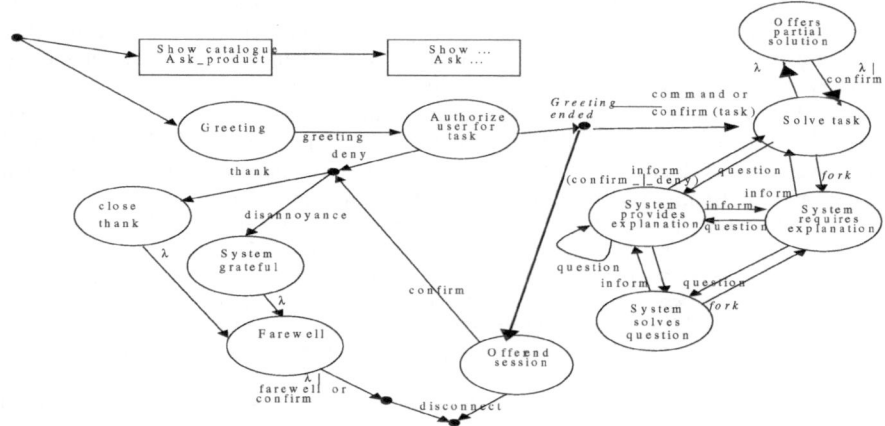

Fig. 2. Partial view of the state Manager

2.3   Discourse Maker

The discourse maker has to validate that last intention committed does not imply the performance of a specific task (event) from the system. The event represents the aim of the system of reaching some state. But, since events are the result of some task, and task are forced by the input of the user, it might be said that those initiatives are, in fact, system reactions to the interventions of the user. So, some tasks are not forced at all by the user, but programmed by the system manager: A timer, for example, pointing a process that the interlocutor is too long since last input from him.

Finally, notice that some events would produce new speech, and some others could even lead to new task processing. As a result, one event can influence the content of the static information storage (with the acquisition of new information, or the refinement of existing information), change the state of the dialogue in the thread joint, or even propose new threads (the system ones). The informational structure for the implementation of the discourse maker is based on:

```
generation(State,Thread,Event,Init_Session,F_Session)
State: the target state
Thread: actual thread
Event: event raised in that response
Init_Session: information about the session before task
F_Session: information about the session after task
```

State	Thread	Event	Effect
2	ident <> 0	*previous aims*	Check if there were previous aims
4	intention=command, obj=purchase		React with intention of *search*
4	intention=command, obj=search		Call the intelligent agent for search
4	intention=request, obj=data	*reask*	
4	intention=request,obj=confirmation	*reask*	
25		*disconnect*	

The task of	Might end with an event of
– calling the intelligent agent	– final sol - null_sol - partial_sol - fork
– checking if there were previous aims	– previous aims - no aims
– checking if basket has anything	– basket empty - basket full

When a user requires information about some object and the system detects the need of new information (not contained explicitly in the dialogue so far), it is started a request for the performance of this task, but can happen that there is not enough information available for the intelligent agent to accomplish it. Therefore, it is proposed to the interaction agent to introduce some new thread to obtain the information needed before to perform that task successfully.

3. Interaction Agent Performance

To perform the co-ordination between the different agents, a communication language is needed. The messages will contain the semantic information involved during the user or agents interaction.

KQML [11] observe three levels (communication, message and content) as candy wraps [12], covering fore with higher level layer. However, our approach is based in the fact that *the suitable set* of communicative acts for a concrete system in an specific domain has to fit the particular needs of the domain. Regarding dialogue processing challenges, some examples could be presented. For instance, Reithinger and Klesen [13] found within Vermobil dialogue corpus a set of 27 dialogue acts, which they distributed into 18 abstract classes. On the other hand, Mittal and Moore [14] propose a set of just four speech acts.

The communicative acts used to communicate interface and interaction agents [15] consists of thirteen communicative acts distributed into six categories: *Representative*, the emitter shows a link with the reality, sharing with his interlocutor; *Directive*, the emitter should direct his interlocutors next actions; *Authorizative*, the emitter wants his interlocutor to perform some action; *Courtesy*, social conventions that both interlocutors should observe just for protocol, tuning, or politeness; *Non-verbal*, Required for non-verbal social conventions such us connection; and *Null*, when there is no effective communication. Several parameters characterise the occurrence of each dialogue act [6] in a way that can be shown as 'labelled' communicative acts to be handled by both interface and interaction agents.

When the communicative acts reach the interaction agent, the information carried by them is interpreted. Regarding the threads management, an intervention can follow the focused thread, any other previous thread, or originate a new one. The threads are arranged as a tree like structure, and leaf nodes should be closed with the inclusion of a 'solve' thread, which means that the thread of that branch has been satisfied. Any interlocutor might at any moment 'jump' to a branch in the thread tree different than the focused one (a previous thread or a new one that is not a descendent of the focused thread, as example in figure 3).

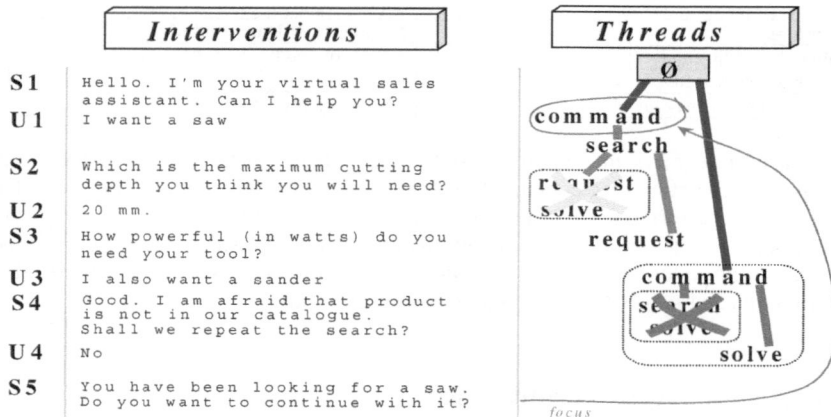

Fig. 3. Threads management

In the example within figure 3, before intervention (S2) the system summoned the intelligent agent for providing a product identification. Since there were several of them, the discourse maker decides to create a new thread heed to obtain from the user more information (particularly, the desired cutting depth for that product) in order to refine the solution. Since the entry point of the discourse maker changes (new focused thread), this component has to restart its process. This time, it has no need of external help for obtaining all needed contents.

4. Conclusions

It was presented a cognitive architecture for supporting an advanced HCI model, as well as an approach for evaluation. A first version of the cognitive architecture presented has been implemented in a virtual assistant for e-commerce during the ADVICE project (IST-1999-11305).

For the evaluation of the interaction agent, was used 10 different dialogs between user and system: (a) within the session model was inspected if the information was registered at a good rate and in an accurate way, and if the relevant information for each dialogue step was available when is needed; (b) the evaluation of the system dynamic information processing, was based on the cost of satisfying the user needs by the average number of interactions needed for successfully accomplish a conversation between user and system, average number of targets or communicative actions to be solved at each intervention (system and user's), and average number of *useless* or *improper* interventions; and (c) the Discourse Maker evaluation was based on its capability for generating different reactions from user interventions (variability).

That evaluation shows that the first prototyped Interaction Agent was no complete and thus, we are now working towards this in the VIP-ADVISOR project for the domain of risk management.

Acknowledgements. We would like to thank the ISYS research group at the Technical University of Madrid for their support during the design and development of the interaction agent.

References

1. García Serrano A., Teruel D., Hernández Diego J., 2001. Intelligent Assistance in E-commerce Scenario, Int. Conference on Intelligent Agents, Web Tech. and Internet Commerce.
2. Larsson, S., Berman, A., Bos, J., Grönqvist, L., Ljunglöf, P., Traum, D., 2000. TrindiKit 2.0 Manual. Task Oriented Instructional Dialogue, LE4-8314. Deliverable D5.3
3. Traum, DR, Bos, J., Cooper, R., Larsson, S., Lewin, I., Matheson, C., Poesio, M., 1999. A Model of Dialogue Moves an Information State Revision. Trindi Project (LE4-8314) deliverable 2.1.
4. Amores,J.G., Quesada,J.F., 2001. Dialogue Moves for Natural Command Languages. Procesamiento del Lenguaje Natural, 27, pp. 81–88. Jaen, sept.
5. Ferguson, G.F., Allen, J.F., Miller, B.W., Ringger, E.K., 1996. The Design and Implementation of the TRAINS-96 System: A Prototype Mixed-Initiative Planning Assistant. TRAINS Technical Note 96–5. Rochester, New York.
6. Ferguson, G.F., Allen, J.F., 1998. TRIPS: An Integrated Intelligent Problem-Solving Assistant. In Procs. of the 15th National Conference on Artificial Intelligence, pp 567–572.
7. Levinson, 1983, Pragmatics, Cambridge University Press.
8. Poesio, M, Mikheev, A., 1998. The Predictive Power of Game Structure in Dialogue Act Recognition: Experimental Results Using Maximum Entropy Estimation. Proc. ICSLP-98.
9. Cohen, P.R., Levesque, H.J., 1991. Confirmation and Joint Action, Proceedings of International Joint Conference on Artificial Intelligence.
10. Cohen, P. R. and Levesque, H. J. 1991. Teamwork, Nous 25(4), Special Issue on Cognitive Science and Artifical Intelligence, pp. 487–512.
11. Finin, T., Weber, J., Wiederhold, G., Genesereth, M., Fritzson, R., McKay, D., McGuire, J., Pelavin, R., Shapiro, S., Beck, C., 1994. Specification of the KQML Agent-Com. Language. DARPA Knowledge Sharing Initiative. External Interfaces W. Group.
12. Patil, R., Fikes, R., Patel-Schneider, P., Mckay, D., Finin, T., Gruber, T., Neches, R., 1992. The DARPA Knowledge Sharing Effort: Progress Report. Proceedings of the Third International Conference on Knowledge Representation and Reasoning, Boston.
13. Reithinger, N., Klesen, M., 1997. Dialogue Act Classification Using Language Models. In EuroSpeech '97, pp 2235–2238. Rhodes.
14. Mittal, V.O., Moore, J.D., 1995. Dynamic Generation of Follow up Question Menus: Facilitating Interactive Natural Language Dialogues. CHI '95 Mosaic of Creativity.
15. Rodrigo, L., García-Serrano, A., Martínez, P., 2001. Gestión Flexible de Diálogos en el proyecto Advice. Procesamiento del Lenguaje Natural, n 27, pp. 319–320.
16. García-Serrano, A., Calle, J., Hernández, J., 2001. Dialogue Management for an advice giving virtual assistant. IJCAI 01 Workshop on Knowledge and Reasoning in Practical Dialogue Systems. Seattle

A Multi-agent Reflective Architecture for User Assistance and Its Application to E-commerce

Antonella Di Stefano[1], Giuseppe Pappalardo[2], Corrado Santoro[1], and Emiliano Tramontana[2]

[1] Dipartimento di Ingegneria Informatica e delle Telecomunicazioni
{adistefa, csanto}@diit.unict.it
[2] Dipartimento di Matematica e Informatica
Università di Catania
Viale A. Doria, 6 - 95125 Catania, Italy
{pappalardo,tramontana}@dmi.unict.it

Abstract. Assisting an user working with an application can involve several tasks of a different nature; thus it can be a complex job which is better performed by several autonomous agents. Accordingly, in many scenarios, several small assistant agents, each dedicated to a single task, are employed to supply help and to enhance the same application.

This paper proposes a software architecture that allows multiple assistants to serve the same application and interact with each other as necessary, while working autonomously from each other. This architecture interfaces assistants with an existing application by means of computational reflection. The latter mechanism allows meaningful user activities to be intercepted by assistants, and the outcomes of their activity to be supplied to the application. No assumptions need to be made about the application or the assistants; assistants can be changed, added and removed as necessary to adapt the application to unforeseen scenarios, conversely an assistant can be employed to support several applications. The usefulness and applicability of the proposed architecture is demonstrated by an e-commerce case study: we show how a suitable assistant set can integrate with and enhance a bare web browser, making it fit to support e-commerce activities.

1 Introduction

Although common widely-known applications provide a user-friendly GUI and a set of functionalities that help users carrying out their work, they can be further improved with *assistant agents* [16,4] that facilitate user operations and/or add support for user-specific activities. In this field, one of the most famous examples is the Microsoft Office assistant, which is an ActiveX object, integrated with the Office suite. Other research proposals provide assistants to help web browsing [13, 6], chatting [14], web mining [11], etc.

Up to now, the techniques used to connect assistant agents with an application need to be (re-)designed each time a new application is extended or a new

M. Klusch, S. Ossowski, and O. Shehory (Eds.): CIA 2002, LNAI 2446, pp. 90–103, 2002.

assistance functionality is integrated; this is because the connection is generally obtained by exploiting the access points provided by the application itself or by the operating system environment (e.g. scripting services). In any case, solutions are application- or environment-dependent and no general technique to interface applications and assistants exists. In addition (with few exceptions like [6,11]), assistants proposed so far consist of a single component which embeds all the supplied functions, thus making it hard to modify assistance functionalities or add further ones.

To overcome the above limitations, this paper proposes a multi-agent architecture for the *modular* design of application assistance software based on a set of cooperative agents. It extends [4] by supporting coordination among various assistants working for the same application. The architecture is conceived not to be tied to a specific application. It exploits *computational reflection* [15] to interface with an existing application written in an object-oriented programming language. We adopt the *metaobject* model [8] to capture control from an application object whenever an operation is performed on it (e.g. a method is invoked), and to bring control within the associated *metaobject*, which can choose to modify the behaviour of the application object. In the proposed architecture, a set of assistant agents, each entrusted with a specific task, cooperate with a special agent, called *Coordinator*, which handles interactions between them and the application. This agent incorporates some metaobjects, which *intercept* control from application objects, and cooperates with assistant agents. It triggers assistant activities and uses their outcomes to change or enrich the behaviour of the application.

The proposed architecture affords a great degree of *flexibility* and *modularity* in the design and implementation of assistants. Each of these can be seen as a "plug-in", which can be added (even at run-time) if its functionality is needed, or can be removed in the opposite case, without affecting the functioning of the entire system.

The architecture has been employed to coordinate a set of assistants aimed at facilitating e-commerce activities. We envisage several types of assistants enhancing a web browser with functionalities for e-commerce and simplifying the steps that users must perform before purchase. An assistant is dedicated to each of the following tasks:

- understanding user preferences from visited web pages and from typed keywords;
- extracting data from web pages to collect features of interesting goods;
- creating *on the client side* a virtual cart that stores potential user's purchases;
- finding offers for user selected goods;
- monitoring the trend of prices of user selected goods.

The outcomes of assistant activities are used to change the browser behaviour, by e.g. re-organising web pages and highlighting important pieces of information on web pages, as the user navigates.

The outline of the paper is as follows. Section 2 presents the reflective soft-ware architecture for coordinating multiple web assistants. Section 3 describes in detail a set of assistants cooperating within the proposed architecture, in or-der to enhance a web browser. Section 4 analyses related work. Conclusions are presented in Section 5.

2   An Architecture for Coordinating Assistants

2.1   Reflection

A software system is said to be reflective when it contains structures, representing some of its own aspects, which allow it to observe, and operate on, itself [15]. A reflective system is typically a two-level system comprising a *baselevel*, intended to implement some functionalities, and a *metalevel*, which observes and acts on the baselevel. A widespread reflective model is the *metaobject model*, which associates each baselevel object for which this is deemed useful, with a corre-sponding metalevel object called *metaobject*. As Figure 1 shows, metaobjects *intercept* control from their associated objects whenever e.g. an object method is invoked (see (1) of Figure 1), or an object changes its state [15,8]. Once control is within metaobjects (2), these are able to *inspect* and change the state of their associated objects, and to modify objects behaviour by activating operations, changing parameters, etc. After control has been captured by metaobjects, it is usually given back to the object invoked initially (3).

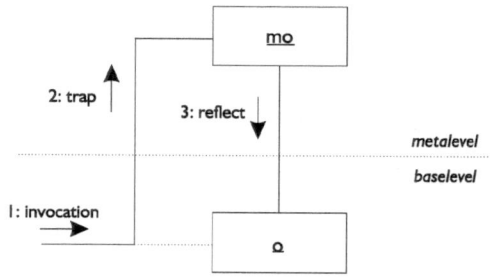

Fig. 1. Metaobject model

Reflective systems have been exploited to transparently provide software sys-tems with synchronisation [21], adaptation to changing conditions of the envi-ronment [22], fine grained allocation of objects in a distributed environment [5], etc.

Metaobjects are associated with objects by means of reflective object-oriented languages, such as OpenC++ [2], Javassist [3], etc. The former language is a re-flective version of C++ that relies on inserting keywords into the source code to provide an application with metaobjects. Then the OpenC++ code is transformed into executable code by a special pre-compiler. Javassis is a reflective version of Java that allows objects to be associated with metaobjects by changing selected bytecode parts, and injecting into objects statements that notify some of their events to metaobjects.

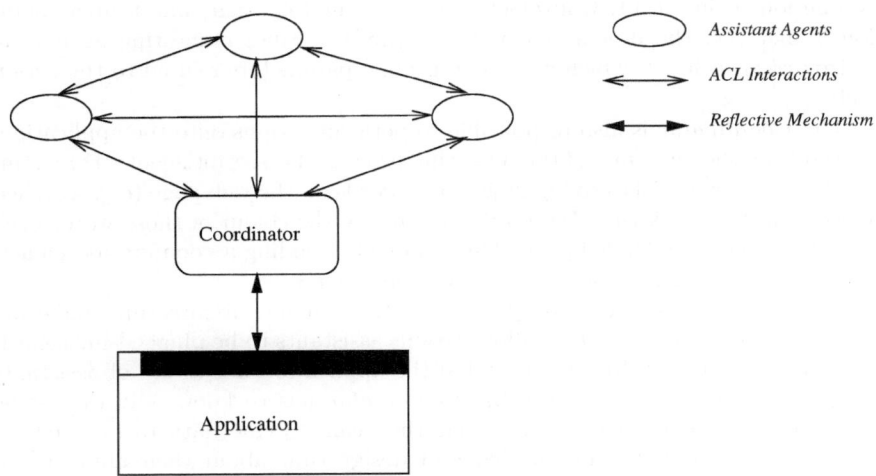

Assistant Agents

ACL Interactions

Reflective Mechanism

Fig. 2. Reflective software architecture coordinating several assistants

2.2   The Architecture

Assistants aim at providing additional information and functionalities to users while they work with an application. For this, assistants need to capture user activities and appropriately react by changing the application behaviour.

The software architecture that this paper proposes exploits computational reflection as a means to integrate assistants into an application. In such an architecture, complexity is handled and the support for modularity is effectively realised by using several autonomous and specialised (assistant) agents.

The architecture consists of an application (typically a web browser, however we are exploiting it also for other applications) at the baselevel, and various agents, i.e. a *Coordinator* and some assistants, at the metalevel (Figure 2). Several assistants enable achieving *modularity* since each of them is built as a small component dedicated to a single task.

Assistants interact with the application by means of the *Coordinator* agent, whose purpose is to communicate to assistants the interesting events of the application, to use assistant outcomes to change some operations of the application, and to allow exchanging data between assistants. Communication between agents—both assistants and *Coordinator*— is performed by using messages, that is Agent Communication Language (ACL) speech acts [12].

Thanks to reflection, the *Coordinator* is able to detect the *effect* of user operations on the application (i.e. method invocations, changes of object attributes, etc.). On the basis of this detection, the *Coordinator* deduces user actions and notifies the occurrence of these to other agents, according to their requests. In particular, each agent interested in being informed of a specific event sends a request-whenever speech act to the *Coordinator* defining, as the condition, the user action to intercept. Conversely, the Coordinator, each time that a condition is met (i.e. the user action is intercepted), notifies requesting agents via an inform speech act, which carries additional parameters related to the action itself.

The *Coordinator* is also responsible to perform actions onto the application, derived from the outcomes of the reasoning process of assistant agents. For example, if an assistant wishes to highlight some words on the web page (e.g. searched keywords), it can ask the *Coordinator* to change the colour of those words each time they occur in a loaded page. This is done by sending a request speech act, containing the action to be done, to the *Coordinator*.

The characteristics of the proposed reflective software architecture, and especially those of the *Coordinator*, allow various assistants to be plugged-in, according to the user needs. Reflection makes the application not aware of assistants changing its behaviour, whereas the *Coordinator* has to know only that some assistants need to be notified and that they can provide data to be used for the application, but has no knowledge at design time about their number and specific task. Indeed, assistants can be of any type and can be created incrementally. The only constraint for assistants, to be able to interact with each other and the application, is the type and meaning of events and data that they are able to exchange. To make it possible for the *Coordinator* to work with several unknown assistants, it exploits the *Observer* design pattern [9] and the *Blackboard* architectural style [19].

Figure 3 shows the proposed reflective software architecture allowing several assistants and an application to be interfaced, and the structure of the *Coordinator*.

2.3   Components of the Coordinator

In order to achieve/perform its operations, the *Coordinator* is based on the set of components shown in Figure 3, which also depicts the dynamic of interactions. These components are: metaobjects Switcher, implementing the interactions with application objects; and metalevel objects Merger and Blackboard realising the interactions with assistants, by means of an ACL. Each component is described in the following.

– Metaobjects Switcher are employed to detect events of the application. They are associated with those application objects that generate events which some assistants are interested in, and those application objects whose behaviour can be changed by assistants.

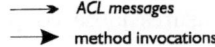

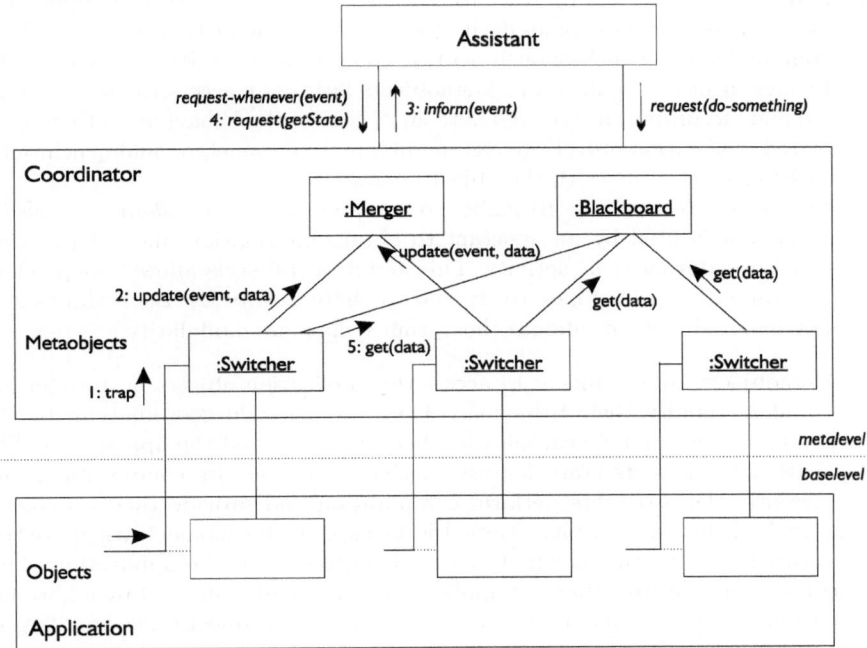

Fig. 3. Coordinator functionalities and interactions with assistant agents

Each metaobject captures all the method invocations and state changes of an application object (see (1) of Figure 3), thus it is able to detect a specific set of events and to intervene to modify the behaviour of the application object. E.g., for e-commerce assistants, the events that metaobjects capture include: downloading a new web page, rendering a web page, displaying a word on the screen, inserting a word in a web form.

– Metalevel object `Merger` receives information on events and data of the application by metaobjects `Switcher` (2). As in the *Observer* design pattern, it handles a list of *observers*—i.e. agents involved in the assistance activity—for each intercepted event and sends them notification (3). If needed, assistants may receive additional data, related with the event, using a suitable `request` speech act (4).

The *Observer* design pattern allows updating the state of the assistants that need to know changes of the application state. It lets assistants change or increase their number without modifying the `Merger` (i.e. the *subject*, in the design pattern terminology) or other observers. It ensures loose coupling between the *Coordinator* and assistants.

- Metalevel object `Blackboard` is a repository for the outcomes of assistants and it constitutes a way to make such results available to the application and to assistants. Outcomes derive from assistants deduction activity and are communicated asynchronously to this component in order to influence the behaviour of the application. Metaobjects `Switcher` access the `Blackboard` (5) and, according to retrieved outcomes, change the behaviour of their associated application object, by e.g. modifying its parameters, and synchronise assistance activities with the object operations.

  In our architecture, the `Blackboard` component is also a *shared knowledge base*, that is used by an assistant to obtain information inferred by other assistants during their activity. This architectural style allows independent assistants to work cooperatively and to share results [1]. Each assistant is not required to know about others, thus enhancing modularity.

Metaobjects are the means to access the application objects both to gather data and to modify their behaviour. They also provide coordination for the assistants activity and synchronisation between them and the application. The application changes its state for user activities and for its computation, and concurrently the assistants perform computation and provide their outcomes, from their deduction activity. Metaobjects exploit the moment when control is captured to pour the assistants (partial) outcomes to the application. This synchronisation ensures that the application is not badly affected by additional concurrent activities and it does not add complexity due to the handling of concurrency, since it is very easy to be implemented.

2.4   A Case-Study: Changing the Behaviour of a Web Browser

In order to better understand the mechanisms of the architecture, in this Section we provide a simple example showing how a web browser is extended by adding user assistance functionalities. We consider a single assistant agent charged with the task of finding and highlighting keywords each time a new web page is loaded and displayed by the browser. The assistant builds a ranked list of keywords by means of a term-frequency algorithm (see Section 3.1), which is updated each time a new page is loaded. The top elements of the list are used to determine the words to highlight.

As discussed in [4], the first step of a programmer wishing to build the connection between the assistance software and an application is *identifying* the *events* that trigger assistant activity. In this case, the relevant events are: downloading a new web page and rendering a web page, which are briefly sketched below.

1. *Downloading a new web page.* The assistant needs, from the *Coordinator*, a notification each time a new page is requested by the user and loaded by the browser. To this aim, at startup, the assistant contacts the *Coordinator*

using a `request-whenever` speech act which expresses the assistant's interest in receiving this notification. Each time a new page arrives, the *Coordinator* answers with an `inform` speech act containing the downloaded HTML source page.

2. *Rendering a web page.* In order to perform keyword highlighting, the assistant executes a `request` speech act that supplies the *Coordinator* a ranked list of tuples, in the form (`keyword,colour`), where the colour indicates how important a word is.

After identifying the set of events triggering assistance, the second design step to be performed is *understanding* which browser objects are involved with the events identified in the first step. Obviously, these objects depend on the implementation of the web browser. E.g., referring to the *Jazilla* Java browser [20], the above events are handled respectively by objects `SimpleLinkListener` and `JTextPaneRenderer`.

The third design step is *connecting* the identified application objects with the *Coordinator* by capturing their method calls by means of metaobjects. For this purpose, we use the reflective extension of Java, called Javassist [3]. In the example at hand, metaobject `SwitcherListen` is associated with object `SimpleLinkListener` and captures control when a new page is downloaded (i.e. when method `hyperlinkUpdate()` is invoked). This informs object `Merger` (see Figure 3) of this event, which, in turn, sends an `inform` message to the assistant. Once this message has been sent, control is returned to the application, which continues its normal execution.

As far as keyword highlighting is concerned, application object `JTextPaneRen- derer`, which displays web pages, is associated with metaobject `SwitcherRender`. The latter traps control before a page is displayed, searches the page for the keywords of the ranked list, stored in the `Blackboard`, and modifies the page formatting to change the foreground colour of the keywords.

3   Web Assistants for E-commerce

By exploiting the architecture proposed in the previous Section, we designed a multi-agent system aimed at assisting e-commerce activities performed through a web browser. The application extended is the web browser Jazilla. At this stage we have developed and tested the *Coordinator* and a simple version of the assistants described in the following. The set of assistant agents envisaged is depicted in Figure 4; they cooperate together to perform the following activities:

- understanding user preferences from visited web pages and typed keywords;
- extracting data about interesting goods from visited web pages;
- storing extracted data into a virtual cart;
- finding offers for some user selected goods.

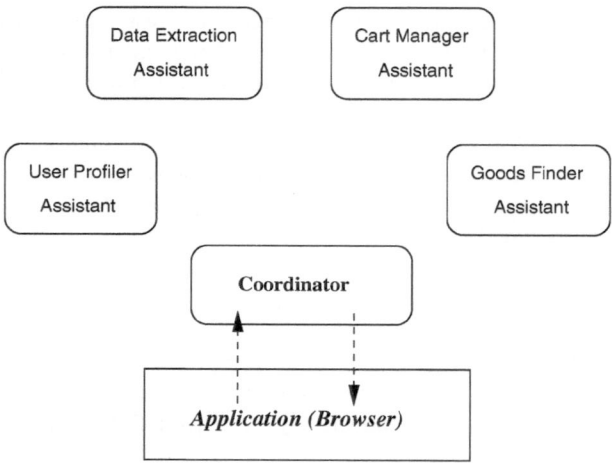

Fig. 4. E-commerce assistants for a web browser

3.1   User Profiler Assistant (UPA)

This assistant is entrusted with the task of profiling the user while he browses the Internet, in order to automatically determine user preferences and interests. For this purpose, it analyses and classifies the visited Web pages. This activity is triggered when a new page is loaded by the web browser and performed *autonomously* and asynchronously from the web browser and its user. UPA is informed by the *Coordinator* that a new page has been loaded.

Once the assistant is triggered, it employs a classification algorithm to characterise the current web page, by finding out its degree of "similarity" to categories of a predefined set. The adopted approach is analogous to the one described in [17]. The latter algorithm uses a set of page *categories* and a set of *weighted keywords* for each category generated in a training phase specialised for e-commerce activities. These two sets are stored into two appropriate local tables. New pages are classified by calculating and ranking the similarity value to each predetermined category.

This classification algorithm finds the frequencies of the words of a web page and normalises them by considering the length of the web page. To take into account user interests, in addition to the algorithm cited above, our assistant changes the keyword weights of each category according to the most recurrent keywords of the visited pages. This allows the keyword weights within a category to be tuned in order to adapt to the user's navigation activity. The outcome of the characterisation of user preferences is a ranked list of keywords, called *WebProfile*, obtained from the keywords of each scored category normalised with the weight of the category itself. UPA sends the *WebProfile* list to the *Coordinator*, which stores it into the Blackboard in order to make it available to other assistants and to the browser application.

Additionally, a user can show his/her interest for some keywords by marking the appropriate text in the web pages. Consistently with the adopted methodology, the latter user operation is captured by the *Coordinator*, which identifies the marked words and notifies them to this assistant. As a result the latter changes the weight of the new keywords in its categories. The ranked list of keywords is used, when pages are displayed on the web browser, to determine which words to highlight, as described in Section 2.4.

Note that this kind of assistant is not e-commerce specific, except for its training phase. Its activities can be used also for other kinds of assistance, which shows that this assistant can be reused as a independent module in several contexts.

3.2   Data Extraction Assistant (DEA)

This assistant is responsible to search for the parts of a web page that refer to goods. It is notified by the *Coordinator* of the downloading of a new web page and *autonomously* performs its page analysis. It uses the keywords previously collected by UPA and stored on the `Blackboard` to find out whether some goods are interesting.

If any relevant goods are displayed on the web page, DEA gathers good names, prices, availability, features, links to other web pages where they are offered, etc. and stores them into a local list, called *GoodList*. By doing so this assistant builds a structured version of the data contained in an unstructured web page, so that data can be easily manipulated. This is achieved by a well-known algorithm [7], using an ontology that describes the data of interest. The ontology allows producing a database scheme. Based on the ontology, it is possible to automatically extract data from web pages and structure them according to the generated database scheme.

Once new data are gathered, the assistant compares these with those previously stored and ranks requested pages goods so that the most accessed ones are on top of the *GoodList*. This list is sent to the *Coordinator* and stored into the `Blackboard` so that it can be read by other assistants when needed. When visiting a new web page any occurrence of a good that had been selected by DEA is highlighted. In order to carry out this service, the rendering of a web page is captured by a metaobject that searches the page for items occurring in the *GoodList* stored in the `Blackboard`.

A user can show his/her interest on specific goods by marking the appropriate text in a web page. Analogously to the previous assistant, this assistant is notified about the marking action performed by the user and carries out its extraction algorithm to update the list of goods.

3.3   Cart Manager Assistant (CMA)

The goods collected by DEA are accessed by the Cart Manager Assistant and presented to the user on request. This assistant shows a new window that graphically compares for each good the prices on different web sites or, depending on the type of data available, the trend of prices over time. These data are transformed on-the-fly by the assistant for more effective presentation; thus, when necessary, currency conversion is performed, additional costs are considered (e.g. V.A.T., delivery fee), etc. The user can interact with the graphical representation of data to notify the assistant which goods are more relevant for her/him. This phase allows the assistant to have hints about user preferences and so to tune its activities.

This virtual cart has many benefits that accrue from the fact that data about goods are stored exclusively at the client side. To begin with, it enhances security and privacy, since such data may be sensitive and personal; thanks to this client side solution, remote web sites are cut off from their handling and only the proper user is given the opportunity to work on them. The second benefit is to simplify user operations on selected data, since the virtual cart handles data provided by several web sites. It provides a common repository that the user can easily access avoiding the fragmentation of data among several web sites and independently of the availability of the network connection. Other benefits of the virtual cart are: handling additional personal information, such as the budget for types of goods; organising goods inside categories, calculating price trends, since it keeps track of the offers for the same goods on different web sites.

By a user/assistant interface, the user can ask to see the list of items in the cart, or graphs comparing prices or displaying their trends.

Data organised by this assistant are converted to some suitable format (such as one a spreadsheet can read) and permanently stored on a file. This allows other applications to further analyse data, separately from the assistant, and permits integration of the collected data into other applications.

3.4   Goods Finder Assistant (GFA)

For some user selected goods, this assistant carries out additional operations, such as seeking on the web further offers, or data. When viewing the data handled by CMA, the user can ask for more detail on a good simply by clicking on it. In response, GFA autonomously searches and accesses web pages where goods can be found, and analyses them in the background looking for the good of interest. If such a good is found, GFA asks DEA to extract the appropriate data from the web page and informs CMA of the new gathered data.

Addresses of web pages and search engines where goods are searched are stored in a list handled by GFA. Each entry of this list contains both the web address, the categories of goods which can be found, and a weight for each category. This weight is constantly updated taking into account whether a search of a good has been successful, thus tuning the effectiveness of a web address for a given category in accordance with the number of hits.

4   Related Work and Discussion

The literature reports many works dealing with agents that support user activities [16,13,6,14,11]. Yet, the majority of them deals with a single agent that embeds all assistance activities and interfaces with the application using *ad hoc* techniques. We have already cited the Microsoft Office Assistant, which is an ActiveX object (MSAgent) catering only for user interactions, while assistance tasks proper must be addressed by the application [18]. The MSAgent is also used in [11] to provide the visual looks for a set of agents which assist the user in web mining activities; however this approach is based on JavaScript and thus assistants can only be used with a (JavaScript enabled) web browser and in a Win32 environment (since the MSAgent is a Win32-ActiveX object). Assistants proposed in [13,14,16] are interfaced with the application by means of AppleScript [10], and thus require an application to be controllable through this technology. In contrast to these approaches, our proposal exploits a general methodology—reflection—which does not require the application, nor the operating system (or GUI libraries) to provide special interface "hooks". It is platform-independent and can be applied to any application provided its source code, or only its Java bytecode, is available.

The second difference with other proposed approaches lies in the modular architecture: each agent is charged with a specific task and can be added or removed at run time without affecting the structure of the entire system. The *Coordinator* allows a complete separation between interfacing and assistance tasks, thus making the assistance activity independent of the particular application to be extended. For example, using the same e-commerce assistants presented here, we can extend different web browsers by simply adapting the *Coordinator* to the specific browser. Moreover, some assistants, originally designed to aid a particular type of application, can be later used to assist another type of application. E.g., a word processor user writing commercial letters advertising some goods for sale could be presented by GFA with a list of similar goods found in the Web.

Finally, the proposed architecture is also suitable to operate in a distributed environment; some agents, such as GFA or an assistant monitoring price trends and goods availability, could operate on some "reference server sites" in the background, irrespective of whether site users are browsing the web; they would provide search results as soon as a user opens her/his browser. In addition, if we include an agent capable of HTTP communication, we could be able to support the "personal mobility" [6], in order to offer search results also when the user is browsing the web from a PC different than his own.

5   Conclusions

This paper has described a reflective software architecture allowing multiple assistant agents to aid an application. The architecture handles the integration of assistants into the application, while enabling assistants to perform their tasks autonomously. Assistants need not be known at design time and can be added, when available, at run time.

Regarding performance issues, we have tackled it by making the interaction loose between application and assistants, e.g. giving assistants sufficient autonomy for carrying out their activities. This has been experimentally observed to avoid the application to be excessively delayed. Moreover, interception of application events, by metaobjects, can be carefully tuned to introduce a bearable overhead, e.g. capturing the rendering of the whole web page and introducing changes once for all is much faster than capturing the rendering of each word.

We have shown the usefulness and applicability of the architecture by means of a set of e-commerce assistants that enhance a web browser. However, the architecture can be easily used in other contexts varying the set of assistants, the application or both.

References

1. G. Cabri, L. Leonardi, and F. Zambonelli. Mobile-Agent Coordination Models for Internet Applications. *IEEE Computer*, 33(2):82–89, February 2000.
2. S. Chiba. A Metaobject Protocol for C++. In *Proceedings of the Conference on Object-Oriented Programming Systems, Languages and Applications (OOPSLA'95)*, pages 285–299, 1995.
3. S. Chiba. Load-time Structural Reflection in Java. In *Proceedings of the ECOOP 2000*, volume 1850 of *Lecture Notes in Computer Science*, 2000.
4. A. Di Stefano, G. Pappalardo, C. Santoro, and E. Tramontana. Extending Applications using Reflective Assistant Agents. In *Proceedings of the 26th Annual International Computer Software and Applications Conference (Compsac'02)*, Oxford, UK, 2002.
5. A. Di Stefano, G. Pappalardo, and E. Tramontana. Introducing Distribution into Applications: a Reflective Approach for Transparency and Dynamic Fine-Grained Object Allocation. In *Proceedings of the Seventh IEEE Symposium on Computers and Communications (ISCC'02)*, Taormina, Italy, 2002.
6. A. Di Stefano and C. Santoro. NetChaser: Agent Support for Personal Mobility. *IEEE Internet Computing*, 4(2):74–79, March/April 2000.
7. D. W. Embley, D. M. Campbell, Y. S. Jiang, S. W. Liddle, Y.-K. Ng, D. Quass, and R. D. Smith. Conceptual-Model-Based Data Extraction from Multiple-Record Web Pages. *Data Knowledge Engineering*, 31(3):227–251, 1999.
8. J. Ferber. Computational Reflection in Class Based Object Oriented Languages. In *Proceedings of the ACM Conference on Object-Oriented Programming Systems, Languages and Applications (OOPSLA'89)*, volume 24 of *Sigplan Notices*, pages 317–326, New York, NY, 1989.
9. E. Gamma, R. Helm, R. Johnson, and R. Vlissides. *Design Patterns: Elements of Reusable Object-Oriented Software*. Addison-Wesley. Reading, MA, 1994.
10. D. Goodman. *Danny Goodman's AppleScript Handbook*. Random House, New York, 1994.
11. Y. Kitamura, T. Yamada, T. Kokubo, Y. Mawarimichi, T. Yamamotom, and T. Ishida. Interactive Integration of Information Agents on the Web. In *Proceedings of CIA 2001*, volume 2182 of *Lecture Notes in Artificial Intelligence*, pages 1–13. Springer, 2001.
12. Y. Labrou, T. Finin, and Y. Peng. Agent Communication Languages: the Current Landscape. *IEEE Intelligent Systems*, pages 45–52, March-April 1999.
13. H. Lieberman. Letizia: An Agent That Assists Web Browsing. In *International Joint Conference on Artificial Intelligence*, pages 924–929, Montreal, August 1995.

14. H. Lieberman, P. Maes, and N. Van Dyke. Butterfly: A Conversation-Finding Agent for Internet Relay Chat. In *International Conference on Intelligent User Interfaces*, Los Angeles, January 1999.
15. P. Maes. Concepts and Experiments in Computational Reflection. In *Proceedings of the Conference on Object-Oriented Programming Systems, Languages and Applications (OOPSLA '87)*, volume 22 (12) of *Sigplan Notices*, pages 147–155, Orlando, FA, 1987.
16. P. Maes. Agents that Reduce Work and Information Overload. In Bradshaw, J., editor, *Software Agents*, pages 145–164. AAAI Press/The MIT Press, 1997.
17. H. Mase. Experiments on Automatic Web Page Categorization for IR system, 1998. Technical Report, Stanford University.
18. Microsoft Corporation. *Microsoft Developer Network Library*, 2000.
19. M. Shaw and D. Garlan. *Software Architecture - Perspective on an Emerging Discipline*. Prentice Hall, 1996.
20. SourceForge. Jazilla Home Page. WWW, 2002. http://jazilla.sourceforge.net.
21. E. Tramontana. Managing Evolution Using Cooperative Designs and a Reflective Architecture. In W. Cazzola, R. J. Stroud, and F. Tisato, editors, *Reflection and Software Engineering*, volume 1826 of *Lecture Notes in Computer Science*. Springer-Verlag, June 2000.
22. E. Tramontana. Reflective Architecture for Changing Objects. In *Proceeding of the ECOOP Workshop on Reflection and Metalevel Architectures (RMA '00)*, Nice, France, June 2000.

Curious Negotiator

Simeon Simoff and John Debenham

Faculty of IT, University of Technology, Sydney
{simeon, debenham}@it.uts.edu.au

Abstract. In negotiation the exchange of information is as important as the exchange of offers. The curious negotiator is a multiagent system with three types of agents. Two negotiation agents, each representing an individual, develop consecutive offers, supported by information, whilst requesting information from its opponent. A mediator agent, with experience of prior negotiations, suggests how the negotiation may develop. A failed negotiation is a missed opportunity. An observer agent analyses failures looking for new opportunities. The integration of negotiation theory and data mining enables the curious negotiator to discover and exploit negotiation opportunities. Trials will be conducted in electronic business.

1 Introduction

The *curious negotiator* is a multiagent system of competitive agents supporting multi-attribute negotiation where the set of issues is not fixed [1]. In 2001 an e-exchange, designed by the authors was built in a joint collaboration with Bullant Australasia Pty Ltd – an Australian software house with a strong interest in business-to-business (B2B) e-business. The actor classes are illustrated in Fig. 1. We have extended the model in [2], adding the sell-side "Content aggregator" component.

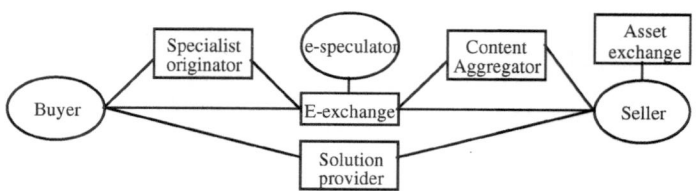

Fig. 1. Major actor classes in the e-market

Central logical components are "e-exchanges" in which one-off deals are done, and "solution providers" through whom contracts are negotiated and business relationships developed. E-speculators take short-term positions in an e-exchange and look for medium term arbitrage opportunities. Sell-side "Asset Exchange" components exchange or share assets between sellers. Content Aggregators—acting as forward aggregators—coordinate and package goods and services from various sellers. Specialist Originators—acting as reverse aggregators—coordinate and package orders for goods and services from various buyers. In simple terms the existing project is

M. Klusch, S. Ossowski, and O. Shehory (Eds.): CIA 2002, LNAI 2446, pp. 104–111, 2002.
© Springer-Verlag Berlin Heidelberg 2002

considering all except the Solution Provider class. The machinery that the Solution Provider class will need to negotiate is not yet clearly understood [2]; the curious negotiator presented in this paper aims to build this machinery and so to complete the whole e-market picture [3]; [4]. Further we present the negotiation process, as it is the focus of the curious negotiator.

2   Negotiation Process, Mechanisms, Strategies, and Contextual Information

Negotiation is the process whereby two (or more) individual agents with conflicting interests reach a mutually beneficial agreement on a set of issues. A negotiation may be assisted by a third-party *mediator* who facilitates and accelerates the process. The individuals involved in a negotiation operate in accordance with a set of rules called the *negotiation mechanism*. Negotiation mechanism [5] specifies how the negotiation will take place, i.e. what each of the negotiating individuals may or should do as the negotiation proceeds, and when they should do it; when offers made are binding and what happens if such commitments are broken. Given a negotiation mechanism, an individual will develop a *negotiation strategy* that aims to ensure the negotiation proceeds in the individual's interests—whether an agreement is reached or not. Early negotiating agents in agent-mediated electronic commerce used several simplistic fixed strategies [6]. A negotiation strategy should generally rely on information drawn from the context of the negotiation. The significance of information to the negotiation process was analysed formally in the seminal paper by Milgrom and Weber [7] in which the Linkage Principle, relating the revelation of contextual information to the price that a purchaser is prepared to pay, was introduced. Their analysis is limited to single-issue negotiation using conventional auction mechanisms. The information generated during the negotiation process should assist each player to gauge and accommodate the interests of their opponent [8]. "Good negotiators, therefore, undertake integrated processes of knowledge acquisition that combine sources of knowledge obtained at and away from the *negotiation table*. "They learn in order to plan and plan in order to learn" [9]. The curious negotiator encapsulates this observation.

Contextual information can be characterised as unexpected, interesting, and even novel. Curious negotiator is designed to incorporate data mining and information discovery methods [10] that operate under time constraints, including methods from the area of topic detection and event tracking research [11]. We consider novelty and unexpectedness of discovered patterns with respect to a belief system (the current belief system of the negotiator), similar to [12]. The identification of novel strategies that emerge during the negotiation process is based on evolutionary algorithms, following the approach presented in [13]. As people and agents are the participants in negotiation, trust and reputation are other key elements of contextual information in negotiation, together with information about people types. To enable agents to evaluate the reputation of other agents (parties) involved, the curious negotiator incorporates a computational representation of trust. Closer to the curious negotiator is the computational approach of reputation management developed in [14].

Negotiation is goal-directed in the sense that individual agents involved in a negotiation may—probably will—have agendas of their own. But the agendas of the negotiating agents may be incompatible—there may be no solution that satisfies them all. Further the existence of a solution is unlikely to be known when the negotiation commences. So it may not be useful to consider negotiation as a search problem because the solution space may be empty whilst the negotiating agents may believe that it is not so. In some cases the deal space is unknown. In summary, there appears to be little virtue in attempting to manage negotiation as a goal-directed process. What then drives negotiation? Using an alternating offers mechanism, multi-issue negotiation consists of a sequence of offers where each offer is the derived from the history of offers considered, including the current offer, and from information that is either part of the offers or has been derived from the negotiation context because of the offers. So the direction that a negotiation takes is determined by the agents' responses to this accumulated wisdom. All of this has much in common with knowledge-driven processes that are the hallmark of emergent processes. A multiagent system for emergent process management is described in [15].

Curious Negotiator deals with multi-issue negotiation with an open negotiation set using an alternative offers mechanism. After the process commences, each agent receives an offer, checks the set of issues in the offer for consistency, evaluates the offer and determines a response. All of this is done using the process knowledge and information that can be gleaned from the context and from the opponent. The construction of the response can reasonably be expected to be achieved within a certain time, and so the whole business of gathering information to determine the response is in general time constrained. This is illustrated in Fig. 2.

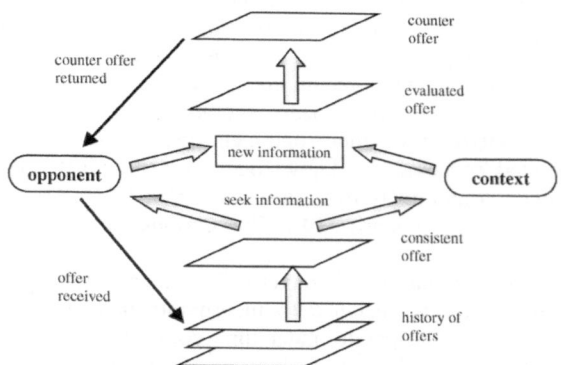

Fig. 2. High-level view of the interplay between the e-market player and the context.

An offer may contain apparent inconsistencies such as "the item has a full and unconditional warranty for twelve months" and "once the item has been supplied and delivered to the purchaser the vendor is not responsible for any subsequent transportation charges". The determination of a consistent offer is concerned with the removal of such apparent inconsistencies. This is a complex problem even if the terms of the offer can be represented in Horn clause logic due to the amount of common and background knowledge required. The contextual investigations that are an integral part of the negotiation process can typically be conducted by managing a suite of data and text mining bots as time—and maybe cost—constrained goal-driven processes. From a process management point of view, negotiation processes are interesting in that they are knowledge-driven emergent processes that can be fully managed provided that, first, full authority to negotiate is delegated to the agent and, second, sufficient contextual information can be derived from the market data, from the sources, available on the Internet (news feeds, company white papers, specialised articles, research papers) and other sources by the data mining bots.

3 Outline Design of Curious Negotiator

As mentioned earlier, the overall goal of this design is to exploit the interplay between contextual information [16] and the development of offers in negotiation conducted in an electronic environment. The curious negotiator is a multiagent system containing three types of agents: negotiation, mediation and observer agents, as illustrated in Fig. 3. *Negotiation agents* apply the negotiation strategies in the negotiation process [17], including strategies for developing the set of issues in an offer as well as identifying, requesting and evaluating contextual information including determining what information to table as the negotiation proceeds. The impartial *mediation agents* assist two or more negotiation agents. The role of *observer agents* is to observe and analyse what is happening on the 'negotiation table' and to look for opportunities particularly from failed negotiations.

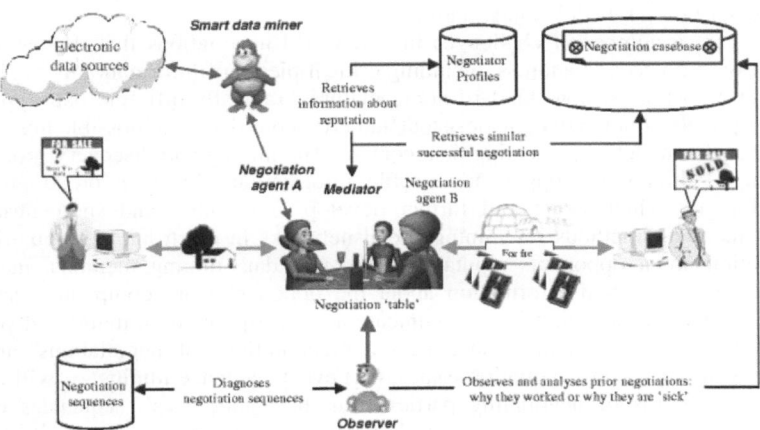

Fig. 3. The initial design of the curious negotiator (includes Negotiation agent, Mediation agent, Observer agent and the Smart data miner)

---

[1] Avatars, used to denote software agents in the diagram, are adapted from MIT project "BodyChat" and Bonzi Buddy (www.bonzi.com).

Successful negotiation relies on an understanding of how to 'play' the negotiation mechanism [18] and on contextual information. This contextual information is derived from what happens at the bargaining table and away from it. To do this the curious negotiator includes a *smart data mining system* — the "Smart data miner" in Fig. 3, which operates in tandem with the negotiation agent. The smart data miner extracts contextual information from relevant markets and from the Internet generally. The main components of the 'curious negotiator' are described in more detail below.

The **negotiation agents** are the core agents in the 'curious negotiator'. The negotiation agents operate in two modes: as an assistant that works with an individual who makes some of the decisions, and as an autonomous agent that has delegated authority to negotiate [19]. To operate as an assistant, the negotiator will require an interface that enables high-level interaction with its user. Hence, virtual worlds are considered as a possible implementation technology. The negotiation agent architecture is illustrated in Fig. 4a. The negotiation agent strategies [20] are governed by the rules of the negotiation mechanism [5]. In addition to governing the development of the offers, the negotiation mechanism governs, in part, the information exchange [21], hence negotiation strategies deal with information gathering and verification as well as with issue modification. A strategy determines: (i) the modification of the existing issues, and modification of the issue set; (ii) requests for information from the opponent agent and from information gathering bots, as illustrated in Fig. 4a; (iii) verification of, or establishment of a measure of belief in, information provided. Obtaining and verifying information takes time and resources— the negotiation strategy will accommodate those delays and will manage those costs as part of the overall cost of the negotiation. To reduce some of the delays, the Smart data miner in Fig. 4a can also 'pre-fetch' some of the information that is expected to be necessary for a scheduled negotiation.

There are a number of challenges in real world negotiations that the smart data mining system needs to address, including critical pieces of information being held in different repositories; non-standard nomenclatures; radically different data types and models; possible duplicative, inconsistent and erroneous data; and possible high rate of change of the models representing data content. The mining and discovery procedures include: (i) mining the opponent's profile information (this is a broad group of methodologies which adapt and further develop user-centric and site-centric data mining methods, methods for mining social networks in electronic communities for information about opponents reputation [14], text data mining methods, including discovering unexpected information about the opponent from competitors sources, methods for topic detection in communication transcripts); (ii) mining deal profiles information — these methods analyse the preconditions of negotiations, and the dynamics of change in negotiation issues; (iii) event sequence mining — will extract behaviour patterns of negotiating parties from the 'utterances', sequences of key events that can change negotiation (based on past experiences and current situation on the 'negotiation table').

The role of the **mediation agents** is to assist negotiations to converge on the basis of the type of the two negotiation agents (for example, one could be representing a student), the subject of the negotiation (for example, a personal computer system), the negotiation history and the current negotiation state. Achievement of this functionality requires broadly-based shallow reasoning [22]. The inclusion of mediation agents in the curious negotiator resolves an intractable problem by partly removing the need for each negotiation agent to model its opponent—that could be a very costly exercise. The mediation agent maintains a "profile book" of the negotiations that it has observed and mediated. The 'input' to the mediation agent is a long history of negotiations each of which has an identifiable type. Each player has attributes that enable them to be typed as well. The mediation agent then accelerates the negotiation process by suggesting new issues or combinations of issues triggered by the state of the negotiation, the type of the negotiation and the types of the players. The initial design of the curious negotiator employs a combination of case-based reasoning and 'collaborative filtering' for its mediation agent. The idea is presented in Fig. 4b. The mediation agent operates only over the positive examples from the negotiation case base. When confronted with a situation where mediation is necessary, it retrieves a successful negotiation that is the "closest" (according to the implemented distance metric) to the current situation on the negotiation table. The mediation agent also provides the negotiation agent with information about opponent's reputation that is based on previous experience with that negotiator.

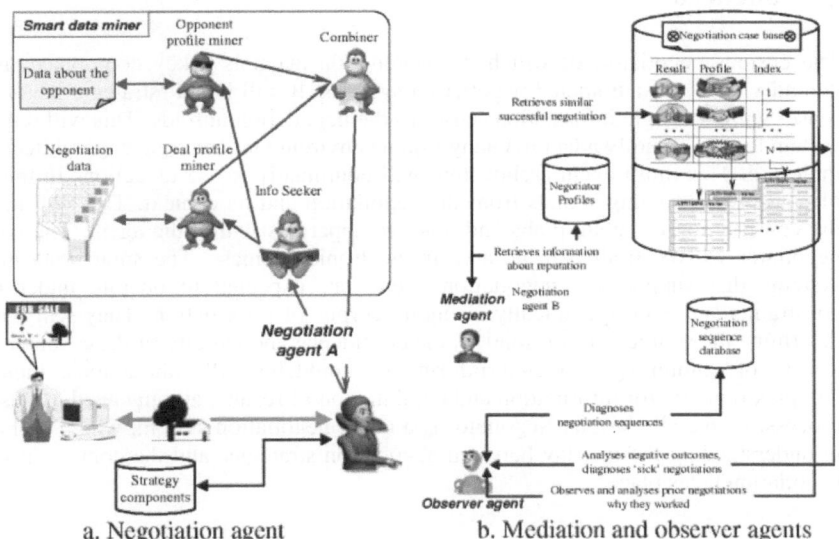

a. Negotiation agent   b. Mediation and observer agents

Fig. 4. The three types of agents (including the smart data mining system).

The *observer agents* do not contribute directly to an existing negotiation process. They observe negotiations looking for failed, or otherwise unsatisfactory, negotiations. Failed negotiations are lost business opportunities. The observer agent analyses these failed negotiations to determine why they failed and then synthesises these reasons for failure into new forms of transactions designed to prevent similar lost opportunities in the future. The introduction of an observer agent enables the curious negotiator to discover innovative, new forms of transaction. The data mining algorithms that support the observer agent are oriented towards discovery of unexpected information about the lost opportunities — information that is relevant to the negotiation process, but is unknown to the negotiation and mediation agents, and may even contradict their beliefs (expectations). Some of the analysis techniques that are included in the initial design are: (i) knowledge-based diagnostic methods for diagnosing 'sick' negotiations; (ii) mining trust chains [23] and relating them to the negotiating agents and the results of negotiation (we will investigate what will the length and branching of such chain tell us about the failure); and (iii) mining outliers in the behaviour of negotiating agents and mediation agent (outliers usually are thrown out, however, they can be containing the answer to what went wrong.) The observer agents address the deep issue in the curious negotiator of devising creative, innovative forms of transactions and ways of negotiating that should prevent lost opportunities. Each negotiation, including the information gathering, verification, combination and distillation, is managed as a business process. This is a novel approach, especially in managing data mining bots under tight time and cost constraints by ensuring that the best available advice is provided when required.

4 Conclusion

The curious negotiator, of which the negotiation agent is a key component, is our "grand vision" for automated negotiation systems. It will blend 'strategic negotiation sense' with 'strategic information sense' as the negotiation unfolds. This will require a system that can readily adapt to changes in its environment and so agent architecture is indicated. This multi-agent architecture will continually revise its actions in the light of possibly conflicting signals from the negotiation and its context. This will involve the construction of subtle plans and reactive apparatus within the agent. The curious negotiator will be trialled in an area in electronic business. The smart data mining systems that support the negotiation agent, are expected to operate under time-constraints and over dynamically changing corpus of information. They will need to determine the sources of information, the confidence and validity of these sources and a way of combining extracted information (models). All transactions, including complex requests for information and combination of results, are managed as business processes. Overall Curious Negotiator is a novel negotiation system, which will assist in understanding the interlay between negotiation strategies and the context in which negotiation takes place.

References

1. Gerding, E.H., van Bragt, D.D.B. and La Poutre, J.A.: Multi-issue negotiation processes by evolutionary simulation: validation and social extensions. Proceedings Workshop on Complex Behavior in Economics. Aix-en-Provence. France, May 4–6 (2000)
2. Wise, R. and Morrison, D.: Beyond the Exchange; The Future of B2B. Harvard Business Review. Nov-Dec (2000) 86–96
3. Tennenholtz, M.: Electronic Commerce: From Economic and Game-Theoretic Models to Working Protocols. Proceedings Sixteenth International Joint Conference on Artificial Intelligence, IJCAI'99. Invited Paper, Stockholm, Sweden Invited Paper (1999)
4. Bichler, M.: The Future of E-Markets: Multi Dimensional Market Mechanisms. Cambridge University Press, Cambridge, MA (2001)

5. Faratin, P.: Multi-Agent Contract Negotiation. In: Dautenhahn, K., Bond, A., Canamero, L. and Edmonds, B. (eds): Socially Intelligent Agents – creating relationships with computers and robots. Kluwer Academic Publishers (2002)
6. Klusch, M.: Agent-Mediated Trading: Intelligent Agents and e-Business. In: Hayzelden, A.L.G. and Bourne, R.A. (eds): Agent Technology for Communication Infrastructures. John Wiley and Sons, Chichester (2001), 59–76
7. Milgrom, P. and Weber, R.A.: Theory of Auctions with Competitive Bidding. Econometrica. 50 (1982)
8. Benn, W., Görlitz, O. and Neubert, R.: An Adaptive Software Agent for Automated Integrative Negotiations. Int. J. of e-Business Strategy Management. 1 (1999)
9. Watkins, M.: Breakthrough Business Negotiation-A Toolbox for Managers. Jossey-Bass (2002)
10. Hand, D., Mannila, H. and Smyth, P.: Principles of Data Mining. MIT Press, Cambridge, MA (2001)
11. Franz, M., Ittycheriah, A., McCarley, J.S. and Ward, T.: First Story Detection: Combining Similarity and Novelty Based Approaches. (2001) Available from http://www.nist.gov/speech/tests/tdt/tdt2001/PaperPres/ibm-pres/tdt2001_nn.ppt
12. Padmanabhan, B. and Tuzhilin, A.: A Belief-Driven Method for Discovering Unexpected Patterns. Proc. 4th ACM SIGKDD Conf. On Knowledge Discovery and Data Mining, KDD-98 (1998) 27–31
13. Smith, R.E., Dike, B.A., Ravichandran, B., El-Fallah, A. and Mehra, R.K.: Discovering Novel Fighter Combat Maneuvers: Simulating Test Pilot Creativity. In: Bentley, P.J. and Corne, D.W. (eds): Creative Evolutionary Systems. Academic Press (2002)
14. Yu, B. and Singh, M.P.: A Social Mechanism of Reputation Management in Electronic Communities. In: Klusch, M. and Kerschberg, L. (eds): Cooperative Information Agents IV: The Future of Information Agents in Cyberspace. Springer (2000), 154–165
15. Debenham, J.K.: Supporting knowledge-driven processes in a multiagent process management system. Proceedings 20th International Conference on Knowledge Based Systems and Applied Artificial Intelligence, ES'2000: Research and Development in Intelligent Systems XV. Cambridge, UK (2000) 273–286
16. Gomes, A. and Jehiel, P.: Dynamic process of social and economic interactions: on the persistence of inefficiencies. London (2001)
17. Krauss, S.: Strategic Negotiation in Multiagent Environments. MIT Press, Cambridge, MA (2001)
18. Ströbel, M.: Design of Roles and Protocols for Electronic Negotiations. Electronic Commerce Research Journal, Special Issue on Market Design (2001)
19. Wong, W.Y., Zhang, D.M. and Kara-Ali, M.: Towards an Experience Based Negotiation Agent. In: Klusch, M. and Kerschberg, L. (eds): Cooperative Information Agents IV: The Future of Information Agents in Cyberspace. Springer (2000), 131–142
20. Fatima, S.S., Wooldridge, M. and Jennings, N.R.: Optimal negotiation strategies for agents with incomplete information. Proc. 8th Int. Workshop on Agent Theories, Architectures and Languages (ATAL). Seattle, WA (2001)
21. Milgrom, P.: Auction Theory for Privatization. Cambridge University Press, Cambridge, MA (2002)
22. Leake, D. and Kolodner, J.: Learning through case analysis: Encyclopedia of Cognitive Science. Macmillan, London (2001)
23. Castelfranchi, C. and Tan, Y.H.: Trust and Deception in Virtual Societies. Kluwer Academic Publishers, Dordrecht, Netherlands (2000)

Measuring Behaviour-Based Trust between Negotiating Agents

Michael Grimsley[1] and Anthony Meehan [2]

[1] School of Computing & Management Science, Sheffield Hallam University, Pond Street, Sheffield S1 1WB, UK
m.f.grimsley@shu.ac.uk

[2] Faculty of Mathematics & Computing, The Open University, Walton Hall, Milton Keynes MK7 6AA, Buckinghamshire, UK.
A.S.Meehan@open.ac.uk

Abstract. We describe a metric to assess agent trustworthiness from the earliest stages of a dialogue between two web agents. There is no assumption of a transaction history between the agents nor is there a requirement for the agents to fully share the semantics of the set of alternatives over which negotiation occurs. The metric is designed to recognise a form of co-operative negotiation behaviour, so-called logrolling, which is known to induce trust between human negotiators. The metric requires an agent to be able to infer the issue priorities of the other party over a series of proposals and to correlate these with its own priorities. An example is used to illustrate how this may be achieved.

1 Introduction

Agents are readily trusted to find or exchange information on items, products or services but they are less commonly trusted to complete a transaction by procuring the same. And very few people are prepared to trust an agent to complete a transaction if an exact match to requirements is not available and a best alternative must be negotiated with a provider. This may remain the case for some time [1]. Improving the ability of web-based agents to reliably assess the trustworthiness of other agents with whom they negotiate is one of the prerequisites for expansion of electronic trading.

The concept of trust is multifaceted and no one dimension can be used to capture it. Early approaches to trust tended to conflate trust with security but, whilst undoubtedly contributing to trust, security is quite distinct. Security can be viewed as a mechanism to transfer trust, e.g., as a certificate, between where it is held and where it is needed [2]. Certification poses its own problems in relation to trust: an agent is trusted because a trusted authority has given it a certificate of trust. If the certification authority is a trusted third party, one introduces the assumption that trust is transitive, but this assumption may be unsafe [1], [2]. Mutual trust between the parties to a transaction is preferable [3].

M. Klusch, S. Ossowski, and O. Shehory (Eds.): CIA 2002, LNAI 2446, pp. 112–122, 2002.
© Springer-Verlag Berlin Heidelberg 2002

A common approach to trust depends upon prior experience of interaction with an agent: a trusted agent is one that has reliably performed some task in the past. This dimension of trust will remain an important part of trust assessment, however, it is of little value when dealing with a new or unfamiliar agent and it does not contribute to the assessment of trust *during* a transaction.

This problem of dealing with new and unfamiliar agents is of significance because the security and trust constraints commonly imposed limit quite profoundly the autonomy of agents in finding the best deals or solutions. This paper begins to tackle this problem. It describes a means to assess agent trustworthiness from the earliest stages of a dialogue between two web agents. There is no assumption of a familiarity (transaction history) nor is there a requirement for the agents to fully share the semantics of the set of alternatives over which negotiation occurs: the agents are essentially solipsistic. Our approach is based upon giving agents the ability to recognise a form of cooperative negotiation behaviour, so-called logrolling, which is known to induce trust between human negotiators [4]. This ability requires an agent to be able to infer the issue priorities of another party, over a series of proposals made by that party, and to correlate these with its own priorities. We show how these may be realised and an example is provided to illustrate the approach.

As indicated earlier, trust is multifaceted and the measure of trust we describe is intended to complement, rather than supplant, existing trust metrics.

2   Trust

We begin by looking at some of the recognised dimensions of trust. We then look at human negotiation behaviour that is known to build trusting relationships.

2.1   Dimensions of Trust

A number of researchers have attempted to identify the underlying dimensions of trust. Trusted agents should not compromise private information or deviate beyond specified constraints [1]. Agents should be reliable, though they need not always be successful. Here, trust is proportional to probability of success assessed over prior deployments of the agent [2]. Another, complementary, view is that trust is inversely proportional to risk. Risk variables not already mentioned include transaction cost and indemnity [5]. Higher transaction costs imply higher risk. Trust is viewed as directly proportional to the fraction of a potential loss that is indemnified by a third party.

A human centred view of trust introduces less tangible dimensions. A review the social-psychological literature reveals a multiplicity of definitions of trust, an undeveloped understanding of the dynamics of trust creation [6]. A more behaviour-based approach to trust assessment in humans uses concepts of honesty/dishonesty and straight/crooked [2]. Honesty is defined as adherence to agreement and straightness is defined as keeping to the rules of some protocol. By this definition, honesty is comparable to reliability in that a judgement can be based on prior performance. Straightness is more difficult to measure if agents enjoy a degree of autonomy from each other because one needs access to the reasoning of the agent being assessed.

Each of the dimensions above contributes to an assessment of trust (note: they are not necessarily orthogonal). Many of them depend upon prior experience of an agent. None are of value *during* a negotiated transaction.

2.2 Negotiation and Trust

Human-centred negotiation theory documents a number of negotiation styles that can be adopted. Of particular relevance in this context is the integrative negotiation style [4]. In this case, each party seeks to identify and accommodate the interests of the other. The goal is to find an agreement that allows everyone to feel that his or her priority objectives have been acknowledged. It may produce joint gain solutions. From the point of view of human relationship building, integrative behaviour has distinct benefits. Agreements are less likely to be repudiated, there is a stabilising effect on relationships because parties enjoy the relationship more and seek to help the relationship persist. Integrative behaviour fosters trust and this opens up the possibility of measuring the degree of integrative behaviour displayed by another agent as an indirect indication of its trustworthiness. If all agents exhibit a high degree of integrative behaviour then a virtuous spiral of mutually reinforced trust may be achieved.

An important tactic in integrative negotiation is logrolling. An uninformative term in itself, logrolling involves trading concessions on different issues or dimensions of an agreement. Typically, agents concede on issues that are (relatively) unimportant to them but which are perceived to be important to the other party. Clearly, for an agent to engage in logrolling, it must have knowledge of its own issue priorities. It must also attempt to infer the issue priorities of the other party over a series of proposals. This done, the trustworthiness of the agent can be measured by correlating these estimated priorities with its own priorities.

3   Assessing Issue Priorities

In human negotiation, issue priorities are explored through dialogue and behavioural observation. For computer-based agents, these requirements can pose problems. There is no fundamental obstacle to an agent being aware of its own priorities, though acquiring and representing and maintaining this knowledge can be an appreciable knowledge engineering task. Designing agents that can communicate about their respective goals and objectives is possible and a number of such systems have been proposed and implemented [7], [8], [9], [10], [11]. However, insisting that agents that share a protocol that facilitates argumentation over alternatives in a negotiation space can restrict the set of agents that can be party to the negotiation. Research is ongoing to develop sharable ontologies [12] to which agents may be committed [12], and standards for a semantic web [13] that would allow much wider participation and interaction of agents. However, the requirement to make significant ontological commitment may be seen as restriction on the scope of the operability of an agent. The semantic web project imposes a similar restriction and there is even some scepticism as to its feasibility [14].

Currently, our preferred approach is to use solipsistic agents. Such agents represent and interpret any proposal by reference to their personal world framework. Only those terms used to name alternatives within the negotiation space need be shared between agents. We have shown that this scheme corresponds well to the way in which humans interpret proposals from others during negotiation [15]. Solipsistic agents do not use argumentation, they communicate only by rejecting or accepting proposals and by identifying and offering counter proposals. Whilst this may seem to be an appreciable limitation. The advantage is ease of implementation and accessibility to new agents. The technique for measuring trust described below does not depend upon this restriction and can be applied by agents with more extensively shared semantics over the domain of negotiation.

3.1 Representation of the Negotiation Space

Each agent represents alternatives in the negotiation space on the basis of a set of issues (also called or attributes or dimensions in the information and other domains). Some of these may be public and shared whilst some are private [15]. Quite generally, any negotiation can be viewed as taking place over a set of alternative contracts. (The contract may relate to the provision of information, the supply of a car, a holiday, an insurance policy, a book, etc.) An agent-centred representation of a contract is

$$c^a = (..., p_i, ..., q_j, ...); (p_i, q_j \in P^a). \tag{1}$$

P^a is the set of public (p_i) and private (q_j) issues for agent a (note: as suggested above, we do not require agents to share representations).

During the conduct of a negotiation, any one agent generates a sequence of proposals or counter-proposals until agreement is reached or the negotiation terminated. As the negotiation progresses, the proposals from an agent evolve in such a way as to preserve the values on those issues that are most important to the proposing agent. Characteristically, the issues of most importance are conceded last. The issues of little importance seem, from the recipient's perspective, to vary without any obvious goal.

Table 1 provides an example of a sequence of eight contract proposals, $c(i)$, over six issues generated by an agent. The issues and the values associated with them are determined by reference to the representational framework of the solipsistic agent that receives and interprets the contract. Later, we show how the receiving agent can use this sequence to infer the degree integrative behaviour, and hence measure, in part, the trustworthiness of the party that has generated sequence. In this illustrative example, the agent concedes issue *1* most reluctantly: issue *2* is conceded gradually from the outset, as perhaps is issue *5*, but in this case relatively larger concessions are made earlier on. Issues *4* and *6* seem to vary without any obvious intent or target level. (Note: the issues are not necessarily independent of each other.)

Table 1. Example sequence of proposals from an agent. The agent need only communicate the name of the contract, $c(i)$. The issues and their associated values are determined by reference to the representational framework of the interpreting agent. (The data is taken from a case study involving the search for, and negotiation of a plastic that would satisfy a product design [15].)

c(i)	Issue (p)					
	1	2	3	4	5	6
1	700	610000	7900	10	300	40
2	600	940000	10000	100	200	30
3	700	1100000	10000	60	400	40
4	900	1250000	12000	200	1500	200
5	1500	1800000	25000	110	1400	240
6	1650	1980000	27500	121	1540	264
7	2400	1800000	43000	120	2700	300
8	18000	2330000	20200	1000	3300	20

3.2 Inference of Issue Priorities for Another Agent

Having found no work in the literature on assessing the relative importance of issues over such short temporal interaction sequences we have developed an empirical metric that scores issues for importance over a short sequence of multidimensional proposals [16].

For each agent, a, the function, Pen, penalises relatively large early concessions and/or seemingly non-goal directed variation in the values taken by issue p over a sequence of k contract proposals:

$$Pen_{p,k}^{a} = \frac{b_k}{R_p} \max\left(\left| c_k(p) - c_i(p) \right|_{i=1}^{(k-1)} \right) \qquad (2)$$

R_p is the range of values for issue p known to agent a. b_k is chosen to be decreasing over $1..k$ so as to penalise relatively early concessions.

The obvious cumulative penalty, $CPen$, for issue p after k proposals is simply,

$$CPen_{p,k}^{a} = \sum_{i=2}^{k} Pen_{p,i}^{a}. \qquad (3)$$

High values of $CPen$ indicate issues of low priority to the proposing agent.

3.3 Determining an Agents Own Issue Priorities

Determining an appropriate issue evaluation function for a given agent can be a significant knowledge engineering task. A number of concerns need to be addressed.

A methodological concern is the extent to which people do or do not use decision theoretic issue evaluation functions as opposed to some simple ecological heuristic or some Gestalt process [17]. Many traditional decision theoretic approaches entail assumptions which, whilst attractive, are often unfounded. Examples of assumptions to be explored relate to independence of the issues in the contract [18], transitivity of alternative contracts and the independence from irrelevant alternatives [19]. (See [19] for a useful critical account of the treatment of assumptions).

A practical concern relates to the number of issues. If the number of issues is small, it may be possible to ask the user to assign priorities directly. However, even with a small number of issues, it can be arduous and time consuming if they are not independent and a transformed, orthogonal, representation of the issues is desirable (see [17] for a discussion of the role that rotated principal components can play).

Further, it is not uncommon for the priority of issues, especially private issues, to change relatively frequently, perhaps reflecting organisation wide factors such as production and inventory management.

For all of these reasons, our preferred approach is to elicit priorities indirectly, treating a human user as another agent. To do this, we ask the human user to order a set of example contracts from the negotiation space, and apply the priority inference scheme of expressions **2** and **3**.

3.4 Evaluating Integrative Intent and Trustworthiness

Recall that logrolling behaviour involves making proposals that concede issues of high importance to the other party and of relatively low importance to oneself. In correspondence with know human relations, a higher degree of trust can be attributed to an agent that is exhibiting such integrative behaviour [4]. Given the priority inference scheme of section 3.3, one agent can now measure the integrative intent of another by correlating their respective issue priorities.

We have found that ranking the inferred issue priorities of the respective agents after each contract proposal and computing Spearman's r, a robust measure of the correlation between priorities, gives a measure of integrative intent of one agent with respect to another (expression 4).

$$r_k = 1 - \frac{6\sum_{i=1}^{p}(d_i)^2}{p^3 - p}. \qquad (4)$$

d_i is the difference in the ranks assigned by the respective agents to issue i; p is the number of issues, k indexes the proposal sequence.

Perfect integrative behaviour would result in $r = -1$ given that ranked priorities should run counter to each other: non-integrative behaviour would result in values of r near to +1. (Of course, for very short sequences of contracts, r is unlikely to be significant in the statistical sense but sometimes some any information is better than no information and this is the view we take in this context.)

In determining trustworthiness, one approach is simply to take the current value of r equating $r = -1$ to high trust and $r = 1$ to zero trust. We prefer to look at r-values over the proposal sequence and look for r tending to -1, and to use a weighted average of r-values computed over the k proposals with greatest weight given to the most recent r-values.

This approach gives usable information on trustworthiness from the earliest stages of an encounter with a possibly unfamiliar agent.

4 An Example

Table 1, above, presents a sequence of proposals, revealed one at a time by a proposing agent, and interpreted over a number of issues by a receiving agent. Table 2 facilitates comparison between issues by fuzzifying the raw data of Table 1.

Table 2. Fuzzy Classification of the data in Table 1.

Contract (i)	Issue (p)					
	1	2	3	4	5	6
1	2	1	2	1	1	1
2	2	2	3	3	1	1
3	2	2	3	2	2	1
4	2	2	3	4	4	5
5	3	3	4	3	4	5
6	3	4	4	3	4	5
7	3	3	5	3	5	5
8	5	4	4	5	5	1

Table 3 illustrates the application of expression **2** to the data in Table 2 in order to compute the penalty function associated with concessions on issues over the sequence of k proposals.

Table 3. Penalty scores (Pen_p) computed over k proposals using expression **2**. (Note: here, R_p has been taken as the number of fuzzy categories used (6), and b_k chosen as $n-(k-1)$.)

K	Issue (p)					
	1	2	3	4	5	6
2	0.0000	1.1667	1.1667	2.3333	0.0000	0.0000
3	0.0000	1.0000	1.0000	1.0000	1.0000	0.0000
4	0.0000	0.8333	0.8333	2.5000	2.5000	3.3333
5	0.6667	1.3333	1.3333	1.3333	2.0000	2.6667
6	0.5000	1.5000	1.0000	1.0000	1.5000	2.0000
7	0.3333	0.6667	1.0000	0.6667	1.3333	1.3333
8	0.5000	0.5000	0.3333	0.6667	0.6667	0.6667

Table 4 gives the cumulative penalties generated from Table 3 using expression **3**. Note how the priority of issues 5 and 6 are significantly reassessed over the sequence.

Table 4. Cumulative penalty scores ($CPen_p$) for each issue from **3**.

K	Issue (p)					
	1	2	3	4	5	6
2	0.0000	1.1667	1.1667	2.3333	0.0000	0.0000
3	0.0000	2.1667	2.1667	3.3333	1.0000	0.0000
4	0.0000	3.0000	3.0000	5.8333	3.5000	3.3333
5	0.6667	4.3333	4.3333	7.1667	5.5000	6.0000
6	1.1667	5.8333	5.3333	8.1667	7.0000	8.0000
7	1.5000	6.5000	6.3333	8.8333	8.3333	9.3333
8	2.0000	7.0000	6.6667	9.5000	9.0000	10.000

At this stage, it is necessary to introduce the issue priorities of the agent receiving the proposal sequence. Table 5 gives the cumulative penalty scores for issues over the contract preferences of such an agent. These values have been computed as for the proposing agent but they have been obtained following the approach advocated in section 3.3 above. Accordingly, the row associated with $k=8$ represents the priorities of this agent to be used when computing the correlation with the priorities of the other agent. (Note: there is no special significance to the fact that the k values in the tables for the proposing and receiving agent are the same: this simply serves to facilitate a discussion point below.)

Table 5. Cumulative penalty scores for each issue for a second, receiving, agent (relative priorities in bold – high value indicates low priority).

k	Issue (p)					
	1	2	3	4	5	6
2	1.0000	0.5000	0.5000	0.0000	1.0000	1.0000
3	2.0000	0.5000	0.5000	0.0000	1.0000	2.0000
4	3.0000	1.2500	1.2500	0.2500	1.2500	2.0000
5	4.0000	1.9167	1.9167	0.9167	1.5833	2.0000
6	5.0000	2.5833	2.5833	1.5833	1.9167	2.0000
7	6.0000	3.2500	2.9167	2.2500	1.9167	2.0000
8	**6.5000**	**3.7500**	**3.9167**	**2.2500**	**1.9167**	**2.0000**

Tables 6a and 6b are derived from tables 4 and 5 respectively and represent the ranked issue priorities obtained for each of the two agents.

Table 6a. Ranked issue priorities for 1ˢᵗ (proposing) agent (from table 4).

k	Issue (p)					
	1	*2*	*3*	*4*	*5*	*6*
2	1	4	4	6	1	1
3	1	4	4	6	3	1
4	1	2	2	6	5	4
5	1	2	2	6	4	5
6	1	3	2	6	4	5
7	1	3	2	5	4	6
8	1	3	2	5	4	6

Table 6b. Ranked issue priorities for 2ⁿᵈ (receiving) agent (from table 5).

k	Issue (p)					
	1	*2*	*3*	*4*	*5*	*6*
2	4	2	2	1	4	4
3	5	2	2	1	4	5
4	6	2	2	1	2	5
5	6	3	3	1	2	5
6	6	4	4	1	2	3
7	6	5	4	3	1	2
8	**6**	**4**	**5**	**3**	**1**	**2**

Table 7 gives the values r over the contract sequence and shows how the perceived integrative intent of the proposing agent changes over the sequence of proposals. The sequence of r-values shows an initial, highly integrative proposal at the 5ᵗʰ proposal ($k=4$), followed by a slight decline which then recovers towards the conclusion of the sequence. On this metric alone, the proposing agent seems relatively trustworthy.

Table 7. r-values for the ranked issue priorities of the two agents over the sequence of proposals. (Note: the correlations use only the final issue priorities of the receiving agent.)

k	r_k
2	0.1751
3	-0.0826
4	-0.8155
5	-0.7611
6	-0.7714
7	-0.8286
8	-0.8286

5   Discussion

This aim of this paper is to describe and illustrate a means by which one agent may assess partially the trustworthiness of another agent on the basis of a measure of integrative intent. The principal advantages of this our approach is that it is an objective, behaviour-based measure; that it assumes no previous interaction between the agents; and that it allows assessment of trust from the earliest stages of a new interaction.

A minor modification of the scheme enables a third agent to observe a sequence of proposals exchanged between two agents and hence to infer the integrative intent of the respective agents towards each other. Such an observation may be of value in forming an independent assessment of the reputations of the observed agents. To do this, an agent would compute *r-values* for the each of the corresponding rows of the tables 6a and 6b and look for a sustained or increasing measure of integrative behaviour.

6   Conclusion

This paper has presented a means to assess the trustworthiness of another agent during the negotiation of a contract and without relying on a previous transaction history. This has been done by exploiting the human association between integrative negotiation behaviour and trustworthiness. The method is intended to complement existing trust variables, not to substitute for them. For example, the measure of trust exhibited towards an agent at the end of a transaction could be reported to a certification authority to update any trust index maintained by that authority and referenced by the same or other agents in future.

References

1.   Nwana, H.S., Sandholm, T., Sierra, C., Maes, P. Guttman, R.: Agent-mediated electronic commerce: issues challenges and some viewpoints. Autonomous Agents 98, Minneapolis MN USA. ACM (1998) 189–196
2.   Jøsang, A: The right type of trust for distributed systems. 1996 ACM New Security Paradigm Workshop, Lake Arrowhead. ACM (1997) 119–131
3.   Manchala, W.D.: E-commerce trust metrics and models. IEEE Internet Computing, Volume: 4 Issue 2 (2000) 36–44
4.   Pruitt, D.G.: Negotiation Behaviour. Academic Press (1981)
5.   Yahalom, R., Klien, B., Beth, T.: Trust relationships in secure systems - a distributed authentication perspective. In Proc. IEEE Symp. on Research in Security and Privacy. IEEE (1993) 150–164
6.   Castelfranchi, C. and Pedone, R.: A review on Trust in Information Technology. National Research Council – Institute of Psychology, Rome, Italy.
7.   Kraus, S. Sycara, K., Evenchick, A., 1998. Reaching agreement through argumentation: a logical model and implementation. *Artificial Intelligence* 104:1–69.

8. Zlotkin, G., Rosenschein, J.S., 1996. Mechanisms for automated negotiation in state oriented domains. *Journal of Artificial Intelligence Research* 5:163–238.
9. Zlotkin, G., Rosenschein, J.S., 1996. Mechanism design for automated negotiation and its application to task oriented domains. *Artificial Intelligence* 86:195–244.
10. Faratin, P., Sierra, C., Jennings, N.R., 1997. Negotiation Decision Functions for Autonomous Agents. *Int. J. of Robotics and Autonomous Systems* 24 (3-4) 159–182.
11. Sierra, C., Faratin, P. and Jennings, N.R., 1997. Deliberative Automated Negotiators Using Fuzzy Similarities. Proc EUSFLAT-ESTYLF Joint Conference on Fuzzy Logic, Palma de Mallorca, Spain, 155–158.
12. Gruber, T.R.: A translation approach to portable ontologies. *Knowledge Acquisition*, 5(2):199-220, 1993 (see also http://www-ksl.stanford.edu/kst/what-is-an-ontology.html).
13. Hendler, J.: Agents and the semantic web. IEEE Intelligent Systems no. 2 March/April 2001, 30–37 (This special issue contains a number of other relevant articles on the semantic web.)
14. Hayes, P.: Keynote address to Fifteenth International Florida Artificial Intelligence Research Society Conference (FLAIRS 2002) Pensacola, Florida, 14–16 May 2002.
15. Barker, R., Holloway, L.P., Meehan, A.: Supporting Negotiation in Concurrent Design Teams. Proceedings Sixth International Conference on CSCW in Design, July 12-14, 2001, London, Ontario, Canada, National Research Council of Canada, NRC Research Press, p243–248
16. Grimsley, M.F., Meehan, A.: A web-based selling agent that maintains customer loyalty through integrative negotiation. 2nd International Conference on Adaptive Hypermedia and Adaptive Web-based Systems (AH'2002) Malaga, Spain, May 2002, Lecture Notes in Computer Science (LNCS 2347), Springer-Verlag, Berlin Heidelberg New York (2002) 397–400
17. Gigerenzer, G. and Todd, P.M.: Fast and Frugal Heuristics: the Adaptive Toolbox. Oxford University Press (1999) 3–34
18. Keeney, R.L. and Raiffa, H.: Decisions with Multiple Objectives: Preferences and Value Tradeoffs. John Wiley & Sons (1976) 224–273
19. French, S.: Decision Theory. Ellis Horwood (1986)
20. Grimsley, M., Meehan, A.: Perceptual Scaling in Materials Selection for Concurrent Design. In Haller, S and Simmons, G (eds.) Proceedings of the Fifteenth International Florida Artificial Intelligence Research Society Conference (FLAIRS 2002) Pensacola, Florida, 14-16 May, AAAI Press (2002) 158–162.

Acquiring an Optimal Amount of Information for Choosing from Alternatives[*]

Rina Azoulay-Schwartz[1] and Sarit Kraus[1,2]

[1] Department of Computer Science, Bar-Ilan University, Ramat-Gan, 52900 Israel
[2] Institute for Advanced Computer Studies
University of Maryland, College Park, MD 20742

Abstract. An agent operating in the real world must often choose from among alternatives in incomplete information environments, and frequently it can obtain additional information about them. Obtaining information can result in a better decision, but the agent may incur expenses for obtaining each unit of information. The problem of finding an optimal strategy for obtaining information appears in many domains. For example, in ecommerce when choosing a seller, and in solving programming problems when choosing heuristics. We focus on cases where the agent has to decide in advance on how much information to obtain about each alternative. In addition, each unit of information about an alternative gives the agent only partial information about the alternative, and the range of each information unit is continues. We first formalize the problem of deciding how many information units to obtain about each alternative, and we specify the expected utility function of the agent, given a combination of information units. This function should be maximized by choosing the optimal number of information units. We proceed by suggesting methods for finding the optimal allocation of information units between the different alternatives.

1 Introduction

An agent which has to choose from among alternatives in an incomplete information environment, would like to obtain information about them. The information about an alternative may enable the agent to compute its expected utility from choosing this alternative, and also the risk associated with this alternative. Given this knowledge, the agent will be able to make a better choice between the available alternatives.

Often, there is an expense associated with obtaining information. This expense may be for the time used to seek on-line information, the time spent talking to friends, the cost of buying relevant journals or the cost of searching a commercial database. We focus on situations where the information obtained is only partial. A unit of information about an alternative means one observation of the result due to the choice of this alternative. Thus, as the agent increases the number of information units about an alternative, it has better knowledge

---

[*] This work was supported in part by NSF under Grant No. IIS-0208608.

M. Klusch, S. Ossowski, and O. Shehory (Eds.): CIA 2002, LNAI 2446, pp. 123–137, 2002.

about the average value of this alternative. For example, an information unit in the ecommerce domain may be an impression of one customer from a product it bought. In choosing between heuristics, an information unit may be a result of one simulation. When using a remote information agent, one information unit may be a result of one query to an external database, etc.. The agent should evaluate its utility from additional information units about each alternative, in order to decide which information to obtain before making a decision.

This problem appears in ecommerce. A customer in an electronic market often has to choose between several suppliers of a product or a service. In ecommerce, the customer cannot view the product before buying it, and cannot form a personal impression of the supplier. Moreover, the price of the product cannot identify its quality, as shown in [4]. Thus, the customers have to collect information about the suppliers in order to learn about the quality of their products. The quality of the goods in ecommerce is measured by its properties, such as supply time, life time of the product, customer support, etc. The utility of the customer given a particular item depends on the item's quality and its price, and the customer should choose the supplier that will maximize its expected utility.

Another domain where information is crucial is in choosing between heuristics when developing a software or hardware product. Each heuristic can be tested a priory by simulations, but testing requires time and resources. Once a heuristic is chosen, it will be implemented in the product, and provided to the customers. The agent should determine the optimal number of trials to run on each heuristic in order to decide which heuristic will be integrated in the commercial product. Suppose the programmer has to decide how many simulations to run during the night for each heuristic. The problem can be formalized as a decision about allocation of information units, since each simulation result can be considered an information unit. Running a simulation has costs of computational power, and there is a limit on the total simulations that could be run in a given time period. In this case, there is a limit on the total number of information units, but not on the number of units for each alternative. Obviously, obtaining more information will improve the agent's knowledge about the different alternatives and will improve its decision making process. Since obtaining information incurs costs of time, communication and other resources, the agent should determine the optimal number of units of information to be obtained about each alternative, in order to optimize its utility from the final decision.

We assume that the agent should decide in advance on how many information units to obtain about each alternative, and it cannot change its decision during the information obtaining process. This assumption holds in different situations. For example, consider an agent that interacts with a search engine. The agent should specify how many answers it would like to obtain about each alternative. It cannot ask for additional answers from the search engine, since the answers will overlap with the previous ones. Thus, the agent should decide how many answers it wants. Another situation where the number of trials should be determined in advance is in sending queries or jobs to multiple machines. Consider, for example, the heuristics domain. Suppose the tester has M machines where he can test its heuristics, but he has to decide how many machines should be allocated to each heuristic. Again, the decision should be taken in advance, and it cannot be changed after observing part of the results, since the results are obtained simultaneously from all the machines.

A similar problem can be found in running a survey. Suppose an agent wants to ask clients of different companies about their satisfaction. The agent sends email to the clients of the different companies, and waits for answers. The agent should decide how many emails to send, assuming that there is a cost of sending emails. (time, communication, etc.) Also in this domain, the decision on the number of information units to be obtained on each alternative is made before answers are obtained.

Our problem is different from the k-armed bandit problem [5], since no costs or benefits are associated with the result of an observation, whereas in the bandit problem, the utility of the agent is composed of the results of the observations. In addition, in our problem, after the sampling process is over, the agent decides about the alternative to be used, while in the k-armed bandit problem, an item is chosen repeatedly, and the decision on the chosen item may be changed over time, according to the observed results. In ecommerce, a bandit problem arises when the agent has to choose repeatedly which item to buy, while our problem of optimal amount of information arises when the item is bought only once, but information can be collected from other entities prior to the buying event.

Furthermore, our problem can be distinguished from classical *value of information* literature [17, 7]. In the latter, it is usually assumed that a piece of information means an exact evidence about the value of some random variable, while in our case, each observation gives only partial information about a given alternative. In addition, in our situations, there is an infinite number of possibilities of information units, since the value of the mean of each alternative, and the value of each observation has a continuous distribution. The assumption about a continuous set of possible answers seems to be more realistic in real world domains. For example, in ecommerce, the quality of an item can be a real number (such as weight, lifetime, etc.) and also an evidence of the quality of a particular item can be, again, a real number. Also in the heuristic domain, the time or the quality of the result can, again, obtain any real number in a given interval. Thus, different methods than those used in the classical literature should be used to solve the current problem.

In this paper, we first present relevant related work. We proceed by describing the case of deciding between two alternatives, and then we consider the general case of deciding between multiple alternatives. For both cases, we introduce a formal model of the problem and identify the utility from obtaining a given combination of information units for each alternative. We suggest how to decide on the optimal combination of information units to be obtained, in order to optimize the agent's expected utility. We also propose some heuristics for the case where there are multiple alternatives and a large possible number of information units for each of them. Finally, we conclude and propose directions for future work.

2   Related Work

In this section we describe research related to the information acquiring problem in AI and in statistics. Some work in AI has considered the decision about acquiring information, during the process of planning or decision making in incomplete information environments.

The problem of *value of information* was widely discussed in Artificial Intelligence, e.g., [8, 17, 7, 6]. However, as specified by Russel and Norvig, 'Usually, we assume that exact evidence is obtained about the value of some random variable.' In this paper, we consider the case where the acquired data gives only partial information, as described in Section 1. In particular, each unit of information about a particular alternative includes one evidence about the alternative.

Grass and Zilberstein [6] developed a decision theoretic approach that uses an explicit representation of the user's decision model in order to plan and execute information gathering actions. However, their system is based on information sources that return perfect information about the asked query. Similarly, Dean and Wellman [2] studied the problem of decision making on information acquisition to improve planning, but consider only cases where the answers consist of complete knowledge about the questions asked. In our paper, the information obtained about an alternative consists of a sample of this alternative, but does not provide a complete answer on the value of the given alternative.

Lesser et al. [11, 10] developed BIG, which is a sophisticated information gathering agent that retrieves and processes on-line information to support decision making. They supplied BIG with a design-to-criteria scheduler in order to control the following three factors: (a) the money spent on acquiring information from sites that charge a fee for accessing their information; (b) the balance between the coverage of information gathered and the precision of the results; and (c) the time of the overall process of information gathering. The design-to-criteria scheduler analyzes the agent's set of problem solving actions and chooses a course of actions for the agent. Lesser et al. consider the overall process of decisions about information gathering, but do not provide a formal model for optimal information acquisition, considering the precision of the results, and the time of the overall process.

Some ongoing research considers also the case of partial evidence about the missing information (the hypothesis) [7, 18]. Tseng and Gmytrasiewicz [18] considered sampled answers, but they assume that the number of possible answers for a query in the information gathering process is finite while in this paper we consider a continuous set of possible answers. Moreover, Tseng and Gmytrasiewicz consider a myopic sequential procedure for the information gathering process. Thus, their solution is not optimal: they only consider the nearest step of information gathering, assuming that in each step the agent can decide about the next information to be obtained. However, in our case the combination of information units to be obtained should be decided in advance and we are looking for optimal solutions.

Heckerman et al. [7] consider the case of partial information obtained about a hypothesis, but they consider a simplified model where there is one binary hypothesis, and the data that can be learned is based on binary evidences about several unknown variables. They suggest to consider all possible sets of results, in order to choose the next data item to obtain. In a case of a large number of binary variables, they suggest to use a normal approximation. The problem addressed in this paper is different, since each data item has a continuous set of possible values, so different computation techniques should be used. Moreover, the decision in this paper is which alternative to choose out of N possibilities, and not just to accept or reject a particular hypothesis. Thus, our problem is more complex than that of Heckerman et al.

Poh and Horvitz [16] consider a situation where the information obtained due to the model refinement is only partial, and it can have continuous probability distribution. They consider several types of model refinements, and they also consider the problem of which refinement to choose, when there are different alternative refinement steps. They consider the case where after each refinement, a new decision is made about the next refinement to do, and they suggest a greedy-myopic algorithm for the decision about the next refinement to be performed in each step. In this paper, we consider the problem of how to decide optimally about the sample allocation, in cases where the decision should be taken in advance.

A set of problems related to ours is the family of the bandit problems [1, 5]. In this kind of problems, the agent has to choose sequentially between alternatives. Each alternative when observed produces a result, and the agent's utility is based on a weighted sum of the results obtained over time. Our problem is different from the bandit problem since costs or benefits are associated with the result of each observation. However, in our problem the utility of the agent is composed only of the outcome of the final decision . In addition, in our problem, after the sampling process is over, the agent decides about the alternative to be used. In the k-armed bandit problem an item is chosen repeatedly, and the chosen item can be replaced over time, according to the observed results. For example, in the heuristics domain, if the final software includes a mechanism that can choose which heuristic to use in each step, and can change its decision using the results of the previous steps, then the problem will be similar to the k-armed bandit problem, since the result of each step is important. But, if there is a trial step, where all alternatives are tested, and only the winner is implemented in the final software, then there is a problem of the value of information: the agent does not care about the results of the sampling tests, and is only concerned with the final decision and the cost of performing the tests.

Most of the work done in statistical research in the context of determining the size of a sample, considers a criteria of reaching a required accuracy of the result of the sample units [13, 9]. Few researches deal with trying to maximize future benefits. Dunnett [3] considers the problem of determining the number of samples to be taken when deciding among multiple alternatives. However, he considers only the case of an equal number of samples to be taken about each alternative. Moreover, he assumes equal standard deviation of the different alternatives. Based on these assumptions, the optimal number of samples can be found analytically, at least for the case of two alternatives. However, in reality, the standard deviation of the different alternatives can be different, and there is also no reason for the number of samples to be the same for all the alternatives. Thus, the general case is much more complex and an analytical solution can not be found in most of the cases.

Lindley [12] describes a full Bayesian treatment for the problem of sample size determination, and compares it to other approaches. However, he considers a decision regarding whether to accept or reject a particular hypothesis, while in our research, the final decision is a choice between several alternatives.

Pezeshk and Gittins [15] consider the problem of sample size determining in the context of medical trials. They suggest how to choose the optimal number of trials to perform on a new medicine, in order to maximize the social benefits, or to maximize the benefits of the medical company. They also consider only a decision about accepting or rejecting one alternative, where the decision to be made is whether or not to accept the alternative.

In this paper, we consider the problem of sample size determination, where an agent that has to decide between several different alternatives by sampling them. Similar to the statistical research, we consider a continuous distribution of the values of each alternative. However, we suggest procedures for choosing from multiple alternatives, while current research in statistics mostly considers the decision of whether to accept or reject a particular hypothesis.

3   Environment Description

Consider a risk neutral agent that has to choose from among k alternatives. After choosing alternative i, the agent will obtain a value of x_i, which is unknown in advance. x_i has a particular distribution, but the distribution is unknown to the agent. In particular, we assume that for each alternative i, x_i is normally distributed, with an unknown mean μ_i, and a known standard deviation σ_i.[3] The agent does not know μ_i, but it has some prior beliefs about its distribution. The agent believes that the mean μ_i for each alternative i is normally distributed, with mean ζ_i and standard deviation τ_i. Formally, $x_i \sim N(\mu_i, \tau_i)$ and $\mu_i \sim N(\zeta_i, \tau_i)$. The prior beliefs are based on the knowledge of the agent about the world. For example, its knowledge about the average quality of an item, etc., but its prior beliefs may be inaccurate.

The agent has some available information about each alternative. For each alternative i, it has $n_i \geq 0$ units of information, with an average value of $\overline{x}_i$ per unit. The agent is able to obtain additional information units about the different alternatives, but this operation is costly. Collecting each unit of information takes one time period, and the agent has a discount factor of $0 < \delta \leq 1$ for each time delay. Suppose also that asking a query has a direct cost of $c \geq 0$. This may be

---

[3] In order to simplify the model, we assume a known standard deviation. If the standard deviation is unknown by the agent, then we can use the student (t) distribution, and analyze it accordingly.

the payment to the answering agent, the cost of a phone call, or other expenses associated with the query process.

Using the above parameters, the posterior distribution of x_i can be calculated, and used to calculate the value of information. We suggest that the final decision about the winner alternative be made only according to the collected information, and the prior distribution of x_i be considered, since this distribution is based on beliefs that are inaccurate. Dunnett [3] refers to this type of procedure as Procedure D_0. Therefore, the parameters x_i and n_i, which are used both for the calculation of posterior beliefs and for the final decision, and the parameters ζ_i and τ_i, which are used only for the calculation of posterior beliefs should be considered in a different manner.

Given the cost of time, δ, and the direct cost c, and given the list of alternatives, and the parameters $(\sigma_i, \zeta_i, \tau_i, x_i, n_i)$ for each of the alternatives, the agent should decide how much information to obtain about each alternative. We denote by m_i the number of information units to be obtained about alternative i. Thus, the agent should choose the combination $(m_1, m_2, .., m_n)$. We assume that $m_i \in \{0, .., M-1\}$, i.e., the maximum number of information units for each alternative is $M - 1$. Thus, there are M possibilities for the number of units to be obtained about each alternative. There are also situations where the total number of samples is limited, i.e., $\sum m_i < M$. For example, this is the case in the heuristics domain when there are M machines and the agent has to decide how to divide its trials among them. In this case, there is only a limit on the total number of samples, which is supposed to be at most $M - 1$.

In the following example, we present a particular ecommerce problem where there are two alternative suppliers and the agent has to choose between them. This example will be used in order to illustrate the evaluation process and the algorithm to determine the optimal amount of information to obtain.

Example 1. Suppose a customer has to buy a particular item, that can be sold by two different suppliers, A and B. Suppose the price of the item is the same for both suppliers, but the quality of the item cannot be observed in advance. The average quality of supplier A is μ_A and the average quality of supplier B is μ_B, but the customer does not know the values of μ_A and μ_B. However, the customer can collect information from friends or from the Web about these suppliers, in order to be able to decide between them. Since the prices of the suppliers are equal, the expected utility of the buyer depends on μ_A and μ_B. Obviously, the customer would like to choose the better supplier, but first it has to decide how much information to obtain about each of the suppliers.

We consider a case where the customer does not have specific beliefs about the suppliers A and B, but has prior beliefs about the distribution of μ_i for any unknown supplier i (suppose these are the average and standard deviations of the item given any arbitrary supplier). In particular, the customer believes that $\mu_A \sim N(\zeta_A = 50, \tau_A = 50)$ and $\mu_B \sim N(\zeta_B = 50, \tau_B = 50)$. Suppose also that σ_A and σ_B are equal and known to be 50. Finally, suppose that the discount factor of the agent is $\delta = 0.9$ and the cost is $c = 0$.

Suppose that the agent was able to obtain available information about both suppliers from some external sources (such as a free search engine), and it has collected 10 units of information about each alternative, with the results $\overline{x}_A = 49, \overline{x}_B = 47$. Given this available information, it is clear that without additional information, the agent will choose to buy the product from supplier A. However, the agent is able to collect additional information about each supplier, from some information source (for example, from another search engine, but reading each answer takes time, so a discount factor exists).

The agent should decide how much additional information to collect about each supplier. It should decide in advance how many units it wants for each alternative: it cannot ask for additional answers from the search engine, since the answers will overlap with the previous ones. Formally, we would like to find the optimal numbers M_A, M_B, where M_A is the number of information units to be obtained about supplier A, and M_B is the number of information units to be collected about supplier B.

In the following section we show how the agent should decide on the number of information units to obtain about each alternative i, given its prior beliefs about i, and given $\overline{x}_i$ and σ_i.

4   Choosing between Two Alternatives

Suppose the agent has to decide between alternatives A and B. Currently, $\overline{x}_A > \overline{x}_B$. Since the agent is risk neutral, and since the decision is made according to the collected information, alternative A will be chosen if no additional information is obtained. If additional information will be acquired the decision may be changed either because of additional negative information about A, or because of additional positive information about B. Thus, we should evaluate the expected utility resulting from the additional information.

Suppose that it is possible to obtain m_A additional units of information about alternative A and m_B additional units of information about alternative B. Denote by $\overrightarrow{x}_A$ and $\overrightarrow{x}_B$ the average value of these additional units, for alternative A and B, respectively. We start by calculating the value of the information from obtaining these additional units.

The agent has to evaluate its utility from obtaining additional information about the alternatives. In order to do so he has to evaluate the probability that the additional information will change his decision. We denote this probability by $Fchange(\mu_A, \mu_B, \sigma_A, \sigma_B, \overline{x}_A, n_A, m_A, \overline{x}_B, n_B, m_B)$. In the following lemma, we find the value of $Fchange$, as a function of its arguments.

Lemma 1. Calculating Fchange

The value of Fchange, is as follows:
$Fchange(\mu_A, \mu_B, \sigma_A, \sigma_B, \overline{x}_A, n_A, m_A, \overline{x}_B, n_B, m_B) = Pr(Z > Z_\alpha)$
where Z is a random variable, having the standard normal distribution (see [13]), $Pr(Z > Z_\alpha)$ is the probability that the random variable Z will take a value greater

than Z_α, and

$$Z_\alpha = \frac{\mu_A m_A (m_B + n_B) - \mu_B m_B (m_A + n_A)}{\sqrt{m_A^2 (m_B + n_B)^2 \cdot \sigma_A^2 + m_B^2 (m_A + n_A)^2 \cdot \sigma_B^2}} + \frac{n_A \overline{x}_A (m_B + n_B) - n_B \overline{x}_B (m_A + n_A)}{\sqrt{m_A^2 (m_B + n_B)^2 \cdot \sigma_A^2 + m_B^2 (m_A + n_A)^2 \cdot \sigma_B^2}}$$

Sketch of proof: Given the additional m_A, m_B units of information, the new average quality of A will be $(m_A \overrightarrow{x}_A + n_A \overline{x}_A)/(m_A + n_A)$, and the new average of B will be $(m_B \overrightarrow{x}_B + n_B \overline{x}_B)/(m_B + n_B)$. In order for the average of B to outperform the average of A, the following should hold: $(m_B \overrightarrow{x}_B + n_B \overline{x}_B)/(m_B + n_B) > (m_A \overrightarrow{x}_A + n_A \overline{x}_A)/(m_A + n_A)$. Manipulating the above formula, the above condition is $\overrightarrow{x}_B m_B (m_A + n_A) - \overrightarrow{x}_A m_A (m_B + n_B) > n_A \overline{x}_A (m_B + n_B) - n_B \overline{x}_B (m_A + n_A)$. Denote $e_A = m_A (m_B + n_B)$ and $e_B = m_B (m_A + n_A)$. Then we prove that $e_B \cdot \overrightarrow{x}_B - e_A \cdot \overrightarrow{x}_A \sim N(e_B \cdot \mu_B - e_A \cdot \mu_A, \sqrt{e_A^2 \cdot \sigma_A^2 / m_A + e_B^2 \cdot \sigma_B^2 / m_B})$. Based on this,

$$\frac{e_B \cdot \overrightarrow{x}_B - e_A \cdot \overrightarrow{x}_A - (e_B \cdot \mu_B - e_A \cdot \mu_A)}{\sqrt{e_A^2 \cdot \sigma_A^2 / m_A + e_B^2 \cdot \sigma_B^2 / m_B}} \sim N(0, 1).$$

Using the above, we find the value of Z_α, such that

$$Z_\alpha = \frac{n_A \overline{x}_A (m_B + n_B) - n_B \overline{x}_B (m_A + n_A) - (e_B \cdot \mu_B - e_A \cdot \mu_A)}{\sqrt{e_A^2 \cdot \sigma_A^2 / m_A + e_B^2 \cdot \sigma_B^2 / m_B}}$$

and the probability for a change is the probability of a normal variable to be more then Z_α. □

In the following example we will calculate *Fchange* for different combinations of m_A and m_B, in the suppliers examples, and show how *Fchange* will be affected by changing m_A or m_B.

Example 2. We return to the case of Example 1. Recall that the data collected before the decision should be made includes 10 units of information about each alternative, where $\overline{x}_A = 49$ and $\overline{x}_B = 47$. In order to calculate the values of *Fchange* for different combinations of m_A and m_B, we should consider all possible values of mean value μ_A and mean value μ_B. Intuitively, the influence of m_A and m_B on *Fchange* depends on the values of μ_A and μ_B.

For example, suppose that $\overline{x}_A = 49$, and additional units are obtained only about alternative B. In this case, the additional units may cause a change if the combined average, which includes $\overline{x}_B$ and $\overrightarrow{x}_B$, will be above 49 (since the average quality of alternative B is 49). Whenever $\mu_B > 49$, the probability of a new example to have a value higher than 49 is greater than the probability of it to have a lower value. Thus, as we collect more data about alternative B, the probability for a change increases, since more often the collected data will be higher than 49, and will push the combined average above 49. Whenever this value will be over 49, alternative B will win (since the average of alternative A is 49). But, if $\mu_B < 49$, then obtaining additional information units about B will more often cause the average of alternative B to remain less than the average of alternative A, so a change will occur more rarely. The global influence on *Fchange* depends on the probability for each value of μ_A and μ_B.

In the following table, we display the different values of $Fchange$. The values of $Fchange$ for $m_A = 0$, and $m_B = 0, .., 5$ are presented in the second column. We see that the positive influence of enlarging m_B is higher than the negative one, i.e., as m_B increases, the probability of a change increases too. The third column presents the influence of enlarging m_A when $m_B = 0$. Again, the total positive effect is higher than the negative effect: as m_A increases, the probability of a change increases.

m	$Fchange$ $(m_A = 0, m_B = m)$	$Fchange$ $(m_A = m, m_B = 0)$
1	.41543	.41055
2	.43648	.42998
3	.44536	.43784
4	.45041	.44217
5	.45371	.44492

The next evaluation step is the calculation of the gains due to the additional information. We should consider all possible pairs μ_A, μ_B, and for each pair, calculate the expected benefits from m_A and m_B additional information units, and multiply this by the probability for μ_A, μ_B being the actual mean values.

The expected benefits from obtaining additional m_A units of information on A and m_B units on B, is $Fchange \cdot (\mu_B - \mu_A)$, since obtaining these additional units can cause the final decision to be changed from choosing A to choosing B with a probability of $Fchange$, and in this case, the expected utility of choosing B instead of A is $\mu_B - \mu_A$. In order to compute the probability for each particular assignment of μ_A and μ_B, we evaluate their posterior distribution, using their prior distributions, and the collected information $n_A, n_B, \overline{x}_A$ and $\overline{x}_A$.

The following lemma provides the expected benefits from obtaining additional information about each alternative, by considering all possible distributions of both alternatives, i.e., by considering each possible pair μ_A, μ_B. In this lemma, we use the following notations. Denote by $f(\mu_i | \zeta_i, \tau_i, \sigma_i, n_i, \sigma_i, \overline{x}_i)$ the probability for alternative i to have a mean of μ_i, given the prior belief $\mu_i \sim N(\zeta_i, \tau_i)$, given σ_i, and given a sample with n_i units, and average $\overline{x}_i$. Denote by $f(u_i = \mu_i | u_i \sim N(\mu(i), \sigma(i))$ the probability of the variable u_i to have the value μ_i, given that u_i is normally distributed, with mean $\mu(i)$ and standard deviation $\sigma(i)$.

Lemma 2. Calculating the benefits *The benefits due to obtaining m_A units of information about A and m_B units of information about B are as follows*

$$benefits(m_A, m_B) =$$
$$\int \int Fchange(\mu_A, \mu_B, \sigma_A, \sigma_B, \overline{x}_A, n_A, m_A, \overline{x}_B, n_B, m_B) \cdot$$
$$(\mu_B - \mu_A) \cdot f(\mu_A | \zeta_A, \tau_A, \sigma_A, n_A, \overline{x}_A) \cdot f(\mu_B | \zeta_B, \tau_B, \sigma_B, n_B, \overline{x}_B) d\mu_A d\mu_B =$$

$$= \int_{-\infty}^{\infty} \int_{-\infty}^{\infty} Fchange(\mu_A, \mu_B, \sigma_A, \sigma_B, \overline{x}_A, n_A, m_A, \overline{x}_B,$$
$$n_B, m_B) \cdot (\mu_B - \mu_A) \cdot f(u_A = \mu_A | u_A \sim N(\mu(A), \sigma(A)))$$
$$\cdot f(u_B = \mu_B | u_B \sim N(\mu(B), \sigma(B))) d\mu_A d\mu_B$$

where

$$\mu(i) = \frac{\sigma_i^2 \zeta_i + n_i \tau_i^2 \overline{x_i}}{\sigma_i^2 + n_i \tau_i^2}, \sigma(i)^2 = \frac{\sigma_i^2 \tau_i^2}{\sigma_i^2 + n_i \tau_i^2}. \tag{1}$$

Sketch of proof: We should consider all the possible pairs of μ_A, μ_B, and for each pair, to evaluate the expected value of additional m_A and m_B units of information, given the pair μ_A, μ_B, multiplied by the probability for this pair. The expected value of the additional units is equal to the probability of a change, multiplied by the gains $\mu_B - \mu_A$ due to a change. The probability for each value μ_i is evaluated, by calculating its posterior distribution, by the Bayesian estimation [13]. □

Finally, we will also consider the various costs involved in obtaining $m_A + m_B$ units of information and present the agent's utility. Recall that there is a discount factor of $0 < \delta \leq 1$ on the utility of the agent, and a direct cost of c for each unit. Given δ and c, the expected utility of the agent from obtaining a utility of x_i from the alternative chosen, after collecting m units of information, is $(x_i)\delta^m - \sum_{i=0}^{m-1} c \cdot \delta^i$. The explicit value is $x_i \delta^m - c(\frac{\delta^m - 1}{\delta - 1})$. Considering all possible values of x_i, we obtain the following theorem. The proof is immediate from lemma 2 and from the cost of each data unit.

Theorem 3. *The expected utility from obtaining m_A and m_B additional information units about alternative A and B, respectively, is $utility(m_A, m_B) = benefits(m_A, m_B) \cdot \delta^{m_A + m_B} - c \frac{\delta^{m_A + m_B} - 1}{\delta - 1}$.*

If there is no discount factor, then $\delta = 1$. In this case, the utility of the agent is $benefits(m_A, m_B) - cm$. If there are no direct costs, then $c = 0$, and in this case, the utility of the agent is $benefits(m_A, m_B)\delta^m$. Based on the above theorem, we proceed by presenting an algorithm that computes the optimal number of units to obtain for each alternative. The agent's goal is to find the pair m_A and m_B, that yields the highest value of $utility(m_A, m_B)$, i.e., we should find the values M_A and M_B such that, $(M_A, M_B) = argmax_{m_A, m_B} utility(m_A, m_B)$.

We suggest to consider all possible combinations of information units about A and B, and choose the optimal combination. Since there are only two alternatives, this process is polynomial. We proceed by implementing the above process on a particular problem, and then we generalize the problem and consider $k > 2$ alternatives to choose from. In the following suppliers example, we show how the values of m_A and m_B should be determined.

Example 3. We return to the situation of Examples 1-2. One may hypothesis that as m_A and m_B increase, the benefits due to the additional information increase, since the additional information results in more knowledge about the alternative, and a better decision. However, an increase of m_A and m_B also has a negative effect, due to the cost of time. The following table, that describes $Utility(m_A, m_B)$ for each pair m_A, m_B, shows that there is a peak level for the optimal values of m_A and m_B, and an additional increment of them can only reduce the expected utility of the agents.

m_B m_A	0	1	2	3	4	5
0	0	2.0241	2.5998	2.7867	2.795	2.711
1	1.7951	2.6685	2.9528	2.9959	2.920	2.784
2	2.3551	2.8884	**3.0344**	3.0055	2.889	2.729
3	2.5547	2.9113	2.9794	2.9118	2.776	2.609
4	2.5831	2.8319	2.8529	2.7647	2.622	2.455
5	2.5205	2.6982	2.6899	2.5915	2.449	2.287

In the above example, the optimal combination of m_A and m_B is $m_A = 2, m_B = 2$, which gives a utility of 3.0344. As the number of units about alternative A or B decreases or increases, the utility decreases. Note that if there are at most 5 available information units for both alternatives, i.e., when $M = 6$, then we should consider only the part of the table from the main diagonal and up, while $m_A + m_B < 6$, but the same result will be obtained in our case, since the pair $m_A = 2, m_B = 2$ is valid also in the case of a total of $M - 1$ units.

There are cases where the optimal M_A and M_B can be found by analytically finding the optimal value of $utility(m_A, m_B)$, as done by [3] for a simpler case. This calculation can be performed in simple situations. For example, if μ_A and μ_B have a uniform distribution. But, in more complex situations, analytical derivation of the optimal values of M_A and M_B becomes hard or even impossible.

In the above example, we could simply use a greedy algorithm in order to find the optimal allocation of samples. The algorithm should choose in each step the most beneficial sample to add, and it should stop when there is no additional sample that increases the expected utility. However, in the following lemma, we show that the greedy algorithm is not optimal. The reason being that there may be situations where obtaining one unit of information about a particular alternative is not worthwhile, but obtaining two and more may be worthwhile to the agent, as stated in the following lemma.

Lemma 4. *(1) There are situations where obtaining one unit of information about a given alternative is not beneficial, but obtaining more than one is beneficial. (2) There are situations where obtaining information about one alternative is not beneficial, while obtaining information about two or more is beneficial.*

Proof. Both claims will be proven by examples. In order to show claim (1), consider a case where prior beliefs of the user are: $\mu_A \sim N(\zeta_A = 10, \tau_A = 27), \mu_B \sim N(\zeta_B = 10, \tau_B = 76)$, and $\sigma_A = 34$, $\sigma_B = 50$. Suppose that the discount factor is $\delta := 0.968$, and the cost is $c = 0$. Suppose that there are ten collected information units about alternative A and only two units about B, with the results $\overline{x}_A = 9.5, \overline{x}_B = 12.9$. In this case, $utility(m_A = 1, m_B = 0) = -.02551$, while $utility(m_A = 2, m_B = 0) = .63431$. Thus, although it is not worthwhile to obtain one unit of information about alternative A, it may be worthwhile to obtain 2 units of information about this alternative.

We proceed by an example to show claim (2). Suppose the prior beliefs of the agent are $\mu_A \sim N(\zeta_A = 27, \tau_A = 72), \mu_B \sim N(\zeta_B = 27, \tau_B = 72)$. Suppose also that $x_A \sim N(\mu_A, 89)$ and $x_B \sim N(mu_B, 67)$. The discount factor is $\delta := 0.991$, and the cost of time is $c = 0.03$. Eight units of information were collected about each alternative, A and B, with the results $\bar{x}_A = 31.05$ and $\bar{x}_B = 34.83$. In this case, $utility(m_A = 1, m_B = 0) = -0.85096$, $utility(m_A = 0, m_B = 1) = -0.62808$, but $utility(m_A = 1, m_B = 1) = 0.86613$. This means that although it is not worthwhile to obtain one unit of information about alternative A or B, it becomes beneficial to obtain one unit about each of these two alternatives.   □

5   Choosing from Multiple Alternatives

We proceed by considering a general case, where there are $k > 2$ alternatives, and the agent can obtain up to $M - 1$ units of information about each of them. Thus, there are M^k possible combinations of information units that can be obtained by the agent, and if there are a total of $M - 1$ units to be used, then there are $(M + k)!/((M - 1)! \cdot (k + 1)!)$ possible combinations (Each sample can be allocated to a particular alternative or not be allocated at all). In the following, we describe the agent utility function given a combination of information units.

In order to calculate the value of each combination of information units, we should know the prior beliefs ζ_i, τ_i about each alternative i, and also the value of $\bar{x}_i$ for the k_i information units that were already obtained. In the case of two alternatives, we presented the expected utility to be the additional utility due to replacing alternative A with alternative B. In this section, for simplicity reasons, we calculate the absolute utility from each alternative, without comparing it to the previous winner. Of course, given the utility from each alternative, the new winner could be identified.

Let $comb = (m_1, m_2, ..., m_k)$ denote a combination of m_i units of information about alternative i, and $totalM$ the total number of information units obtained about all the alternatives, i.e., $totalM = \sum_{i=1}^{k} m_i$. Also $\vec{x}_i$ will denote the average of the m_i information units about alternative i. Finally, let $R_{mi} = m_i/(m_i + n_i)$ and $R_{ni} = n_i/(m_i + n_i)$. The following theorem expresses the utility of the agent, given the information units combination $comb$, the prior beliefs about each alternative and the prior average value of each of them.

Theorem 5. *Suppose that given $\bar{x}_i$ and n_i, alternative 1 will be chosen. The utility from obtaining m_i additional information units about each alternative i is*

$$Util(comb) = \sum_{i=2}^{k} \int_{-\infty}^{+\infty} f(i, \mu_i) \cdot \int_{-\infty}^{+\infty} f(1, \mu_1) \cdot (\mu_i - \mu_1) \cdot$$
$$f(wins_i|\mu_i, \mu_1, comb) d\mu_i d\mu_1 \cdot \delta^{totalM} - c \frac{\delta^{totalM-1}}{\delta - 1},$$

where

$$f(wins_i|\mu_i, \mu_1, comb) = \int_{\vec{x}_i = -\infty}^{\infty} f(\vec{x}_i|\mu_i) \cdot$$
$$\left(\int_{-\infty}^{(R_{mi} \cdot \overline{x_i} + R_{ni} \cdot \overline{x_i} - R_{n1} \cdot \overline{x_1})/R_{m1}} f(\vec{x}_1|\mu_1) d\vec{x}_1 \cdot \right.$$
$$\prod_{j>1, j \neq i} F\left(\frac{(R_{mi} \cdot \overline{x_i} + R_{ni} \cdot \overline{x_i} - R_{nj} \cdot \overline{x_j})/R_{mj} - \mu(j)}{\sqrt{\sigma_j^2 + \sigma(j)^2}} \right) d\vec{x}_i$$

where $f(i, \mu_i) = f(u_i = \mu_i | u_i \sim N(\mu(i), \sigma(i))$ as defined in equation 1, $f(\vec{x}_i|\mu_i) = f(x = \vec{x}_i | x \sim N(\mu_i, \sigma_i/\sqrt{m_i}))$ and finally, $F(z)$ is the standard normal density of the random variable z.

Sketch of proof: Given *comb*, for each alternative i we consider the probability for it to win, and the expected utility in this case, and we also consider the cost of obtaining the combination *comb* of information units. Thus, we run all the values of μ_i and μ_1, which is the default alternative to be chosen. For each pair, we calculate the probability for this pair, and the utility from the additional information, which is $\mu_i - \mu_1$ (since we changed the decision from alternative 1 to alternative i). We multiply the above by $f(wins_i|\mu_i, \mu_1, comb)$, the probability for alternative i to win.

In order to evaluate $f(wins_i|\mu_i, \mu_1, comb)$, we run each possible value of $\overrightarrow{x}_i$, and calculate its probability to win, i.e., we require that for each $j \neq i$, $(n_j \cdot \overline{x} + m_j \cdot \overrightarrow{x}_j)/(m_j + n_j) < (n_i \cdot \overline{x} + m_i \cdot \overrightarrow{x}_i)/(m_i + n_i)$. So, the maximum value of $\overrightarrow{x}_j$ should be $(R_{ni} \cdot \overline{x} + R_{mi} \cdot \overrightarrow{x}_i - R_{nj} \cdot \overline{x})/R_{mj}$.

The distribution of the average of alternative $j > 1, j \neq i$ depends on μ_j. Denote $M' = (R_{ni} \cdot \overline{x} + R_{mi} \cdot \overrightarrow{x}_i - R_{nj} \cdot \overline{x})/R_{mj}$. Then, calculate $\int_{-\infty}^{\infty} f(j, \mu_j) \cdot \int_{-\infty}^{M'} f(\overrightarrow{x}|\mu_j)$. Manipulating the above formula, and using integration rules of the normal distribution from [14], we reveal that the above formula is equal to $F(\frac{M'-\mu(j)}{\sqrt{\sigma_j^2 + \sigma(j)^2}})$. Finally, we consider the cost of obtaining the additional information: we multiply the expected utility by δ^{totalM}, and subtract $c\frac{\delta^{totalM-1}}{\delta-1}$.   □

Given the ability to evaluate the expected utility from a particular combination of additional information units, we are also able to calculate a beneficial combination, in order to maximize its expected utility. There are two methods for finding the optimal combination. First, this can be done analytically, by finding the derivation of the expected utility according to the $m_1, .., m_k$, and finding the values of $m_1, .., m_k$ for which the derivation is equal to 0. This method was performed by Dunnett [3] for the case of equal standard deviation σ for the different populations, and equal sample sizes k. In cases of multiple $m_1, .., m_k$ and $\sigma_1, .., \sigma_k$, the calculation becomes very complex, or even analytically impossible. In such cases, we consider different combinations of $m_1, .., m_k$, and choose the combination that maximizes *Util*.

We can suggest an optimal algorithm that considers all possible pairs of $m_1..m_k$, but this algorithm is clearly exponential in the number of alternatives. Different heuristics for the choosing problem can be used such as greedy-myopic heuristic [16], or a local search technique. In future work we intend to compare the different heuristics by simulations, and to compare their results with the optimal solution.

6   Conclusion

In this paper, we consider the problem faced by an agent that has to choose from alternatives, and is able to acquire additional information about them. We consider situations where the agent should decide in advance how much information it would like to obtain about each alternative, before it obtains any answer. We describe the expected utility of the agent due to the acquired information units, and we provide an optimal and polynomial decision procedure for the case of choosing between two alternatives, and demonstrate it with a particular example. We proceed by considering the case of choosing from multiple alternatives, and we describe the expected utility of the agent given this case. We suggest an optimal algorithm for this case, which has an exponential complexity, and suggest how sub-optimal solutions can be found.

References

1. D. A. Berry and B. Fristedt. *Bandit Problems: Sequential Allocation of Experiments.* Chapman and Hall, London, UK, 1985.
2. T. L. Dean and M. P. Wellman. *Planning and Control.* Morgan Kaufman, Publishers, California, 1991.
3. C. W. Dunnett. On selecting the largest of k normal population means. *Journal of the Royal Statistical Society. Series B (Methodological)*, 22 (1):1–40, 1960.
4. C. Eric, K. Hann, and I. Hitt. The nature of competition in electronic markets: An empirical investigation of online travel agent offerings. WP, The Wharton School of the Univ. of Pennsylvania, 1998.
5. J. C. Gittins. *Multi-armed Bandit Allocation Indices.* John Wiley & Sons, 1989.
6. J. Grass and S. Zilberstein. A value-driven system for autonomous information gathering. *Journal of Intelligent Information Systems*, 14:5–27, 2000.
7. D. E. Heckerman, E. J. Horvitz, and B. Middleton. An approximate nonmyopic computation for value of information. *IEEE Transactions on Pattern Analysis and Machine Intelligence*, 15:292–298, 1993.
8. R. A. Howard. Information value theory. *IEEE Transactions on Systems Science and Cybernetics*, 2:22–26, 1966.
9. L. Joseph and D. B. Wolfson. Interval-based versus decision theoretic criteria for the choice of sample size. *Statistician*, 46 (2):145–149, 1997.
10. V. Lesser, B. Horling, F. Klassner, A. Raja, T. Wagner, and S. Zhang. Big: An agent for resource-bounded information gathering and decision making. *Artificial Intelligence*, 118:197–244, 2000.
11. V. Lesser, B. Horling, A. Raja, T. Wagner, and S. X. Zhang. Sophisticated information gathering in a marketplace of information providers. In *Proceedings of IEEE Internet Computing, Agents on the Net*, volume 4 (2), pages 49–58, 2000.
12. D. V. Lindley. The choice of sample size. *The Statistician*, 46:129–138, 1997.
13. I. Miller and J. E. Freund. *Probability and Statistics for Engineers.* Premtoce-Hall, Inc., 1985.
14. J. K. Patel and C. B. Read. *Handbook of the normal distribution.* Marcel Dekker, Inc., 1996.
15. H. Pezeshk and J. Gittins. Sample Size Determination in Clinical Trials. *Student*, 3 (1):19–26, 1999.
16. K. L. Poh and E. Horvitz. Reasoning about the value of decision model refinement: Methods and application. In *UAI-99*, pages 174–182, Washington DC, 1993.
17. S. Russel and P. Norvig. *Artificial Intelligence: a Modern Approach.* Prentice-Hall Inc., 1996.
18. C. Tseng and P. J. Gmytrasiewicz. Time sensitive sequential myopic information gathering. In *Proc. of HICSS-32*, Maui, Hawaii, 1999.

A Competitive Information Recommendation System and Its Behavior

Yasuhiko Kitamura, Toshiki Sakamoto, and Shoji Tatsumi

Osaka City University, Osaka 558-8585, Japan
{kitamura,sakamoto,tatsumi}@kdel.info.eng.osaka-cu.ac.jp
http://www.kdel.info.eng.osaka-cu.ac.jp/

Abstract. Information recommendation systems draw attention of practitioners in B-to-C electronic commerce. In an independent recommendation system such as in www.amazon.com, a user cannot compare the recommended item with ones from other information sources. In a broker-mediated recommendation system such as in www.dealtime.com, the broker takes the initiative of recommendation, and the information provider cannot recommend its item directly to the user.
In this paper, we propose a competitive information recommendation system consisting of multiple animated agents that recommend their items competitively, and discuss the advantages through showing a prototype developed for restaurant recommendation. Each agent recommends restaurants from its own point of view and the user tells good or bad about them. In our competitive information recommendation system, the user can compare items recommended from multiple agents, and the information providers can recommend their items directly to the user through its animated agent. We also show that the competitive nature affects the output depending on the number of participating agents.

1 Introduction

Electronic Commerce (EC) is one of most successful application domains of the Internet. We can access a large number of shopping sites that deal with various goods through a Web browser. A simplest and easiest way of starting a shopping site is just to create a Web page on which items for sales are listed up. When there are too many items to be contained in plain Web pages, we may deploy an information retrieval tool to help customers find their preferred items.

Recently, to make the shopping sites more attractive, new technologies are added to them. Recommender systems initiatively recommend items to customers by using collaborative and/or content-based filtering techniques [2]. They try to reduce customers' burden of searching for their preferred items. Life-like animated agents, such as developed by Extempo (www.extempo.com), are also available to navigate customers to their preferred items in the site. They can build a close and friendly relationship between the shop and the customers.

Most of conventional shopping sites, such as amazon.com, are running in an independent and closed manner. In such a site, customers receive information

M. Klusch, S. Ossowski, and O. Shehory (Eds.): CIA 2002, LNAI 2446, pp. 138–151, 2002.

for sales items from the site only and any devices for comparing the items with those from the other sites are not facilitated.

To make the comparison easy, a number of comparison shopping sites, such as Bargain Finder, Jango[3], DealTime (www.dealtime.com) and so on, have been developed. However, such a site is run by a third party, which is independent from buyers and sellers, and the design of how to compare and what (attribute) to compare depends on the third party. It is told that many owners of shopping site are not happy with such comparison services because they just raise price competitions ignoring the other additional services offered by the sites.

In this paper, we propose a new multiagent based platform for EC where multiple shopping sites or information recommendation sites are integrated in a flexible and interactive manner. The platform provides a virtual space where multiple animated agents, each of which is delivered from an information site, interact with each other and the user to recommend items in a competitive manner.

In this platform, the customer can compare recommended items with those by other agents and find a preferred one by watching competitive recommendations performed by multiple agents on a browser. Through interactions with the customer, agents can learn his/her preference and use it for further recommendations. From a viewpoint of shopping site, this platform provides a virtually open market place where agents can interact with the customer, and the agents can directly recommend items to the customer without intervention of an information broker such as a comparison shopping site.

In Section 2, we show a prototype of competitive information recommendation system called Recommendation Battlers and how multiple animated agents recommend items in a competitive manner. In Section 3, we discuss the system architecture of Recommendation Battlers and in Section 4, we discuss the rational recommendation method employed in the system. In Section 5, we show a macroscopic behavior of Recommendation Battlers through simulation experiments and show how both utilities of agents and the user change depending on the number of agents and the number of items. Finally, we discuss related works and future work in Sections 6 and 7 respectively and summarize this paper in Section 8.

2 Recommendation Battlers: A Prototype for Competitive Restaurant Recommendation

Recommendation Battlers is a prototype of competitive information recommendation system. As shown in Fig. 1, two restaurant recommendation agents; Peedy and Genie appear on a Web browser. Responding to a request from the user such as "I would like to find a good Indian restaurant near Shinsaibashi station," Peedy starts to gather relevant restaurant pages from Yahoo! Gourmet[1] and extracts their addresses and average cost. It then calculate the distance from the

---

[1] http://gourmet.yahoo.co.jp/

nearest station by referring to the addresses. Genie also do the same process but it uses another information source called Kansai Walkerplus[2].

After gathering restaurant information from Web sites, Peedy and Genie start to recommend restaurants in a competitive manner. A typical dialogue is given below.

(1) **User:** "I would like to find a good Indian restaurant near Shinsaibashi station."

(2) **Genie:** (After gathering information from the Kansai Walkerplus) "Do you like Restaurant A? The average cost is around 2,000 Yen and the distance from Shinsaibashi station is 90m."

(3) **User:** "Good."

(4) **Peedy:** (After gathering information from the Yahoo! Gourmet) "Do you like Restaurant B? The average cost is around 2,500 Yen and the distance from Shinsaibashi station is 80m."

(5) **User:** "No good."

(6) **Peedy:** "Do you like Restaurant C? The average cost is around 2,200 Yen and the distance from Shinsaibashi station is 80m."

(7) **User:** "Good."

(8) **Genie:** "I am sure that you like Restaurant D. The average cost is around 1,500 Yen and the distance from Shinsaibashi station is 70m."

(9) **Peedy:** "I have no more restaurant to recommend."

The recommendation is performed by two character agents interacting with each other and the user. An agent recommends a restaurant not only by showing the Web page that contains the restaurant information, but also by telling comments about the average cost and the distance from the nearest station. When needed, it asks whether the user likes the restaurant or not by showing a dialogue box. The user responds to the question by telling "Good" or "No good." Referring to the responses, the agents try to learn the user's preference about the cost and the distance and use it for further recommendations. When either of agents has no more restaurant to recommend, the process terminates.

The order of recommendation depends on the agent's strategy. For example, in the above dialogue, Peedy recommends Restaurant B before Restaurant C although Restaurant C apparently looks better than Restaurant B from the viewpoint of the average cost. In this case, Restaurant B is more beneficial for Peedy because we assume the agent receives more fee from the information provider when it succeeds to broker the restaurant. In this sense, agents in Recommendation Battlers are not cooperative but are competitive. In Section 5, we analyze the macroscopic behavior of agents and show how both utilities of agents and the user change depending on the number of agents and the number of items. However, in any way, agents should recommend restaurants in a rational manner such as recommending items in decreasing price order. We discuss more about a rational recommendation method we employ in Section 4.

Recommendation Battlers has the following advantages.

---

[2] http://www.walkerplus.com/kansai/gourmet/

Fig. 1. A snapshot of Recommendation Battlers. Peedy on the left shows a Web page of an Indian restaurant from YAHOO! Gourmet and says "Do you like Restaurant Gautama? The average cost is around 800 Yen and the distance from Shinsaibashi station is 170m." Genie on the right also shows a Web page of another restaurant called "New Light" from Kansai.Walkerplus.com and the user compare the two restaurants.

- It provides a platform where multiple information sources are integrated in an interactive manner. By preparing another character agent, we can add another information source into this platform.
- It provides a virtual space where multiple animated agents can recommend items in an active and interactive manner. They are just like sales persons who come from different companies. Each sales person talks about his/her goods from his/her own viewpoint. By comparing the talks, we can understand the advantage and disadvantage of goods more than just by hearing from one.
- It provides a space shared among agents. A response from the user to an item recommended by an agent helps other agents learn the user's preference.
- It provides a friendly and easy-to-use interface to the user. Animated agents recommend items to the user in a friendly and active manner, and the user just watches the process of recommendation performed on a browser. Even when requested a response, he/she just does it by telling "Good" or "No good."

3   System Architecture

Recommendation Battlers consists of multiple agents, a recommendation blackboard, and a browser with animated characters, as shown in Fig. 2.

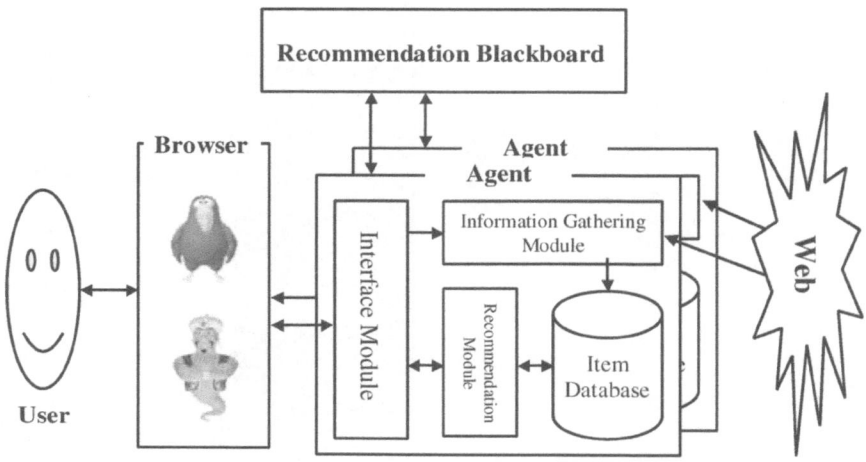

Fig. 2. System Architecture of Recommendation Battlers

3.1   Agent

Agents play the most important role to gather information from WWW information sources and to recommend items through the character interface. An agent consists of an information gathering module, an item database, a recommendation module, and an interface module.

Collecting Information. The information gathering module gathers information from a WWW information source by using an information extraction wrapper. The information extraction wrapper consists of MetaCommander[4] and Template Filter.

MetaCommander is a tool to download Web pages by interpreting a given script. It downloads not only simple Web pages designated by URLs but also those that are accessible through the CGI. This module automatically translates a request from the user into a MetaCommander script depending on the target Web site.

For example, let us assume the user submits a request such as "I would like to find a good Indian restaurant near Shinsaibashi station." The module first extracts keywords "Indian" (a recipe name) and "Shinsaibashi" (a place name in Osaka). Currently we just use a simple keyword matching method between keywords in the user's request and those in the tables of recipe and place names, so the system may misinterpret a request such as "I want to find an Italian restaurant in the Indian quarter."

An example of MetaCommander script is shown as follows.

```
getURL( "http://gourmet.yahoo.co.jp/bin/g_searcho",
  "a1" = "15" ,
  "a2" = "270004" ,
  "oc" = "0" ,
  "jl" = "0205" ) {
  file( "yahoo/searchResult.html" ) {
    print
    }
}
```

getURL is a MetaCommander command to get a Web page through the CGI. The first parameter is the URL of Web page and the other parameters are optional for the CGI depending on the Web site. In this case, "a1=15" means Osaka, "a2=270004" means Shinsaibashi, and "jl=0205" means Indian food. The information gathering module has a table that translates a recipe or place name into a site-dependent code such as "15" for Osaka, "0205" for Indian food, and so on. The command file is to specify the name of file that stores the downloaded Web page.

Template Filter is a tool to extract the designated data by filtering the data from a Web page through a template. Many of Web-based information sites provide information in a fixed format in HTML, so our Template Filter works effectively for such a site.

Gathered items are stored in the Item Database as a set of records in the XML format as below.

```
<?xml version="1.0" ?>
<restaurantData>
  <name>Gautama</name>
  <recipe>Indian</recipe>
  <address>1-18-2 Higashi Shinsaibashi, Chuo-ku, Osaka </address>
  <budget>700--800 Yen (Lunch) <br /> 1100--1500 Yen (Dinner) </budget>
  <url>www.gautama.co.jp</url>
</restaurantData>
```

Currently, we use a very rigid method for wrapping Web information sources. Depending on the target Web source, we have to write a program by using Meta-Commander and Template Filter. We, of course, can reduce the programming task by using these tools much more than by just using a naive programming language such as C or Java.

Recommending Items. Each agent controls the Web browser to display a Web page as a recommendation to the user. At the same time, it also controls the character to utter a comment about the recommendation. When it needs to get a feedback on the recommendation from the user, the character asks a question to the user through a dialogue box. By using a character, we can recommend items in an interactive and friendly manner.

In Recommendation Battlers, we use Microsoft Internet Explorer for the browser and Microsoft Agent as the character interface as shown in Fig. 1. The detail of recommendation method is discussed in Section 4.

3.2   Recommendation Blackboard

The recommendation blackboard is used to share information among agents. Recommendation blackboard shares the following information.

Request from the user: It keeps requests for recommendation from the user. For example, when the user submits a request "I would like to find a good Indian restaurant near Shinsaibashi station," a record `<request> <location> Shinsaibashi </location> <recipe> Indian </recipe> </request>` is stored in the blackboard.

Recommended items: It keeps information on items recommended by agents as a set of records consisting of the recommended item, the list of their attributes and values, and the agent that recommended the item.

Feedback from the user: It keeps feedbacks on recommended items from the user as a set of records consisting of the recommended item and the feedback from the user. The feedback is given by "Good" or "No good."

4   Rational Recommendation

In Recommendation Battlers, multiple agents recommend items in a competitive manner, but also they need to do it in an rational order. For example, when the user has accepted a restaurant whose cost is 2,000 Yen and the distance from the nearest station is 150m, he/she is unlikely to accept another candidate whose cost is 3,000 Yen and the distance is 300m. Agents need to recommend items in a way that the user likely to accept, and we propose a rational recommendation method.

The process of information recommendation is as follows.

1. A request from the user is stored on the recommendation blackboard.
2. Each agent accesses the recommendation blackboard to get the request.
3. Each agent gathers information that meets the request from its own Web information source.
4. An agent proposes an item to the user. If there is no agent that has appropriate items to propose, then the flow terminates.
5. The user gives a feedback to the recommended item when needed.
6. Each agent accesses the recommendation blackboard to get the feedback from the user.
7. Go to step 4.

At the step 4 of the above procedure, each agent monitors the other agent's proposals and the user's responses. It then proposes a new item that is more appropriate given the course of dialogue. We here use a rational recommendation method to make agents propose appropriate items.

To simplify the discussion, we make the following assumptions.

- Each of item targeted has only two attributes (cost and distance). We associate item p with cost c and distance d using the tuple $< p, c, d >$
- The lower an attribute value is, the better it is for the user.
- The user can respond to any proposal using either "Good" or "No good."

Our method categorizes items into three groups: R, I, U.

R: A group of items that the user is likely to accept.
I: A group of items that the user is likely not to accept.
U: A group of items for which it is unknown whether they would be accepted or not by the user.

Items placed in R are those whose attribute values are better than those of the items already accepted. On the other hand, items placed in I are those whose attribute values are worse than those of the items already accepted. Items that do not fall into R or in I are placed into category U. For example, let us assume that only one item $< p_1, 2000, 150 >$ has been accepted. It follows that item $< p_2, 1500, 100 >$ would be placed into R because its attribute values are better than those of p_1. Item $< p_3, 3000, 200 >$ is placed in I because its attribute values are worse than those of p_1. Item $< p_4, 1500, 200 >$ and $< p_5, 2500, 100 >$ are placed in U because it is unknown which attribute is more important to the user at this time.

It is obvious that items in I should not be proposed to the user. On the other hand, items in R and U could be of interest to the user. For an item in U, it is unclear if the user will accept it or not, so the agent needs to ask for confirmation, as in utterances (2), (4), and (6) in Section 2. It is highly likely that the user will accept an item in R, so the agent does not need to ask for confirmation as in utterance (8) in mentioned Section 2.

In the rational recommendation method, the three groups, R, I, and U, must be updated according to the last proposal and the response from the user. We here explain how to update the groups.

Proposal from R. Let us assume that $< C, 2200, 80 >$ has been accepted and one agent proposes $< D, 1500, 70 >$. As D is in R, the agent does not need to seek the user's confirmation. When the agent proposes D, group boundaries are updated as shown in Fig. 3. Items in region $(x > 1500)$ and $(y > 70)$ become members of I, items in region $(x \leq 1500)$ and $(y \leq 70)$ become members of R, and the remaining items fall into U. This update corresponds to utterance (8) mentioned in Section 2.

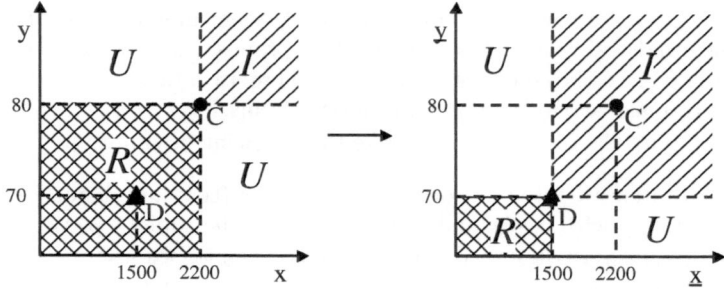

Fig. 3. Update of boundaries when a proposal is made from R.

Proposal from U. Let us assume that $< A, 2000, 90 >$ has been accepted and the agent proposes $< C, 2200, 80 >$. As C is in U, the agent needs to get confirmation from the user. If the user answers "Good," the boundaries change as shown in Fig. 4. Items in region $(x > 2000)$ and $(y > 90)$ and region $(x > 2200)$ and $(y > 80)$ become members of I, and items in region $(x \leq 2000)$ and $(y \leq 90)$ and in region $(x \leq 2200)$ and $(y \leq 80)$ become members of R. The remaining items fall in U. This corresponds to utterances (2) and (6) mentioned in Section 2.

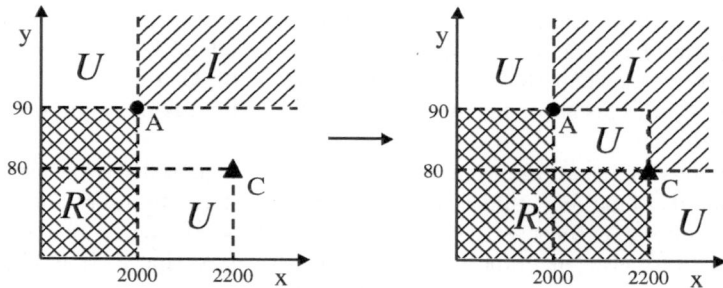

Fig. 4. Update of boundaries when a proposal is made from U and the response is "Good."

In the above situation, if the user answers "No good," boundaries change as shown in Fig. 5. As B is not accepted, boundaries for R do not change. Boundaries for I are updated in the same way as when the user answers "Good." This corresponds to utterance (4) mentioned in Section 2.

With the rational recommendation method, an agent can propose items that are appropriate given the course of dialogue. There may be multiple items in regions R and I, but how to choose one of them depends on the agent's strategy. If the agent is rewarded for securing the user's acceptance, it may well propose items in decreasing order of the reward amount.

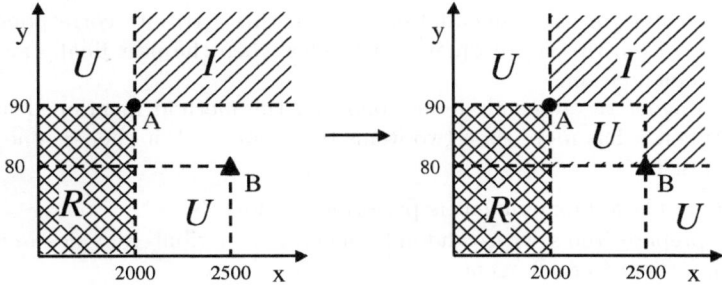

Fig. 5. Update of boundaries when a proposal is made from U and the response is "No good."

Here we discuss cases where agents deal with only two attributes for simplicity of discussion, but we can apply the above method to more than three attributes cases.

5   Macroscopic Behavior of Recommendation Battlers

In this section, we show the competitive nature of Recommendation Battlers affects the output (an item that is finally accepted by the user) of the system from a macroscopic view. It is supposed that the behavior of Recommendation Battlers changes depending on the number of agents. When there is only a single agent, it is clear that it behaves like an independent recommendation system and no competition occurs. As the number of agents increases, the agents become more competitive to recommend items to the user, and that leads to an increase of the user's utility and an decrease of the agents' utility. In this section, we verify the above supposition through simulation experiments.

5.1   Simulation Settings

As settings for simulation, we have the following assumptions.

- Each item C_i has three independent attributes $x_{i,1}, x_{i,2}, x_{i,3}$ and each attribute takes a value from 0 to 1 at random.
- The user's utility, when he/she accepts an item C_i, is calculated from the first and second attribute values as follows.

$$U_u(C_i) = \frac{1}{2}x_{i,1} + \frac{1}{2}x_{i,2}, \tag{1}$$

where C_i is an item whose attribute values are specified as $x_{i,1}$ and $x_{i,2}$. In a restaurant recommendation system, these attributes correspond to the average cost and the distance from the nearest station.
- The agent's utility, when its recommended item is finally accepted by the user, is identical with the third attribute value of the item.

$$U_a(C_i) = x_{i,3} \tag{2}$$

In a restaurant recommendation system, this attribute corresponds to the reward from the an information provider when the user finally accepts the recommendation.

– Each agent recommends items following the method mentioned in Section 4. When it has more than two items to recommend, it chooses one with the highest $U_a(\cdot)$.

Our simulation experiment is performed as follows.

1. We prepare items with randomly generated attributed values and equally assign them to each agent.
2. We then run a system to get an item that is finally accepted by the user and calculate the utility values of the user and the wining agent.
3. We perform the above experiments 1000 times and calculate the average of the utilities.

5.2   Results

We show the utilities of the user and the winning agent in Fig. 6 and Fig. 7 respectively when we change the number of agents and the number of items.

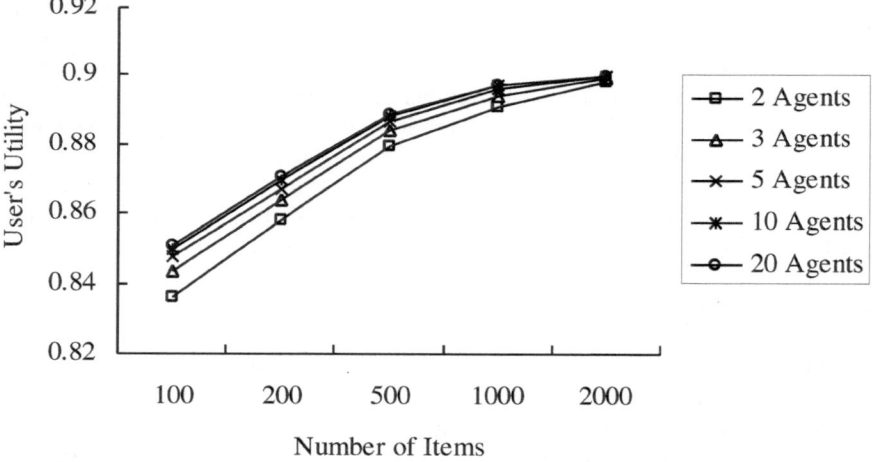

Fig. 6. User's Utility

Fig. 6 and Fig. 7 show that the user's utility increases but that the agents' utility decreases as the number of agents increases. This is because more agents raise more competitions among them and this makes a benefit to the user. The user can get an item that is more preferred. The results also show that both of agent's and the user's utilities increase as the number of items increases. This is because the probability that the finally accepted item is beneficial for both of the user and the agent increases as the number of items increases.

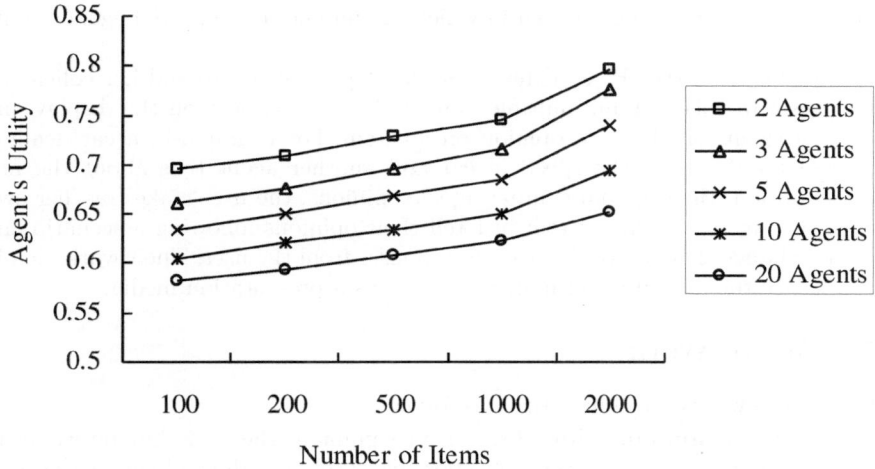

Fig. 7. The Winning Agent's Utility

6   Related Work

Information recommendation system provides information to the user from the system side. This is contrasting with conventional information retrieval systems in which the user needs to operate a system by forming and submitting a query. In other words, for a user to obtain information, the user is passive in an information recommendation system, and he/she is active in an information retrieval system. In general, an information recommendation is effective when the user does not have clear requirement or preference nor has a prior knowledge about information sources. Hence, information recommendation systems facilitate a function to estimate the true preference of the user and a function to interact with the user. ATA(Automated Travel Assistant)[6] and Expert Clerk[7] are examples of information recommendation systems.

ATA is a system for assisting the user in his/her travel planning. In ATA, CCA(candidate/critique agent) learns the user's model through conversational interactions with the user. CCA represents the user's model as a multi-attribute utility function and learns it by adjusting the function and the weight.

ExpertClerk is a system that navigate a customer on the Internet by using a commodity database and a life-like agent. In ExpertClerk, a life-like agent talks with the customer in a natural language by using two navigation modes; NBA(Navigation by asking) and NBP(Navigation by proposing). NBA produces questions that gain most information on the user's preference by using a hierarchical concept base. NBP displays three contrasting goods to the user to know the user's preference from another viewpoint.

Both of ATA and ExpertClerk are information recommendation systems that try to recommend items to the user through interactions with him/her, but each of them is a single agent system in which the number of employed agent is only one.

Inhabited Market Place[1] has been developed by Andre and her colleagues at DFKI. In this system, multiple animated agents appear on the display and each of them tells its own opinion on an item. For example in a car dealing, an agent tells about the speed of car and another agent tells about the fuel consumption. Hearing and comparing the opinions, the user makes his/her own decision. Agents in this system just tell their opinions following a scenario and do not change them according to the responses from the user. Their work mainly emphasize the advantage of multiple agents as a presentation media.

7   Future Work

Our future works are summarized as follows.

Efficient recommendation. From a viewpoint of the user, he/she wants to obtain preferred items as soon as possible rather avoiding a long transactions with the agents. We need to continue to study how to reduce the number of recommendations when there are a large number of items to recommend.

Shared Ontology. Recommendation Battlers provides a platform where multiple agents compete to recommend items. In the framework, an agent can use responses from the user to items recommended by other agents. To facilitate this mechanism in a general context, agents need to mutually understand the attributes of recommended items. To this end, we need a common ontology that can be shared by agents.

Conversation Capability. In our current prototypes, the user interact with agents by saying only "Good" or "No good," but this is restrictive as a relevance feedback mechanism. For example, a user may respond "No good" because of an experience of bad taste not because of the price or the location of restaurant, but the agent cannot understand the true meaning of "No good." For more complex interactions with the agents, natural language processing or conversation capability is required for agents.

Scalability. In this paper, we just discuss Recommendation Battlers consisting of two or three agents. We need to further study cases where many agents compete to recommend items. At first, it seems difficult that a single user interacts with many agents one time because of at least two reasons. First, the user gets tired of a long transaction of recommendation involving many agents. Second, it is difficult to display many agents on a single browser on the user's PC at once.

A possible solution maybe employ a middle agent between the user and the recommendation agents. At first, a user interacts with a small number of agents and the middle agent records the interactions. When there are more agents to recommend items, they first interact with the middle agent, and the middle agent checks them whether they have at least one item worth to recommend referring to the history of previous recommendations. Only when the middle agent permits, a recommendation agent can directly interact with the user.

8 Conclusion

We proposed a competitive information recommendation system where multiple animated agents recommend items in a competitive and interactive manner. We discussed the advantages of the framework through showing a prototype applied to restaurant recommendation. We also showed how its macroscopic behavior was affected by the number of participating agents.

Including the future work discussed in the previous section, we also continue to work to show the applicability of this framework to real-world domains.

Acknowledgement. This work is partly supported by grants from NEDO (New Energy and Industrial Technology Development Organization), Hitachi Cooperation, and the Ministry of Education, Culture, Sports, Science and Technology.

References

1. Andre, E., Rist, T.: Adding Life-Like Synthetic Characters to the Web. Cooperative Information Agents IV, Lecture Notes in Artificial Intelligence 1860. Springer (2000) 1–13
2. Balabanovic, M., Shoham, Y. Fab: Content-Based, Collaborative Recommendation. Communications of the ACM, 40(3). (1997) 66–72
3. Doorenbos, R.B., Etzioni, O., Weld, D.S. A Scalable Comparison-Shopping Agent for the World-WIde Web. International Conference on Autonomous Agents (1997) 39–48
4. Kitamura, Y., Nozaki, T., and Tatsumi, S. A Script-Based WWW Information Integration Support System and Its Application to Genome Databases, Systems and Computers in Japan, 29(14). (1998) 32–40
5. Kitamura Y., Yamada T., Kokubo T., Mawarimichi Y., Yamamoto T. and Ishida T. Interactive Integration of Information Agents on the Web. Cooperative Information Agents V, Lecture Notes in Artificial Intelligence 2182. (2001) 1–13
6. Linden, G. N. L., Hanks, S. Interactive Assessment of User Preference Models: The Automated Travel Assistant, Proceedings of the Sixth International Conference on User Modeling. (1997) 67–78
7. Shimazu, H. ExpertClerk: Navigating Shoppers' Buying Process with the Combination of Asking and Proposing. Proceedings of the Seventeenth International Joint Conference on Artificial Intelligence (2001) 1443–1448.

Agents That Model and Learn User Interests for Dynamic Collaborative Filtering

Gulden Uchyigit and Keith Clark

Department of Computing,
Imperial College of Science, Technology and Medicine,
London SW7 2BZ.
{gu1,klc}@doc.ic.ac.uk

Abstract. *Collaborative Filtering* systems suggest items to a user because it is highly rated by some other user with similar tastes. Although these systems are achieving great success on web based applications, the tremendous growth in the number of people using these applications require performing many recommendations per second for millions of users. Technologies are needed that can rapidly produce high quality recommendations for large community of users.

In this paper we present an agent based approach to collaborative filtering where agents work on behalf of their users to form shared "interest groups", which is a process of pre-clustering users based on their interest profiles. These groups are *dynamically* updated to reflect the user's evolving interests over time. We further present a multi-agent based simulation of the architecture as a means of evaluating the system.

1   Introduction

The huge amount of Information available in the currently evolving world-wide information infrastructure can easily overwhelm end-users, a situation that is likely to worsen in the future, unless the end user has the ability to filter information based on its relevance. *Content-based filtering* systems infer a user's profile from the contents of the items the user previously rated and recommends additional items of interest according to this profile. In contrast, *Collaborative filtering* systems [2], [4], [13], [7], [12], work by collecting human judgements (known as ratings) for items in a given domain and correlating people who share the same information needs or tastes. These systems generally have the following problems. They rely on an overlap of user rated items (i.e if the user's did not rate any common items then their profiles can not be correlated). The enormous number of items available to rate in many domains makes the probability of finding user's with similar ratings significantly low. Since, recommender systems are used by a large number of users, correlation based algorithms need to search through a large neighbourhood of user's in real time.

An alternative approach and one that we use is *content based collaborative filtering* techniques. Such systems [19], [20], [21] combine both the content and collaborative information.

M. Klusch, S. Ossowski, and O. Shehory (Eds.): CIA 2002, LNAI 2446, pp. 152–163, 2002.
© Springer-Verlag Berlin Heidelberg 2002

We utilise the content of the items the users have rated to infer their interest profile and we then use these profiles to *dynamically form* interest groups which are continuously updated with changing user interests. These interest groups are smaller to analyse compared with the correlation based algorithms where a large neighbourhood of users need to be analysed every time a collaboration recommendation is to be given.

The paper is structured as follows. We first present the multi-agent architecture of our system, along with a brief description of the functionality of the agents involved. We then explain the method of constructing and updating a user's interest profile. This is followed by a description of the collaborative filtering framework, in which we present our algorithm for dynamicaly updating the different interest groups. This is followed by an overview of the multi-agent based simulation of the framework. Finally, our intended future work is presented.

2   System Overview

The personalised TV recommender (for more details see [8]) provides the user with recommendations from online TV guides and other web accessible TV program information. It creates, learns and modifies the user profile automatically based on user feedback on the programs that they have already seen.

A recommended list of programs is displayed to the user upon request or regularly on a daily basis. The user can also request more detailed descriptions or reviews of the recommended programs. The user can decide to watch recommended programs or make his own entirely different selection. The user is asked to give feedback on the programs that they watched the next time they view new recommendation.

A network of agents work behind the scenes, completely hidden from the user to model and learn user preferences in order to provide the program recommendations. A pictorial overview of the agent architecture is given in Figure 1. For each user interacting with the system there is an associated *interface agent* and a *recommender agent*. The interface agent handles all user interactions with the system. It is also able to map user requests and actions into a form understandable by the recommender agent. The recommender agent, on the other hand, does not directly interact with the user but it is the only agent in the system that knows about the user's viewing preferences. Since the recommender agent has to accomplish numerous complex tasks related both to the user and the other agents, it needs to have a picture of the current state of affairs. In particular its knowledge component has a representation for:

- *the user's world*, the kind of viewing habits a user has, his current viewing interests and his past history with respect to the viewed programs. This information is represented in the form of a user profile.
- *the available agents* and their capabilities. It is able to coordinate a number of agents and knows what tasks they can accomplish, what resources they have and their availability.

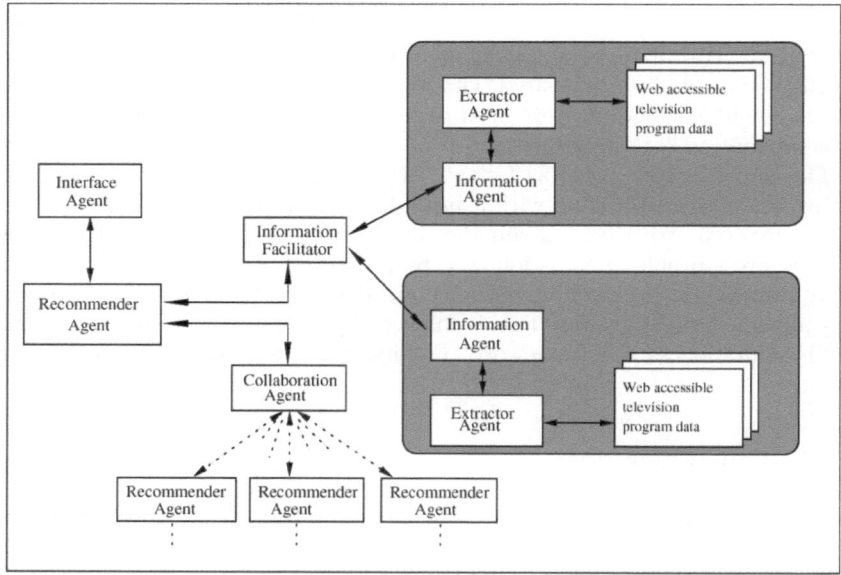

Fig. 1. Overview of the Agent Architecture

The system also supports a collection of information sites. The notion of an information site is used to describe a logical entity that contains a set of WWW sites. At each site there is an *extractor agent* and an *information agent*. The role of the former is to extract Television guide information, the role of the latter is to maintain a database of extracted information. For all the sites there is only one *information facilitator agent* that is able to accept queries from the network of recommender agents. It is then able to route these queries to the information agents that are able to answer the query. The inter-agent communication is based on standard Knowledge Query Manipulation (KQML) [11] performatives.

For the collaborative recommendation component one *collaboration agent* exits. Recommender agents register their user's interest profile with this agent. It then uses these registered interest profiles to automatically and dynamically create and maintain interest groups within main categories of programs. For example, there is a set of interest groups for *situation comedies*, another set of interest groups for *documentaries* and so on. When one of the users reports that they have unexpectedly enjoyed a program (unexpectedly because the program was not recommended by their agent) their recommender agent will immediately inform the collaboration agent. This will then route this information to all the recommender agents in the same interest group. Each of these agents will recommend this new program to its user if the user hasn't yet seen it. They can then catch the program on a repeat or on its next episode, if it is a series or a serial.

More generally, each time the user gives feedback on the programs they have watched the recommender agent updates the user's profile using descriptions of the viewed programs. This in turn causes the interest groups to be updated. It may be the case that an updated user profile is moved from one interest group to another by the collaboration agent, or it may be used to form the nucleus of a new grouping.

3   User Profiling: Initialisation and Updating

In this section we briefly describe the format of a user's interest (or viewing) profile. Each user's profile is divided into categories corresponding to program categories such as *Dramas, Comedies,* in total we have 29 fixed categories that a profile can be divided into. Each category in turn is represented as weighted tuples of keywords (actually word stems) produced from the descriptions of programs the user has liked and disliked. For instance Table 1 is an illustration of a user's preferences in the Drama category (i.e the types of Drama programs the user likes). The fact that this user has a drama category in his profile indicates his interest in Drama programs in general but the existence of "hospital" (i.e hospit) in his profile indicates his *high* interest in hospital drama programs.

Table 1. Keywords representing a user's program preferences for the Drama category

drama	murder
doctor	victim
hospit	killer

This type of keyword representation of the user interests has the problem that small amounts of training data will lead to selection of keywords that accidentally appear in the data and that are really irrelevant in discriminating between interesting and uninteresting programs. Using irrelevant features makes the learning task much harder and leads to a lower classification accuracy. As a solution to this problem alternative methods have been proposed to initialise the user profile. For instance in [3], these keywords are elicited *explicitly* from the user. However, this process of profile initialisation is too tedious for the user and will often result in a user being unable to specify the words that best describe his interests in a particular domain, especially if the user is unfamiliar with this domain. To overcome this problem we use a *rapid profile initialisation method* (for more details see [10]), where the agent automatically and continuously extracts web accessible program information and determines the informative terms that most frequently occur in the descriptions of TV programs for each program category. This is done in the following way. Textual content of program descriptions for different categories are extracted from web sources. The content is then parsed and all *stop-words* (or non informative terms such as "a", "the", "and", "to" etc.) are removed. The words are then stemmed using the porter stemmer algorithm [22]. Then our feature selection algorithm (for details of the algorithm see [9]) is used to assign a weight to each word. These words are then sorted according to their weights and the top scoring words are selected as the representative keywords for each category.

As a result of this process each category is described with a set of informative terms (keywords). Table 2 shows some of the keywords which have been automatically extracted from the content of random selection of *Drama* program descriptions.

Table 2. Feature words extracted from a set of drama programs

blackmail	dilemma	law	anger	crime	secret	disast	suspens
terrifi	catastroph	mysteriou	affair	drama	investig	hostag	victim
hunt	fight	doom	tragic	destroi	evil	trial	court
judg	crimin	murder	viciou	scam	violent	romanc	emergen
hospit	hostag	danger	ritual	pressur	war	victim	diseas
doctor	captiv	polic	threaten	guilti	stalker	fear	pain
shock	physiolog	deadli	plot	blood	killer		

Recommender agents then use these sets of pre-defined keywords to initialise a user profile using user feedback. At first registration the user is asked to rate some programs he has seen within the past two weeks. The agent then uses the descriptions of the programs the user rated and the list of pre-defined keywords to initialise the user profile. For instance consider the program description illustrated in Figure 2, further consider that this program was liked by the user. To initialise the user's profile the agent repeatedly searches for occurrences of the pre-defined keywords from Table 2 within the description of this rated program to produce the subset of keywords of Table 1. Each time a keyword from Table 2 is found its count is incremented by 1. Finally, a probability is determined for each found keyword using the total number of times it appears in the set of programs which has been liked with the total number of times the keyword appears in the descriptions of any program which has been viewed, and rated for that program category. The advantage of the prior keyword selection process is that a user need only rate a few items for the agent to be able to determine which keywords to select for representing in the user profile. Our previous results [10] show that this process of rapid profile initialisation significantly improves classification accuracy.

Later on, as the user gives more feedback, the agent uses this feedback to update the user profile to reflect the users changing interests. This involves an updating of the prior probabilities of the keywords within the user profile. For

---

Murder on the Hour.
Lighthearted drama about a hospital doctor
who uses his sleuthing skills to help the crack
baffling cases. A serial killer appears to be
selecting victims who had recently come close
to death, but were on their way to making full
recoveries. In addition, every murder is taking
place on the hour.

Fig. 2. A description of a Drama program which has been liked by the user.

this we use *conjugate priors* [3]. Conjugate priors are a traditional technique
from Bayesian statistics to update probabilities from data [17].

4   Building and Maintaining Interest Groups

In our system the collaboration agent clusters user's into interest groups based on
the similarity of their profiles for each interest category. Users are not clustered
based on their entire profile contents since it may be the case that two users
have similar tastes in *comedies* but quite different tastes with respect to *sports*
programs.

For the process of clustering we adapted the Hierarchical Agglomerative Clustering (HAC) algorithm [14], [15], [16], to cluster user profiles. The HAC process
repeatedly merges the two most similar clusters until only one cluster remains.
This results in a *single* hierarchy or *dendrogram* to use the correct terminology.

Our adaption of this algorithm for clustering users based on their profiles
is as follows. The first phase involves *initialisation* where each separate interest
profile is represented as one element cluster. There then follows the process of
merging the two most similar clusters until one of the *two* possible termination
conditions are satisfied. Either, the similarity of any two clusters is less than 0.7
or only one cluster remains. For the similarity measure between clusters, we use
vector similarity [5]. Figure 3 is the pseudo-code of our algorithm for clustering
the user profiles in a given category.

Figure 4 shows the clusters formed for three different categories of interest.
At present we keep the similarity levels fixed for every category. One of our future
plans is to determine experimentally the *optimal* similarity levels for the different categories. For the formation of the *interest groups*, the collaboration agent
generates the clusters that have an internal profile similarity greater than 0.7. In
Figure 4 the Drama category has three clusters (clusters are determined by hor-
izontal lines in the dendrogram). These are $\{d_1, d_2, d_3, d_4\}$, $\{ d_5, d_6 \}$, $\{d_7, d_8, d_9\}$
where, $d_1, d_2, d_3, d_4, d_5, d_6, d_7, d_8, d_9$ are the individual interest profiles for the
drama category of nine people.

For maintaining the interest groups the agent re-clusters the profiles on a
weekly basis. As a result of re-evaluating the clusters, the clusters are updated

Input

P=$\{p_1, p_2, ..p_N\}$

Initialise

- start with clusters that contain a single user profile
  $C=\{c_1, c_2, ..c_N\}$ *a set of clusters*
  $c_i=\{p_i\}$ for $1 \leq i \leq N$
  $S = 0$

– Repeat the following steps iteratively until there is only one cluster left **or** $S \leq 0.7$
  for $k = N - 1$ **to** 1 **do**

– identify the two clusters that are most similar

$$S = (c_j, c_m) = arg\max sim(c_j, c_m)$$

where, $sim(c_j, c_m)$ is the cosine similarity

$$\frac{\mathbf{c}_j \bullet \mathbf{c}_m}{|\mathbf{c}_j| \times |\mathbf{c}_m|}$$

– merge them to form a single cluster
  $c^* = \{c_j \cup c_m\}$

– update the clusters
  $C_k = C_{k-1} - \{c_{i,j}, c_{i,m}\} + c^*$

Fig. 3. Pseudo-code of our clustering algorithm

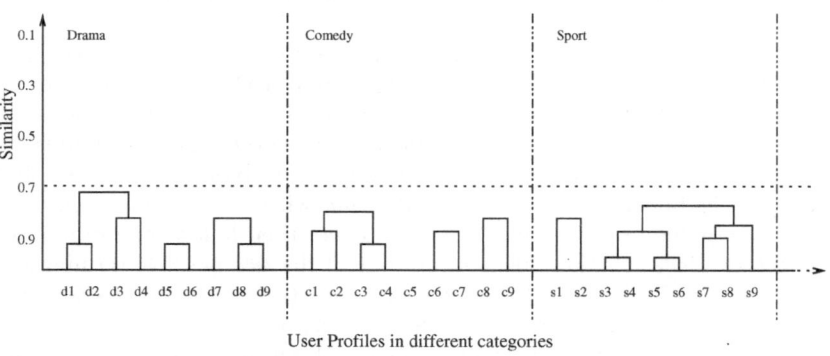

Fig. 4. Profile hierarchies for different categories

to reflect the user's changing interests. This may result in new clusters being formed or existing clusters being augmented.

5   Implementation and Evaluations

5.1   Multi Agent Based Simulation of the User Community

The collaborative recommendation component based on viewing recommendations that come from users with similar tastes requires a reasonable large community of users. We have not got the resources for such a field trial of the system, so instead we decided to simulate such a large user community, representing each user as an agent (see figure 5).This presents the problem of how to represent

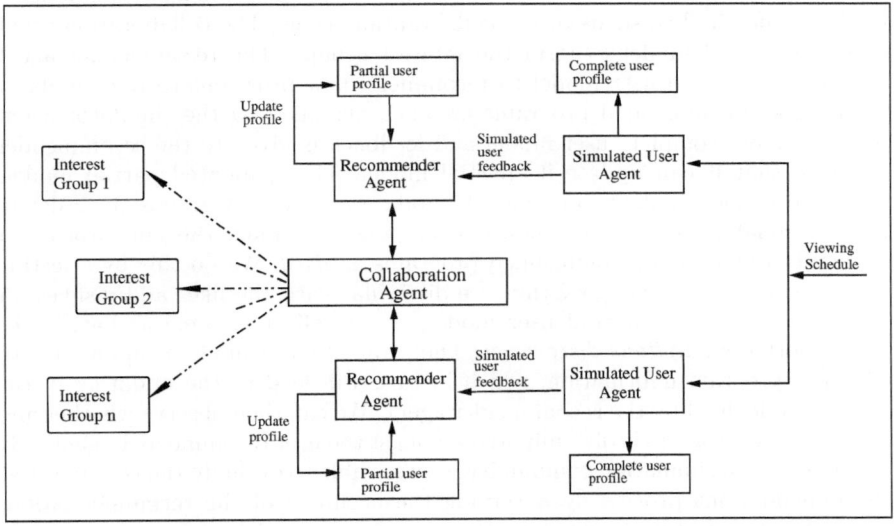

Fig. 5. The Simulation Process

the viewing tastes of each user, tastes that have to be approximated to by the user's recommender agent, as it develops its user model. We decided that the way in which the recommender agent models the user, by weighted tuples of words for liked and disliked types of programs in each program category, was a reasonable way to model a user in their simulating agent. This model is hidden inside the simulating agent and is used by that agent to give 'viewing' feedback to its recommender agent which is trying to learn this model.

This approach reduced the problem of simulating a user community to the need to generate a set of different user profiles, each of which was reasonable internally consistent, to represent some plausible community of viewers. We did this by randomly choosing for each program category, a set of programs that some viewer might have liked and disliked over a three months viewing schedule. Text descriptions of these programs were then used to build the same user model for that program category that would be built by a recommender agent. We then rejected those profiles in which the liked and disliked profiles were too similar. This is so that simulated user profiles have differing likes and dislikes to represent each interest category. We then constructed a complete user model by randomly selecting a set of likes and dislikes profiles to cover all the program categories.

The next process is to simulate the user feedback process which is used by the recommender agents to learn the user profiles. We start by having the simulation agent use its assigned user model to classify as liked or disliked each program in a three week viewing schedule and to give this information to its recommender agent. The recommender agent uses this to build a partial model of its user which it then sends to the collaboration agent. The collaboration agent uses this partial model to form the interest groups. The recommender agent also uses its partial user model to recommend new programs to the simulator agent. The recommended programs are then classified by the simulator agent using its more complete user model and feedback is given to the recommender agent so that it can update its partial model. These updated partial models are used by the collaboration agent to update the interest groups. In order to test the collaborative recommendation component we make the simulator agent randomly report non-recommended programs as *liked*. We do this by selecting programs from each category that are dissimilar with the likes and dislikes for each category of the partial user model, this in effect is same as having the user report *serendipitous discoveries*. The complete user model is updated with this new program information, which in turn will lead to the updating of the partial model held by the recommender agent. We can then observe whether and how this new program is disseminated amongst the user recommender agents. By building such a simulation community we were able to evaluate the collaborative recommendations process by observing the accuracy of the recommendations given. We could also observe how the partial user model evolves over time to become a near complete user model and also to observe how these changes will be reflected in formation and updating of the interest groups.

5.2   Experimental Results

We conducted a number of simulation experiments to assess the validity of our architecture. One of which was to observe the performance with the changing user interests. To do this we observed what would happen to the performance when there is a sudden change in the user profiles. Figure 6 shows results of the simmulation experiments performed within the Drama category. We report the average accuracy of the predictions given to all the interest groups over 45 iterations. At each iteration the partial profiles are re-clustered (i.e the interst groups are updated). After iteration 13 we purposely got the simmulated user agents to report programs that are different to the partial profiles. This is like having user's discover new programs that were not recommended to them by their recommender agents. Only some of the simmulated user agents had their complete profiles updated with this new program information. At iteration 14 this rapid change within the simmulated user's profile is indicated as a sudden drop in the average accuracy of the predictions. But this is followed by a steady increase in the accurcy of the predictions with the other iterations indicating recovery of the interest groups as they are dynamically updated.

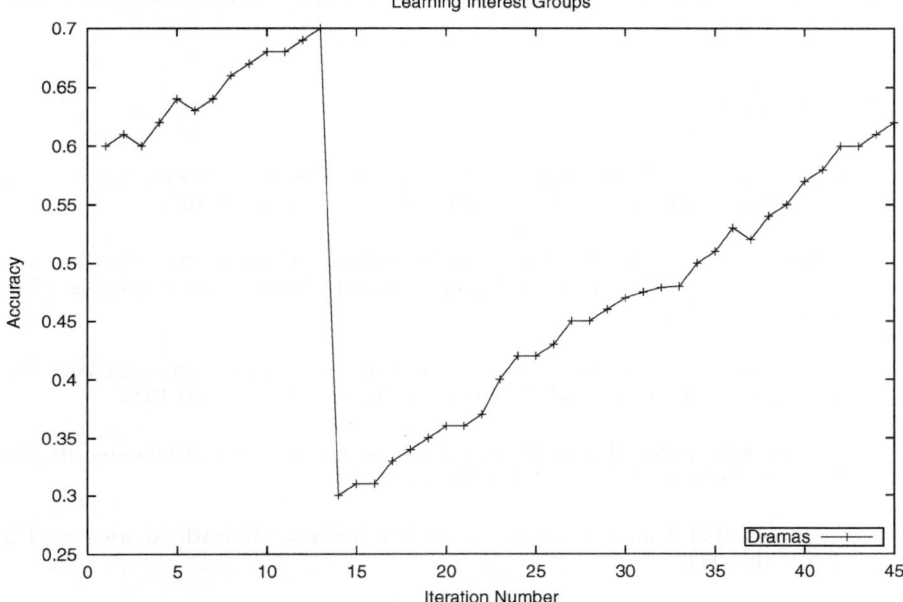

Fig. 6. Results of the simulation

6   Summary and Future Work

In this paper we presented an agent-based collaborative filtering technique that gives users TV program recommendations. The system automatically learns a user profile for each user. The user intrest profiles for each category are then clustered by the agents on behalf of their users in order to form interest groups of users with similar interests. When one user in the group then discovers an interesting program then every user in their interest group for the category of the program are informed. Our approach to collaborative filtering makes it possible for users evolving interests to be considered in the collaborative filtering process.

Further, we presented the evaluation of our algorithm with a multi-agent based simulation, where agents have been used to simulate users and their viewing preferences, along with simulation of user feedback. The results of the simulation demonstrated that the accuracy of recommendations increases as interest groups are updated with changing user interests.

In our future work we intend to determine experimentally optimal similarity measures for the clusters of each category. We would also like to expand this idea to have the agents automatically determine these similarity measures. We also intend to evaluate our system with real users and compare its performance with that of other collaborative filtering methods and also measure its performance in different domains.

References

1. Kautz H, Selman B and Shah M. Refferal Web: Combining Social Networks and Collaborative Filtering. Communications of the ACM. March 1997.

2. J. Konstan, B. Miller, D. Maltz, J. Herlocker,L. Gordon and J.Riedl.: GroupLens:Applying Collaborative Filtering to Usenet News. Communications of the ACM. March 1997.

3. M. Pazzani and D. Bilsus.: Syskill and Webert: Identifying Interesting Web sites. Proceedings of 13th National Conference in AI. pp. 54-61. AAAI 1996.

4. P. Maes. Agents that Reduce Work and Information Overload. Communications of the ACM, Volume 37, No. 7, July 1994. pp.30-40.

5. G.Salton and M. Gill. Introduction to Modern Information Retrieval. McGraw-Hill, New York, 1983.

6. Goldberg, D., Nichols, D. Oki, B.M. and Terry D, Using Collaborative Filtering to Weave an Information Tapestry. Communications of the ACM 1992.

7. Shardanand, U., and Maes, P. Social information Filtering: Algorithm for Automating "Word of Mouth". In Proceedings of CHI'95 1995.

8. Uchyigit G, Carlin B, Quak E, and Cunningham, J. Agents in the Box. Proceedings of HCI International '99 (8th International Conference on Human Computer Interaction) Munich, Germany 1999.

9. Uchyigit, G. and Clark, K. An Agent Based Electronic Program Guide. Workshop on Personalization in Future TV in conjunction with 2nd International Conference on Adaptive Hypermedia and Adaptive Web Based Systems , May 2002 Malaga Spain, (Springer-Verlag Lecture Notes in Computer Science).

10. Uchyigit, G. Feature Selection for Rapid Profile Initialisation: Implementation and Design. Technical Report ICSTM-756-01, Dept of Computer Science, Imperial College, Science Technology and Medicine. 2001.

11. Tim Finin, Y. Labrou and J. Mayfield.: KQML as an agent communications language. Software Agents edited by J. Bradshaw AAAI Press/MIT Press. 1997 p.391-316.

12. Loren Terveen, Will Hill, Brian Amento, David McDonald and Josh Creter.:PHOAKS: A System for Sharing Recommendations. Communications of the ACM. March 1997.

13. Henry Kautz, Bart Selman and Mehul Shah.: Refferal Web: Combining Social Networks and Collaborative Filtering. Communications of the ACM. March 1997.

14. Everitt, B. "Cluster Analysis", Haslsted Press (John Wiley and Sons), New York, 1980.

15. Rasmussen, E. "Information Retrieval, Data Structure and Algorithms", Chapter 16: Clustering Algorithms, W. B. Frakes and R.Baeza-Yates, eds., Prentice Hall 1992.

16. Willett P. , "Recent trends in hierarchic document clustering: a critical review", in Information Processing and Management, 34:5, 1988.

17. Heckerman, D. A tutorial on Learning with Bayesian Networks, Technical Report, MSR-TR-95-06, Microsoft Corporation 1996.

18. Blekin N. J. and Croft W. B., Information filtering and Information Retrieval: Two sides of the same coin?. Communications of the ACM, 35(12):29-38 December 1992.

19. Basu C, Hirsh H. and Cohen W. Recommendation as classification: Using Social and content-based information in recommendation. In proceedings of the Fifteenth National Conferenece on Artificial Intellegence, pages 714-720, 1998.

20. Claypool M, Gokhale A. and Miranda T. Combining content-based and collaborative filters in an online newspaper. In proceedings of the ACM SIGIR Workshop on Recommender Systems- Impelementation and Evaluation, 1999.

21. Good N, Schafer J. B, Konstan J. A, Brochers A, Sarwar B. M, Herlocker J. L, and Riedl J. Combining collaborative filtering with personal agents for better recommendations. In proceedings of the Siteenth National Conference on Artificial Intellegence, pages 439-446 1999.

22. Porter, M. (1980) An Algorithm for suffix stripping. Program (Automated Library and Information Systems), 14(3):130-137

Opinion-Based Filtering through Trust

Miquel Montaner, Beatriz López, and Josep Lluís de la Rosa

Institut d'Informàtica i Aplicacions
Agents Research Laboratory
Universitat de Girona
Campus Montilivi
17071 Girona, Spain
{mmontane, blopez, peplluis}@eia.udg.es

Abstract. Recommender systems help users to identify particular items that best match their tastes or preferences. When we apply the agent theory to this domain, a standard centralized recommender system becomes a distributed world of recommender agents. Therefore, due to the agent's world, a new information filtering method appears: the opinion-based filtering method. Its main idea is to consider other agents as personal entities which you can rely on or not. Recommender agents can ask their reliable *friends* for an opinion about a particular item and filter large sets of items based on it. Reliability is expressed through a trust value with which each agent labels its neighbors. Thus, the opinion-based filtering method needs a model of trust in the collaborative world. The model proposed emphasizes proactiveness since the agent looks for other agents in a situation of lack of information instead of remaining passive or providing either a negative or empty answer to the user. Finally, our social model of trust exploits interactiveness while preserving privacy.

1 Introduction

Recommender systems make recommendations to users according to the information available. Such information includes data on items as well as different profiles of other users on the web. Since there is so much information, a fundamental issue is to select the most appropriate information with which to make decisions. In other words, an information filtering method is essential. Usually, three information filtering approaches have been used in the state of the art for making recommendations [11]: demographic filtering, content-based filtering and collaborative filtering. Moreover, hybrid approaches among them have been proved useful.

However, when we apply the agent theory to recommender systems, a standard centralized recommender system becomes a distributed world of recommender agents [7]. Each user has his/her own recommender agent that is able to interact with others. In an open environment such as Internet, however, the interaction of a recommender agent with all possible agents in order to obtain the best recommendation for the user seems unapproachable. The solution we propose in this paper is a new information filtering method: the opinion-based

M. Klusch, S. Ossowski, and O. Shehory (Eds.): CIA 2002, LNAI 2446, pp. 164–178, 2002.
© Springer-Verlag Berlin Heidelberg 2002

filtering method. Its main idea is to consider other agents as personal entities which you can rely on or not. Reliability is expressed through a trust value with which each agent labels its neighbors. Trust is one of the most important social concepts that helps human agents to cope with their social environment, and is present in all human interaction [5]. Some efforts have been made in the study of social models of trust in market environments [12], where several agents compete for their individual profit as well as in other environments where agents need to delegate actions to other agents [2]. Trust, however, is also important in filtering information environments where recommender agents asses users. Just as in the real world people ask their friends for advice on interesting items, an agent should be able to ask only reliable agents. For example, a common situation is when somebody asks a friend for advice about a new restaurant. Another common situation is when someone discovers a new restaurant and wants to know the opinion of his/her friends about it or when somebody tells you something about a new restaurant, you want to check this information with your friends. If they already know the restaurant, they can give you their opinion, whereas if they do not know it, as from the features of the restaurant (e.g., cuisine, price,...) they can guess an opinion. But people do not ask just anyone for advice. People only ask for advice to friends with similar tastes and interests who can be trusted. And, how do people know whether other people have similar tastes and interests? Usually, through interaction. If you want to know someone's tastes and interests, you ask him/her his opinion. For instance, in the restaurant example, you ask someone his/her opinion about restaurants that you love and about restaurants that you hate. If this person has a similar opinion, you consider him/her someone with similar preferences. In the information filtering context, agents are not considered reliable either because their honesty or their trustworthy information but because of similar preferences, interest, styles.

Therefore, the opinion-based filtering method we propose is based on a model of trust in the collaborative world of recommender agents. Mainly, we provide recommender agents with a technology that allows them to look for similar agents that can offer them advice. The model proposed emphasizes proactiveness since the agent looks for other agents in situation of lack of information instead of remaining passive or providing either a negative or an empty answer to the user. Finally, our social model exploits interactiveness while preserving privacy.

The new approach of the information filtering method is presented as follows. Section 2 justifies the need of trust in recommender agents. With trust, a new information filtering method comes up that is explained in section 3. Section 4 introduces the formal social model of our approach to trust for recommender systems. Section 5 presents related work and, finally, in section 6 we provide some conclusions.

2   The Need of Trust in Recommender Agents

Recommender agents are used to asses the user by filtering information. Three information filtering methods have been proposed in the current state of the art [11]: demographic filtering, content-based filtering and collaborative filtering. Demographic filtering approaches use descriptions of people to learn about a relationship between a single item and the type of people that like that object. Content-based filtering approaches use descriptions of the content of the items to learn a relationship between a single user and the description of the items. Collaborative filtering approaches use the feedback of a set of people on a set of items to make recommendations, but ignore the content of the items or the descriptions of the people. Recently, researchers claim the outperformance of hybrid systems. Hybrid systems exploit features of content-based and collaborative filtering, since they will almost certainly prove to be complementary.

Traditional collaborative filtering systems employ a simplistic approach that directly recommends new items on the basis of the similarity among profiles of different users. This means that users with similar profiles exchange recommendations. However, when a similar user gives unsuccessful advice, there is no way of ignoring it. Over and over again this agent causes a descent in the performance of the other agents.

Marsh proposes the concept of trust to make our agents less vulnerable to others [8]. Trust is basic in any kind of action in an uncertain world; in particular it is crucial in any form of collaboration with other autonomous agents [1]. There is no standard definition for trust [5,2]. Elofson gives a definition closer to our approach [3]. He claims that observations are important for trust, and he defines trust as:

"Trust is the outcome of observations leading to the belief that the actions of another may be relied upon, without explicit guarantee, to achieve a goal in a risky situation"

Elofson notes that trust can be developed over time as the outcome of a series of confirming observations (also called the dynamics of trust). From his experimental work, Elofson concludes that information regarding the reasoning process of an agent, more than the actual conclusions of that agent affect the trust in those conclusions.

Trust is formed and updated over time through direct interactions or through information provided by other members of society about experiences they have had. Each event that can influence the degree of trust is interpreted by the agent either as a negative or a positive experience. If the event is interpreted as a negative experience the agent will loose his trust to some degree and if it is interpreted to be positive, the agent will gain trust to some degree. The degree to which trust changes depends on the trust model used by the agent. This implies that the trusting agent carries out a form of continual verification and validation of the subject of trust over time.

When applying the concept of trust in the collaborative world approach, we can solve the problem that arises when a similar agent gives frustrated recommendations by decreasing the trust in this agent and ignoring its advice in the future. Trust provides, therefore, a new method for filtering information. Taking advantage of the communication among them, an agent can ask other agents for the opinion of a given item. It differs from the typical collaborative filtering approach in the way that the agent does not ask for a recommendation, but an opinion. The opinion is the interest that the other agent thinks that his/her user has about the given item. Instead of using this opinion directly as a recommendation, the agent includes it in its own reasoning and combines it with other agents' opinions in order to decide whether to recommend a given item. We call this new process of filtering information based on agents opinions the opinion-based information filtering method.

It is important to note that this new approach emphasizes proactiveness of agents. That is to say, when an agent has not enough knowledge to decide about a recommendation, it will turn to other agents on the web, in order to look for similar agents from which to gather information.

3 The Opinion-Based Information Filtering Method

The main idea is to consider other agents as personal entities which you can rely on or not. Reliability is expressed through a trust value with which each agent labels its neighbors. The trust value is initially computed through interaction, following a proactive *playing agents* procedure [15]. Each agent ask the other agents about a list of known items and gathers their opinion on such items. The agents ask the queried agents about their opinion on the item that the user either "loves" or "hates". According to similarity between the opinion provided and their own, agents are able to infer a trust value for each neighbor. Only the contact address of *friend* agents (i.e. agents with a high trust value) are kept.

Once the agent has a set of *friends*, it can use them to filter information. When the agent is not sure about a recommendation or discovers a new item, it asks the reliable agents for their opinion and uses their trust values to decide whether the item is interesting for the user or not (see Figure 1). Once the agent has the opinion of the other agents, a consensus is achieved through the use of an aggregation measure. The result of the consensus provides a confidence value upon which the agent can decide on the convenience of recommending an item to the user or not.

We suppose that similar agents will provide pertinent opinions, but they may also give inadequate ones. Trust, therefore, should be modified as goes by depending on the results of the recommendations, in order to improve acquaintance.

When applying an agent-based approach to recommender systems with trust in the collaborative world, the typical information filtering methods (content-based and collaborative filtering) can also be applied. The performance of the content-based filtering method is the same in this approach, but the collaborative filtering method is improved, since agents only believe in the recommendations of agents with a high trusting value. Finally, we get a hybrid approach among opinion-based, content-based and collaborative filtering.

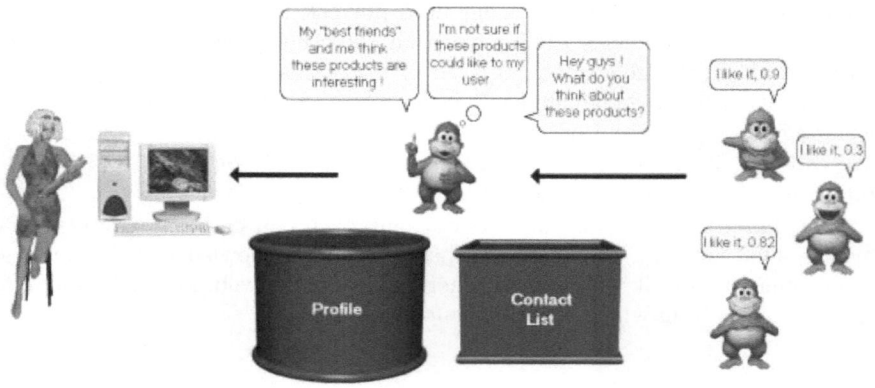

Fig. 1. Information Filtering based on Opinion

4   Social Trust Model for Recommender Agents

The opinion-based filtering method is based on a social model of trust that
we describe following the main dimensions of recommender agents identified in
[11]: user profile representation, initial profile generation, profile exploitation,
relevance feedback, and profile adaptation.

4.1   User Profile Representation

The process of filtering information is based on user profiles which are somewhat hypothesis of unknown target concepts of user preferences. Recommender
systems build and exploit these profiles. The construction of accurate profiles
is a key task since the success of the system will depend to a large extent on
the ability to represent the user's actual interests. Our model considers a user
profile representation based on past experiences and a list of agents which the
agent trusts. It is described as follows:

Given a set of agents: $A = \{a_1, a_2, \ldots, a_r\}$ and a set of products: $P = \{p_1, p_2, \ldots, p_s\}$. Each product is characterized by a set of objective attributes
such as name, price, etc. Thus

$$p_i = \{at_{i_1}, at_{i_2}, \ldots, at_{i_n}\}$$

being At the set of all possible attributes.

Each agent can be interested in one product. Such interest can either be
expressed by the user (explicit attributes) or be captured automatically by the
system as a result of the user interactivity (implicit attributes). Explicit interests
provide more confidence in the recommendation process. However, they are not
always available. Implicit interests are useful to decide upon interesting items

for the user. In our model we distinguish both kinds of user interactions: explicit from implicit, and therefore it is a hybrid approach. We name the set of explicit interest as

$$Int^e = \{int^e_1, int^e_2, \ldots, int^e_m\}$$

and the set of implicit interest as:

$$Int^i = \{int^i_1, int^i_2, \ldots, int^i_l\}$$

Both int^e_j and int^i_j are defined in [0,1].

Each agent has experiences in several products. An experience keeps information about the objective attributes of a given product, as well as subjective information regarding the interest of the user in that product. Thus,

$$E_i = < p_i, Int^e_i, Int^i_i, \delta_i >$$

Where $p_i \subset P$ is the set of objective attributes of the product, $Int^e_i \subset Int^e$ is the set of explicit interest, $Int^i_i \subset Int^i$ is the set of implicit interest, and δ_i is a temporal parameter in [0,1] that indicates the relevance of the experience. Initially δ is set to 1, and it is updated according to the evolution of the agent. For the sake of simplicity we will not deal with this parameter in this paper; see [9] for further information.

Experience of agent a_i in product p_j is $E_{i,j}$, and the set of all possible experiences is denoted as $\mathcal{E}$.

For example, in the restaurant domain products and interests are represented as:

$$A_t = \{name, address, phone\ number, cuisine,$$
$$approximate\ price, capacity, web\ page\}$$

$$Int^e = \{general\ evaluation,$$
$$quality/price\ relation,$$
$$quantity\ of\ food\}$$

$$Int^i = \{web\ page\ visits\ rate,$$
$$retrieved\ queries\ rate,$$
$$rate\ of\ time\ spent\ on\ the\ web\ page\}$$

A single experience of the user in a restaurant recommended by its agent is:

$$E = < \{\text{``}Mallorca\ Restaurant\text{''},$$
$$\text{``}2228\ East\ Carson\ St,\ Pittsburgh, PA\text{''},$$

$$\text{``(412)4881818", ``}Spanish\text{", ``\$70", } 300,$$
$$\text{``}www.mallorcarestaurant.com\text{"}\},$$
$$\{0.83, 0.76, 0.91\},$$
$$\{0.72, 0.36, 0.81\},$$
$$0.83 >$$

Each agent a_i has a list of contact neighborhood agents on which it relies:

$$C_i = \{(a_{i_1}, t_{i,i_1}), (a_{i_2}, t_{i,i_2}), \ldots, (a_{i_n}, t_{i,i_k})\}$$

where $a_{i_j} \in A$ and t_{i,i_j} is a numerical value between [0,1] that represents the truth value the agent a_i has on agent a_{i_j}.

The set of all experiences of a given user and the set of selected agents that the agent trusts constitute the user profile:

$$Prof_i = < \mathcal{E}_i, C_i >$$

where $\mathcal{E}_i \subset \mathcal{E}$.

4.2   Initial Profile Generation

In order to start recommending to a user, the agent needs to fill in the user profile. Initial experiences are generated through the use of a training set. That is, the user is prompted to a set of products and he/she must fill in information regarding his/her interest in the products. We have chosen this technique because, as we will prove later, a training set provides the opportunity to calculate an initial trust for agents in the contact list. Other advantages and disadvantages of this kind of experience generation have been broadly discussed elsewhere, as for example in [11].

The training set consists of a collection of selected products $P^t \subset P$. For each product in the training set, the agent asks the user about the explicit interest and also gathers information related to implicit interests. Thus, the agent has an initial set of experiences.

The next step of the initial profile generation is to obtain *friend* agents for the contact list. Initially the list is empty. However, we assume that there is a server that provides the list of the currently available agents in the world that the agent runs. Such an assumption is reasonable taking into account that most of the multi-agent system platforms currently developed and FIPA [4] compliant provide such a service.

Then we elaborate the initial trust of agents in the world using a procedure that we have called *playing agents* following [15]. The querying agent asks other agents in the world (enquired agents), one by one about, an item of the training set. We can apply this procedure because each agent has been generated from the same training set, so they are able to provide answers about items belonging

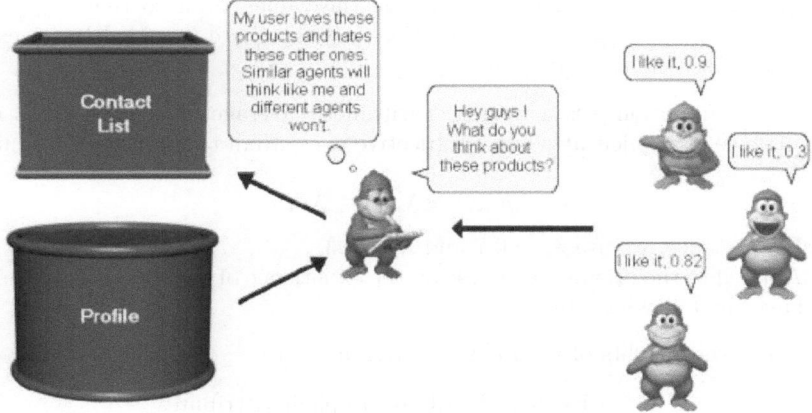

Fig. 2. "Playing Agents"

to such set. Then, the agent asks the enquired agent about the items that the user "loves" or "hates" (see Figure 2).

Note that the answer provided by the enquired agents does not consist of the set of their interest regarding the item asked about, since it would violate its privacy. The implementation of the *playing agents* procedure emphasizes interactiveness in the open world, but the information exchanged (the interest value) hides detailed information about the other users and preserves its personal data. Hence, the answer consists of a quantitative value, between 0 and 1, that represents the degree of interest the agent has in the product (0-hates, 1-loves). This *interest value* of an agent a_i in a product p_j, $v_{i,j}$ is calculated as follows:

$$v_{i,j} = \delta_j * g(f^e(Int_j^e), f^i(Int_j^i)) \tag{1}$$

where f^e is the function that combines the explicit interest of agent a_i in product p_j, f^i is the function that combines the implicit attributes, g is the function that combines the results of f^e and f^i, and finally δ_j is the temporal parameter related to the relevance of the product explained above. Aggregation techniques like [17] can be used for implementing f^e and f^i. For example, the Ordered Weighted Average (OWA) operator [20] is suitable because we are dealing with different preferences of the user and such preferences can be ordered according to their relative importance. The OWA operator is defined as follows:

$$f = \sum_{j=1}^{|p_i|} w_j * Int_j \tag{2}$$

Where:

- $|p_i|$ is the cardinality of the product, that is, the number of attributes that characterizes it; and

- $\{\sigma(1), ..., \sigma(|p_i|)\}$ is a permutation of the values 1,...n so that $v_{i,\sigma(j-1)} \geq v_{i,\sigma(j)}$ $\forall j = 2, ...|p_i|$; in addition, the weights w_j are provided by an expert and must belong to [0,1] and $\sum_j w_j = 1$.

Finally, function g is a weighted arithmetic average (WA) that gives more importance to explicit attributes (objective ones) than to implicit ones (subjective):

$$g(e, i) = \lambda_e * e + \lambda_i * i \tag{3}$$

For instance, we use $\lambda_e = 0.7$ and $\lambda_i = 0.3$.

Applied to the previous example on the experience of the user in a restaurant, we have the following values:

- First, the weights of the interests attributes are:

Explicit Attributes		Implicit Attributes	
$j\ v_{i,\sigma(j)}$	w_j	$j\ v_{i,\sigma(j)}$	w_j
1 0.91	0.5	1 0.81	0.5
2 0.83	0.33	2 0.72	0.33
3 0.76	0.27	3 0.36	0.27

- Second, the application of the OWA operator to aggregate the different explicit attributes and then the different implicit attributes is calculated as follows:

$$f_j^e = 0.5 * 0.91 + 0.33 * 0.83 + 0.27 * 0.76 = 0.93$$

$$f_j^i = 0.5 * 0.81 + 0.33 * 0.72 + 0.27 * 0.36 = 0.74$$

- Then, the application of the WA operator to aggregate explicit and implicit attributes is calculated as follows:

$$g(f_j^e, f_j^i) = 0.7 * 0.93 + 0.3 * 0.74 = 0.87$$

- Finally, the interest value is computed:

$$v_{i,j} = 0.83 * 0.87 = 0.72$$

The current querying agent, a_q, gathers a total of $|P^t|$ interest values of each enquired agent a_{e_i}, one for each product in the training set.

Then, the trust that agent a_q has in agent a_e, noted as $t_{q,e}$ is computed as follows,

$$t_{q,e} = \frac{\sum_{i=1}^{|P^t|} \delta_{p_i}(1 - |v_{q,i} - v_{e,i}|)}{\sum_{i=1}^{|P^t|} \delta_{q_i}} \tag{4}$$

This function computes the similarity between both agents, a_q and a_e, weighted by the relevance of the products (δ_{p_i}) according to a_q's interests (the querying agent). The result of the function is a normalized value in [0,1].

The agent only keeps the agents that have similar interests in the contact list. This is achieved by means of a fixed length contact list: only the n closest

Table 1. Interest values gathered by the querying agent

	p_1	p_2	$\ldots$	$p_{|P_t|}$
a_{e_1}	$v_{e_1,1}$	$v_{e_1,2}$	$\ldots$	$v_{e_1,|P_t|}$
a_{e_2}	$v_{e_2,1}$	$v_{e_2,2}$	$\ldots$	$v_{e_2,|P_t|}$
$\vdots$				
a_{e_n}	$v_{e_n,1}$	$v_{e_n,2}$	$\ldots$	$v_{e_n,|P_t|}$

agents will be kept in the list. The *playing agents* procedure is repeated periodically in order to update the contact list according to the evolution of the user interests. Moreover, the trust value of each agent is updated as a result of a recommendation, as explained in section 4.5. In this sense, acquaintance among agents is improved over time.

Finally, we want to add that the number of agents in the collaborative world is also a matter of constraint in the *playing agents* procedure. That is, it will be very time-costly if any agent, in order to build a contact list, starts a *playing agents* procedure with all the agents in the world. For example, in a platform where agents recommend restaurants from Girona, up to 75.000 agents, one for each citizen, could be considered in the *playing agents* procedure. To reduce the number of agents to be queried, in each *playing agents* execution only a subset of all available agents is considered.

4.3   Profile Exploitation for Recommendation

The agent that recommends items to a user can receive a new product from its environment, or it can also proactively look for new products (for example, asking a server).

When an agent receives a new product, p_{new}, the agent computes the degree of similarity between the new product and the previous ones, according to the similarity measure based on the Clark's distance:

For all experiences E_p in the user profile,

$$sim(p_q, p_new) = \sqrt[2]{\sum_{i=1}^{|p_q|} \frac{|at_{q,i} - at_{new,i}|^2}{|at_{q,i} + at_{new,i}|^2}} \quad (5)$$

where $at_{p,i}$ is the i attribute of the product in the experience E_p and $at_{new,i}$ is the i attribute of the new product. Clark's distance is defined in $[0,1]$ and has been proved useful in several domains. Then:

- If there is some product above a given threshold τ^+, the system recommends it. This process coincides with content filtering.

- If the best similar product is under a threshold τ^-, that means that the user has no interest in it and therefore the agent does not recommend it to the user.
- If the similarity of the products is in $[\tau^-, \tau^+]$ then the agent turns to the opinion filtering method to provide a recommendation.

The opinion filtering method consists of the following steps:

1. Ask the trustworthy agents in the contact list for their opinion on product p_{new}. For each enquired agent a_{e_i} a product value $v_{e_i,new}$ is calculated following equation 1.

Table 2. Product interest values showed by the different enquired agents.

	p_{new}
a_{e_1}	$v_{e_1,p_{new}}$
a_{e_2}	$v_{e_2,p_{new}}$
$\vdots$	
a_{e_n}	$v_{e_n,p_{new}}$

2. Compute a global value for the new product, r_{new} based on the opinion of all the queried agents. Since we are dealing with several sources of information an appropriate combination function is the weighted average (WA) where weights are the trust values of the agents. So,

$$r_{new} = \frac{\sum_i^{|C_q|} t_{q,i} * v_{e_i,new}}{\sum_i^n t_{q,i}} \qquad (6)$$

where $t_{q,i}$ is the trust value that agent a_q has on the queried agent a_{e_i}; and $|C_q|$ is he cardinality of the contact list of the querying agent a_q.

If r_{new} goes above the τ^+ threshold, then the new product is recommended to the user.

It is important to note that if the enquired agents provide the interest values of the product, that is, $int_1^e, ...int_m^e$, and $int_1^i, ...int_l^i$, instead of an aggregated value, $v_{i,new}$, the information gathered by the querying agent will be richer and a more accurate decision can be made. For example, we can use Multicriteria Decision Making techniques (MCDM, [18]) based on the preferences of the querying agent. However, such information can be considered confidential in some environments. So in our approach privacy prevails over accuracy.

4.4   Relevance Feedback

To maintain the user profile, systems need relevant information regarding feedback of the recommendations given to the user. The most common way to obtain relevance feedback from the user is by means of the information given explicitly by the user and the information observed implicitly from the user's interaction with the web. In our model, this relevance feedback information is captured and kept in the Int^e and Int^i sets, included in each experience of users' profiles.

4.5   Profile Adaptation

Objective attributes of products often change, as for example the price. The user can also change his/her interest since human interests change as time goes by. Therefore, the same user can characterizze the same product with a different interest at different times. Then, the update of the user profile is required. In our model we have taken a lazy approach: we do not maintain the interest value of the product explicitly represented in the user profile. We compute it upon demand. Thus, the update process regarding product changes is costless, since it only consists in keeping either the new attribute of the product or the new interest of the user.

The key issue in adaptation is the relevance feedback from previous recommendations. If agents provide a recommendation based on the opinions of our "trustworthy" agents such trust should be updated according to the outcomes. Updating trust and trust dynamics is out of the scope of this paper and is explained in [10].

5   Related Work

There are very few approaches to trust in the collaborative world applied to the information filtering field. Knowledge Pump is an information technology system for connecting and supporting electronic repositories and networked communities [6]. Glance et al. introduce a technique that they call community-centered collaborative filtering (CCCF). In CCCF, the collaborative filter is bootstrapped by the partial view of the social network constructed from a user-input list of "advisors" (people whose opinion users particularly trust). The set of advisors is generated through statistical algorithms that mine the usage data automatically. The main difference from our model is the computation of the trust value since Glance bases it on the person-person correlation. So transparency of user data is required through agents, while in our system privacy prevails. The collaborative filter weighted higher the opinions of his/her most trusted contacts when predicting the user's opinion on items.

In other fields, such as electronic commerce, we can find other trust models that fit the particularities of the domains. For example, Schillo et al. present a formalization and an algorithm for trust so that agents can autonomously deal with deception and identify trustworthy parties in open systems [14]. They demonstrate with results that their approach helps each single agent to establish a model of trustworthiness of other agents. With only few iterations, agents learn who to trust and who to exclude from future interactions. They also show that agents form groups and play among themselves to profit from mutual support.

Before that, they implemented a relevant computational method in the Social Interaction FrameWork (SIF) [13] in which an agent evaluated the reputation of another agent on the basis of direct observation and through other witnesses. The idea of using the opinion of other agents to build a reputation is also applied by Yu and Singh [21]. Their agents build and manage the trust representations not only taking into account the previous experiences of their users, but also communicating with other agents (belonging to other users). They aim at avoiding interaction with undesirable participants and formalizing the generation and propagation of the reputation in electronic communities.

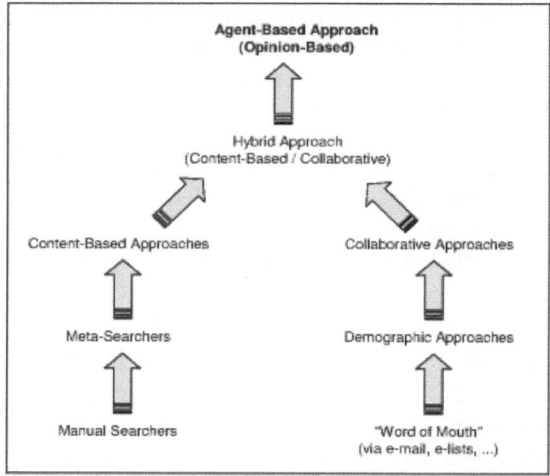

Fig. 3. Evolution of Information Filtering Methods

6   Conclusions

The opinion-based filtering method dealing with an open environment such as Internet is a new approach that seems suitable for recommender agents. Like in the real world, agents rely on certain agents and mistrust others to achieve a purpose. If we provide agents with a technology to evaluate and trust other agents, agents can exploit the collaborative world with a better performance. The model presented in this paper is along this line. We have currently designed and developed a first prototype to test feasibility of the project [19]. Next, we plan to test the model and its advantages and disadvantages through experimentation.

From our point of view, the opinion-based filtering method can be considered as an evolution of the collaborative filtering methods due to the agent's world. If we consider that the hybrid approaches between content-based and collaborative filtering provide better results [11], we can consider this approach as an evolution of the information filtering methods in general (see Figure 3).

As future work, it is also important to show the cost of trust compared to traditional information filtering methods. We are also considering an extension of our model that would take into account the representation of user's interests through fuzzy values, in an attempt to make a more suitable measure. Moreover, we are currently analyzing the applicability of algorithms that automatically generate the different weights needed to apply aggregation measures, like the ones defined in [16]. These algorithms will provide flexibility to our model.

Acknowledgments. This research has been developed within the DAF-DAF Project supported by the CICYT grant DPI2001-2094-C03-01.

References

1. C. Castelfranchi. Information agents: The social nature of information and the role of trust, 2001. Invited Contribution at Cooperative Information Agents V (CIA'01). Modena (Italy).
2. C. Castelfranchi and R. Falcone. Principles of trust for MAS: Cognitive anatomy, social importance, and quantification. In *Demazeau, Y. (ed.), Proceedings of the Third International Conference on Multi-Agent Systems*, pages 72–79. IEEE Computer Society, Los Alamitos, 1998.
3. G. Elofson. Developing trust with intelligent agents: An exploratory study. In *Proceedings of the First International Workshop on Trust*, pages 125–139, 1998.
4. FIPA. http://www.fipa.org/specifications/index.html, 2001.
5. D. Gambetta. Can we trust trust? In *Trust: Making and Breaking Cooperative Relations*, pages 213–237. Gambetta, D (editor). Basil Blackwell. Oxford, 1990.
6. N. Glance, D. Arregui, and M. Dardenne. Knowledge pump: Supporting the flow and use of knowledge. In *Information Technology for Knowledge Management*, pages 35–45. Eds. U. Borghoff and R. Pareschi, New York: Springer-Verlag, 1998.
7. M. Klusch. Information agent technology for the internet: A survey. In *Journal on Data and Knowledge Engineering, Special Issue on Intelligent Information Integration*, volume 36:6. D. Fensel (Ed.), Elsevier Science, 2001.
8. S. P. March. Formalising trust as a computational concept. In *Phd Thesis, Department of Computing Science and Mathematics, University of Stirling*, 1994.
9. M. Montaner. Personalized agents based on case-based reasoning and trust in the collaborative world. In *Thesis Proposal, University of Girona*, 2001.
10. M. Montaner, B. López, and J. L. de la Rosa. Developing trust in recommender agents. *Accepted as Poster at the First International Joint Conference on Autonomous Agents and Multiagent Systems (AAMAS'02). Palazzo Re Enzo (Italy)*, 2002.
11. M. Montaner, B. López, and J. L. de la Rosa. A taxonomy of recommender agents on the internet. In *Submitted to Artificial Intelligence Review*, 2002.
12. J. Sabater and C. Sierra. Regret: A reputation model for gregarious societies. In *Research Report. Institut d'Investigació i Intel.ligència Artificial*, 2000.
13. M. Schillo and P. Funk. Who can you trust: Dealing with deception. In *Proceedings of the Workshop Deception, Fraud and Trust in Agent Societies at the Autonomous Agents Conference*, pages 95–106, 1999.

14. M. Schillo, P. Funk, and M. Rovatsos. Using trust for detecting deceitful agents in artificial societites. In *Applied Artificial Intelligence, Special Issue on Trust, Deception and Fraud in Agent Societies*, 2000.
15. L. Steels and P. Vogt. Grounding adaptive language games in robotic agents. In *Proceedings of the Fourth European Conference on Artificial Life*, pages 473–484, 1997.
16. V. Torra. the learning of weights in some aggregation operators: The weighted mean and the owa operators. volume 6, pages 249–265. Mathware and Soft Computing, 1999.
17. V. Torra. On the integration of numerical information: from the arithmetic mean to fuzzy integrals. Torra V. (Ed). Information fusion in data mining. Physiin-Verlag. (Forthcoming), 2001.
18. A. Valls. Development of a method for multiple criteria decision making based on negation fuctions. chapter 2: State of the art. Thesis proposal, Artificial Intelligence Program, UPC, 2000.
19. R. Vilà and M. Montaner. Implementació d'un sistema multiagent distribuit format per agents personals que recomanen restaurants aplicant raonament basat en casos i tècniques de trust, 2002. Projecte Fi de Carrera en Enginyeria Informàtica, Universitat de Girona.
20. R. R. Yager. On ordered weighted averaging aggregation operators in multi-criteria decision making. volume 18, pages 183–190. IEEE Transactions on SMC, 1988.
21. B. Yu and M. P. Singh. A social mechanism of reputation management in electronic communities. In *cooperative information agents, CIA-2000*, pages 154–165, 2000.

Data Models and Languages for Agent-Based Textual Information Dissemination*

M. Koubarakis, C. Tryfonopoulos, P. Raftopoulou, and T. Koutris

Dept. of Electronic and Computer Engineering
Technical University of Crete
73100 Chania, Crete, Greece
manolis@ced.tuc.gr, {trifon,rautop,koutris}@mhl.tuc.gr
www.ced.tuc.gr/~manolis

Abstract. We define formally the data models $\mathcal{WP}$, $\mathcal{AWP}$ and $\mathcal{AWPS}$ especially designed for the dissemination of textual information by distributed agent systems using communication languages such as KQML and FIPA-ACL. We also define the problems of satisfaction and filtering and point out that these problems are fundamental for the deployment of our models in distributed agent architectures appropriate for information dissemination. One such architecture currently under development in project DIET is sketched in some detail in this paper. Finally, we present algorithms for the problems of satisfaction and filtering, prove the correctness of these algorithms, and calculate their computational complexity.

1 Introduction

The selective dissemination of information to interested users is a problem arising frequently in today's information society. This problem has recently received the attention of various research communities including researchers from agent systems [16, 22, 12, 28, 29], databases [18, 2, 26, 14], digital libraries [15], distributed computing [6, 4] and others.

We envision an information dissemination scenario in the context of a *distributed peer-to-peer (P2P) agent architecture* like the one shown in Figure 1. Users utilize their *end-agents* to post *profiles* or *documents* (expressed in some appropriate language) to some *middle-agents*. End-agents play a dual role: they can be information producers and information consumers at the same time. The P2P network of middle-agents is the "glue" that makes sure that published documents arrive at interested subscribers. To achieve this, middle-agents forward posted profiles to other middle-agents using an appropriate P2P protocol. In this way, matching of a profile with a document can take place at a middle-agent that is as close as possible to the origin of the incoming document. Profile

---

* This work was carried out as part of the DIET (Decentralised Information Ecosystems Technologies) project (IST-1999-10088), within the Universal Information Ecosystems initiative of the Information Society Technology Programme of the European Union.

M. Klusch, S. Ossowski, and O. Shehory (Eds.): CIA 2002, LNAI 2446, pp. 179–193, 2002.
© Springer-Verlag Berlin Heidelberg 2002

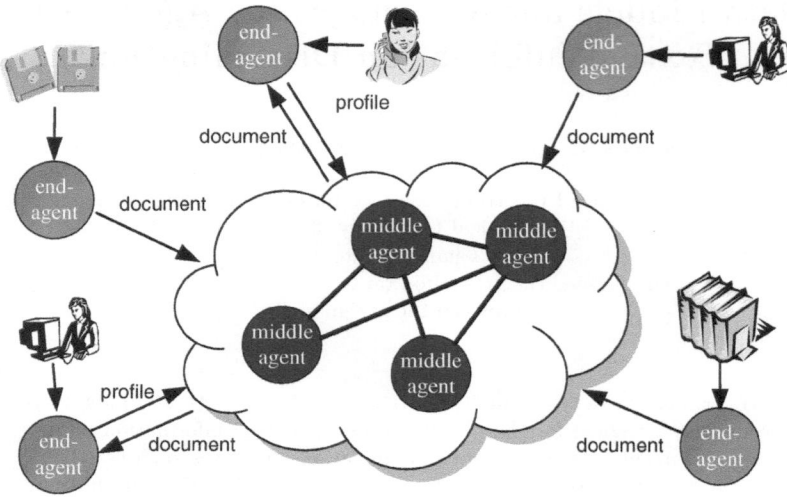

Fig. 1. A distributed P2P agent architecture for information dissemination

forwarding can be done in a sophisticated way to minimize network traffic e.g., no profiles that are less general than one that has already been processed are actually forwarded.

In their capacity as information producers, end-agents can also post *advertisements* that describe in a "concise" way the documents that will be produced by them. These advertisements can also be forwarded in the P2P network of middle-agents to *block* the forwarding of *irrelevant* profiles towards a source. Advertisement forwarding can also be done in a sophisticated way using ideas similar to the ones for profile forwarding.[1]

Our work in this paper concentrates on models and languages for expressing documents and queries/profiles in *textual information* dissemination systems that follow the general architecture of Figure 1.[2] We are motivated by a desire to develop useful agent systems in a *principled* and *formal* way, and make the

---

[1] Most of the concepts of the architecture sketched above are explicit (or sometimes implicit) in the KQML literature and subsequent multi-agent systems based on it [16, 22, 12, 28, 29]. Unfortunately the emphasis in most of these systems is on a single central middle-agent, making the issues that would arise in a distributed setting difficult to appreciate. In our opinion, the best presentation of these concepts available in the literature can be found in [6] where the distributed event dissemination system SIENA is presented. SIENA does not use terminology from the area of agent systems but the connection is obvious.

[2] We use the terms *query* and *profile* interchangeably. In an information dissemination setting, a profile is simply a long-standing query. We do not consider advertisements, but it should be clear from our presentation that appropriate subsets of the query languages that we will present could be used for expressing advertisements as well.

following technical contributions. We define formally the models $\mathcal{WP}$, $\mathcal{AWP}$ and $\mathcal{AWPS}$, and their corresponding languages for textual information dissemination in distributed agent systems. Data model $\mathcal{WP}$ is based on free text and its query language is based on the *boolean model with proximity operators*. The concepts of $\mathcal{WP}$ extend the traditional concept of proximity in IR [3, 8, 9] in a significant way and utilize it in a content language targeted at information dissemination applications. Data model $\mathcal{AWP}$ is based on *attributes* or *fields* with finite-length strings as values. Its query language is an extension of the query language of data model $\mathcal{WP}$. Our work on $\mathcal{AWP}$ complements recent proposals for querying textual information in distributed event-based systems [6, 4] by using linguistically motivated concepts such as *word* and not arbitrary strings. This makes $\mathcal{AWP}$ potentially very useful in some applications (e.g., alert systems for digital libraries or other commercial systems where similar models are supported already for retrieval). Finally, the model $\mathcal{AWPS}$ extends $\mathcal{AWP}$ by introducing a "similarity" operator in the style of modern IR, based on the vector space model [3]. The novelty of our work in this area is the move to query languages much more expressive than the one used in the information dissemination system SIFT [33] where documents and queries are represented by free text. The similarity concept of $\mathcal{AWPS}$ is an extension of the similarity concept pioneered by the system WHIRL [11] and recently also used in the XML query language ELIXIR [10]. We note that both WHIRL and ELIXIR target information retrieval and integration applications, and pay no attention to information dissemination and the concepts/functionality needed in such applications. The models $\mathcal{WP}$ and $\mathcal{AWP}$ are also discussed in [20, 21] but no connection to agent systems and architectures is made. The first presentation of model $\mathcal{AWPS}$ is the one given in this paper.

In the second part of our paper, we built on the formal foundations of the first part and study the computational complexity of the problems of matching and filtering in the three models we have defined. These results are original and are currently leading to an implementation of a prototype information dissemination system in the context of project DIET [24, 30, 19].

The rest of the paper is organised as follows. Section 2 presents data model $\mathcal{WP}$ based on free text and its sophisticated query language. Then Sections 3 and 4 build on this foundation and develops the same machinery for data models $\mathcal{AWP}$ and $\mathcal{AWPS}$. Section 5 presents our complexity results for the problems of satisfaction and filtering. Finally, Section 6 gives our conclusions and discusses future work. The proofs of the results of Section 5 are omitted. They can be found (together with a very detailed discussion of related work) in the long version of this paper which is available at:
http://www.intelligence.tuc.gr/~manolis/publications.html.

2   Text Values and Word Patterns

In this section we present the data model $\mathcal{WP}$ and its query language. $\mathcal{WP}$ assumes that textual information is in the form of *free text* and can be queried by *word patterns* (hence the acronym for the model). The basic concepts of $\mathcal{WP}$ are subsequently used in Section 3 to define the data model $\mathcal{AWP}$ and its query language.

We assume the existence of a finite *alphabet* $\mathbf{\Sigma}$. A *word* is a finite non-empty sequence of letters from $\mathbf{\Sigma}$. We also assume the existence of a (finite or infinite) set of words called the *vocabulary* and denoted by $\mathcal{V}$.

Definition 1. *A* text value s *of length* n *over vocabulary* $\mathcal{V}$ *is a total function* $s : \{1, 2, \ldots, n\} \to \mathcal{V}$.

In other words, a text value s is a finite sequence of words from the assumed vocabulary and $s(i)$ gives the i-th element of s. Text values can be used to represent finite-length strings consisting of words separated by blanks. The length of a text value s (i.e., its number of words) will be denoted by $|s|$.

We now give the definition of word-pattern. The definition is given recursively in three stages.

Definition 2. *Let* $\mathcal{V}$ *be a vocabulary. A* proximity-free word pattern *over vocabulary* $\mathcal{V}$ *is an expression generated by the grammar*

$$WP \to \mathbf{w} \mid \neg WP \mid WP \wedge WP \mid WP \vee WP \mid (WP)$$

where terminal $\mathbf{w}$ *represents a word of* $\mathcal{V}$. *A proximity-free word pattern will be called* positive *if it does not contain the negation operator.*

Example 1. The following are proximity-free word patterns that can appear in queries of a user of a news dissemination system interested in holidays:

$$Athens \wedge hotel \wedge \neg Hilton, \quad holiday \wedge (beach \vee mountains)$$

Word patterns made of words and the Boolean operators $\wedge, \vee$ and $\neg$ should be understood as in traditional IR systems and modern search engines. These systems typically have a version of negation in the form of binary operator *AND-NOT* which is essentially set difference thus safe (in the database sense of the term [1]). For example, a search engine query wp_1 *AND-NOT* wp_2 will return the set of documents that satisfy wp_1 *minus* these that satisfy wp_2. In our information dissemination setting, there is no problem considering an "unsafe" version of negation since word patterns are checked for satisfaction against a single incoming document. Note that the previous work of [9] has *not* considered negation in its word pattern language (but has considered negation in the query language which supports attributes; see Section 3).

We now introduce a new class of word patterns that allows us to capture the concepts of *order* and *distance* between words in a text document. We will assume the existence of a set of *(distance) intervals* $\mathcal{I}$ defined as follows:

$$\mathcal{I} = \{[l, u] : \ l, u \in \mathbb{N}, l \geq 0 \text{ and } l \leq u\} \cup \{[l, \infty) : \ l \in \mathbb{N} \text{ and } l \geq 0\}$$

The symbols $\in$ and $\subseteq$ will be used to denote membership and inclusion in an interval as usual.

The following definition uses intervals to impose lower and upper bounds on distances between word patterns.

Definition 3. *Let $\mathcal{V}$ be a vocabulary. A* proximity word pattern *over vocabulary $\mathcal{V}$ is an expression $wp_1 \prec_{i_1} wp_2 \prec_{i_2} \cdots \prec_{i_{n-1}} wp_n$ where $wp_1, wp_2, \ldots, wp_n$ are positive proximity-free word patterns over $\mathcal{V}$ and $i_1, i_2, \ldots, i_{n-1}$ are intervals from the set $\mathcal{I}$. The symbols $\prec_i$ where $i \in \mathcal{I}$ are called* proximity operators. *The number of proximity-free word patterns in a proximity word pattern (i.e., n above) is called its* size.

Example 2. The following are proximity word patterns:

$$Holiday \prec_{[0,0]} Inn, \quad Mini \prec_{[0,0]} Palace \prec_{[0,0]} Hotel,$$
$$luxurious \prec_{[0,3]} (hotel \vee apartment), \quad hotel \prec_{[0,\infty)} view$$
$$holiday \prec_{[0,10]} beach \prec_{[0,10]} (clean \wedge sandy)$$

The proximity word pattern $wp_1 \prec_{[l,u]} wp_2$ stands for "word pattern wp_1 is *before* wp_2 and is separated by wp_2 by *at least l* and *at most u words*". In the above example $luxurious \prec_{[0,3]} hotel$ denotes that the word "hotel" appears after word "luxurious" and at a distance of at least 0 and at most 3 words. The word pattern $Holiday \prec_{[0,0]} Inn$ denotes that the word "Holiday" appears exactly before word "Inn" so this is a way to encode the string "Holiday Inn". We can also have arbitrarily long sequences of proximity operators with similar meaning (see the examples above). Note that proximity-free subformulas in proximity word-patterns can be more complex than just simple words (but negation is *not* allowed; this restriction will be explained below). This makes proximity-word patterns a very expressive notation.

Definition 4. *Let $\mathcal{V}$ be a vocabulary. A* word pattern *over vocabulary $\mathcal{V}$ is an expression generated by the grammar*

$$WP \to PFWP \mid PWP \mid WP \wedge WP \mid WP \vee WP \mid (WP)$$

where non-terminals $PFWP$ and PWP represent proximity-free and proximity word patterns respectively. A word pattern will be called positive *if its proximity-free subformulas are positive.*

Example 3. The following are word patterns of the most general kind we allow:

$$holiday \wedge (luxurious \prec_{[0,0]} hotel) \wedge \neg Hilton,$$
$$holiday \wedge (hotel \prec_{[0,10]} (cheap \wedge clean)),$$
$$Vienna \wedge ((Dolce \prec_{[0,0]} Vita \prec_{[0,0]} Hotel) \vee (Mini \prec_{[0,0]} Palace \prec_{[0,0]} Hotel))$$

We have here completed the definition of the concept of word pattern. We now turn to defining its semantics. First, we define what it means for a text value to satisfy a proximity-free word pattern.

Definition 5. *Let $\mathcal{V}$ be a vocabulary, s a text value over $\mathcal{V}$ and wp a proximity-free word pattern over $\mathcal{V}$. The concept of s satisfying wp (denoted by $s \models wp$) is defined as follows:*

1. *If wp is a word of $\mathcal{V}$ then $s \models wp$ iff there exists $p \in \{1, \ldots, |s|\}$ and $s(p) = wp$.*

2. *If wp is of the form $\neg wp_1$ then $s \models wp$ iff $s \not\models wp_1$.*
3. *If wp is of the form $wp_1 \wedge wp_2$ then $s \models wp$ iff $s \models wp_1$ and $s \models wp_2$.*
4. *If wp is of the form $wp_1 \vee wp_2$ then $s \models wp$ iff $s \models wp_1$ or $s \models wp_2$.*
5. *If wp is of the form (wp_1) then $s \models wp$ iff $s \models wp_1$.*

The above definition mirrors the definition of satisfaction for Boolean logic [25]. This will allow us to draw on a lot of related results in the rest of this paper.

Example 4. Let s be the following text value:

> *During our holiday in Milos we stayed in a luxurious hotel by the beach*

Then $s \models holiday \wedge Milos$.

The following definition captures the notion of a set of positions in a text value containing only words that contribute to the satisfaction of a proximity-free word pattern. This notion is then used to define satisfaction of proximity word patterns.

Definition 6. *Let $\mathcal{V}$ be a vocabulary, s a text value over $\mathcal{V}$, wp a proximity-free word pattern over $\mathcal{V}$, and P a subset of $\{1, \ldots, |s|\}$. The concept of s satisfying wp with set of positions P (denoted by $s \models_P wp$) is defined as follows:*

1. *If wp is a word of $\mathcal{V}$ then $s \models_P wp$ iff there exists $x \in \{1, \ldots, |s|\}$ such that $P = \{x\}$ and $s(x) = wp$.*
2. *If wp is of the form $wp_1 \wedge wp_2$ then $s \models_P wp$ iff there exist sets of positions $P_1, P_2 \subseteq \{1, \ldots, |s|\}$ such that $s \models_{P_1} wp_1$, $s \models_{P_2} wp_2$ and $P = P_1 \cup P_2$.*
3. *If wp is of the form $wp_1 \vee wp_2$ then $s \models_P wp$ iff $s \models_P wp_1$ or $s \models_P wp_2$.*
4. *If wp is of the form (wp_1) then $s \models_P wp$ iff $s \models_P wp_1$.*

Now we define what it means for a text value to satisfy a proximity word pattern.

Definition 7. *Let $\mathcal{V}$ be a vocabulary, s a text value over $\mathcal{V}$ and wp a proximity word pattern over $\mathcal{V}$ of the form $wp_1 \prec_{i_1} wp_2 \prec_{i_2} \cdots \prec_{i_{n-1}} wp_n$. Then $s \models wp$ iff there exist sets $P_1, P_2, \ldots, P_n \subseteq \{1, \ldots, |s|\}$ such that $s \models_{P_j} wp_j$ and $min(P_j) - max(P_{j-1}) - 1 \in i_{j-1}$ for all $j = 2, \ldots, n$ (the operators max and min have the obvious meaning).*

Example 5. The text value of Example 4 satisfies the following word patterns:

$$luxurious \prec_{[0,0]} hotel \prec_{[0,5]} beach$$
$$luxurious \prec_{[0,0]} (hotel \vee apartment) \prec_{[0,5]} beach,$$
$$(holiday \wedge Milos) \prec_{[0,10]} luxurious \prec_{[0,0]} hotel$$

The sets of positions required by the definition are for the first and second word pattern $\{10\}$, $\{11\}$ and $\{14\}$, and for the third one $\{3, 5\}$, $\{10\}$ and $\{11\}$.

If the structure of *wp* falls under the four cases of our most general definition (Definition 4), satisfaction is similarly defined in a recursive way as in Definition 5 (for Cases 1, 3 and 4) and Definition 7 (for Case 2).

Example 6. The text value of Example 4 satisfies word pattern

$$holiday \wedge (luxurious \prec_{[0,0]} hotel \prec_{[0,5]} beach).$$

3   An Attribute-Based Data Model and Query Language

Now that we have studied the data model $\mathcal{WP}$ in great detail, we are ready to define our second data model and query language. Data model $\mathcal{AWP}$ is based on *attributes* or *fields* with finite-length strings as values (in the acronym $\mathcal{AWP}$, the letter $\mathcal{A}$ stands for "attribute"). Strings will be understood as sequences of words as formalised by the model $\mathcal{WP}$ presented earlier. Attributes can be used to encode textual information such as author, title, date, body of text and so on. $\mathcal{AWP}$ is restrictive since it offers a rather flat view of a text document, but it has wide applicability as we will show below.

We start our formal development by defining the concepts of document schema and document. Throughout the rest of this paper we assume the existence of a countably infinite set of attributes **U** called the *attribute universe*.

Definition 8. *A document schema $\mathcal{D}$ is a pair $(\mathcal{A}, \mathcal{V})$ where $\mathcal{A}$ is a subset of the attribute universe* **U** *and $\mathcal{V}$ is a vocabulary.*

Example 7. An example of a document schema for a news dissemination application is
$$\mathcal{D} = (\{SENDER,\ EMAIL,\ BODY\}, \mathcal{E}).$$

Definition 9. *Let $\mathcal{D}$ be a document schema. A document d over schema $(\mathcal{A}, \mathcal{V})$ is a set of attribute-value pairs (A, s) where $A \in \mathcal{A}$, s is a text value over $\mathcal{V}$, and there is at most one pair (A, s) for each attribute $A \in \mathcal{A}$.*

Example 8. The following is a document over the schema of Example 7:

$\{\ (SENDER, \text{``John Brown''}), (EMAIL, \text{``jbrown@yahoo.com''}),$
$(BODY, \text{``During our holiday in Milos we stayed in a luxurious hotel by the beach''})\ \}$

The syntax of our query language is given by the following recursive definition.

Definition 10. *Let $\mathcal{D} = (\mathcal{A}, \mathcal{V})$ be a document schema. A query over $\mathcal{D}$ is a formula in any of the following forms:*

1. *$A \sqsupseteq wp$ where $A \in \mathcal{A}$ and wp is a positive word pattern over $\mathcal{V}$. The formula $A \sqsupseteq wp$ can be read as "A contains word pattern wp".*
2. *$A = s$ where $A \in \mathcal{A}$ and s is a text value over $\mathcal{V}$.*
3. *$\neg\phi$ where ϕ is a query containing no proximity word patterns.*
4. *$\phi_1 \vee \phi_2$ where ϕ_1 and ϕ_2 are queries.*
5. *$\phi_1 \wedge \phi_2$ where ϕ_1 and ϕ_2 are queries.*

Example 9. The following are queries over the schema of Example 7:

$$SENDER \sqsupseteq (John \prec_{[0,2]} Smith),$$
$$\neg SENDER = \text{``John Smith''} \wedge (BODY \sqsupseteq (Milos \wedge (hotel \prec_{[0,5]} beach)))$$

Let us now define the semantics of the above query language in our dissemination setting. We start by defining when a document satisfies a query.

Definition 11. *Let $\mathcal{D}$ be a document schema, d a document over $\mathcal{D}$ and ϕ a query over $\mathcal{D}$. The concept of document d satisfying query ϕ (denoted by $d \models \phi$) is defined as follows:*

1. *If ϕ is of the form $A \sqsupset wp$ then $d \models \phi$ iff there exists a pair $(A, s) \in d$ and $s \models wp$.*
2. *If ϕ is of the form $A = s$ then $d \models \phi$ iff there exists a pair $(A, s) \in d$.*
3. *If ϕ is of the form $\neg\phi_1$ then $d \models \phi$ iff $d \not\models \phi_1$.*
4. *If ϕ is of the form $\phi_1 \wedge \phi_2$ then $d \models \phi$ iff $d \models \phi_1$ and $d \models \phi_2$.*
5. *If ϕ is of the form $\phi_1 \vee \phi_2$ then $d \models \phi$ iff $d \models \phi_1$ or $d \models \phi_2$.*

Example 10. The first query of Example 9 is not satisfied by the document of Example 8 while the second one is satisfied.

4   Extending $\mathcal{AWP}$ with Similarity

Let us now define our third data model $\mathcal{AWPS}$ and its query language. $\mathcal{AWPS}$ extends $\mathcal{AWP}$ with the concept of *similarity* between two text values (the letter $\mathcal{S}$ stands for similarity). The idea here is to have a "soft" alternative to the "hard" operator $\sqsupset$. This operator is very useful for queries such as "I am interested in documents sent by John Brown" which can be written in $\mathcal{AWP}$ as

$$SENDER \sqsupset (John \prec_{[0,0]} Brown)$$

but it might not be very useful for queries "I am interested in documents about the use of ideas from agent research in the area of information dissemination".

The desired functionality can be achieved by resorting to an important tool of modern IR: the *weight* of a word as defined in the Vector Space Model (VSM) [3, 23, 31]. In VSM, documents (text values in our terminology) are conceptually represented as vectors. If our vocabulary consists of n distinct words then a text value s is represented as an n-dimensional vector of the form $(\omega_1, \ldots, \omega_n)$ where ω_i is the weight of the i-th word (the weight assigned to a non-existent word is 0). With a good weighting scheme, the VSM representation of a document can be a surprisingly good model of its semantic content in the sense that "similar" documents have very close semantic content. This has been demonstrated by many successful IR systems recently (see for example, WHIRL [11]). [3]

In VSM, the weight of a word is computed using the heuristic of assigning higher *weights* to words that are frequent in a document and *infrequent* in the collection of documents available. This heuristic is made concrete using the concepts of word frequency and the inverse document frequency defined below.

---

[3] Note that in the VSM model and systems adopting it (e.g., WHIRL [11]) word *stems*, produced by some stemming algorithm [27], are forming the vocabulary instead of words. Additionally, *stopwords* (e.g., "the") are eliminated from the vocabulary. These important details have no consequence for the theoretical results of this paper, but it should be understood that our current implementation of the ideas of this section utilizes these standard techniques.

Definition 12. *Let w_i be a word in document d_j of a collection C. The* term frequency *of w_i in d_j (denoted by tf_{ij}) is equal to the number of occurrences of word w_i in d_j. The* document frequency *of word w_i in the collection C (denoted by df_i) is equal to the number of documents in C that contain w_i. The* inverse document frequency *of w_i is then given by $idf_i = \frac{1}{df_i}$. Finally, the number $tf_{ij} \cdot idf_i$ will be called the* weight *of word w_i in document d_j and will be denoted by ω_{ij}.*

At this point we should stress that the concept of inverse document frequency assumes that there is a *collection* of documents which is used in the calculation. In our dissemination scenario we assume that for each attribute A there is a collection of text values C_A that is used for calculating the *idf* values to be used in similarity computations involving attribute A (the details are given below). C_A can be a collection of recently processed text values as suggested in [33].

We are now ready to define the main new concept in $\mathcal{AWPS}$, the similarity of two text values. The similarity of two text values s_q and s_d is defined as the cosine of the angle formed by their corresponding vectors:[4]

$$sim(s_q, s_d) = \frac{s_q \cdot s_d}{\|s_q\| \cdot \|s_d\|} = \frac{\sum_{i=1}^{N} w_{q_i} \cdot w_{d_i}}{\sqrt{\sum_{i=1}^{N} w_{q_i}^2 \cdot \sum_{i=1}^{N} w_{d_i}^2}} \tag{1}$$

By this definition, similarity values are real numbers in the interval $[0, 1]$.

Let us now proceed to give the syntax of the query language for $\mathcal{AWPS}$. Since $\mathcal{AWPS}$ extends $\mathcal{AWP}$, a query in the new model is given by Definition 10 with one more case for atomic queries:

- $A \sim_k s$ where $A \in \mathcal{A}$, s is a text value over $\mathcal{V}$ and k is a real number in the interval $[0, 1]$.

Example 11. The following are some queries in $\mathcal{AWPS}$ using the schema of Example 8:

$BODY \sim_{0.6}$ *"Milos is the ideal place for holidays by the beach"*,
$(SENDER \sqsupseteq (John \prec_{[0,2]} Brown)) \wedge$
$(TITLE \sim_{0.9}$ *"Hotels and resorts in Greece"*$)$,
$BODY \sim_{0.9}$ *"Stock options during Easter holidays"*

We now give the semantics of our query language, by defining when a document satisfies a query. Naturally, the definition of satisfaction in $\mathcal{AWPS}$ is as in Definition 11 with one additional case for the similarity operator:

- If ϕ is of the form $\mathcal{A} \sim_k s_q$ then $d \models \phi$ iff there exists a pair $(A, s_d) \in d$ and $sim(s_q, s_d) \geq k$.

---

[4] The IR literature gives us several very closely related ways to define the notions of weight and similarity [3, 23, 31]. All of these weighting schemes come by the name of $tf \cdot idf$ weighting schemes. Generally a weighting scheme is called $tf \cdot idf$ whenever it uses word frequency in a monotonically increasing way, and document frequency in a monotonically decreasing way.

The reader should notice that the number k in a similarity predicate $A \sim_k s$ gives a *relevance threshold* that candidate text values s should exceed in order to satisfy the predicate. This notion of relevance threshold was first proposed in an information dissemination setting by [17] and later on adopted by [33]. The reader is asked to contrast this situation with the typical information retrieval setting where a ranked list of documents is returned as an answer to a user query. This is not a relevant scenario in an information dissemination system because very few documents (or even a single one) enter the system at a time, and need to be forwarded to interested users (see the architecture sketched in Figure 1).

A low similarity threshold in a predicate $A \sim_k s$ might result in many irrelevant documents satisfying a query, whereas a high similarity threshold would result in very few achieving satisfaction (or even no documents at all). In an implementation of our ideas, users can start with a certain relevance threshold and then update it using relevance feedback techniques to achieve a better satisfaction of their information needs. Recent techniques from adaptive IR can be utilised here [7].

Example 12. The first query of Example 11 is likely to be satisfied by the document of Example 8 (of course, we cannot say for sure until the exact weights are calculated in the manner suggested above). The second query is not satisfied, since attribute $TITLE$ does not exist in the document. Moreover the third query is unlikely to be satisfied since the only common word between the query and Example 8 is the word "holiday".

5   The Complexity of Satisfaction and Filtering

For an information dissemination architecture like the one in Figure 1 to become a reality, two very important problems need to be solved efficiently. The first problem is the *satisfaction* (or *matching*) *problem*: Deciding whether a document satisfies (or matches) a profile. The second problem is the *filtering problem*: Given a database of profiles db and a document d, find all profiles $q \in db$ that match d. This functionality is very crucial at each middle-agent and it is based on the availability of algorithms for the satisfaction problem. We expect deployed information dissemination systems to handle hundreds of thousands or millions of profiles.

In this section we present PTIME upper bounds for the satisfaction problem and filtering problem in models $\mathcal{WP}$ and $\mathcal{AWP}$. The reader is reminded that profiles in $\mathcal{WP}$ and $\mathcal{AWP}$ are defined by languages containing all Boolean connectives and not just conjunction as in virtually all previous work in the area of event dissemination systems (a notable exception of this rule is [4]).

5.1   Algorithms for Satisfaction

In previous research, [9] have presented a method for evaluating positive word patterns with proximity operators kW and kN on sets of text values (Fig. 2 of

function $eppf(wp, s)$
if wp is a word of $\mathcal{V}$ **then**
    return $\{\ [x, x] :\ s(x) = wp\ \}$
else if wp is of the form $wp_1 \wedge wp_2$ **then**
    return $\{\ [min(l_1, l_2), max(u_1, u_2)] :\ [l_1, u_1] \in eppf(wp_1, s)$ and
$$[l_2, u_2] \in eppf(wp_2, s)\ \}$$
else if wp is of the form $wp_1 \vee wp_2$ **then**
    return $\{\ [l, u] :\ [l, u] \in eppf(wp_1, s)\ \cup eppf(wp_2, s)\ \}$
else if wp is of the form (wp_1) **then**
    return $eppf(wp_1)$

function $prox(wp, s)$
if wp is a positive proximity-free word pattern **then**
    return $eppf(wp, s)$
else
    Let wp be $wp_1 \prec_i rest$ where $rest$ is a proximity word pattern
    return $\{\ [l_1, u_1] :\ [l_1, u_1] \in eppf(wp_1, s)$ and there exists
                a position interval $[l_2, u_2] \in prox(rest, s)$
                such that $l_2 - u_1 - 1 \in i\ \}$
end

Fig. 2. Some useful functions for deciding whether $s \models wp$

[9]). This method is intended to provide semantics to word patterns, and nothing is said about the computational complexity of evaluation. In this paper we have followed the more formal route of *separating* the definition of semantics from the algorithms and complexity of deciding satisfaction.

We start with the satisfaction problem for proximity-free word patterns of the model $\mathcal{WP}$.

Lemma 1. *Let s be a text value and wp a proximity-free word pattern. We can decide whether $s \models wp$ in $O(\delta + \rho)$ time on average where δ is the number of words and ρ is the number of operators in wp.*

We now turn to proximity word patterns. We first need the following lemma.

Lemma 2. *Let s be a text value and wp a positive proximity-free word pattern. Function $eppf(wp, s)$ shown in Figure 2 returns a non-empty set of position intervals O iff $s \models wp$. Additionally, for every set of positions P such that $s \models_P wp$ there exists an interval $[l, u] \in O$ such that*

$$P \subseteq [l, u],\ min(P) = l\ and\ max(P) = u.$$

The set O can be computed in $O((\delta + \rho)\,|s|^4)$ time where δ is the number of words and ρ is the number of operators in wp.

We now use the above lemma to compute an upper bound on the complexity of satisfaction for proximity word patterns.

Lemma 3. *Let s be a text value and wp a proximity word pattern. We can decide whether $s \models wp$ in $O(n(\delta_{max} + \rho_{max}) |s|^4)$ time where n is the number of proximity free subformulas of wp, δ_{max} is the maximum number of words in a proximity-free subformula of wp and ρ_{max} is the maximum number of operators in a proximity-free subformula of wp.*

We can now show that satisfaction can be decided in PTIME for all formulas in $\mathcal{WP}$.

Theorem 1. *Let s be a text value and wp a word pattern. The problem of deciding whether $s \models wp$ can be solved in $O(\mu n_{max}(\delta_{max} + \rho_{max}) |s|^4)$ time where μ is the number of operators $\wedge$ and $\vee$ in wp, n_{max} is the maximum number of proximity-free subformulas in a proximity word pattern of wp, δ_{max} is the maximum number of words in a proximity-free subformula of wp and ρ_{max} is the maximum number of operators in a proximity-free subformula of wp.*

We will now show that satisfaction can be decided in PTIME for all formulas of $\mathcal{AWP}$ as well.

Theorem 2. *Let d be a document and ϕ be a query in $\mathcal{AWP}$. Deciding whether $d \models \phi$ can be done in $O((E + H)(\alpha + V)MN(\Delta + P)^2 S^4)$ time where E is the number of atomic subqueries in ϕ, H is the number of operators in ϕ, α is the number of attributes in d, V is the maximum size of a text value appearing in ϕ, M is the maximum number of operators $\wedge$ and $\vee$ in a word pattern of ϕ, N is the maximum number of proximity-free subformulas in a proximity word pattern of ϕ, Δ is the maximum number of words in a proximity-free subformula of ϕ, P is the maximum number of operators in a proximity-free subformula of ϕ, and S is the maximum size of a text value appearing in d.*

Now we turn to the complexity of deciding the similarity between two text values.

Lemma 4. *Let s, v be text values. We can decide whether $s \sim_k v$ in $O(\max(|s|, |v|))$ time on average, where $|s|, |v|$ is the size of text values s and v respectively.*

We can now show that the satisfaction problem for $\mathcal{AWPS}$ can also be solved in PTIME.

Theorem 3. *Let d be a document and ϕ be a query in $\mathcal{AWPS}$. To decide whether $d \models \phi$ we need $O((E + H)(\alpha + \max(S, V))MN(\Delta + P)^2 S^4)$ time, where all the parameters are as in Theorem 2.*

Let us now consider the filtering problem introduced at the beginning of this section. Let us assume that we have a database of profiles db and a published event e, how can we find all the elements of db that match e efficiently? In a brute-force fashion could solve a filtering problem by solving $|db|$ satisfaction problems where $|db|$ is the size of the database of profiles db. Thus the filtering problem for models $\mathcal{WP}$ and $\mathcal{AWP}$ can also be solved in PTIME (the exact upper bounds are omitted because they can be easily computed using Theorems 1 and 2).

In practice one would create *indices* over the database of profiles *db* to solve the matching problem more efficiently. This approach has been pioneered in SIFT [32, 33] where queries are conjunctions of keywords interpreted under the boolean or vector space model. Similar indexing algorithms for simple arithmetic constraints have also been presented in [26, 14, 5].

The algorithms of [32] have recently been re-evaluated extensively in [13] and some properties overlooked in the original study of [32] were pointed out. Additionally, it was shown that a main memory version of the most sophisticated algorithm of [32] (called *Key*) can solve the filtering problem for millions of profiles very efficiently. Currently, we are extending this study to the more expressive languages of this paper.

6   Conclusions

In this paper we presented the models $\mathcal{WP}$, $\mathcal{AWP}$ and $\mathcal{AWPS}$ for textual information dissemination in distributed agent systems. We laid down the logical foundations of these models and their corresponding languages, we formalized two fundamental problems arising in information dissemination environments utilizing them, and studied the computational complexity of these problems.

Our current work concentrates on extending the results of [13] to obtain efficient algorithms for solving the filtering problem for queries in the model $\mathcal{AWPS}$. We are also implementing a prototype information dissemination system using the architecture briefly discussed in Section 1 and the API developed in the DIET project and discussed in [24, 30, 19].

Acknowledgements

This work was carried out as part of the DIET (Decentralised Information Ecosystems Technologies) project (IST-1999-10088), within the Universal Information Ecosystems initiative of the Information Society Technology Programme of the European Union. We would like to thank the other participants in the DIET project, from Departmento de Teoria de Senal y Comunicaciones, Universidad Carlos III de Madrid, the Intelligent Systems Laboratory, BTexact Technologies and the Intelligent and Simulation Systems Department, DFKI, for their comments and contributions.

References

1. S. Abiteboul, R. Hull, and V. Vianu. *Foundations of Databases*. Addison Wesley, 1995.
2. M. Altinel and M.J. Franklin. Efficient filtering of XML documents for selective dissemination of information. In *Proceedings of the 26th VLDB Conference*, 2000.
3. R. Baeza-Yates and B. Ribeiro-Neto. *Modern Information Retrieval*. Addison Wesley, 1999.

4. A. Campailla, S. Chaki, E. Clarke, S. Jha, and H. Veith. Efficent filtering in publish-subscribe systems using binary decision diagrams. In *Proceedings of the 23rd International Conference on Software Engineering*, Toronto, Ontario, Canada, 2001.

5. A. Carzaniga, J. Deng, and A. L. Wolf. Fast forwarding for content-based networking. Technical report, Dept. of Computer Science, University of Colorado, 2001.

6. A. Carzaniga, D. S. Rosenblum, and A. L. Wolf. Achieving scalability and expressiveness in an internet-scale event notification service. In *Proceedings of the 19th ACM Symposium on Principles of Distributed Computing (PODC'2000)*, pages 219–227, 2000.

7. U. Cetintemel, M.J. Franklin, and C.L. Giles. Self-adaptive user profiles for large-scale data delivery. In *ICDE*, pages 622–633, 2000.

8. C.-C. K. Chang, H. Garcia-Molina, and A. Paepcke. Boolean Query Mapping across Heterogeneous Information Sources. *IEEE Transactions on Knowledge and Data Engineering*, 8(4):515–521, 1996.

9. C.-C. K. Chang, H. Garcia-Molina, and A. Paepcke. Predicate Rewriting for Translating Boolean Queries in a Heterogeneous Information System. *ACM Transactions on Information Systems*, 17(1):1–39, 1999.

10. T. T. Chinenyanga and N. Kushmerick. Expressive retrieval from XML documents. In *Proceedings of SIGIR'01*, September 2001.

11. William W. Cohen. WHIRL: A word-based information representation language. *Artificial Intelligence*, 118(1-2):163–196, 2000.

12. K. Decker, K. Sycara, and M. Williamson. Middle-agents for the internet. In *Proceedings of IJCAI-97*, 1997.

13. M. Koubarakis et. al. Project DIET Deliverable 7 (Information Brokering), December 2001.

14. F. Fabret, H. A. Jacobsen, F. Llirbat, J. Pereira, K. A. Ross, and D. Shasha. Filtering algorithms and implementation for very fast publish/subscribe systems. In *Proceedings of ACM SIGMOD-2001*, 2001.

15. D. Faensen, L. Faulstich, H. Schweppe, A. Hinze, and A. Steidinger. Hermes – A Notification Service for Digital Libraries. In *Proceedings of the Joint ACM/IEEE Conference on Digital Libraries (JCDL'01), Roanoke, Virginia, USA*, 2001.

16. T. Finin, R. Fritzson, D. McKay, and R. McEntire. KQML as an Agent Communication Language. In N. Adam, B. Bhargava, and Y. Yesha, editors, *Proceedings of the 3rd International Conference on Information and Knowledge Management (CIKM'94)*, pages 456–463, Gaithersburg, MD, USA, 1994. ACM Press.

17. P.W. Foltz and S.T. Dumais. Personalised information delivery: An analysis of information filtering methods. *Communications of the ACM*, 35(12):29–38, 1992.

18. M. J. Franklin and S. B. Zdonik. "Data In Your Face": Push Technology in Perspective. In *Proceedings ACM SIGMOD International Conference on Management of Data*, pages 516–519, 1998.

19. A. Galardo-Antolin, A. Navia-Vasquez, H.Y. Molina-Bulla, A.B. Rodriquez-Gonzalez, F.J. Valvarde-Albacete, A.R. Figueiras-Vidal, T. Koutris, A. Xiruhaki, and M. Koubarakis. I-Gaia: an Information Processing Layer for the DIET Platform . In *Proceedings of the 1st International Joint Conference on Autonomous Agents & Multiagent Systems (AAMAS 2002)*, July 15–19 2002.

20. M. Koubarakis. Boolean Queries with Proximity Operators for Information Dissemination. Proceedings of the workshop on Foundations of Models and Languages for Information Integration (FMII-2001), Viterbo,

Italy , 16-18 September, 2001. In LNCS (forthcoming). Available from: http://www.intelligence.tuc.gr/~manolis/publications.html.

21. M. Koubarakis. Textual Information Dissemination in Distributed Event-Based Systems. Proceedings of the International Workshop on Distributed Event-Based systems (DEBS'02), July 2-3, 2002, Vienna, Austria. Available from: http://www.intelligence.tuc.gr/~manolis/publications.html.

22. D. R. Kuokka and L. P. Harada. Issues and extensions for information matchmaking protocols. *International Journal of Cooperative Information Systems*, 5(2-3):251–274, 1996.

23. C.D. Manning and H. Schütze. *Foundations of Statistical Natural Language Processing*. The MIT Press, Cambridge, Massachusetts, 1999.

24. P. Marrow, M. Koubarakis, R.H. van Lengen, F. Valverde-Albacete, E. Bonsma, J. Cid-Suerio, A.R. Figueiras-Vidal, A. Gallardo-Antolin, C. Hoile, T. Koutris, H. Molina-Bulla, A. Navia-Vazquez, P. Raftopoulou, N. Skarmeas, C. Tryfonopoulos, F. Wang, and C. Xiruhaki. Agents in Decentralised Information Ecosystems: The DIET Approach. In M. Schroeder and K. Stathis, editors, *Proceedings of the AISB'01 Symposium on Information Agents for Electronic Commerce, AISB'01 Convention*, pages 109–117, University of York, United Kingdom, March 2001.

25. C. Papadimitriou. *Computational Complexity*. Addison-Wesley, 1994.

26. J. Pereira, F. Fabret, F. Llirbat, and D. Shasha. Efficient matching for web-based publish/subscribe systems. In *Proceedings of COOPIS-2000*, 2000.

27. M.F. Porter. An Algorithm for Suffix Striping. *Program*, 14(3):130–137, 1980.

28. K. Sycara, M. Klusch, S. Widoff, and J. Lu. Dynamic Service Matchmaking Among Agents in Open Information Environments. *SIGMOD Record (ACM Special Interest Group on Management of Data)*, 28(1):47–53, 1999.

29. K. Sycara, S. Widoff, M. Klusch, and J. Lu. LARKS: Dynamic Matchmaking Among Heterogeneous Software Agents in Cyberspace. *Autonomous Agents and Multi-Agent Systems*, 5:173–203, 2002.

30. F. Wang. Self-organising Communities Formed by Middle Agents. In *Proceedings of the 1st International Joint Conference on Autonomous Agents & Multiagent Systems (AAMAS 2002)*, July 15–19 2002.

31. I.H. Witten, A. Moffat, and T.C. Bell. *Managing Gigabytes: Compressing and Indexing Documents and Images*. Morgan Kauffman Publishing, San Francisco, 2nd edition, 1999.

32. T.W. Yan and H. Garcia-Molina. Distributed selective dissemination of information. In *Proceedings of the 3rd International Conference on Parallel and Distributed Information Systems (PDIS)*, pages 89–98, 1994.

33. T.W. Yan and H. Garcia-Molina. The SIFT information dissemination system. *ACM Transactions on Database Systems*, 24(4):529–565, 1999.

Integrating Distributed Information Sources with CARROT II

R. Scott Cost[1], Srikanth Kallurkar[1], Hemali Majithia[1], Charles Nicholas[1], and Yongmei Shi[1]

University of Maryland, Baltimore County
Baltimore, MD USA
{cost,skallu1,hema1,nicholas,yshi1}@csee.umbc.edu

Abstract. We describe CARROT II (**C2**), an agent-based architecture for distributed information retrieval and document collection management. **C2** can consist of an arbitrary number of agents, distributed across a variety of platforms and locations. **C2** agents provide search services over local document collections or information sources. They advertise content-derived metadata that describes their local document store. This metadata is sent to other **C2** agents which agree to act as brokers for that collection, and every agent in the system has the ability to serve as such a broker. A query can be sent to any **C2** agent, which can decide to answer the query itself from its local collection, or to send the query on to other agents whose metadata indicate that they would be able to answer the query, or send the query on further. Search results from multiple agents are merged and returned to the user. **C2** differs from similar systems in that metadata takes the form of an automatically generated, unstructured feature vector, and that any agent in the system can act as a broker, so there is no centralized control. We present experimental results of retrieval performance and effectiveness in a distributed environment.

1 Introduction

We have developed a scalable, distributed query routing and information retrieval system, CARROT II. It is the successor of an earlier project (Collaborative Agent-based Routing and Retrieval of Text) [9, 7] (originally CAFE [8]). **C2** is composed of a flexible hierarchy of query routing agents. These agents communicate with one another using KQML [10] and the Jackal platform [6], and may be distributed across the Internet. While all agents in the system are alike, they can each control widely varying information systems. Agents interact with information sources via a well-defined interface. Queries presented to any agent in the system are routed, based on the content of the query and metadata about the contents of the servers, to the appropriate destination. Agents themselves are uniform and extremely simple.

C2 contains wrappers that extend several well-known IR systems (e.g. MG [20], Telltale [16]), as well as **C2**'s own, modest IR system. These wrappers present

M. Klusch, S. Ossowski, and O. Shehory (Eds.): CIA 2002, LNAI 2446, pp. 194–201, 2002.

a basic interface to the **C2** system for operating on documents and metadata. Agents are addressable via commands that are communicated in KQML. This means that a **C2** system can be created, configured, and accessed by another information system, and so can be employed to extend the search capabilities of an existing project. We use the Jackal platform to support communication among agents in **C2** and to provide an interface to the outside world. In addition to Jackal's support for agent communication with KQML, we can use its conversation management capabilities to specify and implement higher-level behaviors for the various negotiation and management tasks required within the agent system.

Our research effort has been directed towards testing retrieval performance as well as effectiveness. Since we cannot assume static corpora, we believe in the use of an agent-based retrieval architecture based on a sophisticated communication infrastructure to handle dynamic data and its associated operations. Section 2 discusses the problems areas facing DIR and the efforts so far by the research community, Section 3 describes **C2** architecture and Section 4 describes its operations.

2   Related Work

In the past there have been attempts to introduce the concepts of agent-based information retrieval. Systems like SavvySearch [14] demonstrated a simple approach to querying web search engines and combining their results in a single ranked order.

Historically, Harvest was the first system to demonstrate the use of broker agents in distributed search. The Harvest system [2] is a distributed, brokered system originally designed for searching Web, FTP, and Gopher servers. In Harvest, "gatherer" agents collect metadata from information providers and deliver it to one or more brokers. Metadata objects are represented in Summary Object Interchange Format (SOIF), an extensible attribute-value-based description record. Harvest pioneered the ideas of brokering, metasearch, replication, and caching on the Internet.

2.1   Distributed Information Retrieval

Information Retrieval in a distributed environment normally follows three steps [3]:

1. Information Source Selection: Select best information source per query
2. Query Processing: Send query to source(s) and return ranked list of documents
3. Results Fusion: Create single ranked list from ranked lists of all sources.

For retrieval from text, one of the methods for information source selection is use of automatically generated metadata from the content. Comparing the query to metadata about the sources can reveal the possible relevance of each source to the query. CORI [4] and gGloss [13] are examples of such metadata in information source selection. The CORI model is based on inference networks. CORI creates a virtual document containing Document Frequency (DF) and Inverse Collection Frequency (ICF). The ICF indicates importance of the term across the collections and is analogous to the Inverse Document Frequency (IDF), which is a measure of term importance in a single collection. gGloss creates a virtual document containing DF(s) and Term Frequency (TF), i.e. number of occurrences per document of unique terms of the collection. French et al. [11] showed that CORI performed better than gGloss in terms of retrieval effectiveness, however they could not provide a reason for CORI's better performance.

Gibbins and Hall [12] modeled query routing topologies for Resource Discovery in mediator based distributed information systems. Queries are routed by a referral (of a server) by the mediator or by a delegation of the query to the mediator. Liu [15] demonstrated query routing using processes of query refinement and source selection, which interleaved query and database source profiles to obtain a subset of good databases.

The final step in answering a query is fusing the ranked list from the queried sources to obtain a single ranked list. Voorhees et al. [19] showed the use of query training and query clustering to first query appropriate data sources and then merge the results. The query training approach used a dice biased by the number of documents still to be merged, whereas query clustering applied a factor to the results based on the importance of the source it was from and then rank based on the new scores. Aslam and Montague [1] showed that results fusion based on ranks alone can be as good as regular fusion techniques and that relevance scores are not required.

In general, there is a performance gain by distributing information, but distributed retrieval lags behind centralized retrieval in terms of retrieval effectiveness, i.e. percentage of relevant documents returned for a query. However Powell et al. [17] showed that a distributed search can outperform a centralized search under certain conditions.

3   C2 Architecture

A **C2** system is a collection of coordinated, distributed agents managing a set of possibly heterogeneous IR resources. These agents each perform the basic tasks of collection selection, query routing, query processing, and data fusion. In order to effect this coordination, some amount of underlying structure is required.

There are three components to the **C2** architecture. The central work of **C2** is performed by a distributed collection of **C2** agents. There is also a network of infrastructure agents which facilitate communication and control of the system. Finally, a small set of support agents facilitates access to the system, and coordinates its activities. Each of these components is described in detail below.

3.1   C2 Agents

The **C2** agent is the cornerstone of the **C2** system. It's role is to manage a certain corpus, accept queries, and either answer them itself, or forward them to other **C2** agents in the system. In order to do this, each **C2** agent creates and distributes metadata describing its own corpus to other **C2** agents. All **C2** agents are identical, although the information systems they manage may vary.

A standard interface provides methods for manipulating documents, metadata, and handling queries. The agent maintains a catalog of metadata which contains information about the documents stored by peer agents

3.2   Information Integration

A **C2** agent interfaces with an information source which may be an ordinary IR package, or a database manager.

The **C2** system currently has a wrapper that interfaces with the WONDIR[1] (in-house) IR engine. It can however be extended to support other types of Information sources. As mentioned earlier, metadata is derived from the document collection. The metadata takes the form of a vector of the unique "N-grams" of the collection and a sum of their number of occurrences across all documents in the collection. Hence unlike Harvest, **C2** metadata describes the agent's collection of documents, not a single document. **C2** uses such metadata for source selection per query. The motivation for such a form of metadata comes from relative ease of use, low cost of generation, and the ability to aggregate metadata, such that a single vector may contain metadata about multiple agents.

The **C2** metadata is different from the *CORI virtual document* in that CORI uses document frequency, i.e. the number of documents the term has occurred in the collection. **C2** uses term frequency, i.e. the sum of the number of occurrences of the unique terms over all documents. In many if not most collections, a large percentage of terms have occurrences of 0 or 1. By storing the sum of the terms **C2** metadata adds more weight to terms that appear more often in the collection either in more documents or in fewer documents with larger occurrences per document.*CORI* would favor terms that occurred only in more documents.

The same query operation can now be performed on both documents and metadata. A query operation returns a similarity score using $TF * IDF$ based cosine similarity [18]. Querying a collection returns a ranked list of the documents sorted by their similarity scores. For querying metadata collection IDF is replaced by the ICF (see Section 2). On average from empirical observations the metadata is 8-10% of the size of the document collection. The agent that creates the metadata attaches its signature information to the vector.

3.3   C2 Infrastructure Agents

In order to support the successful inter-operation of potentially very many **C2** agents, we have constructed a hierarchical infrastructure. The infrastructure is

---

[1] Word or N-gram based Dynamic Information Retrieval

largely dormant while **C2** is in operation, serving primarily to facilitate the orderly startup and shutdown of the system, and provide communications support.

The infrastructure is controlled by a single Master Agent, which may be located anywhere on the network. At startup, the Master Agent is instructed as to the number of agents required, and some factors regarding their desired distribution. These include the number of physical nodes to be used, as well as the degree of resource sharing at various levels.

The Master Agent starts a Node Agent on each participating machine, and delegates to it the task of creating a subset of the required agents. The node will be divided into Platforms, or independent Java Virtual Machines, each governed by a Platform Agent. The Node Agent creates an appropriate number of Platforms, and again delegates the creation of a set of agents.

Within each Platform, the Platform Agent creates a set of Cluster agents. The purpose of the Cluster Agent is to consolidate some of the 'heavier' resources that will be used by the **C2** agents. Primarily, this means communication resources. A Cluster Agent maintains a single instance of Jackal. Each Cluster Agent creates a series of **C2** agents; these run as subthreads of the Cluster Agent. Because most agents will be dormant at any one time, we allow a **C2** agent to be assigned more than one collection, creating a set of 'virtual' agents. Thus the virtual agents are the agents visible to all entities external to the system.

3.4   C2 Support Agents

While the agents in the **C2** system work largely independently, a small set of support agents serve to coordinate the system's activities. These are the Agent Name Server, the Logger Agent, and the Collection Manager.

An Agent Name Server provides basic communication facilitation among the agents. Through the use of Jackal, **C2** employs a hierarchical naming scheme, and its operation is distributed through a hierarchy of name servers.

A Logger Agent monitors log traffic, and allows the system to assemble information about the details of operation. This information can then be used to feed monitors or visualization tools.

Finally, a Collection Manager facilitates the distribution of data and metadata. It determines which collection of documents or information source will be assigned to each agent, how each agent will distribute its metadata, and what set of agents will be visible outside the system.

4   C2 Operation

Metadata distribution and query processing are the two main functions of the **C2** agents. Recall from Section 3.2 that the **C2** metadata is an automatically generated feature vector derived from the content itself.

4.1   Metadata Distribution

C2 uses a vector-based representation of metadata which describes the contents of the local corpus (see [9]). Metadata, as well as corpus documents, are managed by an underlying IR engine. This metadata is first order only, and is to be distinguished from information characterizing the set of collections known to a given agent, or higher order metadata. This form of metadata used supports interoperability. The routing of queries should not be hampered by the underlying information source, may it be an IR engine, a search engine on the Internet or an RDF or DAML+OIL [5] based system.

The distribution of Metadata has a profound impact on the system's ability to route queries effectively, and determines the "shape" of the **C2** system. Agents receive instructions on metadata distribution from the Collection Manager. There are three possible metadata distribution modes that can be used by **C2**:

1. Flood: Each agent broadcasts it's metadata to every other agent in the system. Under this scheme, any agent receiving a query would have complete (and identical) knowledge of the system, and be able in theory to find the optimal target for that query.
2. Global: As the original CARROT architecture a designated broker agent has knowledge of the entire system. All agents share their metadata with only this agent.
3. Group: Once the system reaches a certain size, however, both of the above schemes are impractical; the system would become susceptible to bottlenecking. The group scheme based on mathematical, quorum-based distributions, where a group of agents is represented by a chosen (or elected) agent. Metadata sharing would occur inside such groups and amongst the group leaders.

Metadata distribution can be effected by transferring the entire vector, a "difference" vector in case of changes in agent's corpus, or just a URL pointing to the location of the metadata, enclosed in a KQML message.

4.2   Query Processing

Once the system is running, the Collection Manager becomes the primary or initial interface for outside clients. A client first contacts the Collection Manager to get the name or names of **C2** agents that it may query. The names in this set will be determined by the metadata distribution policy. For example, in the case of group-based distribution, the set will contain the group leader agent names. The client then sends queries to randomly selected agents from the given set. It is also possible to model more restricted or brokered architectures by limiting the list to only one or a few agents, which would then feed queries to the remainder of the system.

In response to an incoming query, an agent decides whether the query should be answered locally, forwarded to other agents, or both. In flood mode, for example, the agent compares the query to its local metadata collection , and determines the best destinations. Based on the results, it may send the query to the single best source of information, or it may choose to send it to several. One of those sources may be its own local IR engine. Once answers are computed and received, the results are forwarded back to the originator of the query. If more than one information source is targeted, the agent faces the problem of fusing the information it receives into one coherent response.

Queries may be routed through a number of different agents before finally being resolved; this depends on the scheme used for metadata distribution and the routing algorithm. For example, the simplest scheme is to have each agent broadcast its metadata to every other agent in the system. The corresponding routing algorithm would be to route to the best information source. Since all agents have the same metadata collection and employ the same algorithm, a query will be forwarded at most once before being resolved. For schemes which employ a more efficient distribution of metadata, or possibly higher order metadata, queries may pass through many **C2** agents before finally being resolved.

4.3   Implementation

The current implementation of **C2** uses the flood mode of metadata distribution. This implies that the query given to any agent in the system will return the same answer. The query can be routed either based on a metadata similarity cutoff or to the best N agents, based on the metadata similarity scores. Therefore, as stated in section 4.2, the query needs to be *forwarded* only once. The results fusion is based on Voorhees's query clustering approach [19]. But unlike their method, the importance of the collection is measured by the metadata similarity score generated. The metadata score is simply applied as a factor to the each of the individual document similarity scores of each collection's ranked list. The results are then sorted based on this new similarity score and the top N documents returned as results.

5   Conclusions and Future Work

We presented an initial prototype of a Distributed Information retrieval system that uses an agent-based architecture. We have been able to show with the initial construction of the system a proof of concept, i.e. distributed retrieval in fielded system does actually performs satisfactorily with a slightly deteriorated performance than centralized retrieval.

References

1. J. A. Aslam and M. Montague. Models for metasearch. In *ACM SIGIR*, pages 276–284, 2001.
2. C. M. Bowman, P. B. Danzig, D. R. Hardy, U. Manber, and M. F. Schwartz. The Harvest information discovery and access system. *Computer Networks and ISDN Systems*, 28(1–2):119–125, 1995.

3. J. Callan. *Advances in Information Retrieval*, chapter 6: Distributed Information Retrieval, pages 127–150. Kluwer Academic Publishers, 2000.
4. J. P. Callan, Z. Lu, and W. B. Croft. Searching distributed collections with inference networks. In E. A. Fox, P. Ingwersen, and R. Fidel, editors, *Proceedings of the 18th Annual International ACM SIGIR Conference on Research and Development in Information Retrieval*, pages 21–28, Seattle, Washington, 1995. ACM Press.
5. R. S. Cost, T. Finin, A. Joshi, Y. Peng, C. Nicholas, I. Soboroff, H. Chen, L. Kagal, F. Perich, Y. Zou, and S. Tolia. ITtalks: A case study in the semantic web and DAML+OIL. *IEEE Intelligent Systems*, 17(1):40–47, January/February 2002.
6. R. S. Cost, T. Finin, Y. Labrou, X. Luan, Y. Peng, I. Soboroff, J. Mayfield, and A. Boughannam. Jackal: A Java-based tool for agent development. In J. Baxter and C. Brian Logan, editors, *Working Notes of the Workshop on Tools for Developing Agents, AAAI '98*, number WS-98-10 in AAAI Technical Reports, pages 73–82, Minneapolis, Minnesota, July 1998. AAAI, AAAI Press.
7. R. S. Cost, I. Soboroff, J. Lakhani, T. Finin, E. Miller, and C. Nicholas. TKQML: A scripting tool for building agents. In M. Wooldridge, M. Singh, and A. Rao, editors, *Intelligent Agents Volume IV – Proceedings of the 1997 Workshop on Agent Theories, Architectures and Languages*, volume 1365 of *Lecture Notes in Artificial Intelligence*, pages 336–340. Springer-Verlag, Berlin, 1997.
8. G. Crowder and C. Nicholas. Resource selection in CAFE: An architecture for network information retrieval. In *Proceedings of the Network Information Retrieval Workshop, SIGIR 96*, August 1996.
9. G. Crowder and C. Nicholas. Metadata for distributed text retrieval. In *Proceedings of the Network Information Retrieval Workshop, SIGIR 97*, 1997.
10. T. Finin, Y. Labrou, and J. Mayfield. KQML as an agent communication language. In J. Bradshaw, editor, *Software Agents*. MIT Press, 1997.
11. J. C. French, A. L. Powell, J. P. Callan, C. L. Viles, T. Emmitt, K. J. Prey, and Y. Mou. Comparing the performance of database selection algorithms. In *SIGIR*, pages 238–245, 1999.
12. N. Gibbins and W. Hall Scalability issues for query routing service discovery. In *Second Workshop on Infrastructure for Agents, MAS and Scalable MAS at the Fourth International Conference on Autonomous Agents*, pages 209–217, 2001.
13. L. Gravano and H. Garcia-Molina. Generalizing gloss to vector-space databases and broker hierarchies. In *In Proceedings of the 21st VLDB Conference*, Zurich, Switzerland, 1995.
14. A. E. Howe and D. Dreilinger. SAVVYSEARCH: A metasearch engine that learns which search engines to query. *AI Magazine*, 18(2):19–25, 1997.
15. L. Liu. Query Routing in Large Scale Digital Library Systems. *ICDE, IEEE Press*, 1997.
16. C. Pearce and C. Nicholas. TELLTALE: Experiments in a dynamic hypertext environment for degraded and multilingual data. *Journal of the American Society for Information Science*, June 1994.
17. A. L. Powell, J. C. French, J. Callan, M. Connell, and C. L. Viles. The impact of database selection on distributed searching. In *SIGIR*, pages 232–239, 2000.
18. G. Salton, C. Yang, and A. Wong. A vector space model for automatic indexing. *Communication of the ACM*, pages 613–620, 1975.
19. E. M. Voorhees, N. K. Gupta, and B. Johnson-Laird. Learning collection fusion strategies. In *SIGIR*, Fusion Strategies, pages 172–179, 1995.
20. I. H. Witten, A. Moffat, and T. C. Bell. *Managing Gigabytes: Compressing and Indexing Documents and Images*. Van Nostrand Reinhold, 1994.

Distributed Artificial Intelligence for Distributed Corporate Knowledge Management

Fabien Gandon and Rose Dieng-Kuntz

ACACIA project – INRIA, 2004 route des Lucioles – BP93
06902 Sophia Antipolis Cedex – France
{Fabien.Gandon; Rose.Dieng}@sophia.inria.fr

Abstract. We present a multi-agents architecture that was built and tested to manage a corporate memory based on the semantic Web technologies.

1 Introduction

The advent of information society led organizations to build intranets that are becoming corporate nervous systems. They memorize critical pieces of information and irrigate the organizational entities with them. A corporate memory is an explicit, disembodied and persistent representation of knowledge and information in an organization, in order to facilitate their access and reuse by members of the organization, for their tasks [10]. The stake in building a corporate memory management system is the coherent integration of this dispersed knowledge in a corporation with the objective to promote knowledge growth, knowledge communication and to preserve knowledge within an organization [30].

The field of multi-agents information systems is very active and most promising application areas are, among others, distributed Web-based collaborative work, information discovery in heterogeneous information sources and intelligent data management in the Internet or corporate intranets [21].

Some of these systems are specialized for information retrieval from heterogeneous information repositories. InfoMaster [18] uses a global schema and Carnot [7] a global ontology (Cyc) to build mappings for wrappers of heterogeneous sources. As in RETSINA [9], these systems rely on wrapper agents to provide an homogeneous view of the different sources while the integration is handled by middle agents planning query resolution, information integration and conflict resolution. Information Manifold [23] and InfoSleuth [25] have multiple ontologies but they do not handle mapping between them. SIMS [2] uses Description Logics to handle multiple ontologies and translate queries when there is no loss. Finally OBSERVER [24] takes into account the inter-ontology relationships to tackle the loss of information when translating queries.

SAIRE [26] and UMDL [31] manage distributed large scale libraries of digital documents to offer means to find relevant documents and manage indexing.

M. Klusch, S. Ossowski, and O. Shehory (Eds.): CIA 2002, LNAI 2446, pp. 202–217, 2002.
© Springer-Verlag Berlin Heidelberg 2002

Finally some projects focuses on knowledge management inside organizations. CASMIR [4] and Ricochet [5] focus on gathering information and adapting interactions to the user's preferences, learning interests to build communities and enable collaborative filtering inside an organization. KnowWeb [12] relies on mobile agents to support dynamically changing networked environment and exploits a domain model to extract concepts describing a documents and use them to answer queries. RICA [1] maintains a shared taxonomy in which nodes are attached to documents and uses it to push suggestions to interface agents according to user profiles. Finally FRODO [13] is dedicated to building and maintaining distributed organizational memories with an emphasis on the management of domain ontologies.

The CoMMA project we present here, belongs to this last category. It aims at implementing and testing a corporate memory management framework based on agent technology. Two application scenarios had been submitted by industrial end-users, involving information retrieval tasks for employees:

– *Integration of a new employee to an organization*: the main user of the system is a newcomer that needs to acquire some knowledge to become fully operational and integrated to the organization.
– *Technology monitoring*: assist the detection, identification and diffusion of information about technology movements to disseminate innovative idea in the company and improve the response time by providing the relevant information as soon as possible.

Thus, CoMMA does not target the Internet and the open Web but corporate memory accessible through an intranet based on Web technologies *i.e.* an intraweb. The system does not directly manage documents, but annotations about documents. We suppose documents are referenced by URI and, as explained in section 2, we index them using semantic annotations relying on the semantic Web technologies. CoMMA focuses on three functionalities needed for the two application scenarios: improve precision and recall to retrieve documents, using semantic annotations; proactively push information using organization and user models; archive newly submitted annotations.

On the one hand, individual agents locally adapt to users and resources they are dedicated to: an interface agent adapts to its user; an archivist agent is associated to a repository of annotations and manages it locally providing access to this knowledge base to other agents; etc.

On the other hand, thanks to cooperating software agents distributed over the network, the whole system capitalizes an integrated view of the corporate memory: agents are benevolent with the common collective goal of managing the corporate semantic web; there is no real competition as it could be found in a market place type application; middle agents provide matchmaking for service resolution.

The MAS architecture of CoMMA, detailed in section 3, aims at providing flexibility, extensibility and modularity to allow a deployment above the distributed information landscape of a company, while enabling the user to access an integrated view of its content. CoMMA was a two-year project that ended February 2002 with a system implemented in Java using the FIPA compliant platform JADE [3]. The final prototype was demonstrated and discussed during a trial and an open day and we give our return on experience in the last section on conclusion and discussion.

2 Corporate Semantic Web: An Annotated World for Agents

In their article about "Agents in Annotated Worlds" Doyle and Hayes-Roth [11] explained that annotated environments containing explanations of the purpose and uses of spaces and activities allow agents to quickly become intelligent actors in those spaces. For information agents in complex information worlds, it means that annotated information worlds are, in the actual state of the art, a quick way to make information agents smarter. If the corporate memory becomes an annotated world, agents can use the semantics of the annotation and through inferences help the users exploit the corporate memory.

The Resource Description Framework (RDF) [22] is a foundation to describe the data contained on the Web through metadata: it enables automatic processing and interoperability in exchanging information on the Web by providing a framework to annotate resources referenced by their Uniform Resource Identifier (URI). We use RDF to build *corporate semantic Webs* where software agents use the semantics of annotations and, through inferences, help users exploit the content of the memory. RDF provides a model for representing named properties of resources and property values and an XML syntax. The described resources are of any type. Schemas define the conceptual vocabulary that is used in RDF statements. RDF Schema (RDFS) [6] is a schema specification language that provides a basic type system for use in RDF models. It specifies the mechanisms to define the classes of resources described (e.g. books, Web pages, people, companies, etc.) and the properties used for descriptions (e.g. title, author, name, activity, etc.). Types of classes and properties are organized in two hierarchies. Property types define permitted values (*range*) and classes of resources they can describe (*domain*).

With RDF, we describe the content of documents and the organizational state of affair through semantic annotations and with RDFS we specify the ontology O'CoMMA [17] providing the conceptual primitives used to represent these annotations (Figure 1). Agents use and infer from these annotations to successfully search the mass of information of the corporate memory. The state of affairs includes a description of the organization and profiles of its members.

User profiles capture aspects of the user that were identified as relevant for and exploitable by agent behaviors. A profile is an RDF annotation about a person. It contains administrative information and explicit preferences such as topic interests. It also positions the user in the organization: role, location and potential acquaintance network, enabling the system to target push actions. In addition, the system derives information from the usage made by the user. It collects the history of visited documents and user's feedback and from this it learns some of the user's interests. These derived criteria are then used for results presentation or push technology enabling the emergence of communities of interest.

The enterprise model is an oriented, focused and somewhat simplified explicit representation of the organization. So far, the enterprise modeling field has been mainly concerned with simulation and optimization of the production system design. They provide benchmark for business processes and are used for re-engineering them. But organizations became aware of the value of their memory and the fact that organization models have a role to play in this application too [28]. In CoMMA, the model aims at supporting corporate memory activities involved in the application scenario by giving the agents insight into their organizational context and environment. Thus they can exploit the aspects described in this model for their interactions with other agents and, above all, with users. We used RDF to implement our organizational description, annotating the organizational entities (departments, activities, etc.) with their relations (manages, employs, includes, etc.).

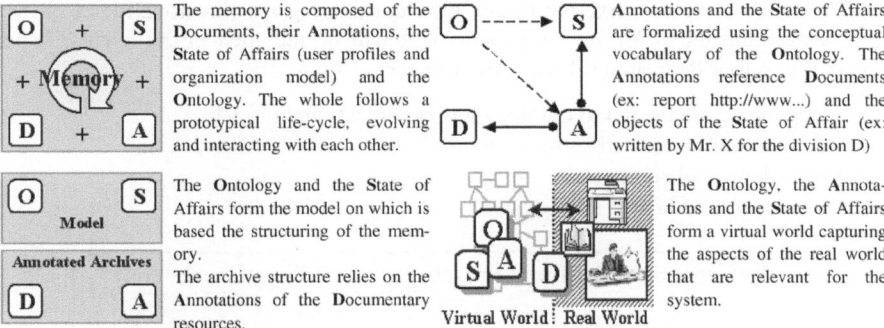

The memory is composed of the Documents, their Annotations, the State of Affairs (user profiles and organization model) and the Ontology. The whole follows a prototypical life-cycle, evolving and interacting with each other.

Annotations and the State of Affairs are formalized using the conceptual vocabulary of the Ontology. The Annotations reference Documents (ex: report http://www...) and the objects of the State of Affair (ex: written by Mr. X for the division D)

The Ontology and the State of Affairs form the model on which is based the structuring of the memory.
The archive structure relies on the Annotations of the Documentary resources.

Virtual World ¦ Real World

The Ontology, the Annotations and the State of Affairs form a virtual world capturing the aspects of the real world that are relevant for the system.

Fig. 1. Structure of the memory

The ontology O'CoMMA plays a pivotal role enabling the description of annotations and organizational and user models that are exchanged between agents. Thus, it provides the semantic ground for the communication and co-operation of the different agents that form the CoMMA architecture. We now detail this architecture.

3   Multi-agents Architecture of CoMMA

The architecture of the CoMMA system was obtained following an organizational approach for designing a multi-agent system (MAS). The design rationale is detailed in [15]. We only describe here the final implemented architecture. We then focus the sub-society dedicated to the management of annotations, its principles and functioning.

3.1 The Societies of CoMMA

The architecture is a structure that portrays the different kinds of agencies existing in an agent society and the relationships among them. A configuration is an instantiation of an architecture with a chosen arrangement and an appropriate number of agents of each type. One given architecture can lead to several configurations. The CoMMA architecture was designed so that the set of possible configurations covers the different corporate organizational layouts foreseeable. The MAS flexibility and modularity is used to provide a maneuver margin and postpone some choices until the very last stage of deployment. In the case of a multi-agents corporate memory system, the configuration depends on the topography and context of the place where the system is rolled out (organizational layout, network topography, stakeholders location, corporate policies). The configuration must be tuned to this information landscape and change with it. Among the possible configuration we also try to choose the one optimizing CPU and network workload.

The architecture was fixed at design time considering the functionalities CoMMA focuses on and the software components that will be included in the agents. It was divided into four dedicated sub-societies of agents (figure 2):

– A sub-society dedicated to ontology and organizational model;
– An annotation-dedicated sub-society;
– A user-dedicated sub-society;
– A connection-dedicated sub-society.

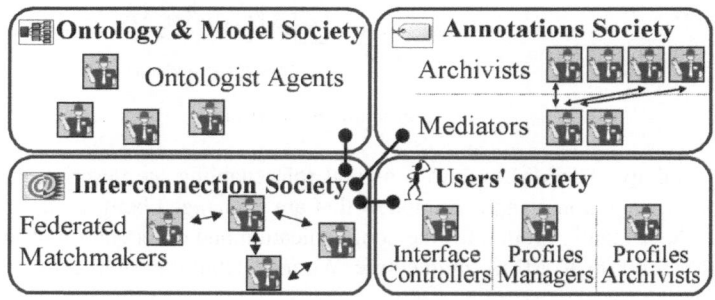

Fig. 2. Architecture of the MAS

In the four societies, ten agent roles were identified and specified and we detail them in the next section. Agent types have been implemented to play those roles and be provided within a complete solution to be deployed on an intranet. Every agent role was assigned to a partner of the project who had the expertise and the tools needed for implementing the corresponding behavior. Then an integration phased was carried out; it was extremely rapid and seamless since the combination of agents, ontology and specified protocols makes the different software components loosely-coupled both at run-time and design-time.

3.2 Specified Agent Roles and Implemented Agent Types

The user-dedicated sub-society relies on the fulfillment of four roles:

- *Interface Controller* (IC): this role is in charge of managing and monitoring the user interface. It is the only role with a limited lifetime which is the login session.
- *User Profile Manager* (UPM): this role is in charge of updating and exploiting the user's profile when the user is logged on to the system. It analyses the users requests and feedback to learn from them and improve the systems reactions.
- *User Profile Archivist* (UPA): this role is in charge of storing, retrieving and querying user profiles when requested by other agents.
- *User Profile Processor* (UPP): this role is in charge of performing proactive queries on the annotations using the user profiles to detect new documents that are potentially interesting for a user and push the information.

The IC role is played by one agent type. The IC agent is created at login and dies at logout. One of the major difficulty in implementing this agent is to try to provide a powerful and yet intelligible interface, that hides the complexity of the MAS and the semantic Web technologies. This agent is implemented using: Java Swing, an XSLT engine and a micro Web-browser to display the processed XML and the results. The IC interacts directly with the agents belonging to the ontology-dedicated sub-society but it relies on a contracted UPM agent to deal with the annotation-dedicated sub-society.

The UPM role is played by one agent type that uses machine learning techniques to learn the interest of the user and build an ordering relation to rank answers of the system and sort them before transmitting them to the IC. This agent was first implemented using the Weka library and then improved as detailed in [20]. The UPM also registers for new annotation notifications and forward them to the UPA.

One agent type, called UPA, is in charge of the UPP role and part of the UPA role concerning storage and retrieval of user profiles. Precise querying on user profiles is handle by another agent type (Annotation Archivist) that belongs to the annotation-dedicated sub-society. The UPA also compares new annotation notifications to user profiles to add consultation suggestions to the profiles.

CoMMA being based on the JADE platform [3], the agents of the connection sub-society play two roles defined by FIPA [14]:

- *Agent Management System* (AMS): this role is in charge of maintaining white pages where agents register themselves and ask for addresses of other agents on the basis of their name.
- *Directory Facilitator* (DF): this role is in charge of maintaining yellow pages where agents register themselves and ask for addresses of other agents on the basis of a description of the services they can provide.

AMS and DF agents are implemented and delivered with the JADE platform. They are directly used by the other agent types developed in CoMMA to form the acquaintance needed for their roles. The current prototype only uses the agent type as a service description, but further service description refinement is done in a second step as it will be detailed for the annotation-dedicated sub-society.

The agents from the ontology dedicated sub-society are concerned with the management of the ontological aspects of the information retrieval activity. The sub-society dedicated to ontology and model relies on two roles:
- *Ontology Archivist* (OA): this role is in charge of storing and retrieving the O'CoMMA ontology in RDFS.
- *Enterprise Model Archivist* (EMA): this role is in charge of storing and retrieving the organizational model in RDF.

Both roles are played by one agent type (OA) since they are really equivalent in their functioning and deployment. A replicated organization (identical roles and knowledge base) for the ontology sub-society is conceivable because CoMMA does not focuses on the maintenance of multiple ontologies.

The agents of the annotation dedicated sub-society must play two roles:
- *Annotation Archivist* (AA): this role is in charge of storing and searching RDF annotations in a local repository it is associated to.
- *Annotation Mediator* (AM): this role is in charge of distributed query solving and annotation allocation. It is a mediator between agents requiring services on the memory and Annotation Archivists attached to one repository. It hides the distributed aspect of the memory from the other agents. This roles also provides a subscription service for agents that whish to be notified of any new annotation added to the memory.

Two agents types were developed to fulfil these two roles. AAs are also used to include user profiles repositories in the query solving process. A hierarchical organization was chosen for this society because it separates the task of maintaining local annotation repositories from the task of managing distributed query solving and annotation allocation which allows us to distribute the workload.

3.3   Agents to Handle Annotation Distribution

We now focus on the annotation dedicated sub-society to explain the principles it is based on and its implementation.

3.3.1   RDF Annotations

RDF(S) was influenced by the graph data models and we manipulate it as a restriction of Sowa's Conceptual Graphs (CGs) [29]. A CG is a bipartite graph, where every arc links a concept node and a conceptual relation node. Both concept and conceptual relation have a type that can be either primitive or defined by a monadic lambda expression. Concept and relation types are organized in two hierarchies which are sets of type labels partially ordered by the subtype relation. Figure 1 shows that RDF schemas and statements can be translated, respectively, into type hierarchies and directed bipartite graphs. The RDF triple model only supports binary relations, thus RDF annotations generate CGs with dyadic relations of primitive type and the signature of relations are derived from the *domain* and *range* constraints.

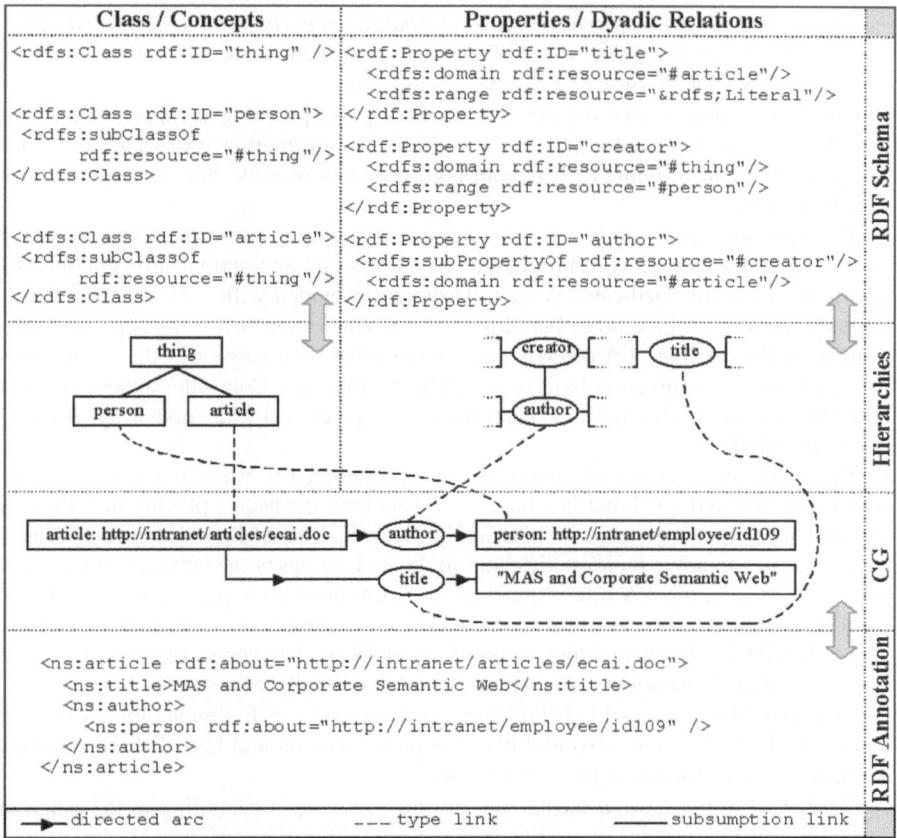

Class / Concepts	Properties / Dyadic Relations	

`<rdfs:Class rdf:ID="thing" />`
 	
`<rdfs:Class rdf:ID="person">`
` <rdfs:subClassOf`
`       rdf:resource="#thing"/>`
`</rdfs:Class>`
 	
`<rdfs:Class rdf:ID="article">`
` <rdfs:subClassOf`
`       rdf:resource="#thing"/>`
`</rdfs:Class>`
	`<rdf:Property rdf:ID="title">`
	`    <rdfs:domain rdf:resource="#article"/>`
	`    <rdfs:range rdf:resource="&rdfs;Literal"/>`
	`</rdf:Property>`
	
	`<rdf:Property rdf:ID="creator">`
	`    <rdfs:domain rdf:resource="#thing"/>`
	`    <rdfs:range rdf:resource="#person"/>`
	`</rdf:Property>`
	
	`<rdf:Property rdf:ID="author">`
	`    <rdfs:subPropertyOf rdf:resource="#creator"/>`
	`    <rdfs:domain rdf:resource="#article"/>`
	`</rdf:Property>`
		RDF Schema

Fig. 3. RDF(S) and CG model mapping

Type hierarchies are at the heart of ontologies for information searching and communication since they support inferences used when querying: specialization, generalization and identification. The CG projection operator is well adapted to annotation retrieval as it performs matching taking into account specialization of relations and concepts. The query language used is RDF with variables to indicate unknown parts and co-references, regular expressions to constrain literal values and operators to express disjunction or negation. The result of the projection is translated back into RDF. This mechanism provides a semantic search engine known as CORESE [8] and an API that we used to implement the behavior of the AA, AM and OA. We shall see now how our agents exploit the underlying graph model, when deciding how to allocate new annotations and when resolving distributed queries.

3.3.2 Annotation Agents
The duality of the definition of the word 'distribution' reveals two important problems to be addressed :

- Distribution means dispersion, that is the *spatial property of being scattered* about, over an area or a volume; the problem here is to handle the naturally distributed data, information or knowledge of the organization.
- Distribution also means the *act of distributing* or spreading or apportioning; the problem then is to make the relevant pieces of information go to the concerned agent (artificial or human). It is with both purposes in mind that we designed this sub-society.

The annotation-dedicated society is in charge of handling annotations and queries in the distributed memory. The submissions of queries and annotations are generated by agents from the user-dedicated society. Users are provided with a graphical interface to guide them in the process of building semantic annotations using concepts and relations from the ontology O'CoMMA (see Figure 6 for a screenshot of the second prototype). From the annotation built in the GUI, the Interface Controller agent generates an RDF annotation; through this agent the user appears just like another agent to the rest of the MAS.

The submitted queries and annotations are then routed to the annotation-dedicated society. As we said, the latter is a hierarchical society: the agents playing the AM role are in charge of managing agents playing the AA role. The AM provides its services to other societies to solve their queries and, to do so, it requests the services of the AAs. On the other side, the AA role is attached to a local annotation repository and when it receives a request, it tries to fulfil it with its local resources in a way that enables the AM to handle the distributed dimension of the problem. The agents playing the role of AA and AM are benevolent and, once deployed, temporally continuous.

Distributed Database field [27] distinguishes two types of fragmentation: horizontal and vertical. By drawing a parallel between data / schema and knowledge / ontology we adapted these notions to RDF annotations.

- *Horizontal fragmentation* means that information is split according to the range of properties; for instance $site_1$ will have reports with a property 'title' ranging from "Criminality in agent societies" to "MAS control" and $site_2$ will have reports from "Naive resource distribution" to "Zeno paradox in loops".
- *Vertical fragmentation* means that information is split according to types of concepts and properties; for instance $site_1$ will have reports with their titles and authors and $site_2$ will have articles with their abstract and keywords. Fragmentation choices are made by the administrators when deploying the agents.

The stake is to find mechanisms to decide *where to store newly submitted annotations* and *how to distribute a query* in order not to miss answers just because the needed information are split over several AAs. These two facets of distribution are linked since the performance of distributed query resolution is closely related to the choices made for the distribution of annotations.

3.3.3 Annotation Distribution

In order to determine which AA should be involved during the solving of a query or to which one an annotation should be given, we compare the content of their archive thanks to a light structure called ABIS (Annotation Base Instances Statistics). It captures statistics, maintained by the AA, about its annotation base: the number of instances for each concept type, the number of instances for each property type and the number of instances for each family of properties. A family of properties is defined by a specialized signature corresponding to at least one instance present in the archivists base:

$$[ConceptType_x] \rightarrow (PropertyType_y) \rightarrow [ConceptType_z]$$

where the concept types are possibly more precise than the signature of *PropertyType_y*. For instance, if there exists a property type *Author* with the following signature:

$$[Document] \rightarrow (Author) \rightarrow [Person],$$

we may have families of properties such as:

$$[Article] \rightarrow (Author) \rightarrow [Student],$$
$$[Book] \rightarrow (Author) \rightarrow [Philosopher].$$

This means that for each of these specialized signatures, there exists, in the archive of the corresponding AA, at least one instance using exactly these types. If a family does not appear in the ABIS, it means there is no instance of this very precise type. The ABIS captures the types for which an AA contributes to the memory. The ABIS of an AA is updated each time an annotation is loaded in the base: the annotation is decomposed into dyadic relations and possibly isolated nodes; for literal properties, the bounding interval $[B_{low}, B_{up}]$ of their literal values is calculated.

When a system is deployed, AAs are started but they may have no annotation in their bases. Their statistics being void, the ABIS is not relevant to compare their bids. Moreover, it is interesting to be able to specialize individual agents according to the topography of the company network (eg. an AA on a machine of the human resources department for users' profile). The CAP (Card of Archives Preferences) is a light structure that captures the RDF properties for which the agent has a preference and, if specified, their range boundaries. Any specialization of these properties is considered to be part of the preferences of the AA and can be used for bidding.

Submitted annotations are not broken down *i.e.* we store them as one block. When a new one is submitted, the AM emits a Call For Proposal and starts a contract-net protocol [14] with the AAs. The AM measures how close a new annotation is from the ABIS and CAP of the candidate AAs in order to decide which one of them should win the bid. Details of the pseudo-distance calculation can be found in [16], it exploits a semantic distance defined on the hierarchies of the ontology and a lexicographical distance for literal values. Figure 4 shows an example of protocol for the allocation of a newly submitted annotation to an archivist agent.

When the annotation has been allocated, the AM that handled the CFP sends the content of the annotation to the UPAs that registered for new annotation notification. This triggers the push chain.

3.3.4 Query Distribution

Query solving involves several annotation distributed bases; answers are a merger of partial results. To determine if and when an AA should participate to the solving of a query, AAs calculate the overlap between their ABIS and the properties at play in the query. The result is an OBSIQ (Overlap Between Statistics and Instances in a Query), a light structure which is void if the AA has no reason to participate to the query solving or which otherwise gives the properties for which the AA should be consulted. Using the OBSIQ it requested before starting the solving process, the AM is able to identify at each step of the decomposition algorithm and for each subquery it generates, which AAs are to be consulted. The communication protocol used for the query solving is an extension of the FIPA query-ref protocol [14] to allow multiple stages with subqueries being exchanged between the AM and the AAs.

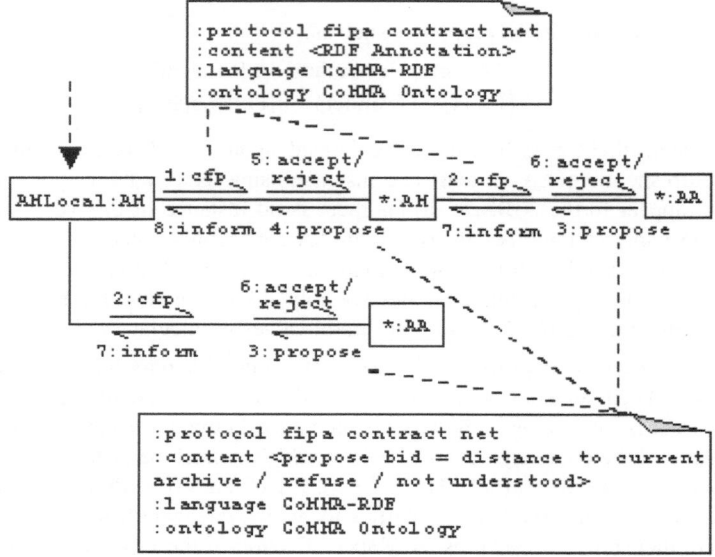

Fig. 4. Protocol for annotation submission

The decomposition algorithm consists of four stages: preprocessing for query simplification (e.g. remove cross-references), constraints solving (e.g. documents with a title containing "XML"), questions answering (e.g. find the name of the author) and final filtering (e.g. cross references such as "the title must contain the name of the author"). These stages manipulate the query structure through the Document Object Model (the DOM is an interface to manipulate an XML document as a forest). In our case, the structure is a tree that represents an RDF pattern and contains nodes representing resources or properties, except for the leaves that may be resources or literals. The resource nodes may have an URI and the AMs use them as cut/join point during query solving to build small subqueries that can be sent to the AAs to gather the information that could be scattered in several archives and merge the partial results. The four stages are detailed in [16].

3.3.5 Role of the Ontology

Figure 5 shows an example of message sent by an agent requesting the title of available memos. There are three nested levels: (a) a level using the FIPA ontology for general speech acts (b) a CoMMA ACL level using speech acts involved in the memory management (c) an RDF level using the O'CoMMA primitives to describe the pattern to look for.

The ontology is the cornerstone of distributed artificial intelligence mechanisms managing distributed knowledge. The ontological consensus provides a foundation on which we can build other consensus as, for instance, computational consensus: here, it is used as a consensual common space that enables us to defined a shared semantic (pseudo)-distances to compare the bids from different agents ; it also provides the primitives used to annotate the memory and to describe the type of knowledge archivist agents have in their base so that the mediator can decide which agent it is relevant to contact to solve a given query. The example of the annotations-dedicated society shows how the ontology, the semantic Web and the agents are complementary to propose solutions from distributed artificial intelligence to the problem of distributed knowledge management.

```
a   (QUERY-REF
     :sender(agent-identifier :name localUPM@apollo:1099/JADE)
     :receiver(set(agent-identifier :name AM@apollo:1099/JADE))
     :content
b     ((all ?x (is-answer-for
                (query
       :pattern
c      <?xml version ="1.0"?> <rdf:RDF xml:lang="en"
       xmlns:rdf="http://www.w3.org/1999/02/22-rdf-syntax-ns#"
       xmlns:comma="http://www.inria.fr/acacia/comma#">
       <comma:Memo><comma:Designation>?</comma:Designation>
       </comma:Memo>
       </rdf:RDF>
b                  ) ?x ) ) )
a    :reply-with  QuerylocalUPM987683105872
     :language    CoMMA-RDF
     :ontology    CoMMA-annotation-ontology
     :protocol    FIPA-Query
     :conversation-id  QuerylocalUPM987683105872 )

   (a)Primitives FIPA (b)Actes du Langage CoMMA (c)Requête RDF
```

Fig. 5. Message from an agent requesting title of memos

4 Results Evaluation and Conclusion

We presented a multi-agent system for the management of a corporate memory. The MAS architecture enabled us to integrate seamlessly several emerging technologies : agent technology, knowledge modeling, XML technologies, information retrieval techniques and machine learning techniques. Using this paradigm and relying on a shared ontology, different teams respectively developed in parallel the agents requiring their specific expertise (knowledge modeling, machine learning , etc.). The prototype functionalities developed were:

- A graphical user interface enabling logging, consultation of pushed documents, user profile edition and queries and new annotations formulation. Queries and annotations are formulated manually but the GUI assists the use of an ontology.
- A machine learning algorithm sorting the results by analyzing users' feedback.
- A mechanism pushing new annotations to potentially interested users; information resources are suggested by comparing new annotations and user profiles.
- Distributed algorithms to allocate new annotations and solve distributed queries.

The prototype was evaluated by end-users from a telecom company (T-Nova Deutsch Telekom) and a construction research center (CSTB) through two trials (at the eighth month and the twenty second month) during the two-year project. The very last prototype was presented and discussed during an open day at the end of the twenty third month.

Since the MAS architecture is used to integrate a lot of different components that are vital to the system (GUI, CG search engine, XSLT engine, machine learning algorithm, etc.) if one of them goes wrong, the whole system evaluation may be hampered. Indeed, it is extremely hard to evaluate a component independently from the other components on which it may relies. A consequence is, for instance, that if there is a problem at the interface level, it may hamper a good evaluation of the information retrieval capabilities as a whole.

The first trial showed that the system meets both group and individual needs (usefulness) but the interfaces were not user-friendly (usability). The reason was that first interfaces were built for designers and knowledge engineers to test the integration, and not for end-users. As a result, users could not have a clear view of the functionalities of the system. Interfaces were completely reengineered.

For the second trial, the evaluation was prepared by a series of iterative evaluations with users-as-designers (*i.e.* end-users who participated directly to the re-design of the interfaces) in a design-and-test cycle. Results clearly showed that the CoMMA system was not only still *useful* (its functionalities were accepted by users), but also now *usable*: the GUIs being less complex (figure 6), users accepted them, and were not reluctant to manipulate them.

The fact that annotations were generated manually was not a problem in our scenarios, however this is not the case in general. To semi-automate the annotation process, we are studying two approaches:

- the use of natural language processing tools as in the SAMOVAR project [19].
- the use of wrappers for semi-structured sources e.g. web pages with a recurrent structure.

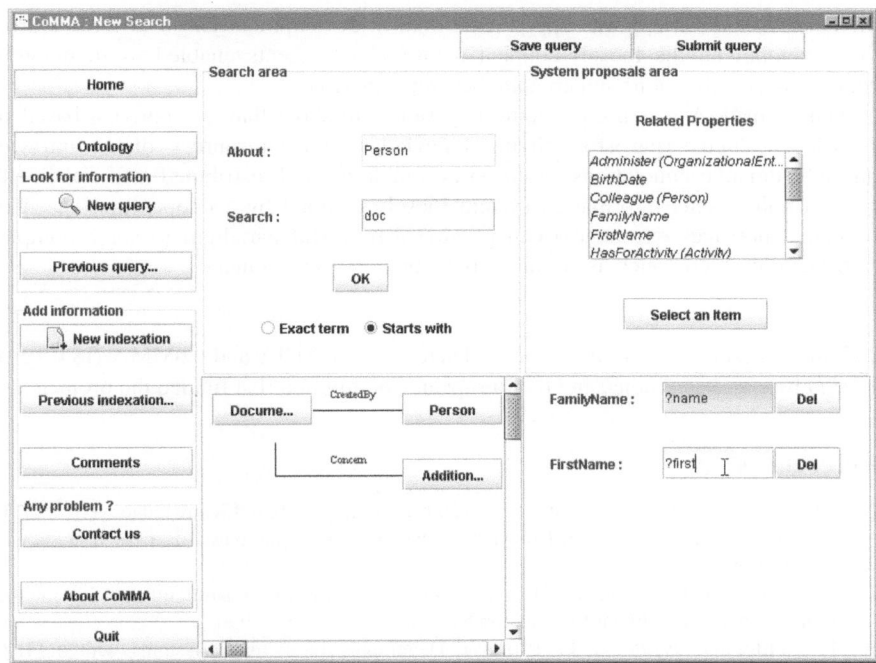

Fig. 6. Query Interface in CoMMA.

Both evaluations were "small-scale" evaluations: small number of users, small number of annotations (about 1000), and small duration of use. This short-period of use did not allow us to observe searching, indexing, and learning phenomena. Larger focused trials are being envisaged.

Trials also showed an effective specialization of the content of the annotation archives. One important point underlined by the first results is that the choice of the specialization of the archives content must be very well studied to avoid unwanted imbalance archives. This study could be done together with the knowledge engineering analysis carried out for the ontology building. It would also be interesting to extend the pseudo-distances to take into account the number of triples present in the archives to balance their sizes when choosing among close bids. We witnessed a noticeable reduction of the number of messages exchanged for query solving – compared to a simple multicast – while enabling fragmented results to be found. However a new algorithm exploiting additional heuristics and decomposition techniques is being studied to further reduce the number of messages exchanged for solving.

From the end-users point of view, the final system was both a real proof of concept and a demonstrator. It is not a commercial tool, but it did play its role in diffusing research results and convincing new partners to consider the MAS solution for distributed knowledge-based systems. From the developer point of view, the ontology-oriented and agent-oriented approach was appreciated because it supported specification and distribution of implementation while smoothing the integration phase. The modularity of the MAS was appreciated both at development and trial time. During the development, the loosely-coupled nature of the agents enabled us to integrate changes in specifications and contain their repercussions.

Thus, CoMMA was a convincing experience to show that an approach based on knowledge engineering (formalizing knowledge about resources of an intraweb through semantic annotations based on an ontology) and distributed artificial intelligence (multi-agents information system loosely coupled by a cooperation based on semantic messages exchanges) can provide a powerful paradigm to solve complex distributed problems such as organizational memory management.

Acknowledgements. We thank our colleagues of ACACIA and CoMMA (IST-1999-12217) for our discussions, and the European Commission that funded the project.

References

1. J.L. Aguirre, R. Brena, F. Cantu-Ortiz, (2000). Multiagent-based Knowledge Networks. To appear in the special issue on Knowledge Management of the journal Expert Systems with Applications.
2. Y. Arens, C.A. Knoblock, W. Shen. Query reformulation for dynamic information integration. Journal of Intelligent Information Systems, 6(2):99-130, 1996.
3. F. Bellifemine, A. Poggi, G. Rimassa, Developing multi agent systems with a FIPA-compliant agent framework. Software Practice & Experience, (2001) 31:103–128
4. B. Berney, and E. Ferneley, (1999), "CASMIR: Information Retrieval Based on Collaborative User Profiling", In Proceedings of PAAM'99, pp. 41–56. www.casmir.net
5. C. Bothorel, and H. Thomas, (1999), "A Distributed Agent Based-Platform for Internet User Communities", In Proceedings of PAAM'99, Lancashire, pp. 23–40.
6. D. Brickley, R. Guha, Resource Description Framework Schema Specification 1.0, W3C Candidate Recommendation 27 March 2000
7. C. Collet, M. N. Huhns, and W. Shen. Resource integration using a large knowledge base in CARNOT. IEEE Computer, pages 55–62, December 1991
8. O. Corby, R. Dieng, C. Hébert, A Conceptual Graph Model for W3C Resource Description Framework. In Proc. ICCS'2000 Darmstadt Germany
9. K. Decker, K.P. Sycara., Intelligent adaptive information agents. Journal of Intelligent Information Systems, 9(3):239–260, 1997.
10. R. Dieng, O. Corby, A. Giboin, M. Ribière. Methods and Tools for Corporate Knowledge Management. In S. Decker and F. Maurer eds, *IJHCS special issue on knowledge Management*, vol. 51, pp. 567–598, Academic Press, 1999.
11. P. Doyle, B. Hayes-Roth, Agents in Annotated Worlds, In Proc. Autonomous Agents, ACM Press / ACM SIGART, Minneapolis, MN USA (1998) pp. 173–180
12. M. Dzbor, J. Paralic and M. Paralic, Knowledge Management in a Distributed Organisation, In Proc. of the BASYS'2000 - 4th IEEE/IFIP International Conference on Information Technology for Balanced Automation Systems in Manufacturing, Kluwer Academic Publishers, London, September 2000, ISBN 0-7923-7958-6, pp. 339–348
13. L. van Elst, A. Abecker, Domain Ontology Agents in Distributed Organizational Memories In Proc. Workshop on Knowledge Management and Organizational Memories, IJCAI, 2001.

14. Foundation for Intelligent Physical Agents, FIPA Specifications, 2001
15. F. Gandon, A Multi-Agent Architecture for Distributed Corporate Memories, Proc. 16th European Meeting on Cybernetics and Systems Research (EMCSR 2002) April 3–5, 2002, Vienna, Austria, pp 623–628.
16. F. Gandon, A Multi-Agent Platform for a Corporate Semantic Web, to appear in Proc. AAMAS 2002.
17. F. Gandon, Engineering an Ontology for a Multi-Agents Corporate Memory System, In Proc. ISMICK'01, Université de Technologie de Compiègne, pp. 209–228.
18. M. Genesereth, A. Keller, O. Duschka, Infomaster: An Information Integration System, in proceedings of 1997 ACM SIGMOD Conference, May 1997.
19. J. Golebiowska, R Dieng-Kuntz, O. Corby, D. Mousseau, (2001) Building and Exploiting Ontologies for an Automobile Project Memory, First International Conference on Knowledge Capture (K-CAP), Victoria, October 23–24.
20. A. Kiss, J. Quinqueton, Multiagent Cooperative Learning of User Preferences, Proc. of European CMLP & PKDD, 2001.
21. M. Klush, *Intelligent Information Agent: Agent-Based Information Discovery and Management on the Internet*, Springer, pages IX–XVII, 1999
22. O. Lassila, R. Swick, Resource Description Framework (RDF) Model and Syntax Specification, W3C Recommendation 22 February 1999
23. A.Y. Levy, D. Srivastava, and T. Kirk, Data model and query evaluation in global information systems. Journal of Intelligent Information Systems 5(2):121–143, September 1995
24. E. Mena, V. Kashyap, A. Sheth and A. Illarramendi, "OBSERVER: An approach for Query Processing in Global Information Systems based on Interoperation across Preexisting Ontologies," Proceedings of the 1st IFCIS International Conference on Cooperative Information Systems (CoopIS '96), Brussels, Belgium, June 1996
25. M. Nodine, J. Fowler, T. Ksiezyk, B. Perry, M. Taylor, A. Unruh, Active Information Gathering In Infosleuth™; In Proc. Internat. Symposium on Cooperative Database Systems for Advanced Applications, 1999
26. J.B. Odubiyi, D.J. Kocur, S.M., Weinstein, N. Wakim, S. Srivastava, C. Gokey, J. Graham. SAIRE – A Scalable Agent-Based Information Retrieval Engine, Proc. Autonomous Agents 97, Marina Del Rey, CA.
27. M.T. Özsu, P. Valduriez, Principles of Distributed Database Systems, 2nd edn., Prentice-Hall, 1999
28. Rolstadås, Development trends to support Enterprise Modeling, in Rolstadås and Andersen *Enterprise Modeling: Improving Global Industrial Competitiveness*, Kluwer, pp. 3–16, 2000
29. J.F. Sowa, Conceptual Structures: Information Processing in Mind and Machine, Addison-Wesley, 1984.
30. L. Steels, Corporate Knowledge Management, *Proc. ISMICK 1993*, pp. 9–30
31. P.C. Weinstein, W.P. Birmingham, E.H. Durfee. Agent-Based Digital Libraries: Decentralization and Coordination. IEEE Communication Magazine, pp. 110–115, 1999

Integrating Information Gathering and Problem-Solving in Open Environments

Santiago Macho-Gonzalez and Boi Faltings

Artificial Intelligence Laboratory (LIA),
Swiss Federal Institute of Technology (EPFL),
IN-Ecublens, CH-1015 Ecublens, Switzerland,
boi.faltings | santi.macho@epfl.ch,
http://liawww.epfl.ch/

Abstract. An important realization driving the development of the semantic web is that people are interested in information in order to *solve problems*. Many researchers have considered techniques for turning information sources into a single database which can then be used for problem-solving tasks. We present a method for integrating problem-solving with information gathering and show that it achieves remarkable efficiency gains.

1 Information Gathering in Open Systems

Information gathering is an important practical problem that arises in particular for information agents on the internet. Most recent work such as Infomaster ([1]) or Infosleuth ([2]) has focussed on turning distributed information sources into a single, coherent database that can be used as a basis for solving problems. This is particularly interesting in the context of the semantic web, which provides information in structured form that is easy to assemble.

When considered in an open environment, however, this approach presents two important problems. The first is that there is an unbounded number of information sources, and there is no clear termination criterion that indicates when the database synthesis is complete. The second is that much of the information that is gathered may turn out to be unnecessary to solve the original problem, resulting in low efficiency. Therefore, we believe that large improvements can be obtained by integrating information gathering directly into a problem-solving process. Rather than first obtaining the information and then carrying out problem-solving on that information, we gather information only as required for problem-solving. In this way, we avoid retrieving large amounts of information that plays no part in a solution to our problem, and can instead focus search on those aspects that are critical to the success of problem-solving. Experiments show that we can obtain very significant efficiency gains in this way.

In this paper, we propose *constraint satisfaction* (CSP) as a problem-solving model. Using CSP as a model for information agents has been introduced in [3, 4] and also in [7] and since used in several operational systems such as [5, 6].

M. Klusch, S. Ossowski, and O. Shehory (Eds.): CIA 2002, LNAI 2446, pp. 218–225, 2002.
© Springer-Verlag Berlin Heidelberg 2002

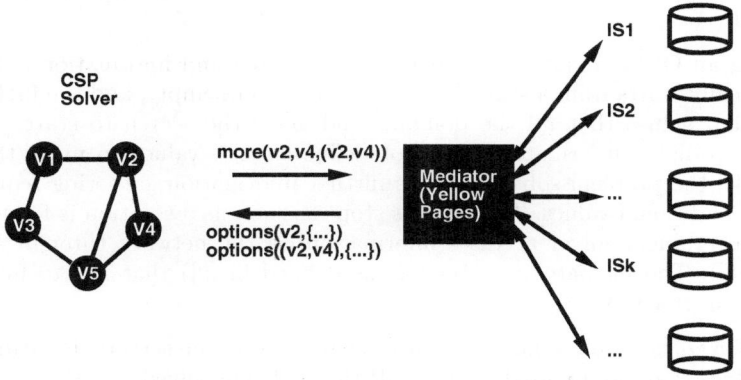

Fig. 1. *Elements of an open constraint satisfaction problem*

2   Open Constraint Satisfaction Problems (OCSP)

We consider the setting shown in Figure 1 which reflects the important elements that occur in an open setting. The problem-solving process is modelled abstractly as the solution of a constraint satisfaction problem. The choices that make up variables domains and relations of the CSP are distributed throughout an unbounded network of information servers $IS_1, IS_2, ...$, and accessed through a mediator ([8]).

More precisely, the CSP is an *open constraint satisfaction problem*, defined formally as follows:

Definition 1. *An* open constraint satisfaction problem *(OCSP) is a possibly unbounded, partially ordered set* $\{CSP(0), CSP(1), ...\}$ *of constraint satisfaction problems, where CSP(i) is defined by a tuple* $< X, C, D(i), R(i) >$ *where*

- *$X = \{x_1, x_2, ..., x_n\}$ is a set of n variables,*
- *$C = \{(x_i, x_j, ...), (x_k, x_l, ...), ...\}$ is a set of m constraints, given by the ordered sets of variables they involve,*
- *$D(i) = \{d_1(i), d_2(i), ..., d_n(i)\}$ is the set of domains for CSP(i), with $d_k(0) = \{\}$ for all k.*
- *$R(i) = \{r_1(i), r_2(i), ..., r_m(i)\}$ is the set of relations for CSP(i), each giving the list of allowed tuples for the variables involved in the corresponding constraints, and satisfying $r_k(0) = \{\}$ for all k.*

The set is ordered by the relation $\prec$ where $CSP(i) \prec CSP(j)$ if and only if $(\forall k \in [1..n])d_k(i) \subseteq d_k(j)$, $(\forall k \in [1..m])r_k(i) \subseteq r_k(j)$, and either $(\exists k \in [1..n])d_k(i) \subset d_k(j)$ or $(\exists k \in [1..m])r_k(i) \subset r_k(j)$.

A solution *of an OCSP is a combination of value assignments to all variables such that for some i, each value belongs to the corresponding domain and all value combinations corresponding to constraints belong to the corresponding relations of CSP(i).*

Solving an OCSP requires an integration of search and information gathering. It typically starts from a state where all domains are empty, and the first action is to find values that fill the domains and allow the search to start. As long as the available information does not define enough values to make the CSP solvable, the problem solver initiates further information gathering requests to obtain additional values. The process stops as soon as a solution is found.

The problem solver accesses information on the network through a mediator ([8]). The mediator is a broker (as defined in [9]) that has to fulfill two important functions:

- a *directory* or yellow pages, it must locate information servers that can supply values that can be used in the CSP that is being solved.
- an *integrator* that reformulates information from the servers to fit a format required by the CSP.

In order to be generally useable, the mediator must be compatible with any CSP that a user might want to solve. This is achieved through ontologies that define the meaning of CSP variables and values:

Definition 2. *An ontological grounding of an open CSP $< V, C, D(i), R(i) >$ is a tuple $< O, M_V, M_D >$ where:*

- $O = \{o_1, ..., o_m\}$ *is a set of ontologies,*
- M_V *is a mapping $V \to O \times C(O) \times P(O)$ that maps each variable $v_j, j = 1..n$ into a tuple $< o_j, c_k, p_l >$ which means that v_j models the property p_l (sometimes called relation in the literature) of concept c_k in ontology o_j. Note that the mapping need not be bijective, i.e. there can be several variables that map to the same concept and property.*
- M_D *is a mapping $V \to O \times 2^{P(O)}$ that maps each variable $v_j, j = 1..n$ into a tuple $< o_j, \{c_1, .., c_k\} >$ that defines the possible values that could be part of the variable's domain.*

The ontological grounding allows the problem solver to define what information is required to fill the different aspects of the problem. It is fixed throughout the problem-solving, and communicated to the mediator either once at the beginning or with each request.

The connection between CSP and information sources is based on its ontological grounding. We make the following assumptions:

- every query for more values refers to some ontology.
- all information sources relevant to an ontology are classified according to this ontology, i.e. an information source that returns values for properties or relations of a concept is indexed under that concept.

We use the technique of [10] to index information sources according to an ontology. In this technique, information servers are classified by the ontological categories of the values they hold.

3   Solving OCSP with Information Gathering

We now address the algorithms for solving OCSP by search interleaved with information gathering. To keep the algorithms simple, we only consider information gathering for variable domains, not for relations associated with constraints. Techniques exist for transforming discrete CSP into CSP where all relations are a form of equality, so this does not limit generality.

When a CSP has no solution, it is often the case that it contains a smaller subproblem that already has no solution. It will not be possible to create a solution by information gathering unless values are added to variables and relations of that subproblem. This fact can be used to more effectively drive information gathering. The idea is to find a variable that must be part of an unsolvable subproblem as a promising candidate for adding extra values. To develop this into a general and complete algorithm, we need to address two issues: how to identify unsolvable subproblems, and how to select all variables in turn to avoid unbounded information accesses while missing a feasible solution.

The following lemma provides the basis for identifying variables that are part of unsolvable subproblems:

Lemma 1. *Let a CSP be explored by a failed backtrack search algorithm with static variable ordering $(x_1, ..., x_n)$, and let x_k be the deepest node reached in the search with inconsistency detected at x_k. Then x_k, called the* failed variable, *is part of every unsolvable subproblem of the CSP involving variables in the set $\{x_1..x_k\}$.*

Proof. In order to reach x_k, the search algorithm has constructed at least one valid assignment to $x_1, ..., x_{k-1}$, so this set of variables does not contain any unsolvable subproblem. However, there is no consistent assignment to $x_1, ..., x_k$, so this set does contain unsolvable subproblem(s). Since the only difference is x_k, x_k must be part of all of these unsolvable subproblems.   □

On the basis of this proposition, we can use the results of a failed CSP search process to determine for which variable additional values should be collected. These are then passed to the mediator, which will search for relevant information on the network. When there are no additional values for this variable, the mediator returns a **nomore** message, and other variables are then considered. The resulting algorithm **fo-search** (failure-driven open search) is shown in Algorithm 1.

Algorithm 1 makes the assumption that variables are ordered by the index i. It assumes that no consistency techniques are used in the search, although the chronological backtracking can be replaced with backjumping techniques to make it more efficient.

It is possible to show the following theorem which proves completeness of Algorithm 1:

Theorem 1. *Supposed that OCSP is solvable, i.e. by calling **more** on every variable a sufficient number of times we eventually reach an instance $CSP(j)$ such that for all $m \geq j$, $CSP(m)$ contains no unsolvable subproblems. Then Algorithm 1 will eventually terminate with this solution.*

```
 1: Function fo-search(X,D,C,R,E)
 2: i ← 1, k ← 1
 3: repeat {backtrack search}
 4:    if exhausted(d_i) then {backtrack}
 5:       i ← i − 1, reset − values(d_i)
 6:    else
 7:       k ← max(k, i), x_i ← nextvalue(d_i)
 8:       if consistent({x_1, ..., x_i}) then {extend assignment}
 9:          i ← i + 1
10:       if i > n then
11:          return {x_1, ..., x_n} as a solution
12: until i = 0
13: if e_k = closed then
14:    if (∀i ∈ 1..k − 1)e_k = closed then
15:       return failure
16: else
17:    nv ← more(x_k)
18:    if nv = nomore(x_k) then
19:       e_k ← closed
20:    d_k ← nv ∪ d_k
21: reorder variables so that x_k becomes x_1
22: fo-search(X,D,C,R,E) {search again}
```

Algorithm 1: *Function* **fo-search** *for solving OCSP.*

4   Experimental Results

We tested the performance of the techniques we described on randomly generated resource allocation problems.

We compare the performance of different combinations of algorithms in the mediator and the problem solver. For the mediator, we consider a **random** selection of any information source that has the right property and concept, and **size** where information sources are additionally ordered by the number of values they carry.

For the problem solver, we consider three algorithms, **OS** for search where variables for information gathering are selected randomly, **FO** for fo-search defined earlier, and **ICSP** for the interactive CSP algorithm defined in [12].

Several metrics for measuring performance have been developed in the field of database selection ([11]). We measure performance by the ratio:

$$R = \frac{Number\ of\ variables\ of\ the\ CSP}{Number\ of\ access\ to\ IS\ until\ a\ solution\ is\ found}$$

Since each variable must have at least one value, solving the CSP requires at least one information source access per variable, so that the ideal value for R is 1. Smaller values of R mean low efficiency. We consider that R provides a good measure of the relative amount of information gathering effort generated by the two methods, but does not take into account possible parallization or buffering.

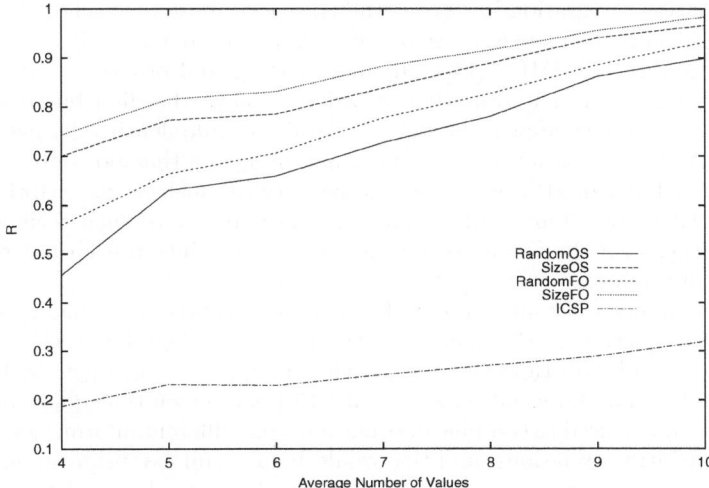

Fig. 2. *Efficiency ratio against number of values for several combination of search/mediator algorithms.*

Figure 2 plots the efficiency ratio against the average number of values available for each variable for a setting in which there are a total of 12 information servers. The more values there are for each variable, the easier the problem is to solve, and we can see that the average efficiency in general increases with the number of available values. The simulations show that integration produces huge efficiency gains over current methods that access all servers beforehand: their efficiency would only be 1/12, whereas with integration we obtain efficiency ratios close to the theoretical optimum of 1. Furthermore, the gains would grow as the numbers of servers increases, thus making it a good tool to improve scaleability. It can also be seen that the ICSP algorithm, in spite of integrating problem solving with information gathering, is not nearly as good as the search methods we presented here.

5   Related Work

Within the CSP community, the work that is closest to ours is *interactive constraint satisfaction* (ICSP), introduced in [12]. Similarly to our work, in ICSP domains are acquired incrementally from external agents. ICSP focuses on settings where value acquisition can be stronly directed using constraints, but does not have an efficient and complete method for deciding what values to gather next. As a result, its performance in an open environment is actually very poor. Using CSP as a model for information agents has been introduced in [3, 4] and also in [7] and since used in several operational systems such as [5, 6]. However, this earlier work does not consider information gathering in a network of servers.

Information integration has been studied by database researchers for a long time ([13]). With the increased use of networking, and particularly the internet, projects such as TSIMMIS ([14]), Infomaster ([1]), and others have addressed dynamic integration of information in order to make the distributed network of informationsources appear as a single database. InfoSleuth ([2]) has built a more elaborate infrastructure using information agents that not only integrate information, but can also provide proactive services such as subscriptions and change notifications. Our work assumes the availability of such techniques in order to transform the results of information sources into the format required for problem solving.

Another important topic is how to locate information sources that are capable of answering queries. In this paper, we assume an ontology-based classification similar to that of [10]. However, the matchmaking process can get significantly more complex. The Information Manifold ([15]) has shown that query planning techniques can be used to combine information from different information sources to obtain arbitrary relations, and this would be a useful extension to our work.

Another important issue is actual matchmaking. Decker and Sycara ([9]) investigate the efficiency of middle-agent systems, and Sycara ([16]) elaborates on their use as information agents. Techniques such as LARKS ([17]) show that much more complex matchmaking than ontology-based classification is possible, and it would be possible to derive such criteria from the problem-solver as well.

Recently, researchers in information retrieval have paid more attention to driving information retrieval from the task that users are trying to solve. Systems such as Watson and I2I ([18]) and just-in-time information retrieval ([19]) automatically retrieve information from databases, mail archives and other information sources by matching it with keywords that occur in the current activity of the user - for example, a document being prepared.

6   Conclusions

We have investigated how to integrate information gathering in a constraint satisfaction problem solver in order to increase the efficiency of accessing information servers. Assuming an information agent infrastructure that corresponds well to what is envisaged for the semantic web, we have shown experimentally that such integration leads to significant efficiency gains.

References

1. Genesereth, M. R., Keller, A. M., Duschka, O.: "Infomaster: An Information Integration System", Proceedings of 1997 ACM SIGMOD Conference, May 1997.
2. Jerry Fowler, Brad Perry, Marian Nodine, and Bruce Bargmeyer: Agent-Based Semantic Interoperability in InfoSleuth SIGMOD Record 28:1, March, 1999, pp. 60-67.
3. Marc Torrens, Rainer Weigel and Boi Faltings: "*Distributing Problem Solving on the Web Using Constraint Technology*" Proceedings of the IEEE International Conference on Tools with Artificial Intelligence (ICTAI'98), pp 42-49, IEEE Press

4. Marc Torrens, Boi Faltings and Pearl Pu: *"Smart Clients: Constraint Satisfaction as a Paradigm for Scaleable Intelligent Information Systems"*, *CONSTRAINTS* **7**(1), 2002, pp. 49-69

5. Pearl Pu and Boi Faltings: *"Enriching buyers' experiences: the SmartClient approach"*, Proceedings of the CHI2000 conference on Human Factors and Computing Systems, April 2000, pp. 289-296, ACM

6. Craig A. Knoblock, Steve Minton, Jose Luis Ambite, Maria Muslea, Jean Oh and Martin Frank: *"Mixed-Initiative, Multi-source Information Assistants,"* Tenth International World Wide Web Conference (WWW10), Hong Kong, 2001.

7. Peter M.D. Gray, Suzanne M. Embury, Kit Y. Hui, Graham J.L. Kemp: "The Evolving Role of Constraints in the Functional Data Model", *Journal of Intelligent Information Systems* **12**, pp. 113-137, 1999.

8. Gio Wiederhold and Michael R. Genesereth: "The Conceptual Basis for Mediation Services" IEEE Expert, 12(5), 1997.

9. Keith Decker, Katia Sycara and Mike Williamson: "Middle-Agents for the Internet," *Proceedings of the 15th International Joint Conference on Artificial Intelligence (IJCAI-97)*, Morgan Kaufmann, 1997, pp. 578-583

10. José Luis Ambite and Craig Knoblock: "Flexible and scalable cost-based query planning in mediators: A transformational approach," *Artificial Intelligence* **118**, pp. 115-161, 2000

11. James C. Freanch and Allison L. Powell :Metrics for Evaluating Database Selection Techniques. 2000

12. Rita Cucchiara, Marco Gavanelli, Evelina Lamma, Paola Mello, Michela Milano, and Massimo Piccardi: "Constraint propagation and value acquisition: why we should do it interactively," *Proceedings of the 16th IJCAI*, Morgan Kaufmann, pp.468-477, 1999

13. A. Sheth and J.A. Larson: "Federated Database Systems," *ACM Computing Surveys* **22**(3), 1990

14. S. Chawathe, H. Garcia Molina, J. Hammer, K.Ireland, Y. Papakostantinou, J. Ullman and J. Widom: The TSIMMIS project: Integration of heterogeneous information sources. In *IPSJ Conference*, Tokyo, Japan, 1994

15. Alon Y. Levy , Anand Rajaraman , Joann J. Ordille: "Querying Heterogeneous Information Sources Using Source Descriptions," *Proceedings of the 22nd VLDB Conference*, Bombay, India, 1996

16. Sycara, K. "In-Context Information Management Through Adaptive Collaboration of Intelligent Agents." In Intelligent Information Agents: Cooperative, Rational and Adaptive Information Gathering on the Internet. Matthias Klusch (Ed.), Springer Verlag, 1999.

17. Katia Sycara, Seth Widoff, Matthias Klusch and Jianguo Lu: "LARKS: Dynamic Matchmaking Among Heterogeneous Software Agents in Cyberspace." Autonomous Agents and Multi-Agent Systems, 5, 173-203, 2002.

18. J. Budzik, S. Bradshaw, X. Fu, and K. Hammond: "Supporting Online Resource Discovery in the Context of Ongoing Tasks with Proactive Assistants," *International Journal of Human-Computer Studies* **56**(1) Jan 2002, pp. 47-74

19. B.J. Rhodes and P. Maes: "Just-in-time information retrieval agents," *IBM Systems Journal* **39**, pp. 685-704, 2000

Supporting Virtual Organisations Using BDI Agents and Constraints

Stuart Chalmers, Peter M.D. Gray, and Alun Preece

University of Aberdeen; Kings College, Aberdeen, AB24 3UE
{schalmer,pgray,apreece}@csd.abdn.ac.uk

Abstract. Virtual organisations underpin many important activities in distributed computing, including e-commerce and e-science. This paper describes a new technique by which software agents can intelligently form virtual organisations to meet some pre-specified requirements. Our approach builds on work in BDI agents and constraint satisfaction techniques. Using a realistic service-providing scenario, we show how an agent can use constraint solving techniques to explore possible virtual organisation alliances with other agents, based on its beliefs and desires. The agent can choose the best among several possible virtual organisations to form in order to meet a customer's requirements. Our approach is to use a deliberative process to construct possible worlds, each corresponding to a potential virtual organisation, and each configured using constraint satisfaction techniques. We also show how an agent can take account of pre-existing virtual organisation relationships in its deliberations.

1 Introduction

Support for virtual organisations is emerging as one of the most significant requirements in modern distributed computing, underpinning many activities viewed as of enormous strategic importance to industry and government. These activities include business-to-business e-commerce, where virtual organisations enable electronic value chains [1], and e-science, where virtual organisations are seen as the fundamental organising principle of the "grid" [9]. The key aspects of virtual organisations that make them such an attractive paradigm are:

- they are composed of a number of autonomous entities (representing distinct individuals, departments, organisations, etc) each of which has a range of problem solving capabilities and resources at their disposal;
- the entities co-exist, collaborate, and sometimes compete with one another in a ubiquitous virtual space (representing a marketplace, meeting room, laboratory, etc);
- service-providing entities may advertise their capabilities to their peers, and then enter into service agreements or contracts with service-requiring entities;
- where appropriate, groups of entities may form a coalition in order to provide some amalgamated service, or carry out some overall activity cooperatively;

M. Klusch, S. Ossowski, and O. Shehory (Eds.): CIA 2002, LNAI 2446, pp. 226–240, 2002.
Springer-Verlag Berlin Heidelberg 2002

– all of the above aspects are highly dynamic: entities may come and go, capabilities may change over time, and coalitions may form, dissipate, and reform.

In the KRAFT project[1] we developed an architecture that offered limited support for virtual organisations, through the following main features [18]:

– entities are represented by *software agents*, which interact with one another in a virtual space defined by *shared communication protocols*;
– an individual entity (agent) may view the world in terms of a *local ontology* (or data model), but to communicate with other entities it must align this local ontology with a *shared common ontology*;
– coordinated activity is achieved by the exchange of *quantified constraints* between entities, and the solving of sets of these constraints; these constraints represent both requirements to be satisfied, and candidate solutions.

Although the KRAFT architecture has been successfully demonstrated in a realistic business-to-business e-commerce scenario [7] it lacks a number of features necessary for adequate support of virtual organisations:

– KRAFT supports very limited agent autonomy, as it assumes the entities are basically cooperative — in particular, *competition* between agents is not supported, because the agents do not have explicit agendas that may be in conflict;
– KRAFT does not allow for *negotiation* between entities over requirements and candidate solutions — there is no general mechanism for relaxing or trading-off constraints in the constraint-solving process.

In this paper, we describe how we are extending the KRAFT architecture to address these limitations, by incorporating recent work using constraint-solving within a *BDI (Beliefs, Desires, Intentions)* agent framework [4]. By adding BDI layers to the KRAFT agents, we aim to support both cooperative and competitive behaviours, and allow agents to negotiate over points of conflict. We have sought to integrate the BDI approach with our constraint-solving approach to coordinated agent interaction, in order to combine the benefits of both. In the context of supporting virtual organisations:

– *beliefs* are the state of the world, as modelled locally by an entity (agent) in the virtual organisation;
– *desires* are the goals of an entity in the virtual organisation;
– *intentions* are the actions an entity plans to carry out.

This paper reports on work-in-progress, specifically on the *formation* of a virtual organisation using BDI agents and constraint satisfaction techniques. In a realistic service-providing scenario, we aim to show how an agent can use constraint solving techniques to explore possible virtual organisation alliances with other

---

[1] http://www.csd.abdn.ac.uk/research/kraft

agents, based on its beliefs and desires. We also show how an agent can take account of pre-existing virtual organisation relationships in its deliberations.

The paper is organised as follows. Section 2 describes our motivating scenario. Section 3 describes the role of constraints in the BDI model, Section 4 describes the design and implementation of the constraint based architecture and Section 5 describes ongoing work on constraint relaxation.

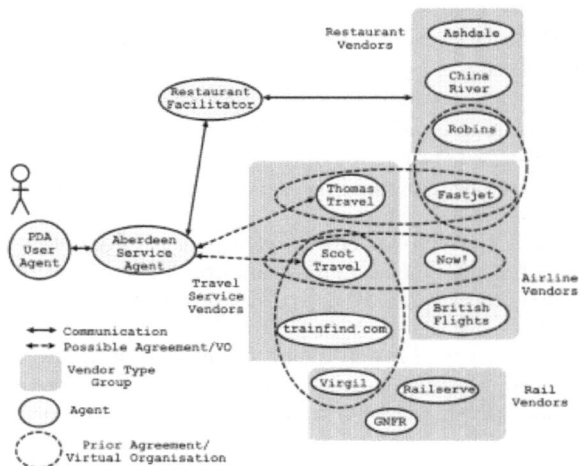

Fig. 1. Motivating Scenario. The Aberdeen Service Agent has to decide whether to enter into a Virtual Organisation relationship with either Thomas Travel or Scot Travel.

2   Motivating Scenario

A lecturer is visiting Aberdeen University for a research meeting. He wishes to travel up from London on the train and arrive in time for his meeting at 2pm on Thursday afternoon. He also wants to eat at a restaurant and travel home that evening on the overnight sleeper train. He would also prefer the cheapest deal, as his funds are extremely limited!

He gives this information to a user agent on his PDA, specifying the following desires:

- Arrive in Aberdeen by 2pm Thursday
- Return to London by 8am Friday
- Eat at a restaurant on Thursday evening
- Get cheapest deal possible
- Travel by train *preferable*

In this scenario we have a number of vendors of different types, which can interact and form *virtual organisations* to provide services and facilities. From the diagram we can see the vendors grouped into service types (airline, rail, etc.) and that some have prior agreements with other vendors (e.g. a relationship exists between Scot Travel and Now!). In this situation the *Aberdeen service agent*, from the information given by the user's PDA, as well as from any relevant information available on other vendors, has to decide on the choice of vendor to enter into a virtual organisation relationship with, that will satisfy as many of the user specified desires as possible. This relationship is then in place for other such requests, or can be renegotiated if any other requirements or services are needed.

In Fig.1 the user agent contacts the *Aberdeen service agent*, which is able to gather information from various resources on local Aberdeen restaurants, and is able to communicate with various *mediator service agents* who can provide possible travel solutions to and from Aberdeen, by consulting train and airline agents for information. There also exists a *restaurant facilitator* which can recommend and book restaurants in the Aberdeen area.

Table 1. Options from the travel mediator agents (* indicates 25% off Robins restaurants)

Name	Travel Type	Price	Arrive	Depart
Now!	Air	€ 70	3:00PM	9:30PM
trainfind.com	Sleeper Train	€ 85	10:00AM	11:30PM
Fastjet*	Air	€ 90	1:00PM	9:30PM

The mediator service agents, Thomas Travel and Scot Travel are asked by the Aberdeen service agent to provide travel details for return journeys from London to Aberdeen. It is their task to find a suitable deal for the service agent.

For Aberdeen/London flights, Thomas Travel are partners of a *virtual organisation* and have negotiated a deal with Fastjet, while Scot Travel have formed two relationships, the first for Aberdeen return flight deals with Now! and the second with trainfind.com and Virgil trains for sleeper services to Aberdeen. Solutions returned from the three mediators are shown in Table 1. After initial contact with restaurant facilitator about restaurant availability in Aberdeen, it receives the options shown in Table 2.

Table 2. Options from the Restaurant Agent

Name	Price	Bookable From:
China River	€ 40	Fully Booked
Robins	€ 40	7:00PM
Ashdale	€ 45	8:30PM

Table 3. Possible package Solutions (*%25 Robins/Fastjet discount offer)

Package	Price	Book From:
Virgil / Ashdale	€ 130	Scot Travel/trainfind.com
Virgil / Robins	€ 125	UK travel/trainfind.com
Now! / Ashdale	€ 115	Scot Travel
Now! / Robins	€ 110	Scot Travel
Fastjet / Ashdale	€ 135	Thomas Travel
Fastjet / Robins	€ 120*	Thomas Travel

From this information the service agent builds a list of possible travel/restaurant combinations (Table 3). From the desires expressed by the user, the service agent decides that the solutions that use Now! are not viable, as the flight would arrive in Aberdeen after the meeting start time. The trainfind/ Robins solution meets the requirements, but the agent decides to commit to the Fastjet/Robins package (Fig. 2), as the virtual organisation relationship between Fastjet and Robins can be exploited *within* this new virtual organisation to provide overall cheaper meal and travel, although the preference of travel by train needs to be relaxed.

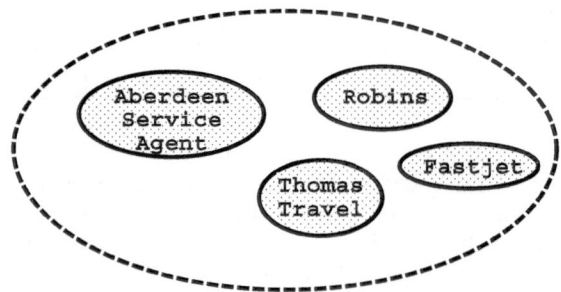

Fig. 2. The VO formed by the Aberdeen Service Agent

We view this decision making process as a constraint problem, where the *available, choices* of travel and restaurant form the set of *possible solutions*, while the users *desires* and *preferences*, as well as information on services and their relationships in *virtual organisations* form the *constraints* over the possible solutions that influence the eventual decision. The *relaxation* of these constraints can also form the basis for negotiation between the vendors in the VO, as in the example relaxtion of the method of travel described here.

This architecture is also used as a basis for the vendor agents when negotiating and forming virtual organisations. In particular, we describe how the autonomy provided by combining CLP with a BDI architecture provides an open and adaptable method for operating in competitive environments.

3   Constraints as Knowledge in an E-commerce Scenario

Recent work has seen constraints being used for knowledge representation in a distributed agent-based environment [5,12]. Our research takes this idea and focuses on using constraints to represent different sources of knowledge, but also to exploit this representation and to use these constraints along with CLP (Constraint Logic Programming) to provide an agent with intelligent decision-making capabilities that can be used in dynamic environments and situations where the choice of solution provided depends on commitments which are transient and can be changed or renegotiated at any time. In doing this, we endeavour to preserve agent autonomy and local decision making.

In the example in Section 2 we are using constraints to represent user desires specifying properties of the solution required, and also to represent specific instances of relationships between companies (e.g. the discount package between Fastjet airline and Robins restaurant). Both these aspects must be combined and used when deciding on a solution.

3.1   Constraints and Agents

Constraints are used to model a description of part of a *desired* goal state which the agent is free to achieve in any number of different ways. In doing so, the agent can take account of other constraints it has undertaken to satisfy by combining all the information into a CLP (Constraint Logic Programming) problem. Therefore an agent in a virtual organisation can take account of commitments with other agents when trying to provide a service or negotiate to join another virtual organisation.

This representation means that the agent is not just responding to a sequence of messages, but is able to deliberate on and *plan* its behaviour by taking into account both the message and other constraints. Further, if the desired state is impossible to achieve (over-constrained) because of too many different desires, it has to relax some constraints, by delegating or exchanging tasks with other agents (See Section 5), which is an important aspect of agent behaviour in multi-agent systems. The constraints thus become mobile [10].

The constraints can refer to the configuration in space of a number of objects, constrained by various relationships and inequalities described in predicate logic. This has been successfully used in the KRAFT project [18], but there the agents were 'information seeking', extracting the constraint information from databases and returning them to a central planner. Here the agents are themselves capable of planning and interacting with other agents and can use temporal as well as spatial constraints[4].

We can transform constraints to use a local ontology or data model as a common basis [13]. Once in this form we can treat the constraints as a CLP and thus provide a decision making process which can take into account many disparate factors, which is vital when providing autonomy in a highly dynamic environment.

```
Do
    options := option_generator(event_queue,B,D,I)
    selected-options := deliberate(options,B,D,I)
    update-intentions(selected-options,I)
    execute(I)
    get-new-external-events();
    drop-succesful-attitudes(B,D,I)
until quit
```

Fig. 3. Main BDI loop

4   BDI Agents

To provide an architecture to contain this CLP mechanism we have constructed
a BDI agent, as its logical reasoning basis allows for easy integration with the
logic approach of the CLP mechanism.

Fig. 3 shows a pseudo-code version of a BDI agent algorithm [19]. We use this
as a basic mechanism for controlling the actions and decision making for each
individual agent. This algorithm controls the agents planning and its interaction
with others.

In a BDI loop, the agent has internal events from the desires (such as required
services) and external events (such as information on the nature and type of
services available) on the `event_queue` and uses these, along with its current
beliefs (B), desires (D) and intentions (I) to generate a set of possible next options,
represented as executable plans. It then selects one of these possible options
based on the status of its B, D and I values. This selection is represented by our
constraint mechanism, which takes the Beliefs and maps them to finite domains
in a constraint problem. It then uses the desires and intentions (represented as
constraints) in the constraint solving mechanism to choose and then execute the
best action from those available. Finally, any new external events (caused by the
execution of the chosen action or otherwise) are added to the `event_queue` and
the agent checks to see whether it can mark as completed any of its goals that
have been achieved, before carrying on.

The algorithm is adopted from the standard BDI loop [19]:

- *Beliefs* represent the views held about the current state of the world, as
  perceived by the agent.
- *Desires* are the goals and aims you wish your agent to achieve.
- *Intentions* are the actual processes being executed so that desires may be
  fulfilled (or sub-goals which are needed for the completion of a desire).

The process of choosing and executing a succession of actions gradually al-
ters the agent's beliefs and provides newer and updated solutions. The agent
may receive new desires in the form of constraints as it progresses but must
take into account all existing commitment constraints until a solution has been
found, when they can then be dropped and marked as being succesful (the
`drop-succesful-attitudes` function in Fig.3).

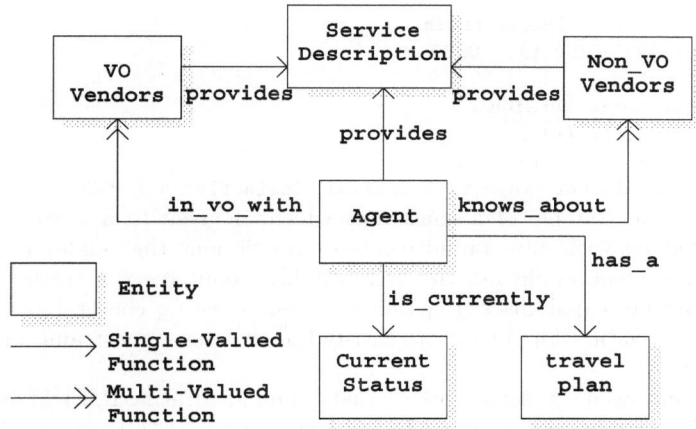

Fig. 4. Agent's Belief data model

4.1 Representing Beliefs, Desires, and Intentions Using CLP – A Functional Data Model Approach

We use an ER-like data model representation for the agent's beliefs (Fig. 4). This holds information on the agents current capabilities, as well as information on the capabilities of others and information on any relationships or coalitions formed. The entities hold the actual data, while the functions represent relationships between the entities. Our data model representation of the agent's beliefs is constructed using P/FDM[2], an object database constructed on semantic data modelling principles from the functional Data Model [21]. This database is constantly updated to reflect changes in the agent's status and current commitments as and when they happen. The advantage of this approach is that the data model can be used to express the semantics of the agent's beliefs as well as the beliefs themselves, and can express complex relationships between objects and data values in those beliefs.

The P/FDM constraint language, Colan [3] (based on Shipman's Daplex language), can be used to express desires in terms of beliefs. Initially Colan was used for specifying database integrity constraints, but since it is based on a range-restricted first order logic, it can be used to describe specifications or mobile fragments of specifications. The following shows an example Colan constraint, based on the scenario described in Section 2. It specifies that if an agent creates a travel plan for a journey, and the journey involves a sleeper train, then the arrival time of the sleeper train must be before 8.30am (For the purposes of simplifying the exposition we have left out contextual information such as date).

Colan Constraint
Constrain all t in travel_plan such that
travel_method(t) = train and....

_____
[2] http://www.csd.abdn.ac.uk/~pfdm

```
travel_class(t) = sleeper_train
to have arrival_time(t) < 0830
```

First Order Logic Version
$(\forall t, a)$ travel_plan(t) &
travel_method(train, t) & ....
travel_class(sleeper_train,t) & arrival_time(a,t)$\rightarrow$ a < 0830

This is an example of a constraint which, if given to a vendor, must be satisfied, along with any commitments or restrictions the vendor might have. The vendor agent would use the beliefs it has about its own status, and that of other agents capabilities, together with any existing constraints (e.g. from current VO relationships) to try to satisfy the given user constraint and provide a solution.

There has been extensive work carried out on integrating P/FDM data model frameworks into finite domain CLP problems in the KRAFT project [13] and in using First Order Logic to express and generate CLP code in terms of this data model. Our techniques for transforming the information from the desires and beliefs into a finite domain constraint problem are largely based on this work, but in KRAFT constraints are used as problem specifications to find solutions to complex distributed design problems.

All components and agents are FIPA compliant, and we have RDF definitions for the COLAN constraint language, as well as for the Daplex database query language [11]. This is possible because of the entity-relationship model shared by both RDF and P/FDM.

4.2   Constructing Possible Worlds

The beliefs are a reflection of how the agent views the current state of the world so they naturally form the basis for the agent's deliberation process. Since we are using a data model approach to hold the agent's beliefs, and to provide the semantics to describe the domain, we formulate agent desires in terms of the entities, attributes and relationships contained in the data model and use these desires as *specifications* of the required tasks.

The advantage of using this data model approach is that each entity class in the data model can be easily viewed as a finite domain, with the object instances themselves as the elements in that domain. The object attributes and functions can then be used to form the basis for variables in the constraints.

The agent deliberation process must take into account current commitments and its current actions (intentions) when looking at any new collaborations. Given that the current environment is constantly changing, and that agents can negotiate and renegotiate commitments with each other at any time, we are unable to plan out and predict the agent's actions. what we *can* do is plan to a specified depth of lookahead and then refine and replan as we encounter changes.

Although the current situation may change, the agent still maintains long term, high level desires which will remain unaffected (e.g. a vendor must be found that can provide travel requirements, but the specific choice of vendor is not stated). What *will* be affected by the changes is the way in which these high level desires are carried out. Thus we are using the CLP process to allow the agent to exercise a degree of *autonomy* in carrying out the high level desires. We provide it with the various implementations of each high level solution and give the agent an intelligent method for choosing the most appropriate implementation.

When the agent begins its deliberation process it first constructs a possible worlds model [19] which contains all possible solutions and the interim states needed to provide those solutions in a connected possible worlds tree like structure. To populate the tree with candidate solutions, we find all the actions possible from the current state, then apply these actions and add these as new branches to the tree. Therefore if the agent is currently at time t, that node of the tree will lead to x_1 possible states the agents beliefs could have at time $t+1$ if a specific action towards the completion of a plan was carried out.

We then take these x_1 states and find the actions available from each of them. We can then apply these, and add the resulting new states to the tree (x_2 solutions at time $t+2$). This process can be continued to a given depth (i.e. how far we want the agent to plan ahead). This also means that we can limit the tree size to avoid a combinatorial explosion with the number of nodes.

The resulting populated structure contains all the possible states of the agents beliefs for the next n specified steps (what states the agent's belief data model would take were it to choose a specific way of carrying out all possible ways of doing these n steps towards completing the high level solution). We therefore have a possible worlds tree-like structure which preserves the information about the hierarchical position of each belief state in relation to the others, with each state containing the agent's beliefs, as they would be if the actions leading to the desired goal state were carried out.

Essentially this can be viewed as a *belief-accessible* world [19], where we can derive the *desire-accessible* and *intention-accessible* worlds, given the assumption that the agent will not desire or intend what it doesn't believe to be true. This can be achieved by constraining the *belief-accessible world* by applying the desires or intentions (represented as constraints).

4.3   From Possible Worlds to CLP

To construct the deliberation process as a CLP, we transform this structure into finite domains in ECLiPSe [3]. The constraints are then posted against these finite domains and any invalid states are eliminated. Fig. 5 shows an example of the constraints that can be posted in the CLP. The constraints come from various sources, but can all be combined to influence the agent's reasoning process.

Each node in the possible worlds structure holds a populated data model (Fig. 4), representing the agent's beliefs for that particular state. The code fragment below shows part of the P/FDM data representation for a small part of one of these states. The entities and their values in the data model are represented using the `object/3` construct, and the functions and their relationships

---

[3] http://www.icparc.ic.ac.uk/eclipse/

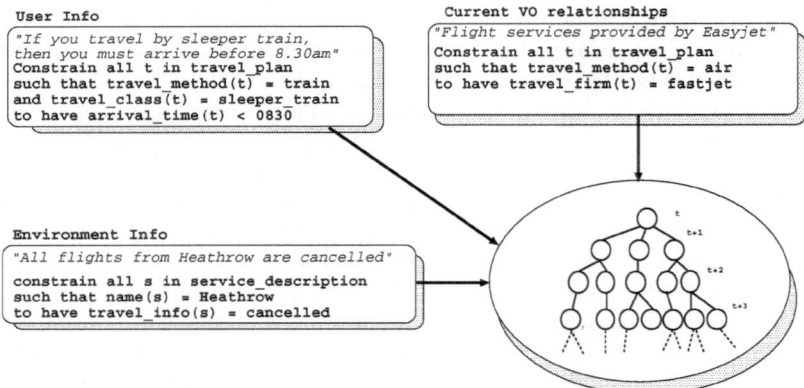

Fig. 5. The Agent's Deliberation Process as a CLP

to other objects are shown by the `fnval/3` construct. The representation of the objects and the object functions as term structures gives us a uniform representation of the agent's beliefs, and allows for easy modification given any additions or changes to the data model representation.

```
object(travel_plan,agent₁).
fnval(travel_method,agent₁,train).
fnval(travel_class,agent₁,sleeper_train).
fnval(arrival_time,agent₁,0758).
fnval(vendor_used,agent₁,vendor₁₂).

object(vendor,vendor₁₂).
fnval(vendor_name,vendor₁₂,fastjet).

object(vendor,vendor₁₀).
fnval(vendor_name,vendor₁₀,Scot Travel).
```

4.4 Solving the CLP Using the ECLiPSe Propia Library

The ECLiPSe *Propia* library supports *generalised constraint propagation*. Using the `infers most` operator we can specify the finite domains for the CLP problem using the following ECLiPSe goals:

```
object(travel_plan,AGENT_NAME) infers most.
fnval(travel_method,AGENT_NAME,METHOD) infers most.
fnval(travel_class,AGENT_NAME,CLASS) infers most.
fnval(arrival_time,AGENT_NAME,TIME) infers most.
fnval(vendor_used,AGENT_NAME,VENDOR_ID) infers most.

object(vendor,VENDOR_ID) infers most.
fnval(vendor_name,VENDOR_ID,VENDOR_NAME) infers most.
```

This makes the possible values of each attribute of each object (as well as the variables representing the objects themselves) into a finite domain CLP variable. For example, the above code fragment would create finite domains for each object and for each `fnval` construct (so `VENDOR_NAME` from the above `fnval` would represent the finite domain containing all vendor names from every state in every node in the tree that contains similar constructs). We can now post constraints from our various sources over these domains. Any elements which are eliminated from the solution space by the constraints will propagate through the rest of the domains, eliminating all belief states which do not satisfy the required constraints. The remaining belief states are the valid options available to the agent in the possible worlds model. What is left therefore is a pruned version of the possible worlds tree structure containing the remaining valid states given the constraints imposed.

From the remaining tree structure a valid chain of actions can be found that, when executed, will lead the agent to the desired state, and therefore the solution to the given task. This can then be returned by the deliberation process as the chosen plan to execute in the main BDI loop. If the problem is over-constrained there is the possibility that no solution is available for this plan, in which case the agent will try to relax the constraints.

5   Constraint Relaxation

While the constraint mechanisms described provide a way of providing autonomy in the decision making process, the agent needs to be flexible so that it can remove or relax possible constraints when the problem is over-constrained and a solution cannot be found.

An agent can find situations where the constraints imposed mean that no valid solution can be found to provide any alternatives for the decision making process. What the agent must do then is *relax* or re-negotiate the constraints it has. In the example shown in section 4.1, the agent has a constraint that if `travel_class` is `sleeper_train` for a journey, then `arrival_time` must be less than 0830.

Suppose this constraint was applied, and no solution can be found. The agent tries *relaxing* the constraint, and tries again using separately the following versions:

```
Constrain all t in travel_plan such that
travel_method(t) = train
and travel_method(t) = sleeper_train
to have arrival_time(t) < 0930
```

```
Constrain all t in travel_plan such that
travel_method(t) = train
to have arrival_time(t) < 0830
```

The first alternative relaxes a *constant*, so that the person only needs to arrive before 9:30am; the second alternative removes a *restrictive term*, so that the person could take a train which was not a sleeper.

6   Current and Related Work

In this paper, we have shown how an agent can choose the best among several possible virtual organisations to form in order to meet some customer requirement. Our approach is to use a deliberative process to construct possible worlds, each corresponding to a potential virtual organisation, and each configured using constraint satisfaction techniques. We are also investigating the scalability of such an approach, given the complexity of constraint satisfaction problems, in a realistic virtual organisation scenario.

Research and development work on technologies to support virtual organisations is not new [16], although it is currently receiving greater attention in the context of Grid computing [9]. In terms of explicit modelling of organisational properties (partner cabailities, service agreements, life cycle stages) the work that has been done using intelligent software agents [8] is well ahead of the mainstream distributed computing work that currently underpins Grid computing. Recent research in the agents area relevant to virtual organisations includes work on coalition formation [2] and formal specification of the rules constituting "electronic institutions" [6]. All of this work is complementary to ours.

As stated earlier, our current work builds on the results of the KRAFT project [18] which in turn was heavily influenced by early multi-agent projects such as SHADE [15], and ADEPT [14]. The novelty in our approach lies in the use of constraints to give a formal yet flexible business knowledge, enabling both the formation and operation of virtual organisations [17].

The Smart Clients project [22] is related to KRAFT in the way they conduct problem-solving on a CSP dynamically specified by the customer, using data extracted from remote databases. Their approach differs from ours in that only data is extracted from the remote databases, no constraints are therefore transmitted across the network; conversely, it is the constraint solver that is transmitted to the client's computer, to work with the constraints specified locally by the customer.

Finally, the Business Rule Markup Language is similar in concept to KRAFT's use of constraints [20]. The difference is that this work uses a rule-based formalism to specify business rules. Logic programming techniques are then used to reason with the rules.

Our current research draws in part on work being done in the context of the Advanced Knowledge Technologies project (AKT) — a multi-site collaboration focussing on the knowledge management life-cycle[4]. AKT shares some basic CLP mechanisms with our current work, as described in 4.1, and is developing RDF definitions for the P/FDM schema language and the Colan constraint language [11].

Our further work in this area will be done as part of the CONOISE project[5], a joint collaboration between Aberdeen, Cardiff and Southampton universities, and BTexact Technologies. CONOISE will look at agent interaction and deploy-

---

[4] http://www.aktors.org
[5] http://www.conoise.org

ment in open systems, and in particular the interplay between constraint-solving and negotiation processes in the formation and operation of virtual organisations.

Initially, we are exploring how Southampton's work in online auctions can be effectively combined with our CSP approach in virtual organisation formation, and how Cardiff's work on service descriptions can enrich the information available to agents during the formation process.

Acknowledgements. The basis of this work is from research supported by an EPSRC grant under the supervision of Prof. P.M.D. Gray and on work previously completed during the KRAFT project, in particular the work of Kit-Ying Hui and Alun Preece. The KRAFT project was funded by grants from BT and EPSRC. The CONOISE project is funded by BTexact Technologies.

References

1. H. Akkermans. Intelligent e-business: From technology to value. In *IEEE Intelligent Systems July/August*, volume 16, pages 8–10, 2001.
2. P. Anthony, W. Hall, V. Dung Dang, and N. R. Jennings. Autonomous agents for participating in multiple online auctions. In *IJCAI01 Workshop on E-Business & the Intelligent Web*, pages 54–64, 2001.
3. N. Bassiliades and P.M.D. Gray. Colan: a functional constraint language and its implementation. In *Data and Knowledge Engineering 14*, pages 203–249, 1994.
4. S. Chalmers and P.M.D. Gray. Bdi agents and constraint logic. In *AISB Journal, Special Issue on Agent Technology*, volume 1, pages 21–40, 2001.
5. P. Eaton, E. Freuder, and R. Wallace. Constraints and agents: Confronting ignorance. In *AI Magazine 19(2):50-65*, 1998.
6. M. Esteva, J.A. Rodriguez, C. Sierra, P. Garcia, and J.L. Arcos. On the formal specification of electronic institutions. pages 126–147. Springer-Verlag, 2001.
7. N.J. Fiddian, P. Marti, J-C. Pazzaglia, K. Hui, A. Preece, D.M. Jones, and Z. Cui. Application of KRAFT in data service network design. In *BT Technology Journal*, volume 17. Chapman and Hall, 1999.
8. K. Fischer, J. Muller, I. Heirnig, and A-W. Scheer. Intelligent agents in virtual enterprises. In *Proc 1st International Conference on Practical Applications of Intelligent Agents*, London, 1996.
9. I. Foster, C. Kesselman, J. M. Nick, and S. Teucke. The physiology of the grid: An open grid services architecture for distributed systems integration. In *http://www.globus.org/research/papers/ogsa.pdf*, 2002.
10. P.M.D. Gray, S. M. Embury, and G. J. L. Kemp. The evolving role of constraints in the functional data model. In *Journal of Intelligent Information Systems*, volume 12, pages 113–117. Kluwer Academic Press, 1999.
11. P.M.D. Gray, K. Hui, and A. Preece. An expressive constraint language for semantic web applications. In *IJCAI01 Workshop on E-Business & the Intelligent Web*, pages 46–53, 2001.
12. P.M.D. Gray, K. Hui, and A. D. Preece. Finding and moving constraints in cyberspace. In *Proc. AAAI Spring Symposium on Intelligent Agents in Cyberspace (SS-99-03)*, pages 121–127, 1999.

13. K. Hui and P.M.D. Gray. Developing finite domain constraints – a data model approach. In *Proceedings of the 1st International Conference on Computational Logic*, pages 448–462. Springer-Verlag, 2000.

14. N. Jennings, P. Faratin, M. Johnson, T. Norman, P. O'Brien, and M. Wiegand. Agent-based business process management. *International Journal of Cooperative Information Systems*, 5:105–130, 1996.

15. D. R. Kuokka, J. G. McGuire, J. C. Weber, J. M. Tenenbaum, T. R. Gruber, and G. R. Olsen. SHADE: Technology for knowledge-based collaborative engineering. *Journal of Concurrent Engineering: Applications and Research*, 1(2), 1993.

16. D. E. O'Leary, D. Kuokka, and R. Plant. Artificial intelligence and virtual organisations. *Communications of the ACM*, 40:52–59, 1997.

17. A. Preece, P.M.D. Gray, and K. Hui. Supporting virtual organisations through knowledge fusion. In *Artificial Intelligence for Electronic Commerce: Papers from the AAAI-99 Workshop*, Menlo Park, CA, 1999. AAAI Press.

18. A. Preece, K. Hui, A. Gray, P. Marti, T. Bench-Capon, Z. Cui, and D. Jones. KRAFT: An agent architecture for knowledge fusion. In *International Journal on Intelligent Cooperative Information Systems (IJCIS)*, 2000.

19. A. S. Rao and M. P. Georgeff. BDI agents: From theory to practice. In *Proceedings of the First International Conference on Multi-Agent Systems*, 1995.

20. D. Reeves, B. Grosof, M. Wellman, and H. Chan. Toward a declarative language for negotiating executable contracts. In *Artificial Intelligence for Electronic Commerce: Papers from the AAAI-99 Workshop*, Menlo Park, CA, 1999. AAAI Press.

21. D. W. Shipman. The functional data model and the data language DAPLEX. In *ACM Transactions on Database Systems 6(1)*, pages 140–173, 1981.

22. M. Torrens and B. Faltings. Smart clients: constraint satisfaction as a paradigm for scaleable intelligent information systems. In *Artificial Intelligence for Electronic Commerce: Papers from the AAAI-99 Workshop*, Menlo Park, CA, 1999. AAAI Press.

An Approach to Agent Communication Based on Organisational Roles*

Juan M. Serrano and Sascha Ossowski

Artificial Intelligence Group
School of Engineering
University Rey Juan Carlos
{jserrano,s.ossowski}@escet.urjc.es
http://www.ia.escet.urjc.es

Abstract. Modern ACLs, such as FIPA ACL, provide standardised catalogues of performatives denoting types of communicative actions, and interaction protocols. They have been designed as general purpose languages to ensure interoperability among agent systems. However, recent work reports a need for new ad-hoc sets of performatives in certain contexts, showing that FIPA ACL does not support adequately all relevant types of interactions. In this paper we first present a formal model that relates performatives, and other ACL-related concepts, to the organisation of MAS. Then, a principled method for the *design* of the ACL of a particular MAS is developed, which account for both, reusability and expressiveness. Finally, we illustrate our approach by an example in the domain of online stock brokering.

1 Introduction

Agent Communication Languages (ACLs) are considered to be the centrepiece of today's multiagent systems (MAS). Modern ACLs, such as the standard FIPA ACL [5], are defined by two major components: a *Communicative Act Library* (CAL) providing a catalogue of performatives [6] which denote a set of illocutionary actions [12], and an *Interaction Protocol Library* (IPL) that comprises a set of interaction protocols based on those message types [7]. These ACLs are designed as general-purpose languages, i.e. they are to provide adequate support for interactions in *every* multiagent organisation.

However, as Pitt and Mamdani [10] rightly argue, this attempt is unrealistic, as not all *social interactions* can be covered at a satisfactory level of abstraction. By consequence, recent proposals of new sets of performatives for argumentation-based negotiation [15], team formation [2], and other domains, have been put forward. Still, it is of foremost importance to find a way of integrating new interaction-specific CAs into a standard ACL in a *principled* fashion, in order to avoid interoperability problems in future large-scale agent systems.

---

* Research sponsored by MCyT, project TIC2000-1370-C04-01, and by CAM, project 07T/0011/2000

M. Klusch, S. Ossowski, and O. Shehory (Eds.): CIA 2002, LNAI 2446, pp. 241–248, 2002.

This paper advocates for the design of *domain-specific extensions to standard ACLs (MAS ACLs)* based on organisational principles. In section 2, we define organisational key concepts by means of the RICA metamodel and analyse the *structure* of FIPA ACL in these terms. Section 3 outlines how this structure can be used to build principled extensions to FIPA ACL, that comply not only with expressiveness requirements but also with reusability and interoperability concerns. This design method is illustrated by an application for the online stock brokerage industry [11]. Finally, we compare our approach to related work, and discuss future lines of research.

2   An Organisational Perspective on ACLs

In order to model the link between communicational and organisational components of MAS, the conceptual framework needs to be identified first. Respecting organisational terms, we draw from Ferber and Gutknecht's Agent/Group/Role metamodel [4], that highlights *Agent*, *Group* and *Role*, as organisational key concepts. As far as the concept of *Role* is concerned, it is customary to define it in terms of the functionality or behaviour associated to some type of agent, within an organisational context [4,17,3]. We employ the term "interaction" in the same way as "protocol" is used in [17]: it refers to the type of *Social Interaction* in which some group of roles participates, specified in terms of the *purpose* of that interaction, rather than to prototypical patterns of message exchange. We reserve the word "protocol" for this latter sense. The Role/Interaction/Communicative Action (RICA) metamodel [14] defines our view of the interrelation between these organisational concepts, in terms of UML class relations. Figure 1 shows the most relevant relations with respect to the purpose of this paper.

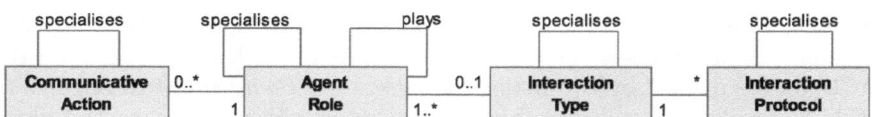

Fig. 1. UML diagram of the RICA metamodel

***Self* Associations.** The usual generalisation and specialisation relationships within classes also apply to the classes of the RICA metamodel, particularly to agent roles [8]. In addition, the RICA metamodel includes the usual *plays*-relation between roles [3]. In the sequel, we will see that these self-associations are crucial for a consistent definition of the interrelation between communicative and organisational concepts.

***Role/Communicative Action* Association.** In general, both the communicative and non-communicative behaviour , together with a set of rights or permissions, are necessary to fully specify a role [17]. As we are concerned with the interplay between organisational and communicative concepts, our standpoint in this paper is similar to [3], where agent interaction is purely dialogic and, consequently, roles are exclusively defined in terms of a set of illocutionary actions. An intelligent tutoring agent, for instance, may request students to perform some exercise, inform them about the examination day, etc. So, its role may be characterised by CAs such as FIPA *request, inform-ref*, etc.

Of course, there are roles in other application domains which will also issue *inform-ref* and *request* messages. This suggests the existence of more generic roles, call them *Requester* and *Information Provider* respectively, that the intelligent tutor and many others may play. Thus, although requests are performed by many different roles, we consider this CA (and others, such as FIPA *cancel, request-when* and *request-whenever*), to be exclusively *characteristic* to the requester role. The one-to-many Role/CA association of the RICA metamodel accounts for this relation between a CA and its *only* characteristic role. Table 1 shows a partition of the FIPA CAL in terms of the characteristic roles of their performatives.

Table 1. Classification Scheme for the FIPA ACL

FIPA ACL				
Message Exchange	Action Performing I	Information Exchange	Action Performing II	Brokering
FIPA CAL				
Communicator	Requester I	Information Seeker	Requester II	Brokering Requester
inform *confirm* *disconfirm* *not-understood*	*request* *request-when* *request-whenever* *cancel*	*query-if* *query-ref* *subscribe*	*cfp* *accept-proposal* *reject-proposal*	*propagate* *proxy*
	Requestee I	Information Provider	Requestee II	Broker
	agree *refuse* *failure*	*inform-if* *inform-ref*	*propose*	
FIPA IPL				
	Request-Prot. *Request-When-Prot.*	*Query-Prot.* *Subscribe-Prot.*	*Propose-Prot.* *ContractNet-Prot.* *IteratedContractNet-Prot.* *English-Auction-Prot.* *Dutch-Auction-Prot.*	*Brokering-Prot.* *Recruiting-Prot.*

If a role is a specialisation of another, the former obviously inherits the attributes of the latter, and in particular all the CAs that characterise the super-role. The sub-role can (but must not) add new illocutionary actions to the catalogue of the super-role, or may *specialise* some of these CAs. For instance, the FIPA *query-ref* message type is a specialisation of the FIPA *request* CA, obtained by overloading its propositional content. This goes in line with a specialisation relationship between the corresponding characteristic roles: the *Requester* and *Information Seeker*. The other specialisation relationships, which can be identified within the FIPA CAL, are shown in figure 2.

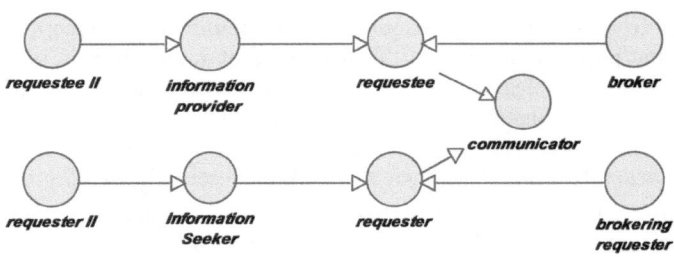

Fig. 2. Role model Implicit in the FIPA CAL

***Role/Social Interaction* Association.** Obviously, several roles may partici-
pate in a certain type of social interaction. For instance, the FIPA Requester
and Requestee roles participate in an interaction about *Action Performing*, and
Exchange of Information is a social interaction jointly performed by the FIPA
Information Seeker and Information Provider roles. Table 1 shows the other
types of social interaction supported by the FIPA ACL.

Still, it is also customary in the organisational literature to acknowledge that
roles may participate in several types of interaction [4]. To account for this multiple cardinality, we make use of the *plays-* relation between roles. For instance, an
intelligent tutor may both, exchange information and interact with the students
regarding action performing. In this example, the intelligent tutor *indirectly* participates in both types of interaction while playing the Requester and Information Provider roles, respectively. The *Role/Social Interaction* relationship of the
RICA metamodel accounts for the *only* characteristic social interaction in which
some role(s) may *directly* participate.

Furthermore note that, as before, the specialisation relationship between roles
also induces a specialisation relationship between the corresponding types of
social interaction.

***Social Interaction/Protocol* Association.** This one-to-many relation ac-
count for that fact that usually *several* protocols are associated to the same
topic, i.e. type of social interaction. For instance, the FIPA-Query-Protocol
and FIPA-Subscribe-Protocol are prototypical patterns of information exchange
among agents. Table 1 shows a partition of the FIPA IPL in terms of the types
of social interaction supported by the FIPA ACL.

Again, given that social interactions can be specialised, the possible protocols
attached to a super-interaction will also be inherited by the sub-interaction,
which might add new protocols and/or specialise existing ones. For instance, the
FIPA-Query-Protocol can be conceived as a specialisation of the FIPA-Request-
Protocol[14].

3   Design Method of the ACL for a Multiagent System

In this section we outline the major steps of a design method for MAS ACLs based on the RICA metamodel, and illustrate them by an example from the domain of online stock brokerage [11]. We focus on the design of the ACL for a personal assistant agent, which extends the basic functionality of traditional Online Stock Brokers with advisory capabilities.

Our ACL design method is driven by an initial organisational model of the particular application at hand. The bottom part of Figure 3 shows this initial model for the Online Stock Broker class.

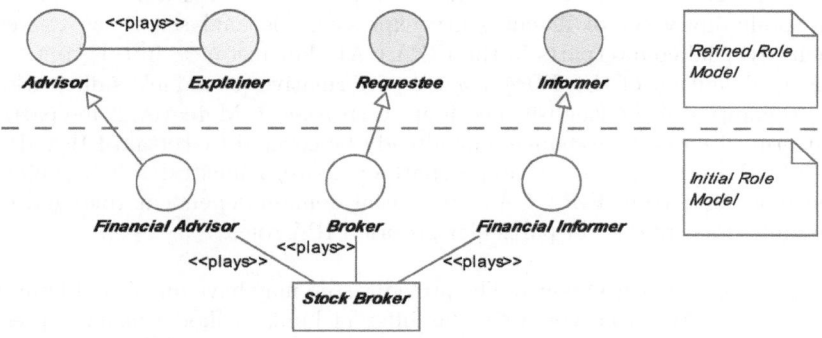

Fig. 3. Role Model of the Stock Broker Agent

Step 1: Collecting Sample Dialogues. The first step in the design of the communication language for our agent application is to collect natural language dialogues characterising the different domain-dependent types of interaction, in which the Online Stock Broker and the Investor participate. Table 2 shows a sample dialogue, whose topic is the trading of a particularly risky stock.

Table 2. Sample Dialogue between Broker and Investor

(1) I-	I would like to buy 500 shares of TERRA	
(2) B-	Be careful, this is a risky order	
(3) I-	Can you explain why?	
(4) B-	Because this stock has a high level of volatility	
(5) I-	Which is exactly the volatility value of TERRA?	
(6) B-	40%	
(7) I-	Which stock would you recommend?	
(8) B-	Some one these stocks might be suitable for you: S1, S2, ...	
(9) I-	Could you recommend me a specific order for S1?	
(10) B-	An order with 50 or 100 shares (current price per share: 10E)	
(11) I-	Forget the initial order. I would like to buy 100 shares of S1	
(12) B-	Ok....	

   Stock Trading   Financial Advice   Exchange of Financial Information

Step 2: Pragmatic Analysis. The second step consists of a pragmatic analysis of the sample dialogues. First, it aims at identifying the types of CAs that best describe the communicative behaviour of the agents participating in the dialogues by means of natural language illocutionary expressions (thus, accounting for the expressiveness requirement). For instance, utterance number 1 of table 2 represents a *request* of the investor, while number 2 is modelled as a *warning not to* perform that order. Second, the patterns of message exchange for each kind of social interaction are identified. As a result, a preliminary natural-language version of the MAS CAL and MAS IPL is obtained.

Step 3: Reuse Analysis. In order to cope with the reusability requirement, the preliminary set of illocutionary expressions is analysed so as to identify their artificial counterparts in the FIPA CAL. For instance, in this context, the formal definition of the *FIPA request* performative [6] models sufficiently well the semantics of the English speech act verb *request*. Moreover, some particular patterns of message exchange may already be covered by certain FIPA IPs.

On the other hand, the upper part of figure 3 illustrates how, guided by the reuse of certain FIPA CAs, the initial domain-dependent roles have been recognised as subroles of particular generic FIPA roles.

Step 4: Extension Design. The previous step may have uncovered limitations of the FIPA ACL to account for the different kinds of illocutionary expressions and/or dialogue patterns that are characteristic for the particular MAS. In our example, *warnings* and *explanations* issued by the financial advisor are out of the scope of the FIPA ACL. Prior to the formalisation of these CAs, the financial advisory role is refined by identifying their characteristic generic roles: the *Advisor* and *Explainer* roles (see figure 3), which participate in advisory and explanatory interactions, respectively.

The formalisation of the illocutionary expressions not covered by FIPA ACL sets out from the linguistic meaning as stated in dictionaries such as [16], but is driven by a *conceptual analysis* from the standpoint of software agent systems. Both, the Natural Semantic Metalanguage (NSM) used in [16], and the FIPA SL are proposed as languages to state the meaning of the new performatives [13].

Concerning interaction protocols, a design proposal exploiting the RICA metamodel is put forward in [14]. It simplifies the formalisation of complex patterns of message exchange based on the role-generalisation and role-playing relationships. In our example, the protocol to be followed by the financial advisor is decomposed into two protocols corresponding to the advisory and explanatory types of social interaction.

As a result, our design method comes up with a MAS ACL whose general structure is shown in table 3(numbers in parentheses refer to the corresponding utterances of table 2). It consists of a generic part (reused from FIPA ACL), and a domain (organisation) dependent part (in this case: Online Stock Brokerage). The latter can be classified further into types of interaction which are potentially reusable, and others that remain idiosyncratic.

Table 3. Agent Communication Language for the Online Stock Broker Application

Online Stock Broker ACL			
Action Perf. I	**Info. Exchange**	**Advisory Interaction**	**Explanatory Interaction**
CAL			
Requestee	**Info. Provider**	**Advisor**	**Explainer**
agree (12) *. . .*	*inform-ref (6)* *. . .*	*warn (2)* *suggest (8)* *recommend (10) . . .*	*explain-inferred-fact (4)* *. . .*
Requester	**Info. Seeker**	**Advisee**	**Explainee**
request (1)(11) *cancel (11) . . .*	*query-ref (5)* *. . .*	*consult (7)(9)*	*request-for-explanation (3)*
IPL			
FIPA-Request-Prot.	*FIPA-Query-Prot.*	*Advisory Protocol*	*Explanatory Protocol*

           FIPA ACL Reused   Potentially Reusable

4   Discussion

In this paper we have described a method for the principled design of domain extensions to the general-purpose FIPA ACL, based on an organisational structuring. This approach follows [10] in the general design strategy, using a core language and providing extended components as required by new types of social interaction. However, it differs significantly in that we explicitly establish and follow the link between the ACL and the types of interaction specified in the organisational model, thus providing clues as to how these types of interaction might inform the design of the ACL. The RICA metamodel also draws upon other methodologies found in the literature, mainly [9]. As with [1] and [3], it focuses on the relation between organisational and ACL components. However, our approach is especially concerned with the reusability and interoperability of CAs and IPs.

The present design method constitutes a conservative extension of the FIPA CAL and IPL, as it does not significantly endanger interoperability. On the one hand, the organisational structuring of the libraries helps the designer to better understand their contents; on the other, formal definitions of new performatives (e.g. based on FIPA SL and NSM) help to enforce a unique interpretation. In addition, our proposal fosters reusability of the extensions, and shows how the reuse of ACL performatives and protocols implies the reuse of the corresponding characteristic components of the organisational model: generic types of social interactions and roles.

We are aware that our design method has been illustrated only in the context of a closed environment (the centrally designed Online Stock Broker application). However, we believe that it also scales up well to open environments. In this case, an agreement between designers or an standardisation body such as FIPA would be required in order to identify specific extensions to performative and protocol catalogues for particularly organisations, as suggested by our structuring approach. In future work we will examine as to how far the organisational analysis of ACLs may have an impact on the current FIPA architecture.

References

1. J. M. Bradshaw, S. Dutfield, P. Benoit, and J. D. Woolley. KAoS: Toward an industrial-strength open agent architecture. In J. M. Bradshaw, editor, *Software Agents*, chapter 17, pages 375–418. AAAI Press / The MIT Press, 1997.
2. F. Dignum, B. Dunin-Keplicz, and R. Verbrugge. Creating collective intention through dialogue. *J. of the IGPL*, 9(2):305–319, 2001.
3. M. Esteva, J. A. Rodriguez, C. Sierra, P. Garcia, and J. L. Arcos. On the formal specifications of electronic institutions. In F. Dignum and C. Sierra, editors, *Agent-mediated Electronic Commerce (The European AgentLink Perspective)*, volume 1191 of *LNAI*, pages 126–147, Berlin, 2001. Springer.
4. J. Ferber and O. Gutknetch. A meta-model for the analysis of organizations in multi-agent systems. In Y. Demazeau, editor, *ICMAS'98*, pages 128–135. IEEE Press, 1998.
5. Foundation for Intelligent Physical Agents. *FIPA ACL Message Structure Specification*. http://www.fipa.org/specs/fipa00061, 2000.
6. Foundation for Intelligent Physical Agents. *FIPA Communicative Act Library Specification*. http://www.fipa.org/specs/fipa00037, 2000.
7. Foundation for Intelligent Physical Agents. *FIPA Interaction Protocol Library Specification*. http://www.fipa.org/repository/ips.html, 2000.
8. Georg Gottlob, Michael Schrefl, and Brigitte Röck. Extending object-oriented systems with roles. *ACM Transactions on Information Systems*, 14:268–296, 1996.
9. H. Van Dyke Parunak and J. Odell. Representing social structures in UML. In J. P. Müller, E. Andre, S. Sen, and C. Frasson, editors, *Proceedings of the Fifth International Conference on Autonomous Agents*, pages 100–101, Montreal, Canada, May 2001. ACM Press.
10. J. Pitt and A. Mamdani. Designing agent communication languages for multi-agent systems. *Lecture Notes in Computer Science*, 1647:102–114, 1999.
11. C. Schmidt, C. Condon, and S. Lee. Online trading skyrockets in europe. *Forrester Research*, January 2000.
12. J.R. Searle and D. Vanderveken. *Foundations of illocutionary logic*. Cambridge University Press, 1985.
13. J. M. Serrano and S. Ossowski. The design of communicative act libraries: a linguistic perspective. *Applied Artificial Intelligence*, In Press, 2002.
14. J. M. Serrano and S. Ossowski. The design of interaction protocols: an organizational approach. In *Proceedings of the Agent Communication Language and Conversation Policies Workshop*, 2002.
15. C. Sierra, N. R. Jennings, P. Noriega, and S. Parsons. A framework for argumentation-based negotiation. *LNCS*, 1365:177–193, 1998.
16. A. Wierzbicka. *English speech act verbs. A semantic dictionary*. Academic Press, Australia, 1987.
17. M. Wooldridge, N. R. Jennings, and D. Kinny. The gaia methodology for agent-oriented analysis and design. *Autonomous Agents and Multi-Agent Systems*, 3(3):285–312, September 2000.

Exploiting Partially Shared Ontologies for Multi-agent Communication

Heiner Stuckenschmidt

Vrije Universiteit Amsterdam
de Boelelaan 1081a
1081 HV Amsterdam, The Netherlands
heiner@cs.vu.nl

Abstract. In has been argued that ontologies play a key role in multi-agent communication because they provide and define a shared vocabulary to be used in the course of communication. In real-life scenarios, however, the situation where two agents completely share a vocabulary is rather an exception. More often, each agent uses its own vocabulary specified in a private ontology that is not known by other agents. In this paper we propose a solution to this problem for the situation, where agents share at least parts of their vocabulary. We argue that the assumption of a partially shared vocabulary is valid and sketch an approach for re-formulating terms from the private part of an agent's ontology into a shared part thus enabling other agents to understand them. We further describe how the approach can be implemented using existing technology and proof the correctness of the re-formulation with respect to the semantics of the ontology-language DAML+OIL.

1 Introduction

An important aspect of multi-agent systems is the communication among different agents, because communication is the basis for cooperation. Ontologies are a technology to support inter-agent communication by providing a definition of the world, an agent can ground his beliefs and actions as well as by providing terms that can be used in communication [13]. In practice, agent communication based on ontologies still suffers from many problems. Uschold [20] identifies a number barriers for agent communication that can be separated in language heterogeneity and in terminological heterogeneity. In the following, we will focus on the latter leaving out the problem of heterogeneous languages for encoding knowledge. In fact, agents will often use private ontologies that define terms in different ways making it impossible for the other agent to understand the contents of a message. In these cases there is a need to align ontologies the ontologies used by different agents. Some principled approaches to overcome this problem have been proposed:

- **Emergence:** A very generic approach is to let shared ontologies evolve within the multi-agent systems. Steels uses language games to generate

M. Klusch, S. Ossowski, and O. Shehory (Eds.): CIA 2002, LNAI 2446, pp. 249–263, 2002.
© Springer-Verlag Berlin Heidelberg 2002

shared ontologies [17]. The approach reported, however, depends on perceptual grounding of agents and assumes an environment that allows for a trial and error phase in communication. In practical applications on the web for example, the situation is different, because legacy ontologies exist and have to be considered.

- **Merging:** In the presence of legacy ontologies, a common approach is to merge existing ontologies resulting in a common one that includes all aspects of the individual ontologies. Stephens and Huhns report an experiment in merging a large number of small ontologies based on matching heuristics [18]. While the result of the experiment is partially convincing, the merging approach is still problematic, because the autonomy of the agents is partially lost by the use of a global ontology.

- **Mapping:** The most often mentioned approach for aligning ontologies on the World Wide Web is the definition of mappings between concepts of different ontologies. Hendler describes this approach that preserves the autonomy of ontological models on a general level [12]. The paper envisions a complex network of ontologies and mappings that enables agents that use different ontologies of the network to communicate via mappings. The use of inter-ontology mappings has been intensively studied in the area of information integration, however, very little work is done on the automatic generation of mappings. As a consequence, the mapping approach requires a lot of manual work and is therefore only pays off for the alignment of ontologies that are frequently used together.

In this paper, we adopt the view of [12] that an intelligent World Wide Web will include a network of different ontologies about various topics that can be used in agent communication. In contrary to Hendler, we do not think that these ontologies will already be linked by mappings, because we expect the effort of establishing these mappings as being too high in many cases. We think that mappings will mostly be established by individual agents that use different available ontologies in order to process a given task. In this view, a connection between the ontologies of different agents is not established by explicit mappings, but rather by existing ontologies that are used by more than one agent.

In this paper, we propose an approach to facilitate agent communication in the situation, where agents share some but not all of their terminology. In the next section, we describe our approach in an informal way. In section 3 we describe the formal framework our framework is build upon in terms of the ontology language DAML+OIL, its semantics and the formal foundation for inter-ontology mappings. The approach for approximating concepts in a language with a limited vocabulary in described in section 4 and a correctness proof is given. In section 5 we describe how the approximation approach can be used to re-formulate agent messages in such a way that another agent can understand it. We summarize with a discussion and some hints towards future research.

2   Communication with Partially Shared Ontologies

In order to get a clearer notion of the problem to be solved we make some simplifying assumptions. First of all we will only consider two agents that want to communicate. Then we assume that there are only two ontologies involved, a shared one and a private one of the agent trying to communicate. We further assume that both ontologies are encoded on the same language, preventing us from the problem of integrating the ontology languages. Figure 1 illustrated the situation.

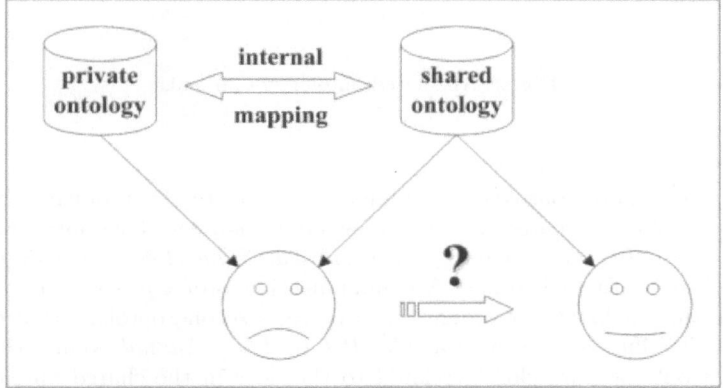

Fig. 1. The communication problem

This simplified communication problem can easily be extended to more realistic scenarios as communication is mostly bi-lateral even in complex multi-agent systems. There might be more than two ontologies involved in the communication, but they will all either be shared or private to one on the agents. The only assumption that really is a simplification is the existence of a single ontology language. Investigating this problem, however, is out of the scope of this paper. For an approach to overcome language heterogeneity, we refer to [8]. In the remainder of this section, we illustrate our approach of translation concepts into a shared terminology.

2.1   Ontology Heterogeneity

In order to perform a task, an agent will use one of more ontologies as an explicit representation of the domain of interest. These ontologies will normally supplement each other to form a sufficiently complete model. Though being supplementary, we can assume that they have sufficient overlap to allow a single agent to find mappings between them. In the following we give a toy example illustrating this idea.

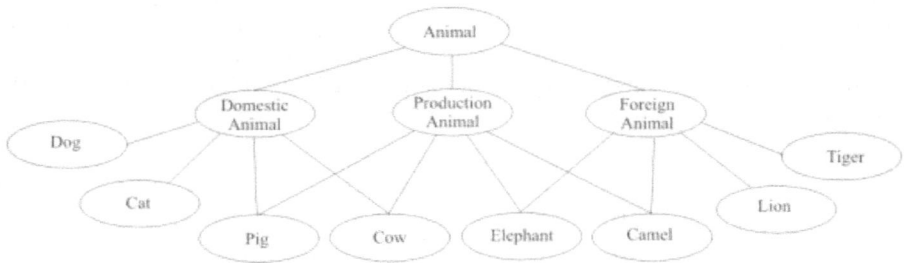

Fig. 2. An shared ontology of animals

We use a simple ontology of animals to illustrate the problem (see figure 2). This ontology is shared by the two agents in figure 1. Therefore, the agents can use terms from this ontology (e.g. *Animal*, *Domestic-Animal* or *Cow*) to communicate with each other. A communication problem arises, because the agent on the left hand side of figure 1 also uses a second ontology that contains different classifications of animal like *Pet* or *Farm-Animal*. While the terms from this ontology are closely related to the ones in the shared ontology, the agent on the right-hand side will not be able to understand them.

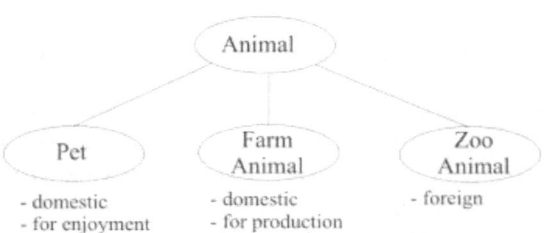

Fig. 3. A private ontology of animals

We can assume that each agent using more than one ontology establishes internal mappings between these ontologies. In our example, these mappings would specify *Pet* as being a subclass of *Domestic-Animal* which is disjoint from *Production-Animal*, *Farm-Animal* to be a subclass of *Domestic-Animal* and of *Production-Animal* as well as *Zoo-Animal* to be a subclass of *Foreign-Animal*.

In the following, we describe, how these internal mappings can be used in order to facilitate external communication.

2.2   Trading-Off Modeling and Reasoning

There are different options for relating ontologies like the ones described above in order to use them for information filtering. The ones most often discussed ones are merging and mapping of ontologies [14]. In this paper, we argue for an approach that is based on on-demand translations rather than a fixed connection of ontologies. .

The merging approach aims at producing a single global ontology based on the ontologies to be related. The integrated ontology will contain class definitions from both ontologies arranged in a single taxonomy. The advantage of this approach is that the merged ontology contains all information that is needed to filter information and the filtering process can be implemented in a straight-forward way. The drawback of this approach, however, is the effort needed to come up with a merged ontology that correctly resembles both ontologies. The situation becomes even worse if we want to include further ontologies. In this case we have to perform further merges that are costly and lead to huge ontology that is hard to handle and maintain.

The mapping approach tries to avoid the creation of large global ontologies. It rather aims at relating concepts from both ontologies using additional knowledge, i.e. mapping rules. These rules can be used to find concepts in the other ontology that correspond to concepts used in a query and retrieve the instances of these concepts as well. The advantage of the mapping approach is that an extension to other ontology does not affect the ones already included in the system. A problem of the mapping approach is the need to specify mappings to all other ontologies already present in a system. Further, static mapping rules can be come very complicated if not only 1:1 mappings are needed like in our example.

Translation with Shared Ontologies tries to combine the advantages of merging and mapping. The idea is to define concepts from different sources using terms specified in a shared model (similar to a partially merged ontology) and relate these concepts only if such a relation is needed using terminological reasoning. The advantages of the translation approach are its scalability - new information sources can be added without affecting other sources - and the fact that we do not have to establish a connection to each other source in the system. Mappings only have to be established with the shared model, because other relations are derived from these mappings.

2.3   Terminology Adaption

We consider the situation, where the agent wants to find information about the concepts specified in its private ontology (figure 3) In order to be able to communicate this information need to other agents that might have valuable information it has to use terminology from the shared ontology (figure 2).

As an example we take the following query $(Animal \wedge \neg(Farm - Animal)$. This query cannot be directly answered, because the term Farm-Animal is not understood. The idea of our approach is to re-write this query in such a way that it covers the same set of answers using terms from the other ontology. In general, an exact re-writing is not possible because the concepts of the private ontology do not have exactly matching concepts in the shared one. In this case, we have to look for re-writings that approximate the query as closely as possible. Re-writings that are an upper approximation of the original query are know from the database area as *minimal subsuming mappings* [4]. While in the area of databases upper approximations are often used in combination with an additional filter that removes irrelevant results, our approach aims for correctness rather than for completeness and therefore uses a lower approximation.

The idea of the re-writing is the following. Based on the mappings between of the classes in both ontologies, we can find those concepts in the ontology of figure 2 that are most closely related to a query concept. Taking a concepts from our query, we can for example decide that *Domestic-Animal* and *Production-Animal* are upper approximations for *Farm-Animal* while Cow and Pig are lower approximations. Using these concepts, we can define lower boundaries for farm-animals $(Cow \vee Pig)$ and use this expression instead of the original concept still getting correct results. In our example, however, the concept occurred in a negated form. In order to return a correct result, we therefore cannot use the lower bound because not all irrelevant resources might be excluded. Based on the considerations made above we can replace the concept farm-animal within the scope of the negation by its upper bound $(Domestic - Animal \wedge Production - Animal)$. Using this rewriting, we get the following query that can be shown to return only correct results: $(Animal \wedge \neg(Domestic - Animal \wedge Production - Animal)$.

In the following, we show how the general idea sketched in this section can be implemented on the basis of available reasoning support for ontology languages, i.e. DAML+OIL.

3   Representation and Reasoning about Ontologies

If we want to guarantee that the re-writing delivers correct results, we need a formal basis for representing and reasoning about the ontologies involved. Recently, the benefits of semantically well-founded ontology languages have been discussed by many authors in connection with the so-called Semantic Web (see e.g. [9]). One of the most important proposals that have been made for well-founded ontology languages for the web is DAML+OIL. In the following, we introduce this language and describe how it can be used to encode and reason about ontologies in order to support our approach.

3.1   The DAML+OIL Language

The DAML+OIL language is a web-based ontology language that has been developed in the DAML programme in order to support intelligent agents to communicate and reason about annotated information on the World Wide Web. Some of the features of the language we can use to precisely define ontological knowledge are the following [22].

Class Building Operations The only possibility to define class structures in RDF schema was the `rdfs:subClassOf` property. DAML+OIL adopts this relation also allowing for multiple inheritance and provides a property for stating that two classes are disjoint.

```
<daml:Class rdf:ID="Domestic-Animal">
    <rdfs:subClassOf rdf:resource="#Animal"/>
</daml:Class>

<daml:Class rdf:ID="Foreign-Animal">
    <rdfs:subClassOf rdf:resource="#Animal"/>
    <daml:disjointWith rdf:resource="#Domestic-Animal"/>
</daml:Class>

<daml:Class rdf:ID="Cow">
    <rdfs:subClassOf rdf:resource="#Domestic-Animal"/>
    <rdfs:subClassOf rdf:resource="#Production-Animal"/>
</daml:Class>
```

The expressiveness of the subclass relation in DAML+OIL is further enriched be the possibility of defining a class to be equivalent to a logical expression over class names.

```
<daml:Class rdf:about="#Animal">
    <daml:disjointUnionOf rdf:parseType="daml:collection">
        <daml:Class rdf:about="#Domestic-Animal"/>
        <daml:Class rdf:about="#Foreign-Animal"/>
    </daml:disjointUnionOf>
</daml:Class>
```

Beside the `daml:disjointUnionOf` property, classes can also be defined to be equivalent to another class, to equivalent to a Boolean expression over classes using `daml:intersectionOf`, `daml:unionOf` and `daml:complementOf` or by enumerating its elements with the `daml:oneOf` property.

Relations DAML+OIL defines two kinds of relations. `daml:ObjectProperty` relates members of different classes to each other. `daml:DatatypeProperty` relates a member of a class to a legal value of a certain data type. The first type of relation is very similar to an RDF property. It has a unique name and can have RDF schema range and domain restrictions like the following example:

```
<daml:ObjectProperty rdf:ID="has-origin">
    <rdfs:domain rdf:resource="#Animal"/>
    <rdfs:range rdf:resource="#Country"/>
</daml:ObjectProperty>
```

The first enhancement to RDF schema employed by DAML+OIL is the possibility of defining one relation to be the equivalent or the inverse of another relation. Using this feature, we can define the **has-child** relation using the one specified above:

```
<daml:ObjectProperty rdf:ID="is-origin-of">
    <daml:inverseOf rdf:resource="#has-origin"/>
</daml:ObjectProperty>
```

Just as RDF schema, hierarchies of relations can be specified using the `rdfs:subpropertyOf` operator. Further, special properties can be assigned to relations, for details we refer to [22].

Property Restrictions Classes define common properties of its members. Different from RDF schema, DAML+OIL provides means for defining these characteristic properties of class members in terms of restrictions on the objects they are related to. In principle there are two kinds of restrictions, type restrictions and number restrictions:

```
<daml:Class rdf:ID="Person">
    <rdfs:subClassOf rdf:resource="#Animal"/>
    <rdfs:subClassOf>
        <daml:Restriction daml:cardinalityQ="1">
            <daml:onProperty rdf:resource="#has-origin"/>
            <daml:hasClassQ rdf:resource=#Country/>
        </daml:Restriction>
    </rdfs:subClassOf>
</daml:Class>
```

The restriction `daml:hasClass` from the example claims that every object related to a member of the class has be be of a certain type. Beside this restriction, `daml:hasClass` claims that every member of the class is related to one object of a certain type, `daml:hasValue` even claims that every object of the class is related to one specific object. Number restrictions `daml:minCardinality`, `daml:maxCardinality` and `daml:cardinality` define lower and upper boundaries and exact values for the number of objects the member of a class is related to via a certain relation. Several restrictions may apply to a relation.

3.2 Semantics of DAML+OIL

In [21] a formal semantics for DAML+OIL is described. The semantics is based on an interpretation mapping into an abstract domain. More specifically, every concept name is mapped on a set of objects, every property name is mapped on a set of pairs of objects. Individuals (in or case resources) are mapped on individual objects in the abstract domain. Formally, an interpretation is defined as follows:

Definition 1 (Interpretation) *An Interpretation consists of a pair $(\Delta, .^{\mathcal{E}})$ where Δ is a (possibly infinite) set and $.^{\mathcal{E}}$ is a mapping such that:*

- $x^{\mathcal{E}} \in \Delta$ *for all individual names x.*
- $C^{\mathcal{E}} \subseteq \Delta$ *for all concept names C*
- $R^{\mathcal{E}} \subseteq \Delta \times \Delta$ *for all role names R*

We call $.^{\mathcal{E}}$ the extension of a concept, a role, or an individual, respectively.

This notion of an interpretation is a very general one and does not restrict the set of objects in the extension of a concept. This is done by the use of operators for defining classes. In our example, we used the `subClassOf` and the `hasValue` operator for restricting the set of objects that are members of the class zoo animals. These kinds of operators restrict the possible extensions of a concept. Figure 4 summarizes the specific interpretations of a part of the operators of DAML+OIL.

Operator	Extension $.^{\mathcal{E}}$
`intersectionOf`	$C_1^{\mathcal{E}} \cap \cdots \cap C_n^{\mathcal{E}}$
`unionOf`	$C_1^{\mathcal{E}} \cup \cdots \cup C_n^{\mathcal{E}}$
`complementOf`	$\Delta - C^{\mathcal{E}}$
`oneOf`	$\{x_1, \cdots, x_n\} \subset \Delta$
`toClass`	$\{y \in \Delta \mid (y,x) \in P^{\mathcal{E}} \implies x \in C^{\mathcal{E}}\}$
`hasClass`	$\{y \in \Delta \mid \exists x((y,x) \in P^{\mathcal{E}}) \wedge x \in C^{\mathcal{E}}\}$
`hasValue`	$\{y \in \Delta \mid (y,x) \in P^{\mathcal{E}}\}$
`minCardinalityQ`	$\{y \in \Delta \mid \mid \{x \mid (y,x) \in P^{\mathcal{E}} \wedge x \in C^{\mathcal{E}}\} \mid \leq n\}$
`maxCardinalityQ`	$\{y \in \Delta \mid \mid \{x \mid (y,x) \in P^{\mathcal{E}} \wedge x \in C^{\mathcal{E}}\} \mid \geq n\}$
`cardinalityQ`	$\{y \in \Delta \mid \mid \{x \mid (y,x) \in P^{\mathcal{E}} \wedge x \in C^{\mathcal{E}}\} \mid = n\}$

Fig. 4. Terminological Operators of DAML+OIL

These kinds of restriction are the basis for deciding whether a class definition is equivalent, more specialized or more general than another. Formally, we can decide whether one of the following relations between two expressions hold:

subsumption: $C_1 \sqsubseteq C_2 \iff C_1^{\mathcal{E}} \subseteq C_2^{\mathcal{E}}$

membership: $x : C \iff x^{\mathcal{E}} \in C^{\mathcal{E}}$

In order to implement information filtering, we need subsumption in order to determine the upper and lower boundaries of a concept. Membership is used in order to retrieve relevant resources that match a query.

3.3   Inter-ontology Mappings

For a long time, representation and reasoning in description logics, which provide the semantic basis for DAML+OIL, has only been investigated in terms of a single homogeneous model. Recently Borgida and Serafini proposed an extension of the formal framework of description logics to distributed knowledge models [3]. The extended framework consists of a set of terminological knowledge bases (ontologies) T_i and a set of so-called bridge rules between concept definitions from different ontologies. Two kinds of bridge rules are considered (the prefixes indicate the ontology a concept definition is taken from):

into rule $i : C \xrightarrow{\sqsubseteq} j : D$
onto rule $i : C \xrightarrow{\sqsupseteq} j : D$

The interpretation of the first rules is that the instances of the concept C in ontology T_i are mapped to a subset of the instances of the concept D in ontology T_j ($i : C^{\mathcal{E}} \subseteq j : D^{\mathcal{E}}$) in the case of the second rule the superset relation is asserted to hold between the instances of the two concepts. Using the formal framework of Borgida and Serafini, we can define the internal mappings between private and shared ontologies informally defined above.

$$Zoo - Animal \xrightarrow{\sqsubseteq} \neg Domestic - Animal \tag{1}$$

$$Pet \xrightarrow{\sqsubseteq} Domestic - Animal \wedge$$
$$\neg Production - Animal \tag{2}$$

$$Farm - Animal \xrightarrow{\sqsubseteq} Domestic - Animal \wedge$$
$$Production - Animal \tag{3}$$

Another important result reported in [3] is the ability to transform a distributed knowledge base into a global one and apply existing description logic reasoner in order to derive new knowledge. In the following, we build on this result whenever we mention terminological reasoning.

4   Approximating Concepts

The classes in a DAML+OIL ontology form a hierarchy with respect to the subsumption relation. In a distributed Description Logic, such a hierarchy can also be computed for separate ontologies that are connected by bridge rules. Therefore, we will always have a set of direct super- and a set of direct subclasses of a class c_1 from the private ontology. We can use those direct sub- and superclasses that belong to the shared ontology as upper and lower approximation for c_1 in the shared ontology:

Definition 2 (Lower Approximation) *Let C_1 be a set of private concepts, C_2 a set of shared concepts of an agent and $c \in C_1$ a class, then a class $c_{glb} \in C_2$ is called a lower approximation of c in IS_2, if the following assertions hold:*

1. $c_{glb} \sqsubseteq c$
2. $(\exists c' \in C_2 : c' \sqsubseteq c) \implies (c' \sqsubseteq c_{glb})$

The greatest lower bound $glb_{IS_2}(c)$ denotes the set of all lower approximations of c in C_2.

Definition 3 (Upper Approximation) *Let C_1 be a private classes , C_2 a set of shared classes of an agent and $c \in C_1$ a private class, then a class $c_{lub} \in C_2$ is called an upper approximation of c in IS_2, if the following assertions hold:*

1. $c \sqsubseteq c_{lub}$
2. $(\exists c' \in C_2 : c \sqsubseteq c') \implies (c_{lub} \sqsubseteq c')$

The least upper bound of $lub_{IS_2}(c)$ is the set of all least upper bounds of c in C_2.

The rational of using these approximations is that we can decide whether an entity x is a member of a class in the private ontology based on its membership in classes of the shared ontology. This decision in turn provides us with an approximate result on deciding whether x is the result of a query stated in terms of a private ontology, based on the following observation:

- If x is member of a lower bound of c_1 then it is also in c_1
- If x is not member of all upper bounds of c_1 then it is not in c_1

In [16] Selman and Kautz propose to use this observation about upper and lower boundaries for theory approximation. We adapt the proposal for defining an approximate classifier M' that assigns members of shared concepts to private ones in the following way:

Definition 4 (Concept Approximation) *Let C_1 be a set of private concepts, C_2 a set of shared concepts of an agent and x the member of a shared concepts then for every $c_1 \in C_1$ we define M' such that:*

- $M'(x, c_1) = 1$ *if* $x : \left(\bigvee_{c \in glb_{IS_2}(c_1)} c \right)$
- $M'(x, c_1) = 0$ *if* $x : \neg \left(\bigwedge_{c \in lub_{IS_2}(c_1)} c \right)$
- $M'(x, c_1) = ?$, *otherwise*

Where the semantics of disjunction and conjunction is defined in the obvious way using set union and intersection .

Based on the observation about the upper and lower bounds, we can make the following assertion about the correctness of the proposed approximate classification:

Proposition 1 (Correctness of Approximation) *The approximation from definition 4 is correct in the sense that:*

1. *If $M'(x, c_1) = 1$ then $x^{\mathcal{E}} \in c_1^{\mathcal{E}}$*
2. *If $M'(x, c_1) = 0$ then $x^{\mathcal{E}} \notin c_1^{\mathcal{E}}$*

Using the definition of upper and lower bounds the correctness of the classification can be proven in a straightforward way [19].

4.1   Quality of Approximation

Unfortunately, proving the correctness of the approximation says nothing about the quality of the approximation. In the worst case, the upper and lower boundaries of concepts in the other hierarchy are always $\top$ and $\bot$ respectively. In this case the translated query always returns the empty set as result. We were not able to investigate the quality of approximations on theoretical level, however, we can provide some rules of thumb that can be used to predict the quality of an approximation:

Depths of hierarchies: The first rule of thumb, we can state is that deeper class hierarchies lead to better approximations. For hierarchies of depth one it is easy to see that we will not be able to find good upper and lower bounds. We can also assume that deeper hierarchies provide finer grained distinctions between concepts that in turn often produce closer approximations.

Degree of overlap: Our approach assumes a shared vocabulary for building class definitions, however, we cannot guarantee that different systems indeed use the same parts of this shared vocabulary. Therefore, the actual overlap of terms used in the existing definitions that are compared is important for predicting the quality of approximations. In general, we can assume that a high degree of overlap leads to better approximations.

Both criteria used in the rules of thumb above strongly depend on the application and on the creator of the corresponding models. At least for the degree of overlap, we can assume that hierarchies that are concerned with the same domain of interest will share a significant part if the vocabulary, thus enabling us to compute reasonable approximations.

5   Adapting the Communication Language

The considerations from last section provide a formal basis for re-writing concepts using in messages an agent uses to communicate with other agents. Having proven the correctness of the approximation we can use them to re-write a concepts by replacing their names by their approximation.

Definition 5 (Concept Re-Writing) *The rewriting of a query c over concepts from a private ontology to an expression over concepts from a shared ontology is defined as as follows:*

- *replace every non negated concept name c by:* $\displaystyle\bigwedge_{c' \in lub_{IS_2}(c)} c'$
- *replace every negated concept name c by:* $\displaystyle\bigvee_{c' \in glb_{IS_2}(c)} c'$

The rewriting a concept can easily be implemented using the Description Logic System RACER [11]. We can compute the re-writing using Algorithm 1. The input for the algorithm is the message to be re-written, the names of shared concepts as well as a unified model of both ontologies.

Algorithm 1 Translate-Message

Require: The Message to be translated: C
Require: A list of shared concepts: S
Require: A terminological knowledge base T
  racer.in-tbox(T)
  for all t is an concept term in C **do**
    if t is negated **then**
      $B[t] := $ racer.directSupers(t)
      $B'[t] := B[t] \cap S$
      $C(t) := (c_1 \wedge \cdots \wedge c_n)$ for $c_i \in B'[t]$
    else
      $B[t] := $ racer.directSubs(t)
      $B'[t] := B[t] \cap S$
      $C(t) := (c_1 \vee \cdots \vee c_n)$ for $c_i \in B'[t]$
    end if
    C' := **proc**   Replace t in C by $C(t)$
  end for
  return C'

As the re-writing builds upon the approximations discussed in the last section we can guarantee that the result of the query is correct. Moreover, we can use subsumption reasoning in order to determine this result. To be more specifically, a resource x is indeed a member of the query concept if membership can be proved for the re-written query.

6   Related Work

The idea of rewriting representations based on the special capabilities of a remote system is first reported in [15]. It has been applied in the area of information retrieval [5] to translate full-text queries and in database systems for translating SQL queries [4]. The use of description logics for query rewriting is described in [10]. Baader and others propose a general framework for rewriting concepts [1]. This work is closest to our approach, however, our goal is not to achieve equivalent rewritings, but rather use an approximation approach that is more handable in practice.

7   Conclusions

We described an approach for exploiting partially shared ontologies in multi-agent communication by translating private concepts into shared ones while ensuring some formal properties. Our approach enables agents on the World Wide Web to exchange semantic information solely relying on internally provided mappings between ontologies. So far, we consider our results as a basic mechanism for facilitating agent communication. However, a lot of work is still necessary in order to apply it in practice. We only want to mention two specific aspects that have to be addressed in this context: First of all, sophisticated communication protocols have to be developed that agents can use in order to find out, which are the ontologies they share and what are the options for re-writing. First investigations in ontology negotiation are reported in [2]. Further [7] suggest to use more complex object and concept definitions in agent messages. Rewriting such complex definitions instead of just concept names requires more sophisticated mechanisms.

References

1. F. Baader, R. Kuesters, and R. Molitor. Rewriting concepts using terminologies. In T. Cohn, F. Giunchiglia, and B. Selman, editors, *Proceedings of the seventh International Conference on Principles of Knowledge Representation and Reasoning KR'2000*. Morgan Kaufmann, 2000.
2. S. Bailin and W. Truszkowski. Ontology negotiation between agents supporting intelligent information management. In *OAS'01 Ontologies* [6].
3. A. Borgida and L. Serafini. Distributed description logics. In *Proceedings of the Internaltional Description Logics Workshop DL'2002*, 2002.
4. K.-C. Chang and H. Garcia-Molina. Approximate query mapping: Accounting for translation closeness. *The VLDB Journal*, 10:155–181, 2001.
5. K.-C. Chang, H. Garcia-Molina, and A. Paepcke. Boolean query mapping across heterogeneous information sources. *IEEE Transaction on Knowledge and Data Engineering*, 8(4), 1996.
6. S. Cranefield, T. Finin, and S. Willmott. Oas'01 ontologies and agent systems. CEUR Workshop Proceedings 52, RWTH Aachen, 2001.

7. S. Cranefield and M. Purvis. Generating ontology-specific content languages. In *OAS'01 Ontologies in Agent Systems* [6].
8. J. Euzenat. An infrastructure for formally ensuring interoperability in a heterogeneous semantic web. In I. F. Cruz, S. Decker, J. Euzenat, and D. McGuinness, editors, *Proceedings of the First Semantic Web Working Symposium*, Stanford, CA, USA, 2001.
9. D. Fensel, I. Horrocks, F. van Harmelen, D. L. McGuinness, and P. F. Patel-Schneider. Oil: An ontology infrastructure for the semantic web. *IEEE Intelligent Systems*, 16(2), 2001.
10. F. Goasdoue and M.-C. Rousset. Rewriting conjunctive queries using views in description logics. 2000.
11. V. Haarslev and R. Moller. Description of the RACER system and its applications. In *Proceedings of the Description Logics Worlshop DL-2001*, Stanford, CA, 2001.
12. J. Hendler. Agents and the semantic web. *IEEE Intelligent Systems*, pages 30–37, March/April 2001.
13. M. Huhns and M. Singh. Ontologies for agents. *IEEE Internet Computing*, pages 81–83, November/December 1997.
14. M. Klein. Combining and relating ontologies: an analysis of problems and solutions. In *Ontologies and information sharing*, number 47, Seattle, USA, August 2001.
15. Y. Papakonstantinou, A. Gupta, and L. Haas. Capabilities-based query rewriting in mediator systems. In *Proceedings of 4th International Conference on Parallel and Distributed Information Systems*, Miami Beach, Flor., 1996.
16. B. Selman and H. Kautz. Knowledge compilation and theory approximation. *Journal of the ACM*, 43(2):193–224, March 1996.
17. L. Steels. The origins of ontologies and communication conventions in multi-agent systems. *Autonomous Agents and Multi-Agent Systems*, 1(1):169–194, October 1998.
18. L. Stephens and M. Huhns. Consensus ontologies - reconciling the semantics of web pages and agents. *IEEE Internet Computing*, pages 92–95, September/October 2001.
19. H. Stuckenschmidt. *Ontology-Based Information Sharing in Weakly-Structured Enviornments*. PhD thesis, AI Department, Vrije Universiteit Amsterdam, 2002.
20. M. Uschold. Barriers to effective agent communication. In *OAS'01 Ontologies in Agent Systems* [6].
21. F. van Harmelen, P. F. Patel-Schneider, and I. Horrocks. A model-theoretic semantics for daml+oil (march 2001). http://www.daml.org/2001/03/model-theoretic-semantics.html, march 2001.
22. F. van Harmelen, P. F. Patel-Schneider, and I. Horrocks. Reference description of the daml+oil (march 2001) ontology markup language. http://www.daml.org/2001/03/reference.html, march 2001.

Evaluation of Distributed and Centralized Agent Location Mechanisms

David Ben-Ami[1] and Onn Shehory[2]

[1]Technion – Israel Institute of Technology, Haifa 32000, ISRAEL
[2]IBM Haifa Research Labs, Haifa University, Haifa 31905, ISRAEL
davb@techunix.technion.ac.il, onn@il.ibm.com

Abstract. With the proliferation of Multi-Agent Systems (MAS), there appears a need to provide effective, robust and scalable agent location mechanisms. Previous studies have presented several solutions to the agent location problem. The majority of those solutions used a centralized approach, however a few distributed solutions were presented as well. Yet, proposed solutions were not compared systematically, and therefore it remains an open question which mechanism should be used, and for which specific MAS parameters. In particular, it is important to compare performance of centralized and distributed solutions, as they are expected to exhibit the most diverse behaviors. This is precisely what we do in this research. We suggest that a distributed peer-to-peer approach [6] to agent location had many advantages over centralized middle-agent location mechanisms [1,2,4]. Via a series of experiments, we show that, in large-scale, overloaded MAS, a distributed approach is more efficient than a centralized one. We also show that through careful planning of the connection model among the agents, one can manage the communication overhead of a distributed location mechanism.

1 Introduction

Agents in a Multi-Agent System (MAS), even when identical in their design and implementation, may be heterogeneous in the sense that they each have different sets of capabilities. They may further differ over the tasks they need to perform. Such heterogeneous agents may need to perform tasks for which they do not have the required capabilities. Cooperation with other agents, possibly in the form of task delegation to the latter, can resolve this problem. Yet, for agents to cooperate with others, they first need to locate those agents that hold the capabilities relevant to the tasks to be delegated. Thus, the first problem to arise in open MAS, where agents do not necessarily know one another in advance, is the agent location problem. Therefore, a designer of MAS needs to provide the individual agents with a mechanism that will enable them to locate other agents.

The solution to the agent location problem was usually provided by centralized mechanisms such as middle agents [1, 2, 4]. The latter provide location services to the rest of the agents in the system. The centralized middle-agent approach has various forms (e.g., matchmakers[1,4], brokers[1] and facilitators[2]), which were explored extensively [7] and were adopted as a natural solution to the location problem.

However, the centralized mechanism might be problematic in large-scale MAS, because central servers tend to be overloaded and to become a bottleneck in

M. Klusch, S. Ossowski, and O. Shehory (Eds.): CIA 2002, LNAI 2446, pp. 264–278, 2002.

distributed systems [5]. In large systems with high reliability requirements, central servers become a potential single point of failure, which can compromise the overall fault-tolerance of the distributed system.

Several different approaches ([3,6]) were suggested to try to overcome those problems. These solutions try to distribute the information about agents' capabilities. The first, distributed matchmaking [3], is using many matchmakers with partial information and coordinating them using a special protocol.

The second approach [6] takes advantage of the fact that each agent already knows about its own capabilities and uses a peer-to-peer (recursive) search for locating an agent with the needed capability. (In a nutshell, an agent broadcasts a request for a reference to its neighbors, and an agent that receives such a request either offers its services to the original caller or broadcasts the request to its own neighbors).

In this work we try to evaluate and compare the suggested distributed peer-to-peer mechanism and the centralized mechanism and try to pinpoint the system characteristics in which each mechanism is more appropriate (performance-wise). We hypothesize that both the centralized location mechanism and the distributed location mechanism provide agents in an open MAS with the references of other agents they seek. Yet, we expect differences in the speed and the quality of the results provided. We believe that the centralized mechanism will work better for smaller systems with small workloads, and that the distributed mechanism will be more appropriate for larger systems with heavy workloads. To examine our hypothesis, we have developed a simulation testbed and performed a series of experiments with both the centralized and the distributed location mechanisms. Simulations details and results are presented in the proceeding sections.

In our experiments we used relatively simple connection models between the agents (mainly random and fixed set of neighbors). We believe that using more sophisticated connection models (such as those found in adaptive social models [8, 9]) can only improve the results of the distributed solution and emphasize its advantages. Our selection of simple models allows us to concentrate on the differences among the distributed and centralized mechanisms and isolate their effects from other phenomena. Additionally, we assume that the success of peer-to-peer solutions in distributed systems such as Chord and FreeNet [10,11] indicates that distributed solutions can be valuable in open MAS as well.

The goal of this study is thus to perform a comparative evaluation of the performance of the distributed mechanism and the standard centralized matchmaker mechanism. This will be performed via simulations of large-scale MAS where both mechanisms are implemented. We aim to evaluate the performance and robustness of the different mechanisms in various configurations (e.g., different system scales, different connectivity models and different workloads). One of the sought results of this research is the ability to specify the algorithmic aspects and parameters that are important in designing an efficient and robust agent location mechanism for dynamic, open, large-scale MAS.

2 Simulation Description

To examine the location mechanisms, we have developed a simulation testbed. The testbed enabled us to define multiple different MAS configurations and to distribute agents on one or more host environments. The testbed was developed using the Java 2 platform and the RMI (Remote Method Invocation) package with an emphasis on flexibility and ability to trace and measure the inter-agent communications. Via communication trace and measurements we can extract results in terms of the metrics defined below. We have implemented in the testbed both the distributed (recursive) agent location mechanism and a centralized agent location mechanism and checked them thoroughly in a wide set of configurations.

To measure and compare the performance of the location mechanisms we test, we have used the following performance metrics:

- The average time for an agent to find another agent with the sought capabilities (that is – to receive a reference to a relevant other agent), denoted as *RefTime*. We also measure the average time for an agent to complete its (delegated) task, denoted by *DoneTime*. A task is considered completed upon receiving an acknowledgement of its execution from the agent to which the task was delegated.
- The average rate of accomplished tasks, denoted as *HitRate*, is the average of the ratio between the number of tasks that were successfully processed by an agent and the total number of tasks assigned to it.
- The average number of messages passed, denoted as *MsgCount*, is the number of mechanism-generated messages passing through an agent (considering both outgoing requests and incoming answers).

In our testbed, we simulate a MAS as a process that runs a group of agent threads. A set of C capabilities, referred to as *system capabilities*, represents the capabilities available in the system. Each agent has its private, randomly generated, subset of C, referred to as *local capabilities*, and a set of randomly generated tasks (each task requires one system capability for its execution). The system further provides a central location mechanism, implemented in an independent thread, referred to as the matchmaker thread. The system monitors agent threads using a monitor thread, which is used to monitor, start and/or stop the agent threads.

All of the agents in our system are identical in their basic code but they differ in their sets of capabilities and tasks. When seeking another agent to perform a task it cannot perform by itself, an agent may use one of the two location mechanisms - central or distributed - to locate a reference for a relevant agent. Upon receiving one or more references, the agent may choose one of the references and request the execution of the task.

The distributed location mechanism relies upon an agent connection graph. This graph is determined at system setup according to a connection model. Note that a connection between one agent A to another agent B does not refer to the existence of a communication line between the two. Rather, it refers to the fact that A knows of B and its capabilities a-priori. Thus, the so-called connection graph is fully expressed by the neighbor lists held by the individual agents. In our tests of the distributed location mechanism, we used 2 principal connection models:

- Grid connection (connecting each agent to its grid neighbors): this model is typical to designed, closed systems, where agents are known in advance to the designer.

- Random connection (connecting each agent to k randomly selected agents): this model is typical to emergent, open systems where, agents build their contact list upon interaction with other agents.

The major parameters in this respect are the size of the neighbor list of each agent (the out-rank of the connection graph) and the search horizon parameter. The latter is determined by the Max_TTL parameter. TTL, which is an acronym of Time To Live, determines the number of hops each query in the system can travel from its originator.

The agents are trying to execute their tasks, while attending to incoming messages from their peer agents. There is a uniform delay (which may also be set to 0) between task executions that enables us to control the average workload on the system.

The communication protocols between the agents and between the matchmaker thread and the agent threads are based on Java RMI. They enable an agent to connect with an agent on remote host (and in a special case – on the same host). This communication method was chosen in order to emulate the performance of a MAS distributed over the network. The RMI implementation is expandable to a multi-host system.

In the following section we provide the details of the activities of each of the entities in our system.

3 Activity Algorithms of System Entities

The simulation system consists of several entities and activities. The details of these entities and their activities are provided below.

Algorithm of the agent thread:

In a nutshell, an agent thread performs the following: Initially, an agent is allocated a set of capabilities and a set of tasks randomly. The agent then successively tries to find a reference to a service provider agent that can perform a task it cannot perform by itself. Upon receiving answers (references to other, relevant agents), the agent chooses one of the references - a service provider agent - and delegates the task to that service provider. A task is considered done after the requester agent receives an acknowledgement from the service provider agent. An agent that receives a request for a reference offers its services to the original requester if it can perform the task, or broadcasts this request to its neighbors (provided that the request TTL counter has not expired). An agent that is requested to perform a task on behalf of another agent does so and sends an acknowledgement to the requesting agent.

The detailed algorithm follows:

1. The agent randomly selects CapNum local capabilities from the set of system capabilities (repetition is allowed, hence the agent may end up with less than CapNum unique capabilities).
2. The agent randomly selects TaskNum tasks: a certain quota of local tasks and a certain quota of foreign tasks (for which it will have to find a reference).
3. When the agent receives a start cue and unless stopped from outside, the agent performs the following loop:
   For each task T from its task list,
   i. If T is local - execute it
   ii. Else – send a query for a reference for T's capability through the system's location mechanism [in case of a centralized mechanism send the query to the matchmaker; in case of distributed mechanism, broadcast query with MAX_TTL counter to the agents in the ContactList]
4. Every X tasks processed poll the incoming message queue and process as many messages as possible (thus empty the queue). Answer these messages according to the following policy:
   A. If the incoming message is a reference proposal to one of the foreign tasks:
   i.   Accept or reject the reference according to the system's reference policy (currently we implement an acceptance of the first reference received).
   ii. Calculate RefTime for this task.
   iii. Send a request for execution to the selected reference.
   B. If the incoming message is a request for a reference (only possible in the distributed mechanism):
   i. If the requested capability is one of the local capabilities - send a reference proposal to original sender of the request.
   ii. Else – decrement TTL counter and broadcast the query to the agents in the ContactList.
   C. If the incoming message is a request for execution - execute the task and send an acknowledgement to the originator of the request.
   D. If the incoming message is an execution acknowledgement - mark the task as done and calculate DoneTime.
   E. Count every message, incoming or outgoing, in MsgCount.

Note: The agent has the right to refuse to execute or propose its services to other agents thus simulating failure or overload - this will be done according to the system failure model.

The Matchmaker Thread Activity

In the case of a central location mechanism, each agent sends its list of local capabilities to the matchmaker thread. Using these inputs, the matchmaker constructs and holds, for each system capability, a list of agents that provide it. To reduce complexity, these lists are not exhaustive. Instead of including all of the agents that provide a specific capability in a capability provision list, only $N^{1/2}$ service providers—

N being the number of agents in the system—are included in each list[1]. Upon receiving a request for a reference, the matchmaker selects (based on a pre-defined selection policy) one service provider from the relevant capability provision list and sends a reference to it to the requester. Currently, the selection policy is to choose a provider by random. The combination of square-root list sizes with random selection from the lists has experimentally shown to minimize the workload of execution on the service provider agents.

The Monitoring Thread Activity

The monitor thread periodically queries all of the agents for their progress ratio. The agents each return their counter of done tasks. When all agents have finished their tasks, or the system is no longer progressing, or a global timeout has reached, the monitor thread stops all agents and closes log files.

Controlling System Workload

The rate in which agents request references depends on the time it takes them to complete tasks. Since in a simulated system this time may be zero, we introduce artificial delays. Hence, in our simulator, each agent waits a constant time (denoted by interTaskDelay) between tasks. This delay reduces the request rate and thus the workload on the location mechanism and on the service provider agents. By varying the value of interTaskDelay, we are able to control the system's workload.

4 Experimental Results

In the following sections we describe the results of a systematic comparison of performance measures between the central location mechanism and the distributed location mechanism. We conducted several sets of experiments on randomly generated simulated systems. Each set of experiments was repeated 5 times and results are the average of these 5 iterations. Each agent in the simulation was allocated 50 tasks. Averaging over tasks was performed as well.

The parameters that could be set in our experiments, their notations and their units are the following:

1. System scale, denoted by AgNum, is the number of the agents in the system.
2. System workload is inversely proportional to the delay between tasks. Therefore, we express it via this delay, denoted by interTaskDelay and measured in milliseconds.
3. Connection model, may be either grid (with 2 or 4 neighbors) or random.
4. Connection range, denoted by Max_TTL, is the maximal number of hops per message.

---

[1] The size of the capability provision list was determined based on experiments in which sizes close to N were proven too complex, and constant-sizes have affected performance negatively. Yet, we have no proof that $N^{1/2}$ is an optimal size.

  5. Capability distribution is the percentage of local capabilities out of
     the system capabilities allocated to each agent.
  6. Failure model refers to the number and type of failed requests. In
     this paper we only refer to zero failures.

In our simulations we were specifically interested in examining the effects of
system scale, system workload, capability distribution and connection model and
range. We have thus conducted 4 sets of experiments in which these parameters were
examined. The experiments were performed such that, when testing (and varying the
value of) a specific parameter, other parameter values were kept constant. The
specific settings of these 4 experiments' sets and their results are described below.

4.1   Experiments' Set 1 – The Effect of System Scale

For this set of experiments, we have constructed configurations with an increasing
system scale, keeping the rest of the parameters constant. The scales we checked
were: 9, 16, 25, 49, 64, 100, 121, 144 and 196. The other parameters were set as
follows: system workload was set to a high load (by setting the delay to 0); the
connection model was a grid connection with 2 neighbors and Max_TTL 5; the
capability distribution was set to 30%; a 0-failures model was set. In these
experiments we measured the response time (RefTime) for the distributed location
mechanism, denoted by DRefTime, and for the centralized location mechanism,
denoted by CRefTime. The results of these measurements are presented in Figure 1.
We have further measured MsgCount, the average number of messages passing
through an agent. The results appear in Figure 2, where DMsgs refers to the average
message count for the distributed location mechanism, and CMsgs refers to the
average message count for the distributed location mechanism.

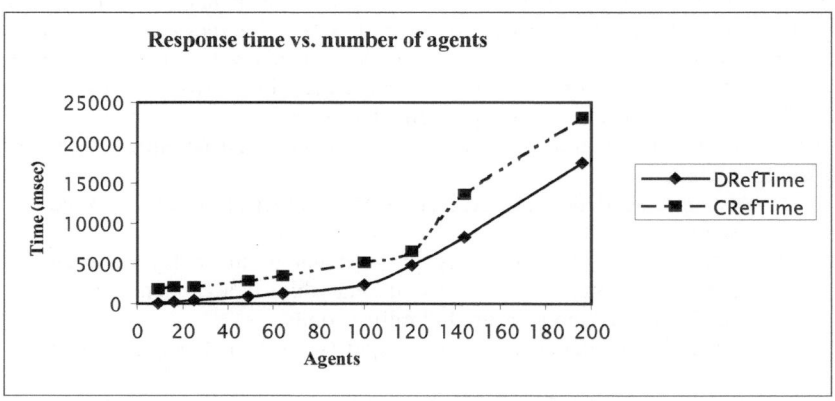

Fig. 1. The response times for the distributed location mechanism are shorter than the response
times for the central location mechanism.

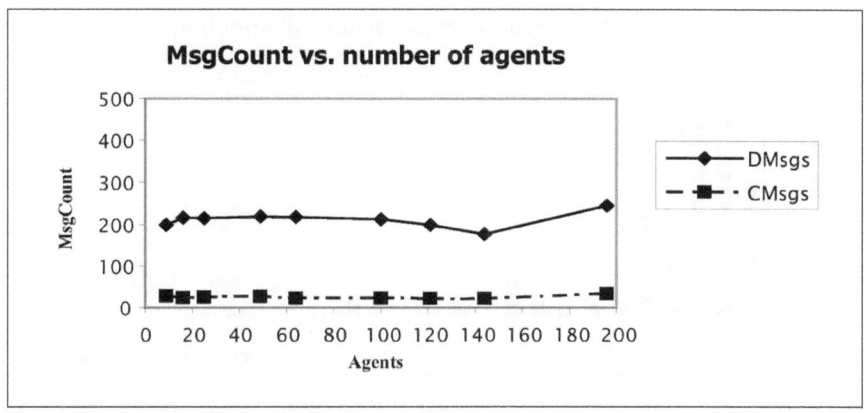

Fig. 2. The average message count per agent is higher for the distributed location mechanism than it is for the central location mechanism.

As appears in Figure 1, the response times in the centralized location mechanism are significantly higher than those of the distributed location mechanism. The message count (Figure 2) is significantly higher in the distributed system, however it is almost independent of the system scale. The distribution of response times is higher in the distributed mechanism (as shown in section 4.2 below). These results suggest that, in terms of responsiveness, the distributed location mechanism is more efficient then the centralized mechanism in systems with high workload, regardless of system size.   Although this advantage of the distributed mechanism results in a communication overhead, this overhead has no dependency on systems size, and therefore does not affect scalability.

4.2   Experiments' Set 1 – Detailed Analysis of Response Times Distribution

In the following graphs we present an interesting phenomenon, observed in the response time measurements of the different mechanisms. Whereas the average time of the distributed location is distinctly lower than the average time of the centralized mechanism, the standard deviation of times in distributed location is much higher.

The following 2 histograms (Figures 3 and 4) depict this phenomenon. It appears that the distributed response times have a densely populated peak at the lower values with a few exceptional samples. Of course, such a distribution increases the standard deviation. The distribution of response times in the central location mechanism is quite different. The results are spread rather evenly over a narrow range (all the values being much higher than in the distributed case).

This phenomenon of a narrow range (though high values) of the response times of the centralized mechanism probably results from the almost equal service provided by the centralized matchmaker. In contrast, the distributed location mechanism is very efficient for most of the requests, however it can have (rare) occasions of "far references" and/or local bottlenecks on a specific agent, which causes the agent to perform relatively bad.

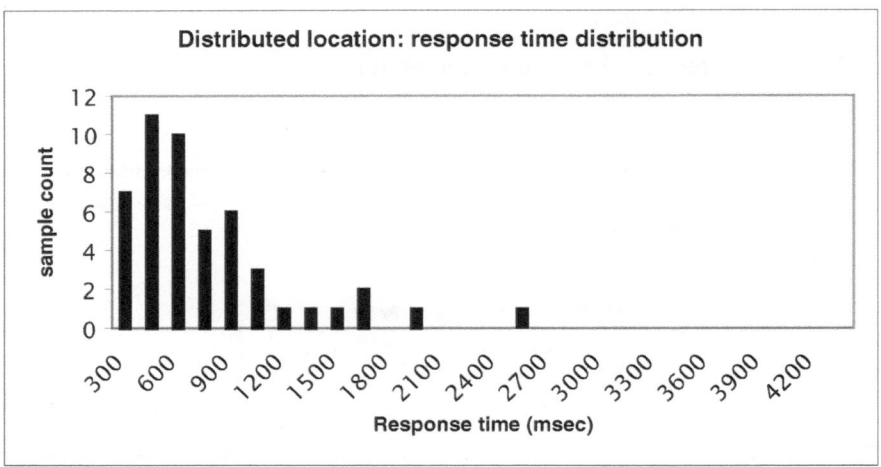

Fig. 3. Distributed location: response time has a peak at lower values, only a few agents have long response times (range of values is very broad, with a high standard deviation) .

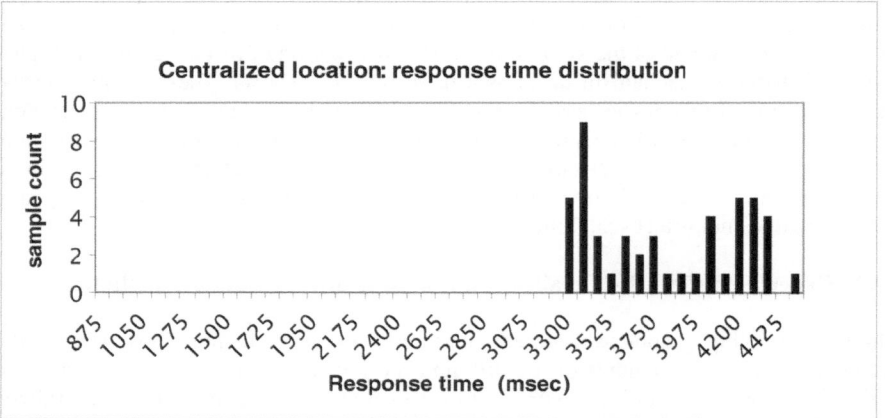

Fig. 4. Centralized location: response time has a relatively narrow range, as most of the agents get the same service quality. Notice that all of the values are higher than the values in the distributed case.

4.3 Experiments' Set 2 – The Effect of System Workload

For the second set of experiments, we have constructed configurations with decreasing workloads (using increasing interTaskDelay), while keeping the rest of the parameters constant. Recall that lower delays mean higher workloads and vice versa. The delay values we checked were: 0, 100, 200, 300, 400, 500, 750 and 1000 milliseconds. The other parameters were set as follows: the system scale was set to two medium sizes (of 49 and 100 agents); the connection model was a grid connection with 2 neighbors and Max_TTL 5; the capability distribution was set to 30%; a 0-failures model was set.

In these experiments we measured the response times (RefTime) for the distributed location mechanism, denoted by DRefTime, and for the centralized location mechanism, denoted by CRefTime. The results of these measurements are presented in Figures 5 and 6, where the former refers to 49 agents and the latter to 100 agents.

Note that in both Figures, at some point—we denote this point as the phase transition point—the response time of the centralized location mechanism becomes better (i.e., shorter) than the response time of the distributed mechanism. Phase transitions occur when the system's workload goes below some threshold.

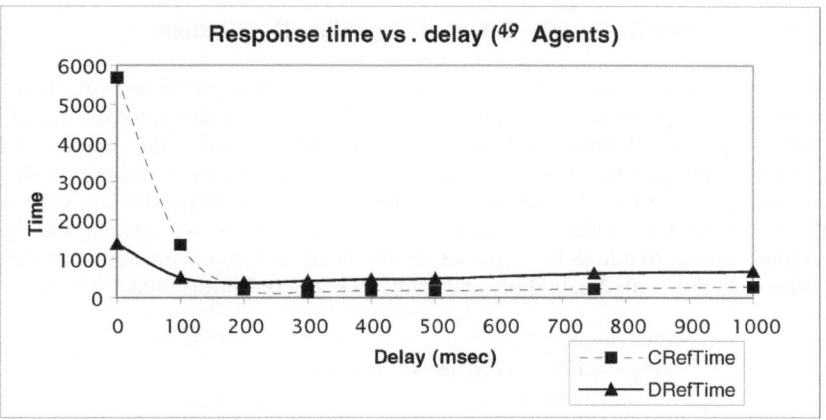

Fig. 5. The response time improves in both mechanisms as workload decreases (and delay increases). The improvement in the centralized case is sharper than it is in the distributed case. The phase transition point in a 49-agent system is at approximately 150 milliseconds.

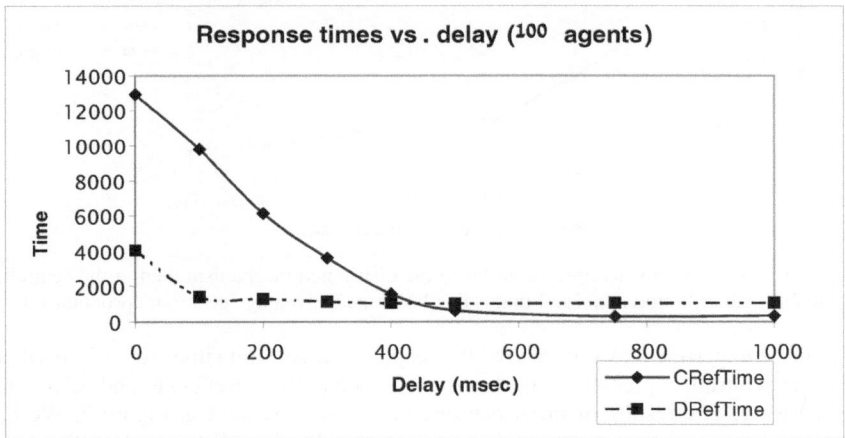

Fig. 6. The response time improves in similarity to the 49-agent system, however phase transition occurs at approximately 400 milliseconds. This means that for a larger system, only a relatively low workload should justify the use of a centralized location mechanism.

From the Figures above we conclude that, as workload decreases, the response time of the centralized mechanism improves. Below some workload threshold, the centralized mechanism becomes better than the distributed mechanism. This workload threshold is lower as system scale increases. On the other hand, for high workloads—the distributed mechanism is significantly better than the centralized one, and this advantage is more prominent for larger systems. Overall, these results show that workload is a dominant factor in the efficiency of the centralized mechanism. Namely, the performance of a centralized location mechanism improves very rapidly as workload decreases. The improvement is less prominent for distributed location mechanism.

4.4   Experiments' Set 3 – The Effect of Capability Distribution

For the third set of experiments, we have constructed configurations with increasing capability distribution, while keeping the rest of the parameters constant. Recall that the term capability distribution refers here to the ratio between the number of local capabilities and number of system capabilities. The capability distributions checked were: 10%, 20%, 30%, 40%, 50%, 60%, and 70%. The other parameters were set as follows: the system scale was set to the medium size of 49 agents; the system workload was set to a high load (by setting the delay to 0); the connection model was a grid connection with 2 neighbors and Max_TTL 4; a 0-failures model was set.

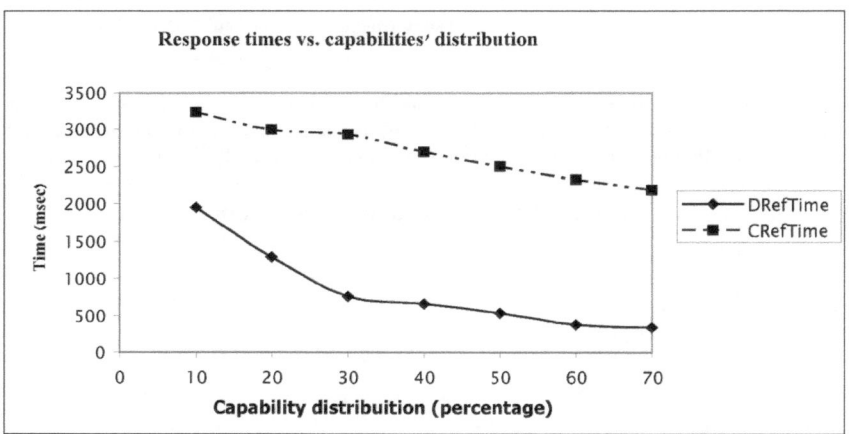

Fig. 7. The response times improves faster in the distributed mechanism than in the centralized as capability distribution increases, that is the distributed advantage gets more pronounced.

In these experiments we measured the response times (RefTime) for the distributed and the centralized location mechanisms, denoted by DRefTime and CRefTime, respectively. The results of these measurements are presented in Figure 7. We have further measured the hit rate (i.e., the average rate of accomplished tasks). The results appear in Figure 8, where DHitRate and CHitRate denote the hit rates of the distributed and the centralized mechanisms, respectively.

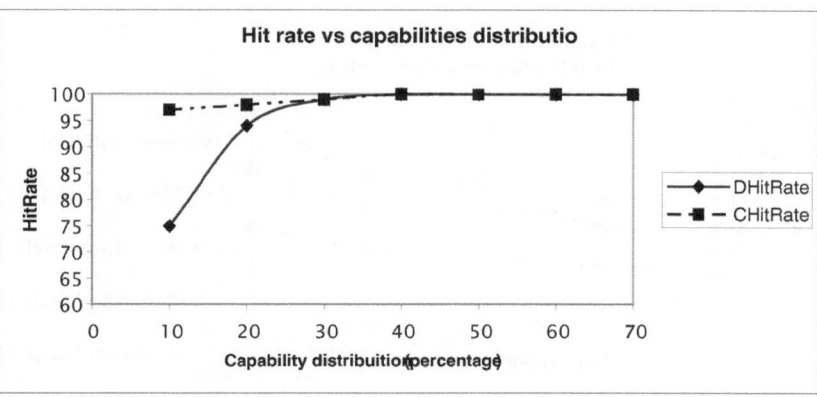

Fig. 8. Hit Rates are very high in both mechanisms (higher than 75% for a 10% capability distribution agent, 95% for a 20 % percent). At 30% and higher capability distributions both mechanism achieve almost perfect results.

The results of measuring the response time (Figure 7) and the message count parameters (the latter is not presented in the graphs) are not surprising: higher values of capability distribution result in shorter response times and lower message counts. This results from a higher probability of finding a closer reference, thus consuming less messages and less time. The interesting result is, however, that the distributed mechanism achieved close to 100% hit rate in all capability distributions above 20% and even in a 10% distribution it achieved a 75-80% hit rate, which is rather high (see Figure 8). We can also conclude that the centralized location mechanism has more reliable results, however this advantage is significant only in systems where the capability distribution is 20% or less.

4.5 Experiments' Set 4 – The Effect of the Connection Model

For the fourth set of experiments, we have constructed configurations with 5 different connection models and search horizons (MAX_TTL) values, while keeping the rest of the parameters constant. The connection models we checked were: *Grid2, Grid4, Random2, Random3* and *Random4*. Here, the number refers to the size of the connection list. The value of MAX_TTL was varied from 2 to 6. The other parameters were set as follows: the system scale was set to the medium size of 49 agents; the system workload was set to a high load (by setting the delay to 0); the capability distribution was set to 30%; a 0-failures model was set.

In these experiments we measured the response times (only) for the distributed location mechanism, as the connection model is irrelevant in the case of a centralized location mechanism. The results of these measurements are presented in Figure 9. We further measured the message count as a function of the size of the search horizon. These results are in Figure 10.

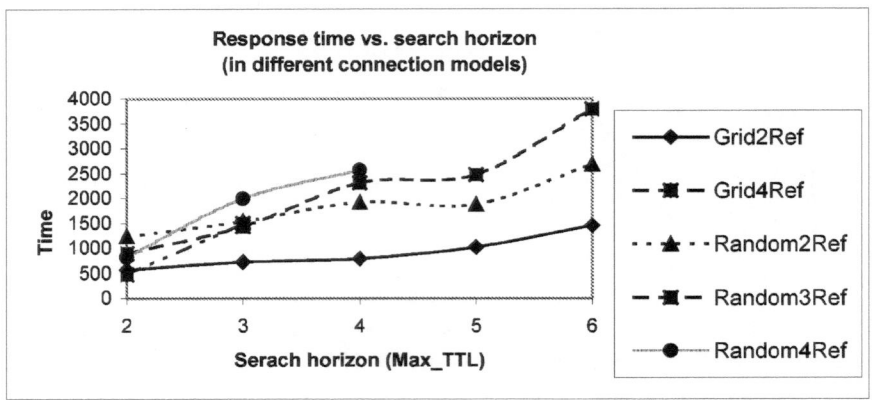

Fig. 9. Response times of the random connection models are consistently higher than those of the grid models.

The response times measured for the random connection models are consistently higher than those of the grid models. On the other hand, the message count parameter is consistently lower for the random connection models. Thus, the use of an ordered model instead of a random model trades off communication overhead for response time. The outrank of the connection graph is the most important parameter in affecting the growth rate of the message count. An outrank of 2 neighbors provides satisfactory results for most TTL values, while maintaining low overhead of messages. An outrank of 4 causes a high, exponential growth rate of the message count. To avoid a communication explosion in such cases, it is necessary to set a low TTL. These results suggest that the distributed location mechanism perform more efficiently in an ordered connection model, although communication overhead is lower in this model. From multiple experiments we conducted we learned that one should use small sizes of contacts' list (2-3) to prevent exponential growth of communication overhead in the distributed model (even a contact list of size of 4 must have a limited search horizon to prevent high communication overhead).

5   Conclusion

The goal of this study was to compare, evaluate and draw conclusions regarding the properties of distributed and centralized agent location mechanisms. To achieve this goal, we have developed a MAS simulation testbed and performed a series of experiments in which both types of location mechanisms were examined and matched. Our major conclusions are in line with our hypothesis. That is, in terms of response time, a distributed location mechanism is significantly better than a centralized one as the system size increases. Yet, in a capability-deprived MAS, a centralized mechanism will be better. It is evident, though, that a centralized location

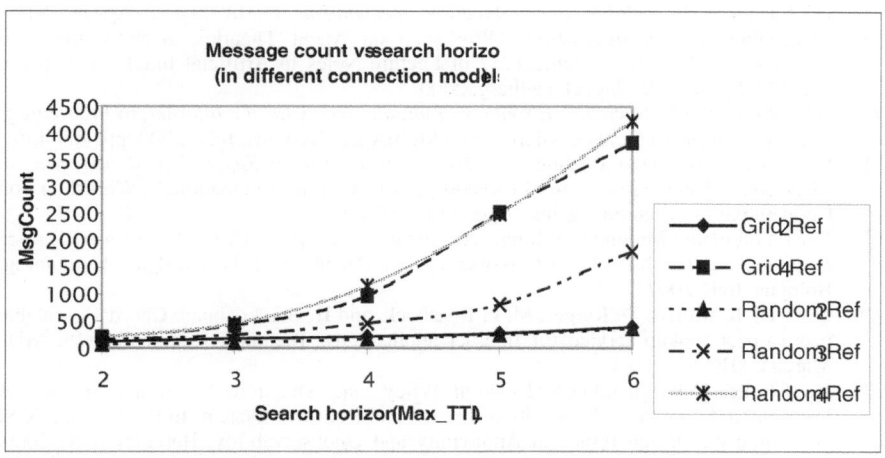

Fig. 10. The message count grows exponentially with TTL value. Outrank is the main factor of growth, although grid connection models have steeper curves than random models have.

mechanism is very sensitive to workloads. A medium to high load, in particular in large MAS, will result in poor performance of the centralized mechanism, whereas the distributed one will hardly be affected. In summary, it appears that a distributed agent location mechanism is the appropriate solution for large MAS with high workloads. Yet, one should bear in mind that the advantages of the distributed solution do not come for free, as it introduces a communication overhead. This communication overhead may pose a severe problem. Nevertheless, as our results suggest, a careful design of the connection model can reduce this risk.

Our study is only a first step towards a better understanding of the advantages and drawbacks of agent location mechanisms. In particular, in future work we intend to examine mixed mechanisms in which agents can decide whether to use peers or to use middle agents to find other agents. We believe that such mechanisms have the potential to perform better than both the pure-centralized and pure-distributed solutions.

References

[1] Keith Decker, Katia Sycara, Mike Williamson. *Middle-Agents for the Internet.* Proceedings of IJCAI-97, pages 578–583, Nagoya Japan 1997.

[2] M. Genesereth and S. Ketchpel. Software agents. Communication of the ACM, 37(7):48–53, July 1994

[3] S. Jha, P. Chalasani, O. Shehory, and K. Sycara. *A formal treatment of distributed matchmaking.* In Proceeding of Agents-98, pages 457–458, Minneapolis, Minnesota, 1998.

[4] D. Kuokka and L. Harada. *Matchmaking for information agents.* In Proceedings of the Fourteenth International Joint Conference on Artificial Intelligence, pages 672–679, 1995

[5] Michael F. Schwartz, *Attribute Distribution and Search for Internet Resource Discovery,* in Internet Society News 1(3), Summer 1992

[6]   O. Shehory. *A scalable agent location mechanism*. In Intelligent Agents VI – Proceedings of 6th International Workshop on Agent Theories, Architectures, and Languages (ATAL'99), volume 1757 of Lecture Notes in Artificial Intelligence, pages 162-172. Springer-Verlag, Heidelberg, 2000

[7]   H.C. Wong and K. Sycara, *A taxonomy of middle-agents for the Internet*, in Proceedings of the Fourth International Conference on MultiAgent Systems, July, 2000, pp. 465-466

[8]   Bin Yu and Munindar P. Singh , *A Social Mechanism of Reputation Management in Electronic Communities*, in Proceedings of Fourth International Workshop on Cooperative Information Agents, pages 154–165, 2000

[9]   Pinar Yolum and Munindar P. Singh, *An Agent-Based Approach for Trustworthy Service Location,* in 1st International Workshop on Agents and Peer-to-Peer Computing, Bologna, Italy 2002

[10]   I. Stoica, R. Morris, D. Karger, M. F. Kaashoek, and H. Balakrishnan. Chord: A scalable peer-to-peer lookup service for Internet applications. Technical Report TR-819, MIT, March 2001

[11]   Ian Clarke, Oskar Sandberg, Brandon Wiley, and Theodore W. Hong. Freenet: A Distributed Anonymous Information Storage and Retrieval System. In Proc. of the ICSI Workshop on Design Issues in Anonymity and Unobservability, Berkeley, CA, 2000. International Computer Science Institute.

Exchanging and Combining Temporal Information in a Cooperative Environment*

Meirav Hadad[1] and Sarit Kraus[1]

Department of Mathematics and Computer Science
Bar Ilan University Ramat Gan 52900, Israel
{hadad, sarit}@macs.biu.ac.il

1 Introduction

This paper considers the problem of exchanging and combining temporal information by collaborative agents who act in a dynamic environment. In order to carry out their cooperative activity the agents perform collaborative planning [2] while interleaving planning and execution. In a former paper [3] we presented a mechanism for cooperative planning agents to determine the timetable of the actions that are required to perform their joint activity. In this paper we expand our former work and compare different methods of reasoning and combining temporal information in a team. Determining the time of the actions in a collaborative environment is complex because of the need to coordinate actions of different agents, the partiality of the plans, the partial knowledge on other agents' activities and on the environment and temporal constraints. Our mechanism focuses on temporal scheduling. Thus, for simplification purposes, the agents do not take into consideration preconditions and effects during their planning process.

One of the main questions in a multi-agent environment is at what stage should an agent commit to a timetable for performing a joint action, and inform the rest of the team of his commitment. If the individual agent commits to a specific timetable early and announces this commitment to the other agents, it may need to negotiate with the others if it needs to change its timetable later. Alternatively, a commitment made and announced as late as possible, e.g., only when requested by other team members, may delay the planning and action of other team members. Another question arises regarding the strategy the team members should use in planning the subactions of their joint activity. If we force all the team members to plan their activity using identical strategies, the flexibility of the individuals is decreased. However, using different strategies may delay the plan of some members of the group. This delay might occur when some member needs certain information about a specific action that it wants to plan, but finds that the other team members chose to delay the plan of this action to some later time. In our work we study these questions by implementing different methods in a simulation environment and by conducting experiments. We also compare the performance of our distributed method with a method in which a team leader is responsible for solving the problem centrally (e.g., [5]).

* This work is supported in part by NSF under Grant No. IIS-9907482. The second author is also affiliated with UMIACS.

M. Klusch, S. Ossowski, and O. Shehory (Eds.): CIA 2002, LNAI 2446, pp. 279–286, 2002.
© Springer-Verlag Berlin Heidelberg 2002

2   Exchanging and Combining Temporal Information

This section briefly describes the major constituents of the exchanging and combining temporal information mechanism; it is based on former works [4, 3].

In order to carry out their cooperative activity the agents perform collaborative planning, which includes processes that are responsible for identifying recipes, assigning actions to agents and determining the time of the actions [2]. A recipe for an action consists of subactions which may be either *basic* actions or *complex* actions. Basic actions are executable at will if appropriate situational and temporal conditions hold. A complex action can be either a single-agent action or a multi-agent action. In order to perform a complex action the agents have to identify a recipe and there may be several known recipes for an action. A recipe may include temporal constraints and precedence relations between its subactions. The general situation of team members A_1 and A_2 performing a joint action α, considering the actions without the associated constraints, is illustrated in figures 1(A) and 1(B), respectively. The leaves of the tree of agent A_k ($k = 1, 2$) represent either basic actions or actions in which A_k does not participate. We refer to this tree as agent A_k's "complete recipe tree for α". The trees of the team members differ with respect to individual actions but are identical with respect to the first level of the multi-agent actions.

The main structure that is used by each agent A_k in the team, when the team members identify the time parameters of their joint activity α, is the temporal constraints graph. The temporal constraints graph is associated with a multi-agent action α and maintains information about the temporal constraints of the actions that constitute the performance of α and the precedence relations among them. Formally, a temporal constraints graph, $Gr_\alpha^k = (V^k, E^k)$ of agent A_k, where $V^k = \{s_\alpha, s_{\beta_1}, \cdots, s_{\beta_n}, f_\alpha, f_{\beta_1}, \cdots, f_{\beta_n}\} \cup \{s_{\alpha_{plan}}\}$ and $\{\alpha, \beta_1, \cdots, \beta_n\}$, represents actions that the agents intend to perform in order to execute the highest level action α (see figures 1(C), 1(D)). The variables s_y and f_y represent the time points at which the execution of an action $y \in \{\alpha, \beta_1, \cdots, \beta_n\}$ can start and must finish, respectively. Some of the vertices may be fixed, i.e., these vertices denote a known time which cannot be modified. The vertex $s_{\alpha_{plan}}$ represents the time point at which agent A_k starts to plan the action α; it is a fixed vertex. Other fixed vertices may be initiated, for example, by a request from a collaborator. The activity of action y is represented by a directed edge between s_y and f_y, that is labeled by the time duration required for the execution of action y. A directed edge from the finish time point of action y to the start time point of another action $z \in \{\alpha, \beta_1, \cdots, \beta_n\}$ denotes that the execution of z cannot start until the execution of y is completed. The interval associated with this edge indicates the possible delay between these actions. A metric constraint $a_{i,j} \leq (v_i - v_j) \leq b_{i,j}$ between two different time points $v_i, v_j \in V$ is represented by the metric edge (v_i, v_j) that is labeled $[a_{i,j}, b_{i,j}]$. The form of this graph is an extension of Simple Temporal Networks [1].

In addition to the temporal information, a temporal constraints graph maintains additional information on each of the graph's actions: (a) whether the action is basic or complex; (b) whether the complex action is a multi-agent or a single agent action; (c) whether a plan for the action has been completed; (d) whether the action has already been executed by the agent(s), and (e) the agent(s) that is (are) assigned to perform the action. We denote the agent(s) that is (are) assigned to perform an action β by Ag_β. This information is determined incrementally by the algorithm which also expands the graph. Each single agent A_k in the system runs the algorithm independently in order to build its temporal constraints graph Gr_α^k. The graphs of individual agents may be different with respect to individual actions, but similar regarding the first level of multi-agent actions. To keep track of the progress of the expansion of the agents' graphs all the vertices in Gr_α^k, of each agent A_k, begin as *unexplored* (UE). The status of both vertices s_β and f_β is changed from unexplored to *explored* (EXP) during the performance of the algorithm by A_k. One of the main purposes of the following mechanism is to determine the values of s_β and f_β.

During the agents' planning process, each agent A_k selects a UE vertex s_β which is associated with action β, from its Gr_α^k. A UE vertex s_β is selected by A_k only if the vertices which precede s_β in the graph are explored. For this selected vertex, A_k checks which of the following conditions is satisfied and performs its

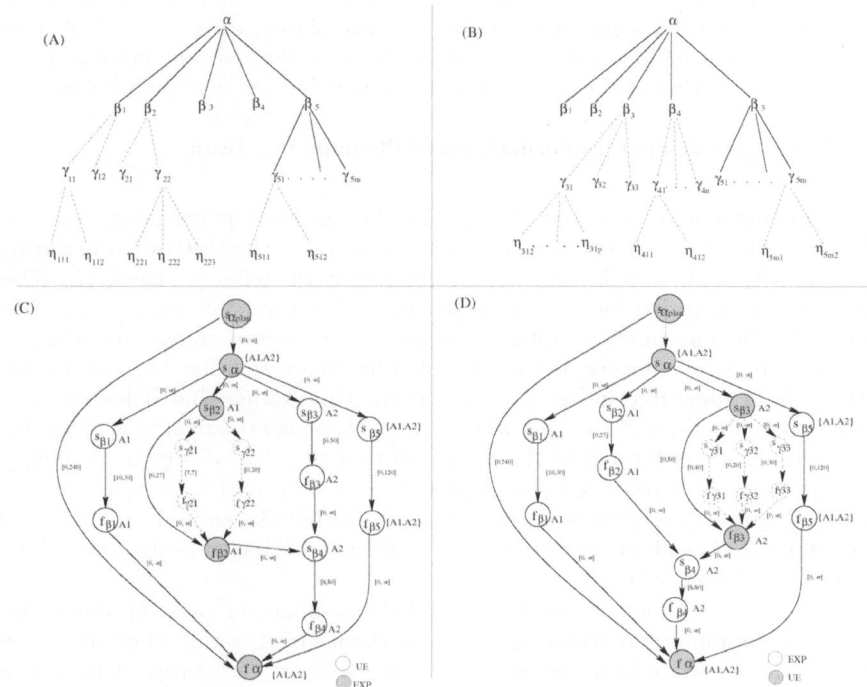

Fig. 1. (A-B) Examples of recipe trees of team members A_1 and A_2, respectively; (C-D) Examples of temporal constraints graphs, Gr_α^1 and Gr_α^2, respectively. The dashed edges represent individual plans.

activities accordingly:

(1) β **is associated with a multi (or single) action, where** A_k **does not belong to the group (or is not the agent) which has to perform the action** (i.e., $A_k \notin Ag_\beta$):

   (1.1) **If the values of** β **are unknown,** A_k leaves this vertex until it receives β's values from the agent(s) who is (are) a member(s) in Ag_β.

   (1.2) **If the values of** β **are known to** A_k, A_k changes the status of the vertices s_β and f_β from UE to EXP.

(2) β **is a multi-agents action and** A_k **participates in performing** β **(i.e.,** $A_k \in Ag_\beta$ **and** $|Ag_\beta| > 1$**):** Ag_β reaches a consensus with the other participants on how they are going to perform the action and who is going to plan this action; after reaching a consensus[1] each agent in Ag_β adds the new information to its temporal graph and determines the new values of its graph's vertices (see [3]). Also, each of them changes the status of s_β and f_β from UE to EXP.

(3) A_k **is the sole performer (i.e.,** $Ag_\beta = \{A_k\}$**):** A_k develops β and determines the new temporal values of the vertices in Gr_α^k as in the individual case (see [4]). Also, it changes the status of s_β and f_β from UE to EXP. After completing the development of β's plan, A_k checks whether β is a subaction in a recipe of a multi-agent action, or if as a result of completing the plan of β its individual plan for a higher level action β' is completed, where β' is a subaction in a recipe of a multi-agent action. If so, it saves the relevant information in order to inform this to the appropriate team members as discussed below.

2.1 Exchanging Temporal Information and Planning in a Team

The development of a shared plan [2] by the agents requires information exchange. Consider the case of two agents, A_i and A_j, that intend to perform a joint activity α. They will exchange information in the following cases: (1) When they identify a recipe for their joint action or for any joint subaction in their plan. (2) When agent A_i completes the plan of a subaction in a recipe of a joint action with A_j, it informs A_j that the plan for this action has been completed. (3) Agent A_i may inform agent A_j about the time values that it identified for its individual actions $\beta_1, \ldots, \beta_m$ when $\beta_1, \ldots, \beta_m$ *delay* the planning of action γ and γ has to be performed by A_j. We assert that $\beta_1 \ldots \beta_m$ *delay* the planning of γ if they directly precede γ. (4) If A_i already sent information to A_j about some action β, but A_i failed to perform β, then A_i backtracks and informs A_j about the failure of β or about new properties of their plan that were determined as a result of its backtracking.

A_i's message about completing its individual plans, in case (2) above, does not include temporal information and other details of A_i's individual plans. The goal of this message is to enable the agents to know the status of their joint plan. The sole case in which the agents send *temporal* information to each other is in case (3) above. Sending the time values of $\beta_1, \ldots, \beta_m$ by A_i to A_j (in case

---

[1] We focus on time scheduling and therefore do not discuss the planning processes for selection agents and recipes.

(3)) causes A_i to commit to these values. Thus, one of the main problems in a cooperative environment is at what stage should A_i commit to a timetable for performing $\beta_1, \ldots, \beta_m$ and inform A_j about this timetable.

One possibility is that when A_i completes the planning of all its actions that directly precede an action γ, which has to be performed by A_j, it commits to their performance times and sends the appropriate values to A_j. This method enables A_j to begin the plan of γ immediately when the planning of all the actions which precede action γ have been completed. Furthermore, A_j does not need to ask A_i for the relevant times since A_i informs A_j about them as soon as it is possible. However, since A_i has to commit to these times, A_i has less flexibility in determining the time performance for its other actions. If it decides to change the announced timetable it will need to negotiate with A_j. Thus, we also consider an alternative mechanism. Following this approach A_j plans its individual actions until it is not able to continue its plan since it depends on A_i's activity. In such a case A_j sends a message to A_i asking for the appropriate time values. When A_i completes the planning of the relevant actions, it sends the appropriate values to A_j. In this manner, the commitment is left to the latest possible time, but, it may delay the planning of the agent waiting for an answer and it requires additional message exchange. In our terminology the first method is called *provide-time* and the second is called *ask-time*.

An additional problem in a collaborative environment involves the order in which the members of the group should plan their activities. As described above, during the planning process, each agent A_k in the group selects a vertex s_β from its Gr_α^k to be expanded. Vertex s_β is selected by A_k only if it satisfies certain conditions. However, since in most cases there is more than one vertex that satisfies all the required conditions, the agent has to decide which of them to select in order to complete its plan. There are several possible selection methods. In the environment that we consider, the order of the vertices selection may affect A_k's decision regarding the time scheduling of its activities. Furthermore, in a joint activity a selection of a specific vertex by an individual agent may influence the activity of the entire team.

In this work we consider three methods for the planning order of the individual in the team. The first is called *random-order*, where A_k randomly selects one of the several actions that can be developed. In the second, called *dfs-order*, A_k selects the action according to the depth-first search order of its Gr_α^k. The third is called *bfs-order*. According to this method A_k selects one of the actions according to the breadth-first search order of its Gr_α^k. In the first method the planning order of the team members differ. In the two latter methods all the agents in the team plan their actions in the same order. In the dfs-order, the agent selects an action from the lowest levels of its recipe tree. Thus, it develops a subaction until it reaches the basic action level and then it continues to the next subaction. In the bfs-order, the agent tries to complete the plans of the highest level actions in each stage of the planning process of its recipe tree. Our simulation results, presented in the following section, demonstrate that the planning order influences the success rate of the agents.

3   Experimental Results

We developed a simulation environment comprising two agents to evaluate the success rate of the system. In our experiments, we made the simplifying assumption that all the time constraints on an agent's action are associated either with the action-type or with the appropriate recipe. We ran the algorithm on several different recipe libraries which were created randomly. Each recipe library included at least one possible solution to the joint activity. For each case we ran 120 experiments with randomly generated parameters from ranges with high success rates of one agent [4].

We tested the provide-time method and the ask-time method when the agents used the random-order method, the dfs-order method and the bfs-order method. The combined methods are called random-provide, dfs-provide, bfs-provide, random-ask, dfs-ask and bfs-ask, respectively. We tested the success rate of each method in a given range of *multi-precedence constraints*. Our goal was to answer the following questions: (1) Does the planning order affect the performance of the system? If so, what is the best method for the planning order in the team? Our hypothesis was that the order in which the agent chooses to plan the actions with the multi-precedence constraints affects the performance. If such actions are selected early, the commitment by the agents will be done at an early stage, and it will reduce their flexibility. However, because the examples

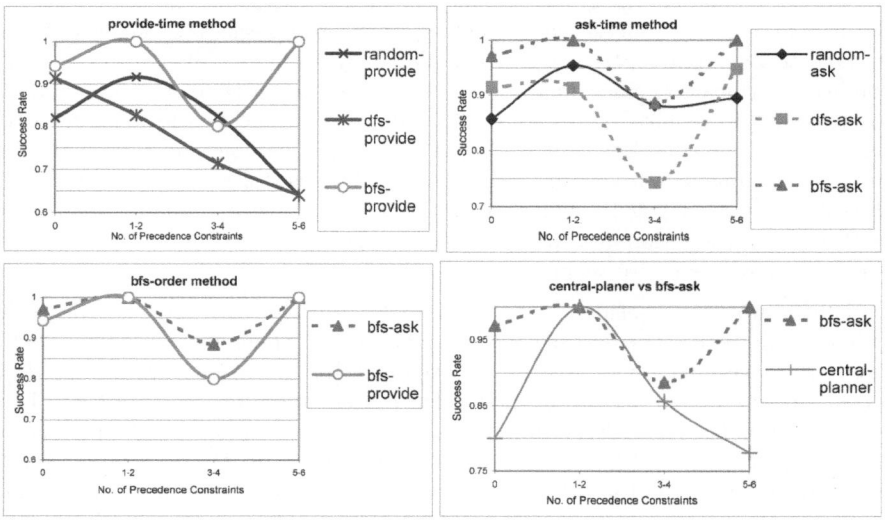

Fig. 2. Comparison between planning order methods when the agents use provide-time (the top left graph) and ask-time (the top right graph); comparison between ask-time and provide-time methods when the agents use bfs-order (the bottom left graph); and comparison between the performance of our distributed method and the central-planner (the bottom right graph).

were drawn randomly, in certain examples using a specific method will cause the agent to select such actions early and in other examples using the same method will cause the agent to select such actions at a late stage. Thus, we assumed that there is not one method that is always the best. (2) At what stage should the agent commit to a timetable for performing joint actions? Is the ask-time method better than the provide-time method? Our hypothesis was that if the commitment is made as late as possible, the flexibility of the agents is higher, thus the performance of the system will be better. (3) Does the number of multi-precedence constraints between complex subactions affect the performance of the system? Our hypothesis was that a high number of multi-precedence constraints would allow the agents less flexibility in deciding the performance time of their activities. Thus, it would reduce the success rate of the system.

The top of figure 2 compares the success rate of the different planning order methods for a given range of multi-precedence constraints, when the agents use provide-time and ask-time methods, respectively. As shown in the right graph bfs-ask (90% − 100% success rate) is better than random-ask (86% − 96% success rate) and dfs-ask (75% − 95%). Also, in the left graph the method with almost always the best results is bfs-provide, with a success rate between 80% − 100%. The success rate of random-provide was between 64% − 92% and of dfs-provide was between 64% − 92%. The only case where random-provide is better than bfs-provide is in the case of 3 − 4 constraints. However, the gap between these methods is very small. Thus, in contrast to our hypothesis for the first question, we can conclude that bfs-order on average is the best planning method for our system. However, as predicted by our hypothesis after carefully examining all the cases, dfs-order succeeded in specific examples where bfs-order failed. We assume that the random order, which is a random combination of bfs-order and dfs-order, drew the wrong order in some examples, which caused it to fail more than the dfs-order. But, in other cases, it drew the best order for the specific example and this is the reason for its good results in certain cases.

We also compared the ask-time method with the provide-time method when the agents use bfs, dfs and the random planning order methods. As we hypothesized, we conclude that in general, the ask-time method is better than the provide-time method (see also the bottom left graph). Thus, when the agents make their commitments as late as possible their performance on average is better. This is also the reason that the success rate of the dfs-provide method is a linear function of the number of the multi-precedence constraints. In the dfs order method the agent tries to complete the entire plan of a selected action before it continues to plan another action. Thus, the planning of certain actions are completed, and the agent provides their timetable and commits to it, at an early stage. As the number of multi-precedence constraints increases, more early commitments are made. In the other methods the success rate does not change monotonically as a function of the number of the multi-precedence constraints. We hypothesize that the reason for this non monotonic behavior results from the fact that a high number of multi-precedence constraints provides more knowledge about the subaction slots. As a result, the precedence constraints lead the scheduler and the other team members to the correct solution (which always exists in our examples). On the other hand, multi-precedence constraints decrease the flexibility of the individuals in the team since they cause them to make more commitments in their timetable. The low flexibility leads to a lower success rate in cases of 3-4 multi-precedence constraints.

We ran an additional set of experiments with the above examples. The goal of this set of experiments was to compare the performance of our distributed method with the alternative method, where a team leader is responsible for solving the multi-agent planning problem centrally. Accordingly, we built a system with a central planner that planned all the actions centrally by using the bfs-order planning method. We can conclude, from the bottom right graph in figure 2, that the success rate of the distributed method ($90\% - 100\%$) is almost always better than the central-planner (between $80\% - 100\%$), except for one case where they perform equally well. We can see that when the joint action does not consist of any multi-precedence constraints, the success rate of the central-planner is low. The success rate of the central-planner is highest when the number of multi-precedence constraints is between $1 - 2$, whereas a high number of multi-precedence constraints reduces the success rate. We believe that the case of zero multi-precedence constraints is identical to the single agent case [4]. The high planning time (of more than 100 basic actions) leads to a delay in sending the basic actions for execution and causes certain basic actions to miss their deadline. This low success rate can be improved by increasing the idle time as in the single agent case. We hypothesize that $1 - 2$ multi-precedence constraints increases the success rate of the system because these constraints force the central-planner to first complete the plans of the actions with the earliest deadlines. This is in contrast to the case of zero multi-precedence constraints, where the partial knowledge of the planner in its uncertain environment does not enable it to predict which actions it has to plan first. However, since the central-planner must plan the actions of all the group members, a high number of multi-precedence constraints causes the central-planner to ask the agents to make more commitments in their schedule. Consequently, these commitments reduce the flexibility of the scheduling process.

References

1. R. Dechter, I. Meiri, and J. Pearl. Temporal constraint networks. *AIJ*, 49:61–95, 1991.
2. B. J. Grosz and S. Kraus. Collaborative plans for complex group action. *AIJ*, 86(2):269–357, 1996.
3. M. Hadad and S. Kraus. A mechanism for temporal reasoning by collaborative agents. In *CIA-01*, pages 229–234, 2001.
4. M. Hadad, S. Kraus, Y. Gal, and R. Lin. Time reasoning for a collaborative planning agent in a dynamic environment. *Annals of Math. and AI*, 2002. (In press) www.cs.biu.ac.il/ sarit/articles.html.
5. N. R. Jennings. Controlling cooperative problem solving in industrial multi-agent systems using joint intentions. *AIJ*, 75(2):1–46, 1995.

Programming Agent Mobility

Rebecca Montanari[1], Gianluca Tonti[1], Cesare Stefanelli[2]

[1]Dipartimento di Elettronica, Informatica e Sistemistica
Università di Bologna
Viale Risorgimento, 2 - 40136 Bologna - Italy
{rmontanari, gtonti}@deis.unibo.it
[2]Dipartimento di Ingegneria
Università di Ferrara
Via Saragat, 1 - 44100 Ferrara - Italy
cstefanelli@ing.unife.it

Abstract. Mobile agents seem an interesting solution for the design and deployment of Web services and applications in the Internet scenario. However, mobility complicates the design of applications and calls for new approaches to facilitate the specification and control of the mobility behaviour without any impact on agent implementation. The paper advocates a policy-based model to specify mobility strategies separately from the agent code and presents a policy controlled mobile agents framework. This approach permits to adapt agent applications to the evolving conditions of the execution environment. The paper also presents a case study to validate our policy-based solution to agent mobility.

1 Introduction

The Mobile Agent (MA) technology seems suitable to provide effective solutions for the design and deployment of new applications and services in the Internet scenario [1],[2]. There is an increasing interest among researchers and practitioners to apply mobile agents in several areas, such as distributed information retrieval, network management, mobile computing, and electronic commerce [3], [4], [5].

However, mobility adds complexity to the design and deployment of applications, because programmers have to decide and express when and where to move agents on the basis of the knowledge of application and environment state. The traditional MA programming approach is to statically hard-code migration rules into the agent code at design time. This lacks flexibility and requires re-engineering efforts to address changes. For instance, this approach is not appropriate when it is not possible to make a-priori assumptions on the logical and physical network topology.

There is the need for new solutions to enable agent mobility adaptation to changes in the underlying operating environment and in the application requirements. The first proposals recognize the principle of separation between mobility and computational concerns as a key design requirement [6].

M. Klusch, S. Ossowski, and O. Shehory (Eds.): CIA 2002, LNAI 2446, pp. 287–296, 2002.
© Springer-Verlag Berlin Heidelberg 2002

We propose a policy-based approach to specify and control agent mobility behavior. Policies are rules governing choices in the behavior of a system, and are separated from the components in charge of their interpretation [7]. In the context of mobility, policies can specify when, where, and which agent parts have to migrate. Policies permit to define dynamically the most appropriate agent migration strategies to adapt to the current environment state.

The paper describes also the infrastructure we are currently developing to apply our policy-controlled mobility to real application scenarios. The proposed infrastructure provides MA programmers with services for application development and runtime support. At design time, developers exploit the Ponder language to easily specify and control agent mobility strategies separately from the application code [8]. At runtime, programmers can dynamically change agent migration strategies to adapt to the evolution of the execution environment. The infrastructure propagates policy variations to interested agents automatically and transparently. In particular, the infrastructure is built on top of the mobile agents SOMA framework that offers a wide range of tools and mechanisms for the support of secure and interoperable mobile agents applications [9].

2   Policy-Controlled Agent Mobility

Most systems that support some forms of mobility exhibit rigid control schemes. The primary limitation derives from the fact that the rules for governing entity mobility are hard-coded into components at design time. This approach does not allow applications to adapt to the evolving condition of a mobile scenario, with roaming users and terminals, and with possibly discontinuous interconnection. Another source of rigidity derives from the assumption about the unit of mobility, i.e. the part of the component that has to move. For instance, the remote evaluation and the code on demand models provide for the shipping/fetching of code only, whereas in the Mobile Agent (MA) paradigm the agent code moves together with the state [1]. Application designers, instead, could benefit from schemes with a finer grain of mobility control [10].

To overcome these drawbacks, this work proposes to rule component migration by means of policies separated from component code. The main advantage of policy adoption is the increased flexibility and dynamicity in the control and change of the mobility behaviour of components. The clean separation between the mobility policy and the coding of components permits to dynamically introduce new migration strategies without impact on component implementation.

A policy-based approach to mobility should provide a clear *policy model* specifying how mobility policies can be expressed and represented and an *enforcement model* that determines how to map policy specifications into low-level implementable policies. Since mobility policies and mobile agents to which policies apply, are separated modules, the enforcement model is responsible for integrating them in a consistent and coherent manner.

2.1 Event-Triggered Policies for Controlled Mobility

Among the various types of policies, we consider a viable solution to model mobility decisions in terms of *event-triggered* policies, i.e. policies triggered by event occurrences. The concept of event-triggered policies has been generally used in the field of policy-based management for distributed systems to handle automated management tasks, such as configuration and security tasks.

In the case of mobility, event-triggered policies specify the migration actions that must be performed when specific events occur. Events can be defined as generic state changes in the system and can uniformly model different changes in application and environment conditions. Some examples of the former case are the completion of an application task and the arrival/departure of new components in/from an execution context. For the latter case, consider the CPU and the memory usage, and the bandwidth occupation. Event-triggered policies require underlying support services for the registration, detection and notification of events.

The exploitation of event-triggered policies facilitates the development of mobile agents capable to adapt to system evolution. Events provide an indication when migration actions should take place within the overall execution flow of agents and, therefore, offer an integrated solution that reduces the difficulties of introducing dynamic changes in the mobility behaviour of agents.

2.2 Ponder for Programming Agent Mobility

Specifying mobility policies in large-scale mobile environments requires an expressive policy language solution that can facilitate the specification of the mobility behaviour of components by providing at the same time a feasible and effective implementation model. We exploit the Ponder language for programming agent mobility [8]. Ponder obligation policies define the actions that policy subjects must perform on target objects when specific events occur. Let us introduce a simple example to illustrate Ponder obligation policies. In Table 1 the P1 policy states that the *Buyer* agent is obliged by the *System* component to migrate to a different node, called G1, when the current node becomes overloaded. The migration action is triggered by the CPU usage exceeding 90%, and the *Buyer* agent is forced to move to G1 and there to perform the *run()* method, if G1 is reachable. Policy P2 differs from P1 because it is the *Buyer* agent that decides to migrate and in this case the agent is both the subject and the target of the policy. When subject and target coincides, there is no need in Ponder to explicitly specify the target.

Note that the triggering event specification follows the on keyword and that it can include events of any type, such as excessive CPU usage, by simply defining the event name and parameters. Event expressions can also be used to combine basic events into more complex ones, to allow to model any sequence of events.

Multiple actions can follow the do keyword. In this case, the policy obligation language provides several concurrency operators to specify whether actions should be executed sequentially or in parallel. For instance, *t.a1 -> s.a2* means that the action *a2* on the object *s* must follow the action *a1* on the object *t*.

In addition, Ponder obligations can include a when clause to let programmers specify the set of conditions for the policy to be considered valid, e.g., the reachability of the G1 node in p1 and p2. These conditions must be explicit in the policy specification and act as constraints for the applicability of a policy. Ponder constraints are expressed in terms of a predicate, which must be true for the policy to apply.

inst oblig **P1** { *on CPU(load,90) ;* *subject s = System ;* *target t = agents/Buyer;* *do t.go_next_Place(G1.toString, run())* *when G1.isReachable()*	*inst oblig* **P2** { *on CPU(load,90) ;* *subject s = agents/Buyer* *do s.go_next_Place(G1.toString, run())* *when G1.isReachable()*

Table 1. Ponder Obligation Policies.

Note that conflicts between policy specifications could arise due to omissions, errors or conflicting requirements of the users specifying the policies. Also run-time policy conflicts can arise. This is the case of two migration policies, one defined by the application user and one by the agent system administrator, that command the same mobile agent to migrate at the same event occurrence, but toward two different nodes. To address this issue, the research already carried out in the field of policy-based management of distributed systems and requirement engineering can offer valuable solutions [11], [12].

3   The Infrastructure to Support Policy-Controlled Agent Mobility

A policy-controlled mobility model requires an integrated infrastructure for the support of policy definition, installation and enforcement. Figure 1 depicts the organisation of the infrastructure for policy lifecycle management in the SOMA system. The infrastructure is designed according to a layered architecture, with a large number of services at different levels. In particular, the upper layer services support policy specification, activation and enforcement. Lower layer services monitor application and environment state and notify mobile agents about changes relevant for their migration decisions.

More in detail, the upper layer includes the following services:
- the *Specification Service* permits programmers to edit, update and remove mobility policy specifications. The service also transforms high-level policy specifications into policy enforcement modules, i.e., suitable code that can be interpreted at run-time by the underlying agent infrastructure;
- the *Repository Service* stores all currently specified and enabled policies and can be queried to retrieve specific policies;
- the *Distribution Service* distributes mobility policies to relevant entities at both policy instantiation time and at any successive change. In particular, it distributes

policies to the policy subjects, either mobile agents (in the case of proactive mobility) or agent system components (in the case of reactive agent migration);

- the *Policy Enforcement Service* is responsible for the enforcement of triggered obligation policies. In particular, at event occurrence the service is delegated to coordinate the retrieval and interpretation of triggered policies and to activate migration and mobility management actions accordingly to policy specification.

At the lower layer, the architecture provides the essential services to support the dynamic adaptation of agent migration strategies to changes in the execution context. The *Monitoring Service* detects the modifications in both application and environment state. The *Event Service* manages the events, i.e., the monitored variations in the whole distributed system, by interfacing with both agents and the Monitoring Service. More in detail, any policy subject can register its interest to one or more specific events with the Event Service. On its turn, the Event Service is responsible for dispatching registered events to interested entities. The Event Service typically receives state information from the Monitoring Service. As a key feature, the Event Service is designed to take into account agent mobility in order to notify events to interested agents even in case of migration.

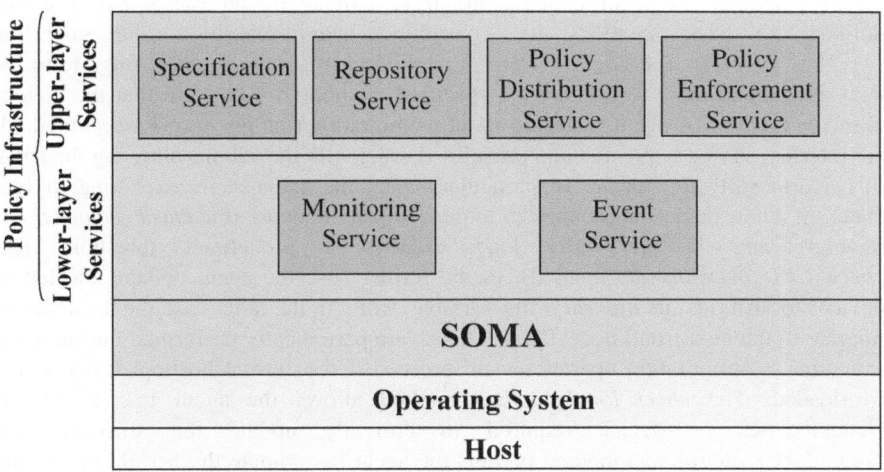

Fig. 1. The Policy-based Infrastructure.

4   Case-Study

We have tested the usability and effectiveness of the policy-controlled mobility model and of the policy infrastructure in the design and implementation of a SOMA application for automatic software configuration and update in the context of a network company composed of distributed and heterogeneous devices that can be either static or mobile. This setting is characterized by a high dynamicity of network topology and calls for a flexible and reconfigurable control of SOMA agent mobility.

SOMA agents are designed to achieve orthogonal goals: software update and migration among all the company network machines. As far as software update is involved, the agent has to check for each company device its current configuration and to retrieve software installation parameters. Then, it has to use such information to determine the set of operations to perform for software update and executes them. With regard to network exploration, the agent owns an initial list of devices to visit and to configure sequentially. The list can vary at run-time, because devices, especially mobile devices, can join/disconnect from the network company. When a device disconnects from the network, its name has to be removed from the list of nodes to visit, whereas when a new device connects, its name has to be added. Moreover, in the case of overloaded devices (for instance, when the CPU load is over 90%), the agent has to skip software configuration tasks and migrate toward the next listed device.

Figure 2 shows two alternative programming methodologies that can be adopted in this application scenario. In the traditional approach, the logic ruling the mobility behaviour is statically embedded into the agent code at development time. As an example, Figure 2A reports the code fragment of the SOMA agent in charge of software update. The agent, called *Configurer1*, extends the abstract *Agent* class that defines the basic methods for controlling agent execution and migration (*go_Next_Place()*). The *go_next_Place()* method instructs the agent to migrate to the next device and there to execute the specified method (*run()*). Note that the actions allowing the SOMA agent to decide about its migration (the *go_next_Place()* method) are interleaved in a sequential and predefined order with the actions allowing the agent to perform software update. In particular, when the agent starts executing, it first checks if a new device has connected to the company network (the *check_connection()* method) and if the CPU load exceeds a predefined threshold (the *check_CPU_overloaded()* method). In the former case the agent updates the list of devices to visit, i.e., its *itineraryPath* variable, while in the latter case the agent has to migrate to the next listed node. These checks are periodically performed during agent execution. Configuration operations can proceed if the current hosting device is not overloaded. The *check_local_config()* method allows the agent to retrieve the characteristics of device required to correctly update the software; the *ToDo_List_elaboration()* method permits the agent to compute the list of configuring actions to perform and the *SW_configuration()* method allows the agent to perform software configuration.

//Traditionally programmed MA:	// Policy-controlled MA:

Public class Configurer1 extends Agent{
Environment env;
VisitedNodes nodes;   **A**
Itinerary itineraryPath;
Place home;
void run() {
if (check_CPU_overloaded)
go_next_Place(NextNode.toString, "run");
check_connection();
check_local_config ();
if (check_CPU_overloaded) go_next_Place(..);
check_connection();
ToDo_List_elaboration();
if (check_CPU_overloaded) go_next_Place(..);
check_connection();
SW_configuration();
Updating_local_vars();
go_next_Place(..) }
boolean check_CPU_overloaded(){
if (env.getCPUload()>90) return true;
return false;}
void check_connection(){
  Place NewConn = env.getNewConnection();
  if (NewConn!= null)
  itineraryPath.addLast(NewConn);}
 	
void check_local_config(){ ... }
void ToDO_list_elaboration(){ ... }
void SW_configuration(){ ... }
}
	Public class Configurer2 extends PolicyControlledAgent{
	Environment env;
	VisitedNodes nodes; **B**
	Itinerary itineraryPath;
	Place home;
	
	  void run() {
	    check_local_config ();
	    ToDo_List_elaboration();
	  }
	......
	}

	inst oblig MobPol1 **on** TaskCompletion(s, "run"); **subject** s= agents/Configurer2; **do** s.go_next_Place(....); **when** NextNode.isReacheable();

	inst oblig MobPol2
	  on NewConnection(PlaceID);
	  subject s= agents/Configurer2;
	  do s.itineraryPath.addLast(PlaceID);

	inst oblig MobPol3 **on** CPULoad(90); **subject** s= agents/Configurer2; **do** s.go_next_Place(...);

Fig. 2. The comparison of a traditional SOMA agent with a Ponder-controlled one.

In the policy-based approach only the application logic is embedded into the agent code part. The agent mobility behaviour, that is likely to evolve with environment conditions, is abstracted away and modelled by means of Ponder obligation policies. In particular, Figure 2B reports the agent code that is executed at each place. In this case the SOMA agent called *Configurer2* extends the abstract *PolicyControlledAgent* class that provides agents with the methods to load/unload policies and to react to event occurrence accordingly to mobility policy specifications. Agent code computation consists in the execution of only the methods required for the software update.

The set of Ponder policies that rule agent mobility are shown in the bottom of Figure 2B. *MobPol1* policy forces the *Configurer2* agent to migrate to the next place in its list of nodes to visit. This policy is triggered by the *TaskCompletion* event that is an event message that notifies the end of an agent method execution (*run()*).The policy can be applied only if the next node is reachable (the *when* field). *MobPol2* policy is used to update the set of devices to visit (addLast()), when new devices connect to the network (the *NewConnection* event). The last policy (*MobPol3*) forces the agent to migrate to the next device when the CPU usage exceeds the 90% percentage usage.

As a final remark, it is worth outlining that policies can vary during the agent lifetime due to changing user preferences. In the case of changes, users can command to disable old policies and to substitute them with new ones. It is the underlying policy infrastructure that transparently disables/enables new policies when required and propagates changes to agents without impacting on agent code implementation.

5   Related Work

The effective design and deployment of MA applications in dynamic environments should consider novel paradigms to provide flexible management of migration strategies and its runtime-time reconfiguration. While traditional applications could be conceived, designed and implemented in quite fixed scenarios of environment conditions, which varied only under exceptional circumstances, this is not possible in the new Internet scenarios. As a consequence, any MA application should be designed and developed with the ability to adapt its execution to all possible operating conditions in which it may be deployed.

This section does not provide a general survey on the state-of-the-art solutions for achieving dynamic adaptability of MA applications, but focuses on the few proposals that, to the best of our knowledge, explicitly deal with dynamic mobility management in applications built with mobile code technologies. All solutions have in common the principle of separation between binding and computational concerns as the key design requirement. However, the proposals differ on how to achieve this separation of concerns.

The approach described in [6] proposes to separate an MA application into three aspects, the function, the mobility and the management aspects, and to program them separately. Each MA is associated with an array with three key/value pairs: a code that gives the code of the agent, a data that gives the data the MA references, and a path that gives the itinerary of the agent.

Another interesting approach is the **FarGo** system that allows to program the layout of a mobile application separately from the basic logic [13]. Dynamic layout policies are encoded within the application by using special API. The use of an event-based scripting language for the specification of layout policies externally to the application code is also considered and is currently under development. However, the language can be used only to express and control the mobility of **FarGo** units of relocation, and not as a general-purpose solution for mobile code applications.

Another recent proposal is represented by the **MAGE** model that introduces the programming abstraction of mobility attributes to describe the mobility semantics of application components [14]. Programmers can attach mobility attributes to application components to dynamically control the placement of these components within the network. However, MAGE relies on the programmer to manually enforce the binding between a program component and its mobility attributes. In addition, MAGE does not currently integrate any security model that controls both the specification and run-time enforcement of mobility attributes.

In [15] another solution is proposed to support incremental insertion or substitution of, possibly small, code fragments at run-time. Differently from the previous proposals that are Java based, **XMILE** exploits XML to achieve more fine-grained mobility than in the approaches based on Java. XMILE enables complete programs as well as individual lines of code to be sent across the network. XMILE is more a model rather than a ready-to-use framework for dynamic application reconfiguration.

Another significant proposal is the **DACIA** framework that provides support for the construction and execution of reconfigurable mobile applications [16]. DACIA provides mechanisms to change the application structure at runtime and for dynamically alter the rules used for application reconfiguration, but no high-level languages are integrated to support the specification of reconfiguration policies clearly separated from the application code.

Our proposal has several points in common with the described approaches; the main difference is in the possibility to specify binding strategies at a higher level of abstraction, to modify them even during the application execution, thus enabling dynamic changes in binding management at deployment time, transparently to service developers. In addition, we believe that our policy infrastructure with its wide set of support services can be considered a useful ready-to-use environment for the design, development and support of adaptive MA applications in a wide variety of application scenarios.

6   Conclusions

Most MA systems exhibit rigid agent migration control schemes. The directives for governing agent mobility are typically hard-coded and tangled within the agent application logic. The lack of separation of concerns forces mobile application designers to take into account at design time both algorithmic and allocation issues and to re-implement agent code in the case migration strategies need to be changed to accommodate evolving conditions.

Only recently few proposals have started to emerge to provide more flexible approaches to mobile application layout reconfiguration. Along this direction, we propose a policy-based approach to mobility and a policy framework for the dynamic control of agent mobility behaviour. The infrastructure results from the integration of a policy-based management system, called Ponder, in the SOMA mobile agent environment. Within this framework, programmers specify agent mobility behaviour in terms of declarative Ponder policies. Dynamic modification of agent mobility behaviour requires to change only policy specifications, whereas the control and enforcement of migration accordingly to policy specifications is delegated to the underlying policy infrastructure, transparently to agent programmers.

As a final remark, we are convinced that our policy-based approach could extend to other application problems not strictly related to agent mobility. Areas that are currently under investigation are the control of both code and device mobility and binding management upon migration of software components. We are convinced that all results shown in this paper could be easily ported to these application domains.

Acknowledgments

This investigation is supported by the University of Bologna (Funds for Selected Research Topics: "An integrated Infrastructure to Support Secure Services"), by CNR (Funds for Young Researchers: "An Integrated Security Infrastructure for Multimedia Services") and by MURST within the framework of the Project "MUSIQUE: Multimedia Ubiquitous Service Infrastructure in a QoS Universal Environment". We also thank Emil Lupu, Naranker Dulay, and Morris Sloman for valuable discussions on policy-based distributed systems management.

References

1. A. Fuggetta, G.P. Picco, and G. Vigna, "Understanding Code Mobility", *IEEE Transactions on Software Engineering*, 24(5), May 1998.
2. J. E. White, Mobile Agents, in J. M. Bradshaw (Ed.) Software Agents, AAAI/The MIT Press, 1997.
3. Baldi, , et al., "Evaluating the Tradeoffs of Mobile Code Design Paradigms in Network Management Applications", *Proc. of ICSE'98*, IEEE CS Press, Los Alamitos CA, 1998.
4. D. Lange, M. Oshima, "Programming and Deploying Java Mobile Agents with Aglets", Addison Wesley, Menlo Park, CA, 1998.
5. P. Bellavista, et al., "Mobile Agent Middleware for Mobile Computing", *IEEE Computer*, 34(3), 2001.
6. K. Lauvset, et al., "Factoring Mobile Agents", *Proc of ECBS'02 Workshop*, Lund, Swe-den, IEEE CS Press, 2002.
7. R. Wies, "Using a Classification of Management Policies for Policy Specification and Policy Transformation", *Proc. of ISINM'95*, Chapman & Hall, 1995.
8. N. Damianou, et al., "The Ponder Policy Specification Language", *Proc. of Policy '01*, Springer Verlag, Bristol, 2001.
9. P. Bellavista, et al., "A Secure and Open Mobile Agent Programming Environment", *Proc. ISADS '99*, IEEE Press, Tokyo, Japan, 1999.
10. G.P. Picco, "μCode: A Lightweight and Flexible Mobile Code Toolkit", *Proc. of MA'98*, Springer Verlag, Stuttgart, Germany, 1998.
11. E. Lupu, et al. "Conflicts in Policy-based Distributed Systems Management", *IEEE Transactions on Software Engineering*, 25(6), 1999.J.P.
12 J. Chomicki, et al., "A Logic Programming Approach to Conflict Resolution in Policy Management", *Proc. KR2000*, Morgan Kaufmann Publishers, 2000.
13. O. Holder, et al., "Dynamic Layout of Distributed Applications in FarGo", *Proc. of ICSE'99*, ACM Press, Los Angeles, California (USA), 1999.
14. E. Barr et al., "MAGE: a Distributed Programming Model", *Proc. of ICDCS'01*, IEEE Press, Phoenix, Arizona (USA), 2001.
15. C. Mascolo et al., "XMILE: an XML based Approach for Incremental Code Mobility and Update", *Automated Software Engineering Journal (Special Issue on Mobility)*, vol. 9, no. 2, Kluwer Publisher, April 2002.
16. R. Litiu, "Providing Flexibility in Distributed Applications Using a Mobile Component Framework", Ph.D. dissertation, University of Michigan, Electrical Engineering and Computer Science, Sep. 2000.

A Method for Protecting Mobile Agents against Denial of Service Attacks

Biljana Cubaleska[1] and Markus Schneider[2]

[1] University of Hagen, Department of Communications Systems
D-58084 Hagen, Germany
`biljana.cubaleska@fernuni-hagen.de`
[2] Fraunhofer Gesellschaft (FhG), Institute for Secure Telecooperation (SIT)
D-64293 Darmstadt, Germany
`markus.schneider@sit.fraunhofer.de`

Abstract. In the world of mobile agents, security aspects are extensively being discussed. In this context, denial of service attacks are of considerable interest. Here, we consider a special kind of denial of service attacks which focuses on malicious hosts that either delete received agents or prevent them from continuing their route. In general, the prevention of such attacks is not possible. This paper discusses a detection method for *a posteriori* identification of such malicious hosts. The output of this identification method can be used by agent owners to avoid contacting these hosts again in the future. Moreover, hosts originally intended to be visited cannot be skipped as a result of one malicious host's misbehavior. We provide solutions to this problem for both the cases of completely dependent and completely independent agent computations.

1 Introduction

Mobile agents are assumed to have a great potential for Internet based electronic markets. Agents migrate through a network of sites to accomplish tasks or take orders on behalf of their owners. The owner of an agent can instruct it to visit many hosts in a network, and thereby execute some desired tasks for him. After having carried out these instructions the agent returns to its home and delivers the results it collected during its journey to its owner.

On the one hand, one of the advantages for using mobile agents technology is that interaction cost for the agent owner is remarkably reduced since after leaving its owner the agent migrates from one host to the next autonomously. On the other hand, the paradigm of mobile agents causes lots of security threats for all involved parties. A serious risk for agents stems from potential denial of service attacks by malicious hosts. In such an attack, the malicious host can prevent an agent from continuing to migrate to another host or may even delete the agent. As a consequence, all results the agent has collected so far from other hosts are lost. This may happen every time the agent passes through this malicious host while the agent owner has no possibility to identify the source of the attack. In general, the term *denial of service* is used for attacks in which the focus is on exhausting resources with the effect that other entities cannot be served anymore. This differs from the kind of attacks we are considering.

M. Klusch, S. Ossowski, and O. Shehory (Eds.): CIA 2002, LNAI 2446, pp. 297–311, 2002.

Unfortunately, there is no possibility for general prevention of *killing* agents. Thus, agent owners need a mechanism which can be used for identification of the culprit host. The knowledge obtained by such a mechanism can be used by the agent owner to exclude the corresponding host from future migration routes.

In this paper, we present solutions that allow an agent owner to identify malicious hosts executing denial of service attacks, both for the cases of *completely dependent* and *completely independent* agent computations. The methods also enable the agent owner to circumvent the activities of a collusion when malicious parties try to skip a host that should be visited. This works if the number of colluding hosts does not exceed a given system parameter. Improper protocol execution from some host can also be detected.

The remainder of this paper is organized as follows. In section 2 we introduce the components of a mobile agent system needed for our solution. A simplified solution for the identification of parties that perform denial of service attacks is given in section 3. In section 4 protocols are presented which solve the problems arising in the simplified solution. Some related work in the area of protecting mobile agents against malicious hosts is discussed in section 5, and section 6 concludes the paper.

2   Some Basics

In the past years, lots of work has been done in the area of mobile agent systems. In the following, we will not focus on a specific mobile agent system. We will consider mobile agents in a rather abstract way. This means that exclusively those components of mobile agents will be considered which are of special relevance for the solution that is presented in this paper. So, in our level of abstraction a mobile agent consists of the following components:

$$agent^j = (uid, bc, in, out^j, r, vc^{\#(c_j)}). \tag{1}$$

Here, the parameter j refers to the agent residing at host c_j after being executed. The parameter uid is a *unique identifier* for the agent. This identifier is created by the agent owner in such a way that all his agents have distinct identifiers. We will use uid later to trace the agent in order to identify an attacker in case the agent does not return to its home host. The parameter bc denotes the *binary code* of the agent to be executed. Furthermore, in serves as input data for agent computations and is given by the agent owner. The component out^j denotes the output data produced by the visited hosts after its execution at host c_j. Furthermore, $r = (c_1, \ldots, c_j, \ldots, c_n)$ describes the mobile agents *route* as an n-tuple (with $n \geq 1$) consisting of hosts that have to be visited. The route is given by the agent owner. Note that the hosts do not necessarily have to be visited in the given order. The last component $vc^{\#(c_j)}$ describes the sequence of already *visited hosts* also including the host c_j when the agent resides at host c_j. This is not necessarily given by the sequence $c_1, \ldots, c_j$ since some of these hosts could possibly not be visited. Here, $\#(c_j)$ denotes the number of hosts that have been visited so far. Thus, $vc^{\#(c_j)}$ is a sequence with $\#(c_j)$ elements. Before the agent starts its first migration residing at its home h the sequence of visited hosts $vc^{\#(h)} = vc^0$ is empty. When the first host c_1 on the agent's journey is visited, then c_1 creates $vc^{\#(c_1)} = vc^1 = c_1$. If we assume that the following visited host is c_3 —host c_2 as intended in the route r could be offline—

then c_3 creates the sequence $vc^{\#(c_3)} = vc^2 = c_1, c_3$. In general, for $1 \leq j \leq n$ we have $vc^{\#(c_j)} = vc^{\#(c_j)-1}, c_j$.

In general, agent systems also allow hosts to extend the route prespecified by the agent owner. But in the following, we assume that agents will exclusively visit hosts which are contained in the route, i.e., dynamic route extensions by hosts are not dealt with. These will be considered in future work.

We can distinguish between two classes of operations in agent systems. In the first class, an agent computation is *dependent*. In a dependent computation at c_j, the results contained in out^{j-1} calculated by c_{j-1} are needed as input for c_j. Such dependencies have an impact on the order of hosts on the journey. We say that an agent journey is *completely dependent* if for $1 < i \leq n$ each c_i requires the results of c_{i-1}. In this case, the hosts have to be visited exactly in the same order as they are prescribed in the route r. This means that the agent cannot fulfill its task when at least one of the required hosts specified in r is either not available or denies its services to the agent. In such a journey, the component $vc^{\#(c_j)}$ is not necessarily required since the order of the hosts is strictly determined by r. The other class deals with computations which are *independent*. Here, the agent computation does not need the results of another host. We say that an agent journey is *completely independent* when there are no dependent computations in it. As a consequence, the hosts contained in the prescribed route r can be visited in any arbitrary order. Note that the properties of being *completely dependent* and *completely independent* are not complementary. But in this paper we restrict our focus on these two cases.

Both the case of hosts being offline or the case of unreachable hosts due to network problems are not considered to be denial of service. However, there are also other attacks which have the same effects for the agent owner which are similar to denial of service. These comprise altering, replacing, or even deleting for example the binary code bc of the agent or its data in, out^j. As in the case of denial of service, in this scenario the agent owner may not receive the desired correct results. Strictly considered, this belongs to another type of attacks —attacks on the agent's integrity. Dealing with integrity attacks —especially concerning the integrity of computation results— is however not in the central scope of this paper. These attacks have been already dealt with in other work, e.g., see [1].

Having a mechanism dealing with the problem of malicious hosts performing denial of service attacks would be very useful for the agent owner. The solutions presented in this paper enables the agent owner to identify malicious hosts *a posteriori*. The information an agent owner can get by using our solution can help him to obtain better knowledge about the hosts he is dealing with.

3   Towards the Solution

In the following, we present a simplified and rather naive solution of the described problem. Later, we point out the shortcomings of this simple approach which will be tackled in the next section. Additionally, we mention briefly the basics of the solution including cryptographic primitives and infrastructure requirements. Furthermore, we show how the agent owner's trust policy can look like.

The underlying idea of our mechanism is based on the usage of undeniable proofs: When an agent owner does not receive his agent after some waiting time, there arouses suspicion that the agent suffered a denial of service by a malicious host. In order to identify the attacking host, the agent owner asks all hosts which were contained in the original agent route r to show him a proof that they correctly dispatched the agent. The attacking host is surely not able to show such a proof.

These undeniable proofs can be realized by the technique of digital signatures —e.g., see [4]. Using digital signatures assumes existance of a public key infrastructure (PKI), where each subject in the system —the agent owner and all hosts— has a private key and a corresponding public key which is certified to be authentic by a certification authority. Generally, a party A that uses the public key of another party B is required to trust B's certification authority to issue only correct certificates. E.g., this implies for our system that the agent owner must trust the certification authorities of all hosts to be visited as will become clear later.

We assume now —more or less naively— that all hosts in the system carry out the following rule: upon receiving an agent, each host c_{j+1} must send a confirmation to its predecessor c_j, where $1 \leq j < n$. This confirmation is actually a digital signature $sig_{c_{j+1}}(uid, bc, in, r)$ created by host c_{j+1} on the unique agent identifier uid, the binary code bc, the agent input in, and the route r. The parameter uid can be understood as a unique name for the agent that remains valid for the agent's whole journey. The uniqueness of the uid is necessary in order to trace the agent in case of denial of service. Loosely speaking, it can be used later for the agent owner's investigations to find who was the last party that saw this specific agent alive. Each host that has received such a confirmation should store it locally in a database. When the agent owner does not receive his agent and starts his investigations, a host c_j having such a confirmation can show it to the owner as an evidence that it properly dispatched the agent to the next host c_{j+1}. This evidence also gives the agent owner the information about which host was visited after c_j. This principle works as long as the hosts being considered did not perform denial of service.

Consider an agent journey on the route $r = (c_1, \ldots, c_n)$. We require that after each migration evidences are sent to the predecessor with two exceptions. These happen in the migrations where the agent owner is involved himself. These two cases need some further explaination. The original goal of our approach was to identify the party that did not send the agent to another host. Therefore, the succeeding host must provide the sending host with an evidence to be shown later to the agent owner to convince him about what happened. But in the first migration $h \to c_1$ the agent owner sends the agent himself, and thus does not need such an evidence from his succeeding host. Requiring confirmation in this step would mean that the agent owner has an evidence to convince himself that he sent the agent —which does not make any sense. The last migration $c_n \to h$ only takes place when no denial of service attack has occured. Thus, there is no necessity for the agent owner to start the investigation procedure.

The decisions of the agent owner when composing the future routes of his agents should be influenced by his experiences made in the past. According to his philosophy concerning security, he can use either a *black list* following an *open trust policy* or a *white list* following a *closed trust policy*. In an open trust policy, all hosts can be visited except those contained in the black list. A closed trust policy means that only the hosts contained in the white list are allowed to be visited.

In all previous considerations, we started from the naive assumption that each host sends a confirmation after having received the agent. Of course, in a real scenario this cannot be guaranteed. Let us consider the case what happens when host c_{j+1} does not send the confirmation to c_j although it successfully received the agent. Assume that c_{j+1} or any other host after it performs denial of service. When the agent owner starts his investigation procedure, host c_j cannot show him an evidence that proves its innocence, although it has done its job properly. Thus, the simplified solution presented so far has to be modified in order to be able to handle such cases in a desired way.

An obvious solution for the problem when c_{j+1} refuses to send a confirmation could be the possibility for c_j to skip c_{j+1} and send the agent to another host, say c_{j+2}. Of course, this is only possible in case of independent results. Then, the agent could return to its home properly, and the agent owner can see from the sequence of visited hosts $vc^{\#(c_n)} = vc^{n-1}$ that host c_{j+1} was not visited. The reason for this remains hidden to the agent owner. From his perspective, c_{j+1} could be offline or refuse to send a confirmation. But this kind of solution could open the doors for another kind of dishonest behavior. To be more specific, a malicious c_j could intentionally skip c_{j+1} without having even contacted it before. Motivations for c_j to do this could be, first, to damage c_{j+1}'s reputation by making the agent owner believe that c_{j+1} is always offline or is not willing to follow the rules for exchanging confirmations. Second, c_j can exclude c_{j+1} from providing its services by simply skipping it.

The protocol proposed in the next section solves all the problems of the simplified version presented above. In the previous consideration, we have mentioned several times the term *investigation procedure* without having explained how this procedure works. This will also be presented in the next section.

4   Detection of Malicious Hosts

Our solutions presented here are distinct for the cases of journeys with *complete dependence* and *complete independence*. The solution of the problem for the case *completely dependent* is quite short. It will be presented in subsection 4.1. The case *completely independent* requires a more sophisticated solution, which is presented in subsection 4.2. The investigation procedure for both cases is given in subsection 4.3.

For security reasons, we modify the agent as it was introduced in section 2. In detail, we assume that the agent

$$agent^j = (uid, bc, in, out^j, r, vc^{\#(c_j)}, m, sig_h(uid, bc, in, r, m)) \tag{2}$$

with $r = (c_1, \ldots, c_n)$ contains also a signature by the agent owner h. With this signature, visited hosts are assured about the integrity and the origine of the signed agent components. Note that there is a new parameter m in this agent abstraction. It is needed for the case *completely independent* and will be explained later. In the case *completely dependent*, m can be ignored. There, also $vc^{\#(c_j)}$ is not necessarily required.

In the following, we assume that visited hosts will always verify the validity of these signatures and we will not mention it again explicitly. The signature verification is done before the hosts start the execution of the protocols presented below. If a host detects an agent with corrupted elements, it will forward the agent directly to its owner. This will be done before any of the sender protocols presented below starts.

4.1   The Protocol in Case of Complete Dependence

Remember that in the case *completely dependent* all hosts must be visited in the order given in the route r, since the agent execution depends on each predecessor's output. The proposed solution combines the mechanism of exchanging confirmations proposed in section 3 and a set of rules for both sending and receiving hosts.

Sender Protocol. The protocol will be started at host c_j after the agent execution has terminated. The steps of the sender protocol are described in pseudo-code. Note that the sender protocol will not be applied in the migrations $h \rightarrow c_1$ and $c_n \rightarrow h$ (section 3).

```
1 Store a copy of the agent
2 Send agent to the next host in the route
3 While (no confirmation received and no time-out)
     wait for confirmation
4 If (confirmation received and valid)
     store confirmation in local database
  else
     send agent to owner
5 Delete agent copy
6 End.
```

Receiver Protocol. The receiver protocol is executed as reaction to the sender protocol. This protocol starts when the sender contacts the receiver to transfer the agent.

```
1 Receive agent
2 Create confirmation
3 Send confirmation
4 End.
```

After protocol termination the receiver can do whatever it wants. It can execute the agent and then execute the sender protocol, or it can be malicious and kill the agent. But if it behaves in such a malicious way, then its confirmation stored at its predecessor can be used to identify it as an attacker in the investigation procedure. The confirmation includes a receiver's digital signature as shown in section 3.

The agent owner's signature on uid, bc, in, and r (see equation (2)) and the exchanged confirmations that also depend on these parameters can be used by the receiving hosts and also by the agent owner in order to detect modifications. The investigation procedure even allows the agent owner to identify the modifying attacker as becomes clear in subsction 4.3.

The copy of the agent at the sender side is stored in order to conserve the agent with its results out^j collected so far. Thus, they will not be lost regardless of how the receiver will behave later. The value of *time-out* can be specified by each host itself and denotes

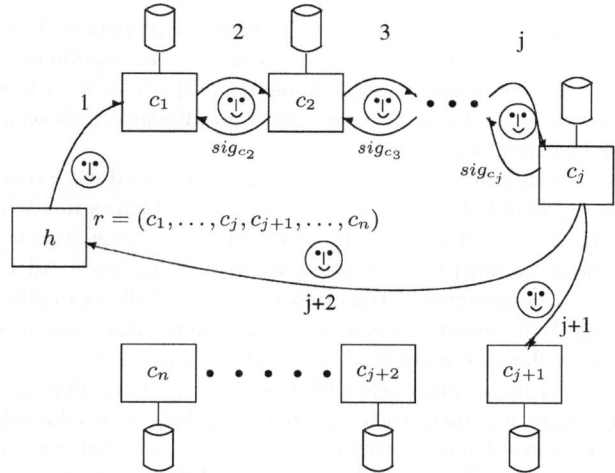

Fig. 1. A scenario for early agent return to its owner

the maximum waiting time for confirmations. The sender is required to verify the validity of the confirmation, i.e., to check that the digital signature is not forged and the receiver's certificate is valid. If the confirmation is valid it must be stored for an adequate period in the sender's database. The length of this period can vary depending on the specific properties of the system. If the sender c_j does not receive a valid response from its successor —receiver could be offline, refuse confirmation, or forge the signature— it sends the agent to its home h. This guarantees that the agent owner receives the results collected so far. Then, the owner can decide himself if his agent should continue its remaining journey $c_{j+1}, \ldots, c_n$ by sending it directly to c_{j+1}. A scenario in which c_j sends the agent to its home before all hosts in the route are visited is depicted in figure 1. In this figure, the numbers $1, \ldots, j+2$ beside the arrows show the order in which protocols are executed.

But what happens when the sender or receiver do not follow the protocol rules? For the following considerations we assume that all sender and receiver protocols have been run properly before the sender protocol is executed by c_j.

If the sender c_j does not follow its protocol in step 2, then it performs denial of service. But this can be detected using its confirmation stored in c_{j-1}'s database.

If c_j does not store the agent copy (step 1) or deletes the copy too early, then c_j can be identified as a denial of service attacker. E.g., this is possible when c_j does not have the agent copy anymore when it receives a forged signature from c_{j+1}. Then, c_{j+1} could delete the agent but the investigation procedure will identify c_j as an attacker. Thus, c_j is interested in having an agent copy for the required time.

If c_j does not verify the signature obtained from c_{j+1} in a correct way (step 4), then it is possible that c_j has no valid evidence in a possible investigation procedure. This would mean that, e.g., c_{j+1} could perform denial of service, but c_j would be identified as the attacker since it cannot prove that it sent the agent to its successor even though it did. Thus, c_j has a natural interest to verify received signatures. The same argument holds for the case when c_j does not store the received confirmation in its database.

If c_j refuses to send the agent to its home (step 4) —e.g., c_{j+1} is not reachable— then, after a certain time the agent owner could start the investigation and c_j would be identified to be the attacker.

Beside the possibilities discussed above, which are in direct connection with the protocol rules, c_j could also perform another action which is in contradiction to the system rules. Host c_j could skip c_{j+1} by sending the agent to another host, even though the hosts in the route must be visited exactly in the prescribed order because of the dependence of the computations. The protocol presented allows in this case to identify the misbehaving host since the investigation procedure allows one to trace the agent, and thereby to see that c_j did not send the agent to c_{j+1}.

Let us consider the receiver protocol. Here, it can be also detected if the receiver c_{j+1} does not follow the rules. The case when c_{j+1} does not send a valid confirmation to c_j is already included in the sender protocol and discussed above —c_j will send the agent to its home. Even if c_{j+1} decides to forward the received agent on its original route without having given a valid confirmation to c_j, it would have no benefit. It can be assumed that it would receive another copy of the agent via the agent owner. The situation is also clear if c_{j+1} sends a valid confirmation to c_j, and then performs denial of service.

4.2   The Protocol in Case of Complete Independence

In the case of completely independent computations a host address appears at most once in the agent route. All results required from a host can be calculated during one visit. This is clear since a host does not require any results calculated elsewhere on the agent's route. Remember that in this scenario the hosts do not have to be visited in the same order given in the route. The solution to be presented combines both the idea of section 3 and a set of rules relevant for hosts that send and receive mobile agents.

The solution here also consists of a sender and a receiver protocol. The sender uses an algorithm *SelectNextHost* as a subroutine. Before we present the algorithm we modify the component containing the list of already visited hosts as it was introduced in section 2. Here, we will have some additional signatures in the list of visited hosts. Assume again that on its journey the mobile agent migrates from host c_k to host c_l, $k \in \{1, \ldots, n-1\}$, $l \in \{2, \ldots, n\}$, and $k \neq l$. Then $vc^{\#(c_l)}$ will be derived from $vc^{\#(c_k)}$ in the following way $vc^{\#(c_l)} = vc^{\#(c_k)}, c_l, sig_{c_l}(vc^{\#(c_k)}, c_l)$. We will give the reason for this modification after the presentation of the *SelectNextHost* algorithm and the protocols. Furthermore, $m \in \mathbb{Z}^+$ as introduced in equation (2) determines the maximum number of hosts that should try to contact another host which is not answering properly or not answering at all. The signature verification of $sig_h(uid, bc, in, r, m)$ and $vc^{\#(c_j)}$ is performed before the sender protocol is started. If either of them is not valid, then the agent is immediately sent to its home.

Let us introduce some notions that are used in this algorithm. For a given element e and set S the predicate $in(e, S)$ returns *true* if $e \in S$, else *false*. The function $card(S)$ returns the number of the elements contained in S. The term $\{vc^{\#(c_j)}\}$ describes the set that contains all the hosts visited so far when the agent is at host c_j. For each agent

to be processed, a host has an own buffer buf in which those hosts are stored that
are not reachable by it, or that did not send a valid confirmation. After forwarding an
agent properly, the host can delete the content of buf. The operator $\neg$ in the following
algorithm represents the negation operator for a given boolean argument. Now, we will
present the algorithm *SelectNextHost* which is used by the *sender protocol*.
Algorithm *SelectNextHost* (at c_j).

```
i = 1
while (i < j)
    if (¬in(cᵢ, {vc#(cⱼ)}) ∧ ¬in(cᵢ, buf))
        if (card({c_{i+1},...,cⱼ} ∩ {vc#(cⱼ)}) < m)
            append cᵢ to buf
            NextHost = cᵢ
            i = n + 2
        else
            i = i + 1
        endif
    else
        i = i + 1
    endif
endwhile
if (i == j)
    i = i + 1
    while (i ≤ n + 1)
        if (i == n + 1)
            NextHost = h
            i = n + 2
        else
            if (¬in(cᵢ, {vc#(cⱼ)}) ∧ ¬in(cᵢ, buf))
                append cᵢ to buf
                NextHost = cᵢ
                i = n + 2
            else
                i = i + 1
            endif
        endif
    endwhile
endif
```

In the first while structure, the hosts checks if there are still some hosts that should
have been visited before itself. If there is such a host that has potentially not been
contacted by m other hosts before, it will be selected as $NextHost$. The following outer
if structure describes the case in which a host selects another host that is contained in
the route after itself.

In the following, we will present the sender and receiver protocols. Compared with
the confirmation introduced in section 3, the confirmation needed here is different. If the
mobile agent is forwarded from host c_k to host c_l then the confirmation to be created
and replied by c_l is

$$sig_{c_l}(uid, bc, in, r, m, vc^{\#(c_k)}).\tag{3}$$

This confirmation signature and also the agent owner's signature on the agent (see equation (2)) can be used for the detection of modification attacks as already mentioned in subsection 4.1. Further reasons for the presence of $vc^{\#(c_k)}$ in the confirmation are given after the presentation of the protocols and the illustrating example.

Sender Protocol. Assume that the agent resides at host c_j. The protocol will be started at host c_j after the agent execution has terminated. The steps of the sender protocol are described in pseudo-code. Note that the sender protocol is not executed in the agent's first migration when it leaves h. If the result of *SelectNextHost* is $NextHost = h$ then the sender protocol can be stopped immediately. Also, no receiver confirmation is required in this case (see section 3).

```
1 Execute algorithm SelectNextHost
2 If (NextHost == h)
    stop
3 Store a copy of the agent
4 Send agent to NextHost found by SelectNextHost
5 While (no confirmation received and no time-out)
    wait for confirmation
6 If (confirmation received and valid)
    store confirmation in local database
  else
    go to step 1
7 Delete agent copy
8 End.
```

Receiver Protocol. The receiver protocol is the reaction to the sender protocol. This protocol starts when the sender contacts the receiver to transfer the agent. This means that when the sender protocol terminates in step 2, the execution of the receiver protocol is not required. Note that the confirmation to be created differs compared to the case *completely dependence*.

```
1 Receive agent
2 Create confirmation
3 Send confirmation
4 End.
```

Both protocols are quite similar compared to the protocols in the case *completely dependent*. The main difference here is that if the sender does not receive a valid confirmation from the receiver, it will not send the agent to h immediately. Instead, it will start the algorithm *SelectNextHost* and the *sender protocol* again in order to send the agent to another host contained in r —as far there is still such a candidate that has not been visited before.

Before we will discuss the achievements of the presented protocols and of the *SelectNextHost* algorithm, we will illustrate both with an example.

Example. Consider an agent owner h that composes an agent with the following parameters: $r = (c_1, \ldots, c_5)$, $m = 3$, and $vc^0 = \{\}$ according to the rules. The agent journey is depicted in figure 2. For the sake of the example we assume that c_2 is offline.

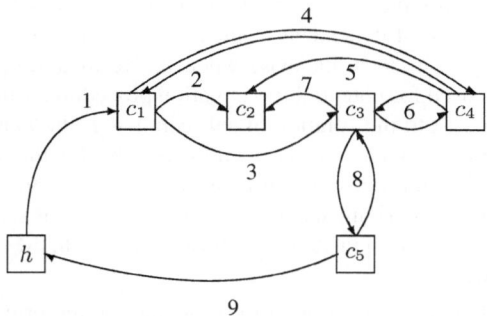

Fig. 2. The agent's journey in the example

In the first migration, h sends the agent to c_1. Here, no confirmation from c_1 is required. Now c_1 updates the list of visited hosts by creating $vc^1 = c_1, sig_{c_1}(c_1)$ and inserts this result in the agent. Then, c_1 starts the sender protocol. With $j = 1$, the algorithm *SelectNextHost* determines $NextHost = c_2$. But since c_2 is offline, the algorithm *SelectNextHost* has to be executed for a second time. With c_2 contained in c_1's buffer it yields $NextHost = c_3$. Assume that c_3 is online, but for some reason it does not respond before time-out. The next execution of *SelectNextHost* yields $NextHost = c_4$. Now, c_4 starts the receiver protocol, creates the confirmation $sig_{c_4}(uid, bc, in, r, m, vc^1)$, and replies with this confirmation to c_1. Then c_4 excutes the agent, updates the agent's list of visited hosts by generating $vc^{\#(c_4)} = vc^2 = vc^1, c_4, sig_{c_4}(vc^1, c_4)$. The start of the sender protocol leads to the execution of *SelectNextHost* for $j = 4$. In iteration step $i = 2$, we have again $NextHost = c_2$ because c_2 is neither contained in vc^2 nor in c_4's buffer. Furthermore, $card(\{c_3, c_4\}) \cap \{c_1, c_4\}) = 1 < 3$. But since c_2 is not reachable *SelectNextHost* is executed again and yields $NextHost = c_3$. Now, c_3 will react in time. It receives the agent, creates the confirmation $sig_{c_3}(uid, bc, in, r, m, vc^2)$, and replies with this confirmation to c_4. The update of the list of visited hosts yields $vc^{\#(c_3)} = vc^3 = vc^2, c_3, sig_{c_3}(vc^2, c_3)$. After the execution of the agent, c_3 starts the sender protocol and obtains $NextHost = c_2$. Without having received an answer from c_2 the next execution of *SelectNextHost* yields $NextHost = c_5$. After having sent $sig_{c_5}(uid, bc, in, r, m, vc^3)$, c_5 creates $vc^{\#(c_5)} = vc^4 = vc^3, c_5, sig_{c_5}(vc^3, c_5)$. For $j = 5$, the application of *SelectNextHost* obtains in iteration step $i = 2$ that c_2 is neither contained in the list of visited hosts nor in c_5's buffer, but $card(\{c_3, c_4, c_5\} \cap \{c_1, c_3, c_4, c_5\}) = 3 \not< 3$. Thus, c_2 will not be contacted by c_5. Further execution of *SelectNextHost* obtains $NextHost = h$, and the agent can be sent without requiring a confirmation. Finally, the agent owner received some part of the desired results. He can see that c_2 was not visited. Of course, he does not know why this happened. But he can assume that c_2 was contacted more than once as far there is no collusion of c_1, c_3, and c_4. We note that in our example, c_2 was contacted by $m = 3$ parties altogether, i.e., first by c_1, second by c_4, and third by c_3. It is up to the agent owner to contact c_2 himself to get the remaining results.   □

Now, we will discuss the achievements of the protocols and the algorithm *Select-NextHost*. As in the case of dependent results, each host checks the confirmation, and stores it persistently to its local database when the verification process was positive. The confirmation is used for potential investigation procedures when a denial of service has occured. In contrast to the solution of subsection 4.1, the journey here will not be completed by sending the agent to its home if the next host in the route is not reachable. Instead, a new destination for the agent is determined by using the algorithm *SelectNextHost*. According to the algorithm and the protocols, the agent is sent to its home if either all hosts in the route have been visited or no host contained in the route to be visited has given a proper answer.

So, it is possible that one or more hosts contained in the original route will not be visited at all when the agent has returned to its home. Then, from the agent owner's perspective it is not clear if the hosts not visited were offline, or refused to handle the agent, or were replying with invalid signatures.

If the protocol and the algorithm are executed correctly then the hosts given in the route can be visited in many orders. If host c_j does not forward the agent even though it received it and confirmed it, then this host can be identified via the confirmation that is stored at c_j's predecessor. Here, signatures in the confirmation also depends on the list of visited hosts $vc^{\#(c_j)-1}$. The reason for this is described in the following.

The fact that the solution allows skipping of hosts could be exploited by a malicious host. E.g., such a host could possibly have the intention to exclude a competitor that is also contained in the route. To do this, it could register the address of the competitor in the list of visited hosts that this host will not be contacted again on the agent's journey, and thus is excluded from the interaction with the agent. Therefore, the list of visited hosts has to be protected so that this attack is not possible. In our solution, each host obtains a signature also depending on the list of visited hosts from its successor that can be used as evidence in order to show that it did not manipulate the list. Thus, the successor signs the list of visited hosts together with other components as shown in equation (3). If something should happen later, then the confirmation proves the correct forwarding of the agent.

It is possible that a host c_j intends to skip another host which is the next host to be visited according to the *SelectNextHost* algorithm. It could claim that this host was not reachable. In such a case it could forward the agent to another host selected by itself out of the set of potential candidates contained in the route. But then this successor of c_j, if honest, would send the agent to the skipped host after having executed it. The only way for c_j to exclude a host is to initiate a collusion, e.g., by bribing. In the context of our solution this would mean for c_j to convince the next $m-1$ consecutive hosts to collude. If only one of these hosts is not willing to collude then the attack does not work. The only possibility would be to skip also the host which refuses to collude. But then, the story starts all over again, i.e., the attacker requires new $m-1$ hosts following the refusing host in order to skip it. Thus, besides a special case to be explained shortly, attacks can only have success if the size of a collusion is at least m —one initiator and $m-1$ partners.

Of course, all this reasoning about collusion size only holds as far as there are at least $m-1$ hosts that can be visited. E.g., consider the case in which we have n route entries and let the agent reside at host c_{n-2}. Here, let $NextHost = c_{n-1}$. Assume that c_{n-2} decides to skip c_{n-1}. In this case, c_{n-2} only has to collude with c_n if all other hosts have been visited before. This means, that here the collusion size is 2 which can be smaller than m. Thus, if some hosts are contained near to the end of the route and have not been visited the agent owner can decide to contact these hosts in a new agent journey. We can also conclude that a manipulation of $NextHost$ does not lead to denial of service (step 1).

In the discussion above we have considered the case in which a host does not properly execute step 1 of the sender protocol, e.g., via skipping. In the remaining considerations we will briefly discuss the implications of improper execution of the other steps. If a host does not fulfill step 4, then it performs denial of service which can be detected, provided that the earlier protocols have been executed properly.

If the host playing the sender role in the protocol deletes the agent copy too early (step 3), then it can be identified as an attacker. Thus, we can assume that the host is not interested in such a behaviour (see subsection 4.1).

A host is also interested in verifying the received confirmation carefully and store it persistently (step 6). If the signature is not valid then it has no proof that it forwarded the agent (see subsection 4.1).

Extra consideration of the receiver protocol is not necessary. For this, we refer to subsection 4.1.

4.3   Investigation Procedure

Now, it remains to show how the investigation procedure works. This procedure works quite similar for the cases *completely dependent* and *completely independent*. Let us assume that the agent owner is waiting for one of his agents that probably should have already returned. When the owner becomes suspicious that some malicious party could have deleted his agent, he starts the investigation procedure. The investigation procedure basically consists of the consecutive application of an investigation protocol which contains two steps: first, the agent owner's request, and second the answer in which a host shows its evidence —as far as it is able to do that.

In the investigation procedure for the case *completely dependent* the agent owner queries the hosts in the same order as they were contained in the initial route until he has found the attacker. The attacker is assumed to be the host not showing a valid evidence.

In the investigation procedure for the case *completely independent* the hosts must not be queried necessarily in the same order as they are given in the route $r = (c_1, \ldots, c_n)$, because the real order of visiting hosts can differ from that one given in the initial route. In fact, the investigation must follow the actual order in which the hosts were visited. This is possible, since all hosts —except the attacker— can provide the agent owner with the identity of their successor by presenting the confirmation. Thereby, the agent owner can easily derive the real route step by step. Thus, the agent owner knows to which party he has to send his next request.

The agent owner starts his investigation procedure by requesting the first host in the agent route, which is the host to which the agent owner sent the agent himself. If c_1 has done its job properly, then it can present its successor's confirmation which contains the signature also dependent on vc^1. Thus, after positive check of the confirmation presented by c_1, he knows c_1's successor to which he will send his next request. Then, the sending of requests and collecting confirmations is repeated according to the same known principle: If the confirmation presented by a host c_i is valid, he sends the next request to the host found in $vc^{\#(c_i)+1}$. The agent owner continues this procedure until he finds a host not able to show a valid evidence. If the attacking host is found, it is up to the agent owner to decide whether to include it in future migration routes or not.

The investigation procedure also works for the identification of attackers that created new agents via usage or modification of original agent components, like uid, bc, in, r, and m. Since exchanged signatures depend on all these components, the party showing an invalid signature for these components will be identified to be the attacker. If we require that all exchanged confirmations are checked by the hosts on receipt then there is no possibility for a sending host to deny that he dispatched a modified agent. If he receives an invalid signature even though he dispatchted the agent correctly, the rules of the game —as given above— prescribe what to do.

5   Related Work

Many of the problems concerning the security of mobile agent systems, both protecting the host from malicious agents and protecting agents from malicious hosts, have been discussed in the literature. Execution tracing [7] is a technique for detecting unauthorized modifications of an agent through recording the agent's behavior during its execution on each host. In [5] Sander and Tschudin introduce the concept of computing with encrypted functions and thus protecting the integrity and the privacy of the agent's computations. Corradi *et al.* present in [1] methods for protecting the agent's integrity —both making use of a Trusted Third Party and without it. In [3], Kim *et al.* presented an adaptive migration strategy that can be used to avoid mobile agents from blocking or crashing. This is achieved by a route reordering algorithm and a backward recovery algorithm. In [8,9] Westhoff *et al.* describe methods for the protection of the agent's route against hosts spying out route information. One technique for ensuring that a mobile agent arrives safely at its destination is through the use of replication and voting [6]. The problem of detecting the *black hole* —a stationary process destroying visiting agents— in an anonymous ring is addressed in [2].

6   Conclusion and Future Work

In this paper we treated the problem of denial of service attacks in mobile agent systems. We proposed methods which use a combination of cryptographic techniques and a set of rules which enable the agent owner to identify malicious hosts who performed denial of service attacks, both for the cases of *completely dependent* and *completely independent* agent computations. The proposed solutions do not strongly prevent the deletion of mobile agents, but it can be assumed that they have some preventive power to a certain extent. This stems from the fact that an attacker can be uniquely identified. These experiences can be used by the agent owner when composing the future routes for his agents.

The results presented so far are an initial approach to deal with the subject of *denial of service attacks* in the world of mobile agents. There is some work to be done in the future. A problem to be solved is given in the case in which the agent route contains entries for the collection of both dependent and independent computations. Another problem to be handled is the question of dynamic routes where hosts or agents initiate migrations to hosts which were not contained in the route once composed by the agent owner. Other work to be done in the future focuses on formal analysis for our solution. Further aspects of interest are analysis of practicability and performance of our system.

Acknowledgement. This work was supported by the Ministry for Education, Science, and Research of Northrhine Westfalia (project *Research Alliance Data Security NRW*), and by the European Commission (contract IST-1999-10288, project *OPELIX*). Thanks to Firoz Kaderali for his support. Also thanks to the anonymous reviewers for their valuable comments.

References

1. Antonio Corradi, Marco Cremonini, Rebecca Montanari, and Cesare Stefanelli. Mobile agents integrity for electronic commerce applications. *Information Systems*, 24(6), 1999.
2. Stefan Dobrev, Paola Flocchini, Guiseppe Prencipe, and Nicola Santoro. Mobile search for a black hole in an anonymous ring. In *Distributed Computing (DISC 2001), 15th International Conference, Proceedings*, number 2180 in LNCS. Springer Verlag, 2001.
3. Dong Chun Lee and Jeom Goo Kim. Adaptive migration strategy for mobile agents on internet. In *Technologies for E-Services (TES 2001), Second International Workshop, Proceedings*, number 2193 in LNCS. Springer Verlag, 2001.
4. Alfred J. Menezes, Paul C. van Oorschot, and Scott A. Vanstone. *Handbook of applied cryptography*. CRC Press series on discrete mathematics and its applications. CRC Press, 1997. ISBN 0-8493-8523-7.
5. Tomas Sander and Christian F. Tschudin. Protecting mobile agents against malicious hosts. In G. Vigna, editor, *Mobile Agents and Security*, number 1419 in LNCS. Springer Verlag, 1998.
6. Fred B. Schneider. Towards fault-tolerant and secure agentry. In *Distributed Algorithms, 11th International Workshop (WDAG'97), Proceedings*, number 1320 in LNCS. Springer Verlag, 1997.
7. Giovanni Vigna. Cryptographic traces for mobile agents. In G. Vigna, editor, *Mobile Agents and Security*, number 1419 in LNCS. Springer Verlag, 1998.
8. Dirk Westhoff, Markus Schneider, Claus Unger, and Firoz Kaderali. Methods for protecting a mobile agent's route. In *Information Security, Second International Workshop (ISW'99)*, number 1729 in LNCS. Springer Verlag, 1999.
9. Dirk Westhoff, Markus Schneider, Claus Unger, and Firoz Kaderali. Protecting a mobile agent's route against collusions. In *Selected Areas in Cryptography, 6th Annual International Workshop (SAC'99)*, number 1758 in LNCS. Springer Verlag, 2000.

Threshold Route Optimization Algorithm for Information Retrieving Mobile Agents

Roman Morawek

Vienna University of Technology, Institute of Communication Networks
Favoritenstr. 9/388, A-1040 Vienna, Austria
Roman.Morawek@tuwien.ac.at

Abstract. Mobile agents often have the task to collect data from several prede-fined sites. This should be done in an efficient way by minimizing the elapsed time. Usually the agents only know the list of sites but not the distances between them. In contrast to former publications this paper presents an algorithm to determine the agent's tour which does not depend on a known distance matrix. The agent repeats traveling over the short routes and avoids longer ones. The paper shows that the optimal threshold point depends on the number of visits the agent takes or, equivalently, the number of tours taken within that period where the collected network information does not get outdated. Using the proposed algorithm the total latency time can be halved (against the common strategy of a random way) when taking 30 runs, without producing additional network traffic. These results are derived analytically and verified by simulation.

1 Introduction

Mobile software agents are getting more and more common in telecommunication systems. They often have the task to collect from or distribute data to several sites, e. g. to search for relevant literature as proposed in [2], [10] or [6]. In many cases the tour taken is not considered and a random path is used. The optimization of the tour by minimizing the total round trip time of the agent corresponds to the well known traveling salesman problem (TSP) which is NP-hard.

There exist many approaches for choosing the tour, e. g. heuristics as the nearest neighbor algorithm, the greedy algorithm, the Lin-Kernighan algorithm [5] or more advanced strategies as simulated annealing, genetic algorithms or neural networks [3,9, 8]. Some papers deal with the TSP adapted to mobile software agents like [1], [2], and [7], which is often called the traveling agent problem (TAP). All of these algorithms depend on a complete identified optimization problem. That means that the cost data (which usually correspond to the network latencies) are assumed to be known in advance. The objective of this paper is to release this assumption because for mobile agents the distances between the sites are often unknown or get outdated in a short time compared to the time between two visits. The problem of finding the optimal tour can therefore be considered as a traveling salesman problem under incomplete information.

Some other approaches for finding a feasible tour do not rely on a known cost matrix, e.g. the ant optimization algorithm [4]. However, these methods make extensive use of network resources while finding an optimal tour. That means they send several packets

M. Klusch, S. Ossowski, and O. Shehory (Eds.): CIA 2002, LNAI 2446, pp. 312–319, 2002.
© Springer-Verlag Berlin Heidelberg 2002

(or mobile agents) through the network while executing the algorithm. The task of this paper is, to find an optimal strategy for the agents to move, without assuming a known latency matrix and without producing more network traffic than necessary.

In the next section I will present the proposed algorithm and derive its performance. Section 3 will illustrate the simulation results of the algorithm and Section 4 summarizes.

2   The Constant Threshold Algorithm (CTA)

As this is the basic idea of this writing, the cost matrix is unknown at the beginning. As the agent migrates through the network it measures the latency taken for each step. So the cost matrix gradually gets filled. Since it is not possible to perform a global minimization of the total cost because of the principle of the traveling salesman problem, the optimization is done by comparing the examined strategy with the common approach of taking a random tour and keeping it for all repetitions.

Even this procedure is only possible with simplifying assumptions and approximative derivations. For the derivation in this section I assume that the costs are independently and normally distributed with the mean value $\bar{c}$ and the standard deviation σ_c. As the simulation will show the results are consistent.

In the rest of this paper I will interchangeably call the route between two nodes also *edge* according to graph theory. This must not be confused with a link between two network nodes. We are only interested in the nodes to visit and an edge is the route between two such nodes. There may be other nodes between them, even nodes we also have to visit. As a consequence we are confronted with a full meshed graph. Also strictly differentiate between tour and route. A route is the way between two nodes and a tour consists of all nodes to visit. Furthermore, the period t corresponds to the number of the tour taken, not to be mistaken with the network latency which corresponds to the cost c.

The proposed algorithm constructs the tours of the agent by repeating the short edges and taking new edges instead of the long ones by random. I use a threshold to decide which edge to repeat and which not to repeat. The edges are taken according to the greedy algorithm in increasing order of cost as long as the minimum observed edge from node i $c_{i,min} < c_{th}$. Otherwise a new unknown edge from node i is taken by random if this is possible (i.e. when there is still a legal unknown edge left to observe). If this is not possible, the minimal-cost edge which is still valid is taken even if the respective cost is higher than the threshold.

Now consider the start of the problem. At $t = 1$, after the first random tour at $t = 0$ which yielded the initial costs $c_i(0)$, we have to choose the route for each node i, resulting in a situation where there are two cases:

1. $c_i(0) < c_{th}$: The agent will permanently use the edge with cost $c_i(0)$ again or
2. $c_i(0) \geq c_{th}$: The agent uses a new random edge at $t = 1$ with cost $c_i(1)$.

The threshold c_{th} is defined as a function of the mean value and the standard deviation of the cost data according to

$$c_{th} = \bar{c} + k\sigma_c \tag{1}$$

where k describes the *threshold factor*.

The performance of the strategy is measured by calculating the expected gain as the difference of the taken tour compared to repeatedly taking the same tour as at $t = 0$ again, normalized to σ_c:

$$g_i(1) = \frac{1}{\sigma_c} E \begin{cases} c_i(0) - c_i(0) & c_i(0) < c_{th} \\ c_i(0) - c_i(1) & c_i(0) \geq c_{th} \end{cases}$$

$$= \frac{1}{\sigma_c} E \begin{cases} 0 & c_i(0) < c_{th} \\ E(c_i(0)) - \bar{c} & c_i(0) \geq c_{th} \end{cases} \tag{2}$$

For calculating $E(c_i(0))$ we have to consider that $c_i(0)$ has the probability density

$$f_{c_i(0)}(x) = \begin{cases} \dfrac{a}{\sqrt{2\pi}\,\sigma_c} e^{-\frac{(x-\bar{c})^2}{2\sigma_c^2}} & x > c_{th} \\ 0 & x \leq c_{th}. \end{cases} \tag{3}$$

Herein, a is a constant factor which is chosen in a way that the total probability is normalized to 1 ($\int_{-\infty}^{\infty} f_{c_i(0)}(x)\,dx = 1$).
Its expected value is

$$E(c_i(0)\,|_{c_i(0)\geq c_{th}}) = \frac{a}{\sqrt{2\pi}\,\sigma_c} \int_{\bar{c}+k\sigma_c}^{\infty} x\, e^{-\frac{(x-\bar{c})^2}{2\sigma_c^2}}\, dx$$

$$= \bar{c} + \mu(k)\sigma_c \tag{4}$$

The function $\mu(k)$ is independent of $\bar{c}$ and σ_c and is strictly increasing in k.

Inserting this result in (2) leads to an total expected gain of node i in period $t = 1$ of

$$g_i(1) = P(c_i(0) \geq \bar{c} + k\sigma_c) \frac{1}{\sigma_c}(\bar{c} + \mu(k)\sigma_c - \bar{c})$$

$$= (1 - \Phi(k))\,\mu(k) \tag{5}$$

since $c_i(0)$ is assumed to follow a normal distribution. The graph of this equation is observable as the lowest line in Figure 1.

As we can see, if the software agent migrates through the network for only two periods, the best strategy after the random first run would be to set the decision threshold factor to $k = 0$ or $c_{th} = \bar{c}$. This result is also intuitive: For all edges with higher costs than the expected costs, try another route.

Now, let us examine what happens in the next period $t = 2$. We are either using the edge with the minimal cost observed so far, $c_{i,min}(1)$, again or choosing a new edge depending on whether $c_i(0)$ or $c_i(1)$ is smaller than c_{th} or not. The expected gain equals

$$g_i(2) = \frac{1}{\sigma_c} \, \mathrm{E} \begin{cases} c_i(0) - c_i(0) & c_i(0) < c_{th} \\ c_i(0) - c_i(1) & (c_i(0) \geq c_{th}) \wedge (c_i(1) < c_{th}) \\ c_i(0) - c_i(2) & (c_i(0) \geq c_{th}) \wedge (c_i(1) \geq c_{th}) \end{cases}$$

$$= \mathrm{E} \begin{cases} 0 & c_i(0) < c_{th} \\ \mu(k) + \mu(-k) & (c_i(0) \geq c_{th}) \wedge (c_i(1) < c_{th}) \\ \mu(k) & (c_i(0) \geq c_{th}) \wedge (c_i(1) \geq c_{th}) \end{cases} \quad (6)$$

using the symmetry for calculating $\mathrm{E}(c_i(1))$.

Since the probabilities for the events are given by $\Phi(k)$, $(1 - \Phi(k))\Phi(k)$ and $(1 - \Phi(k))^2$

$$g_i(2) = (1 - \Phi(k))\Phi(k) \, (\mu(k) + \mu(-k)) + (1 - \Phi(k))^2 \, \mu(k) \quad (7)$$

which is shown as the second lowest line in Figure 1.

The gain in period $t = 2$ is about 1.5 times higher than $g_i(1)$. But there is one more important result: The maximum gain in period $t = 2$ is not reached at $k = 0$ as it was in period $t = 1$ but at $k < 0$. Thus, the mobile agent should try more new edges even though this is not profitable at $t = 1$. The thereby emerging greater repertory of known edges compensates this at $t = 2$.

Carrying on this calculation for all t results in

$$g_i(t) = \begin{cases} 0 & t = 0 \\ \sum_{i=1}^{t-1} (1 - \Phi(k))^i \Phi(k)(\mu(k) + \mu(-k)) + (1 - \Phi(k))^t \, \mu(k) & t \geq 1 \end{cases} \quad (8)$$

which is plotted with the parameter t in Figure 1.

As the attentive reader may have observed, this modeling violates the fact that there may be no unknown valid edge left to try. In this case, the agent has to take a more expensive edge than modeled. So, the gain is less than and the expected costs are higher than the derived ones. Equation (8) is only valid for $t \ll n$. The divergence will be larger with a lower number of nodes n and a higher period t.

Since the costs are assumed to be independent, the expected gain for all n nodes, $g(t)$, can be calculated as

$$g(t) = \sum_{i=1}^{n} g_i(t) = n g_0(t) \quad (9)$$

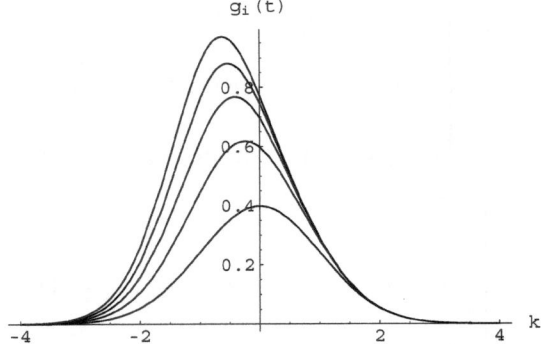

Fig. 1. The expected gain for the periods $t = 1$ (lowest curve) to $t = 5$ (highest curve) as a function of the threshold factor k.

and the cumulated expected gain is the sum of the expected gains $g(u)$ over the whole period scale

$$G(t) = \sum_{u=0}^{t} g(u) \,. \tag{10}$$

The threshold factors are chosen in a way that maximizes the total expected gain by maximizing the equations 8 and 10. They are plotted in Figure 2. Here we can see

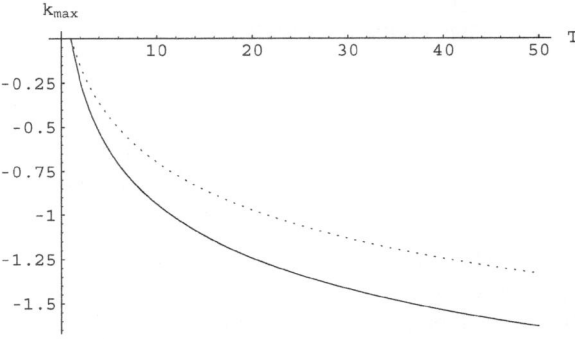

Fig. 2. The optimal threshold factor k for maximizing the gain $g_i(t)$ of period t (solid line) and for maximizing the cumulated gain $G_i(t)$ up to period t, (dotted line).

again, that the optimum threshold factor k to choose is a negatively sloped function on the number of tours the software agent takes. Because of the cumulation of the effects of the individual periods the negative correlation between the maximum gain and k has a lower tendency in the cumulated gain G.

The realized gain per node as a function of the period is shown in Figure 3 with the threshold factor as the parameter.

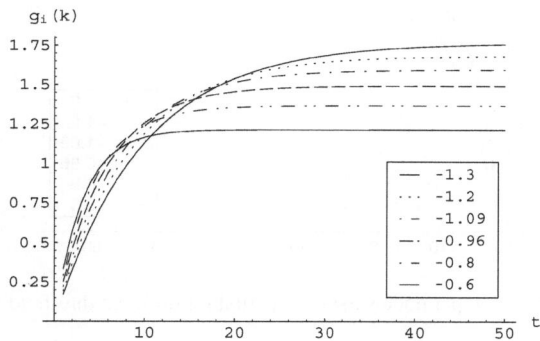

Fig. 3. The gain per node and period by using the specified threshold factor k.

3   Simulation Results

On a sample of 3000 random cost matrices with 50 nodes each I applied the described algorithm for different threshold factors k. The edge costs are calculated as the Euclidean distances between random points in a unit square. Therefore the cost distribution is not a normal distribution as assumed in the derivations but a similar one. The values for the mean value $\bar{c}$ and the standard deviation σ (normalized by $N-1$) are calculated based on the known edges before the generation of each tour. The values for the first pass (when all edges are unknown yet) do not have any influence on the algorithm.

Figure 4 shows the absolute gain per node as a function of the period with the threshold factor as the parameter. As in the former section the gain is scaled in the standard deviation of the cost data. For the first few tours the gains are higher for higher thresholds. This occurs because as long as the threshold is below $\bar{c}$, more *good* edges are avoided the lower the threshold. But the higher threshold has the disadvantage that fewer unknown edges are explored and therefore the tour costs of lower threshold strategies have a larger gain for a higher number of taken tours. So the steady state of the gains is higher the lower the threshold.

The comparison with the equivalent figure of the theoretical section, Figure 3, shows a good consistency. The highest divergence occurs for larg t. As already described, this effect results because of the missing alternatives in the simulation where no unknown edges are left to observe. This lasts in a flattening of the gain curve.

When we compare this simulation result (the optimal threshold for a given t) with the solid line of the theoretical result in Figure 2 we recognize a high agreement. The derived result describes the simulation well despite the simplifying assumptions and the slightly different cost distribution.

318   R. Morawek

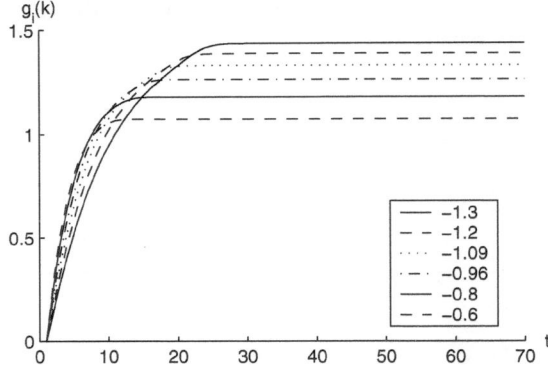

Fig. 4. The gain per node versus the period for different threshold factors k.

To identify the total effect we have to consider the cumulated gain or, equivalently, the cumulated tour costs which are shown in Figure 5. The costs are given as the ratio

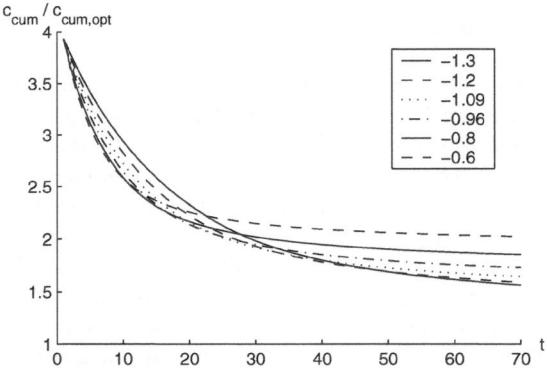

Fig. 5. Cumulated tour costs as a function of the period with the threshold factor as a parameter.

to the optimal cumulated costs under complete information, that means the tour costs obtained by the greedy algorithm with a known cost matrix. You can also see the ratio of the algorithm performance compared to a random tour by rescaling the ordinate by a factor of about a fourth because this is the length of the first, random tour.

The costs of the first tour is equal for all threshold strategies. Afterwards we can see the same effects as before. For lower thresholds (which are less than $\bar{c}$) the total cumulated costs are higher for the first tours and lower for a higher number of taken tours. The points where the optimal strategy changes are shifted to the right compared to Figure 4. You can verify them with the theoretical results of the dotted line in Figure

2. The total cumulated tour costs are about 0.5 the costs of a random tour for 30 taken runs and even less when taking more mobile agent tours.

4   Conclusion

Throughout this paper I presented an algorithm to build the tours of an information retrieving mobile agent. An information retrieving system which periodically sends an mobile agent to e.g. search for relevant information should implement this strategy which determines the tour of each agent in such a way that the total migration latency over all agents is minimized under the given information constraints. The algorithm works by dividing the edges of a communication network into "good" and "bad" edges by using a threshold factor. This threshold factor depends on the number of tours taken by the agents. An equivalent situation occurs when a mobile agent takes an infinite number of tours but the collected network data gets continuously less informative because of a changing network environment. I derived optimal threshold factors and verified these optimal values by simulation. A high correspondence between the theoretical and experimental results was found.

Using the proposed algorithm which is easy to implement and uses only little processing overhead, the cumulated migration time of all information agents (and therefore also the total network usage) can be reduced significantly compared with the common strategy of taking a random tour.

References

1. Baek, J.W., Yeo, J.H., Kim, G.T., Yeom, H.Y.: Cost effective mobile agent planning for distributed information retrieval. In: Proceedings of the International Conference on Distributed Computing Systems (ICDCS), Phoenix, Arizona. (2001)
2. Brewington, B., Gray, R., Moizumi, K., Kotz, D., Cybenko, G., Rus, D.: Mobile agents in distributed information retrieval. In Klusch, M., ed.: Intelligent Information Agents. Springer-Verlag: Heidelberg, Germany (1999)
3. Cerny, V.: Thermodynamical approach to the travelling salesman problem: an efficient simulation algorithme. Journal of Optimization Theory and Applications 45 (1985) 41–45
4. Dorigo, M., Maniezzo, V., Colorni, A.: Ant system: Optimization by a colony of cooperating agents. IEEE Transactions on Systems, Man, and Cybernetics-Part B 26(1) (1996) 29–41
5. Johnson, D.S., McGeoch, L.A.: The Traveling Salesman Problem: A Case Study in Local Optimization. In: Combinatorial Optimization. John Wiley and Sons, Ltd (1997) 215–310
6. Knoblock, C.A., Arens, Y., Hsu, C.N.: Cooperating agents for information retrieval. In: Proceedings of the Second International Conference on Cooperative Information Systems, Toronto, Ontario, Canada, University of Toronto Press (1994)
7. Moizumi, K., Cybenko, G.: The travelling agent problem. Mathematics of Control, Signals, and Systems (MCSS) 14 (2001) 213–232
8. Potvin, J.Y.: The traveling salesman problem: A neural network perspective. ORSA Journal of Computing 5 (1993) 328–347
9. Potvin, J.Y.: Genetic algorithms for the traveling salesman problem. Annals of Operations Research 63 (1996) 339–370
10. Yang, J., Honavar, V., Miller, L., Wong, J.: Intelligent mobile agents for information retrieval and knowledge discovery from distributed data and knowledge sources. IEEE Information Technology Conference, Syracuse, NY (1998)

Author Index

Lecture Notes in Artificial Intelligence (LNAI)

Lecture Notes in Computer Science